C000171113

MICELEE – THE TALE OF A NORTHUMBRIAN VILLAGE

Micelee

The Tale of a Northumbrian Village

by

Ivan Seymour

The Pentland Press
Edinburgh – Cambridge – Durham – USA

First published in 2000
by The Pentland Press Ltd
1 Hutton Close
South Church
Bishop Auckland
Durham

ISBN 1-85821-840-3

Typeset in Monotype Bell 11 on 13
by Carnegie Publishing
Carnegie House
Chatsworth Road
Lancaster

Printed and bound by Bookcraft (Bath) Ltd.

For Betty,
my dear,
stalwart wife

Contents

Acknowledgements ix

Introduction 1

Section One: Setting the Scene

The Wild Places 7
Christianity and Northumbria 9
The Clearing 14
The Coming of the Baliols 17
A Bit of Taxation 26
Names, Skills and Status 30
Life and Death 32
The Nevilles 34
The Reiver Factor 36
Post-Reiver Changes 39
The Village in 1526 40
Wool and England 41
Iron, Steel and a Bit of Art 44
Tudors and their Times 46
Sheep, Trees and Taxes 49
A Different Kind of War 52
Great England 55
A Little Bit of Coal 57
Fenwicks and Humbles 62
Building in Mickley 65
Continuing Progress 67
Bewick the Artist 71
Steam and Railways 73

Section Two: The Second Part

The Second Part 83
Pitmen and their Housing 88
The 'Raas' and Living in them 92
The Daily Round 100
Time Off 108
Waste and Water 111
Pits and Pitmen 117
Personal Finance 120
Coal and the Coal Trade 122
Farming in Industrial Mickley 128
Politics and Education 136

Mickley School	140
New Pit, New Century	144
Churches	149
Gas and Water	154
New Housing	156
The Co-op	158
The Grocery	163
Other Ways to Shop	170
More Shops	173
The Co-op Cobbler	175
The Cart Yard	179
The Butchers	181
The Co-op Manager and his Home	182
Into the Twentieth Century	184
Health Care	186
The Welfare	189
Football	191
The Church Hall	196
Mickley Band	187
The Seaside	202
The 'Royal'	204
The Village Show	206
The 'Hoppins'	208
Turn of the Century	210
Electricity in the Village	214
Blaydon Co-op	216
The New Mickley	218
Stobarts	220
Water and WCs	227
Gas and Gadgets	229
The Bicycle	232
The Cinema	237
The Branch End Connection	239
Longstaffes	241
The Great War	247
A Land Fit for Heroes	250
To Mickley	253
School at Mickley	254
School After Charlie	260
The Other Teachers	261
Riding Terrace	265
The East End	275
Cosy Joe	276
The Wireless	285
The Motor Car	290
The End of the Drift	297
The End of the Forests	302
Mickley at War Again	308
A Fresh Start	333
The Village at Peace	337
Nemesis	344
The End of the Pits	351
A Different World, New Face	353

Acknowledgements

I would like to acknowledge the help of all those past generations of Mickley folk who have made this book possible, as well as those of present times who have supported and encouraged me in what has been a very long labour of love.

I give particular thanks to Gwen Smith, who began it all by insisting Mickley deserved to be written about – and I was the person to do it. Nor did she let it go at that!

Then there is Harry Powell, who took pity on my efforts with an old type-writer and set me off into the world of computing, then guided me towards getting my writing fit to be published.

Thank you all, dear friends.

Introduction

The traveller dashing for the delights of Scotland is unlikely to notice Northumberland from the A1; one looking for Roman remains might turn left at Gateshead, along the A695 up the south side of the Tyne valley towards Hexham. A blink and the sign reading 'Mickley Square' could well be missed – and the chance to wonder, why 'Square'? My aim is to stimulate the enquirer into seeking to know more about this Square which isn't.

So what's in a name? Confusion, if it happens to be the name of a little village on a hill in Northumberland, which began its known existence in Anglo-Saxon times, and is now called Mickley.

In the beginning it could have been a natural space or less dense part of the then widespread forest covering the area; and so given the name 'leah', or clearing, by Anglian settlers.

The first part of the name is less easy; 'micela' is said to mean 'large', whereas in Scotland, not so far away, "Monny a mickle maks a muckle" – many small things make into large, pennies into pounds. So I would say this clearing started 'small' and grew 'big'.

Either way, it was a clearing in the forest. It is when we come to the spelling that the real confusion begins. Variations in pronunciation, influences of language from other places, the written word recorded by scribes of various degrees of competence, with their own ways of spelling, resulted over the centuries in wide choice in construction of the name. Begin if you like, with 'Micela-leah'; then take your pick from Michelleie, Miceleah, Micheleie, Micelee, Mikelee and Mickelee – work out the permutations, they will all have been used. I have chosen 'Micelee' for the early times, then 'Mickelee', and finally Mickley.

There is an excellent little book by Stan Beckenstall, called *Northumberland's Place Names*, published by Butler Publishing, Thropton, Rothbury, NE65 7LP.

Eltringham
Hare & Hounds (P.H.)
Eltringham
Cherry Burn
R I N G
Cherryburn
Cherryburn Cottages
Drift Cottages
Football Ground
Riding Dean
Miners' Arms (P.H.)
P.O.
Riding House
LOW ROW NORTH
LOW ROW SOUTH
WEST STREET
CROSS ROW
HIGH ROW NORTH
HIGH ROW SOUTH
Mickley Squa
Methodist Chapel (Primitive)
Methodist Chapel (United Free)
ASH CLOSETS
FIRST PART OF EAST STREET
A695
B.M. 297·9
G.P.
INCOMPLETE PARISH HALL
INCOMPLETE WEST WYLAM CO-OP
Reading Room
School
HEXHAM
ORDNANCE SURVEY 1896
SHOWING THE FIRST OF THE ASH CLOSETS (NETTIES) EAST END OF LOW ROW, NORTH AND SOUTH AND POSITION OF 'THE SQUARE'

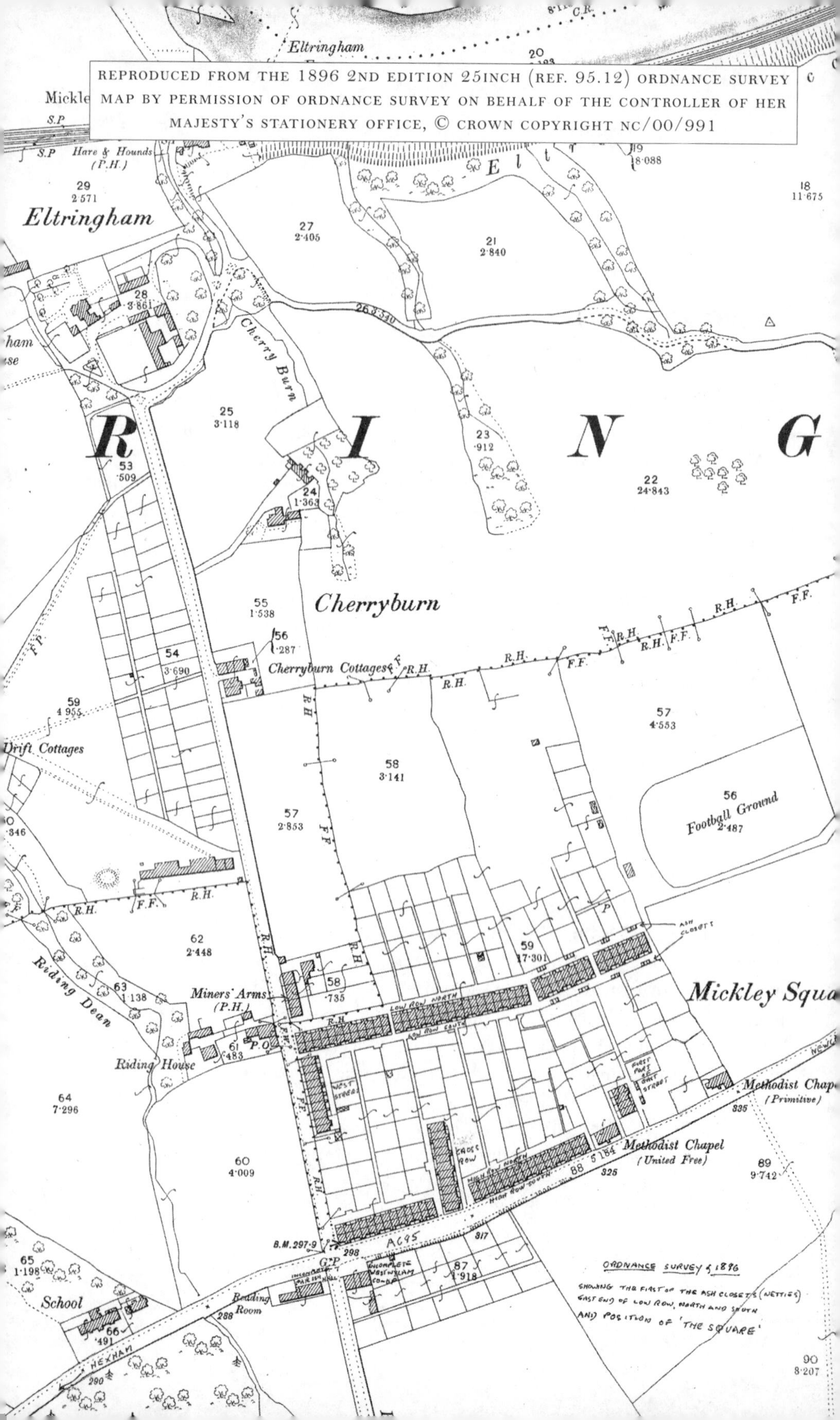

REPRODUCED FROM THE 1939 4TH EDITION 25INCH (REF. 102.1) ORDNANCE SURVEY MAP BY PERMISSION OF ORDNANCE SURVEY ON BEHALF OF THE CONTROLLER OF HER MAJESTY'S STATIONERY OFFICE, © CROWN COPYRIGHT NC/00/991
Cherryburn Cottages
Football Ground
Pavilion
Mickley Square
North View
South View
Low Row North
Low Row South
Riding House
Methodist Church
Picture Theatre
Burnside Cottages
Cross Row
High Row North
High Row South
Methodist Church
Cricket Ground
Club
Mission Room
Reading Room
Pavilion
Bowling Green
Pav.
Children's Playground
Aged Miners' Cottages
Eastgate Bank
Shaft
Vicarage
Grave Yard
St. George's Church
Hall Yards
Collieryclose Wood

Section One:

Setting the Scene

The Wild Places

The evolution of England as one great nation, the development of the nature and character of the English race, which has so greatly influenced the world since the time of Offa, is not for me to record; it is well, if sometimes controversially recorded, from Bede to Churchill and others not so good. My interest lies in the way in which this village evolved with England, never more than on the edge of great events but always close enough to be touched and influenced by them; a microcosm of its history, if you like.

Romans, in their day, were active hereabouts but had little need to bother any Britons who chose to stay and scratch a living from what might have been an early unnamed clearing in the dense forest. A flint axe recently found at Eltringham Farm, a burial place at Prudhoe, and a bronze vessel at Edgewell indicate at least a presence of Britons in the area. Although mobile and thin on the ground, they were widespread in the wilder places – and this was a wilder place, dense with trees for hiding in, and five hundred feet above the fertile river valley where the Romans farmed. When they departed, the Romans left no villa as monument to their presence. Hadrian's breached and useless ungarrisoned wall no longer gave protection from Northern savages to locals perhaps softened by 400 years of 'easy' living. Melting into the forest was their only hope against the fiendish Picts and life after the Romans must have been no life at all in these wilds.

The coming to this island of evil Germanic hordes – the murdering, pillaging Anglo-Saxons – brought no relief, and the natives must have wondered why everyone else wanted to live in their land.

These incomers were essentially lowlanders. When the urge to plunder which brought them gave way to a realisation that here in this verdant, fertile, under-populated land, with the protecting sea at their backs, they could settle down and make a comfortable life, they became colonisers. First they set about wiping out any natives who objected to foreigners filching their land – and a bloody business it was. It went on a long time, perhaps 250 years, with most of the remaining Britons being driven to the hills, from whence they emerged from time to time, and to some effect – they still do . . . The progression which began with the discovery that a flint axe was a better cleaver of skulls than a branch or a bone, an iron sword better than a flint, through steel blades, bullets and high-explosives, to nuclear bombs, became evident in the Saxon invasion in their excellent sword, the SEAX – after which perhaps they were named; it killed a lot of Britons, in the hands of the overwhelming hordes of intruders, who eventually prevailed – in spite of the valiant deeds of the legendary Arthur and his Knightly band of roving cavalry.

The genocide of the southern plains was neither necessary nor possible in the sparsely populated, rugged northern uplands. In the course of time native and invader learned to get along together, eventually intermingling, each to the betterment of the other; and so began the process of mixing races, which produced the 'British'.

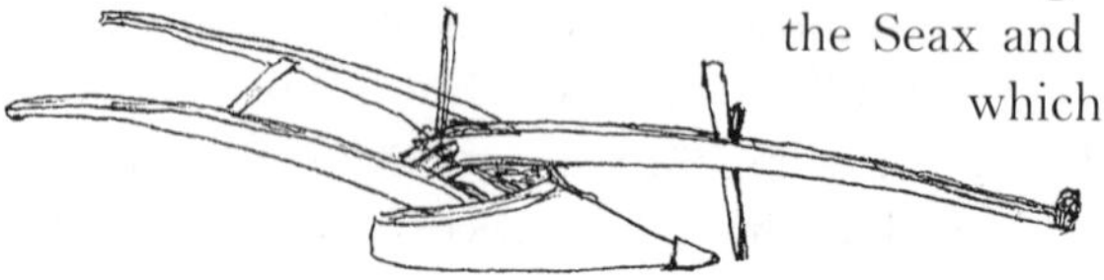

SAXON PLOUGH

The Saxons brought with them, in addition to the Seax and a lust for killing, a plough which constituted a revolution in agricultural practice – it not only dug deep, it turned the earth, unlike the earlier scratching tools. This enabled the Saxons to follow the Roman example in farming the fertile lowland areas. They had no need, initially anyway, to drive the natives off their meagre upland patches, but they gradually put their superior tools to wider use and extended tree clearing and systematic agriculture to the higher ground. Our clearing in the forest on the hilltop grew big enough to justify a name, and the Saxons, or Angles as they would be hereabouts, called it 'Micelee'.

Christianity and Northumbria

The darkness and horror of the years after the Romans left in about the year 400 gradually gave way to a more settled, stable way of life in the area from the river Humber to the narrow neck of Britain, the Forth-Clyde valley. This land, which came to be known as the great and glorious Kingdom of Northumbria, was enlightened by the fires of Celtic Christianity from Ireland, by way of Scotland – a strange phenomenon in view of the barbaric nature of both places – and then by Roman Christianity by way of Canterbury.

After Edwin became king of Northumbria in 616 and dominated all England except Kent, he married a Christian princess of that land, cunning fellow, and when she travelled to him at his capital, York, she brought with her the Roman missionary Paulinus, and before you could blink Edwin was not only married – he was baptised. Thus did Northumbria become Christian.

The qualities of the remarkable Edwin, in 'Kingsmanship, Statesmanship, and Gracious Humanity', guided by the lights of Christianity, brought a state of ordered peace and prosperity to Northumbria unknown since Roman times. It was said that a woman with her child could walk the breadth of the land, from sea to sea, without harm. If this were true the period must have been unique in history – she would be taking a chance today. Edwin had cups hung at drinking places, without their being removed or damaged (which practice continued until recently – within my memory). There again, I doubt if they would survive long in our civilisation – who needs drinking cups anyway? – Coke comes in cans. Penda, the heathen king of Mercia (the Midlands), with Cadwallan, king of the Britons – who continued to emerge from their Welsh hills – destroyed Edwin and with greed and envy (what else?) brought to an end these halcyon days. They temporarily darkened the land and plunged it back into fear and heathen disorder. Only when Penda himself was slain – old-time kings seemed to take turns at it – was the way open for the full flowering of Northumbrian Christianity around the Celtic St Aidan. Then, after the Synod of Whitby of 663 decided the destiny of the Church in the lap of Rome, through Canterbury, and after yet another period of turmoil and strife, Northumbria was finally destroyed as a kingdom and incorporated into the greater kingdom of England. Christians all – but no less savage for all that.

King Ethelbald ravaged Northumbria in 740, but Offa, who succeeded him, was a man of some note. He calmed the land, put England on the map, and influenced the whole of Europe.

Having gained the moral conquest of a more or less united land, under the Saxon invention of supposedly divinely appointed kings within a social system based on power through land ownership, Christianity proceeded to colonise it to some effect. Churches sprang up like mushrooms. Bishops proliferated – by 803 enough could be spared for two, and an Archbishop, to visit Bywell for the ordination of another, in the wooden church, or perhaps on the site of where it was to be built.

Although the Saxons brought with them, in addition to their plough and deadly sword, the skills of making lime-mortar, they used it only for the grandest of places, so the original church at Bywell would be of wood; it was cheap and plentiful – although the clearings were getting bigger ... Unfortunately, wood rots away and we have no evidence of an original wooden church.

There we have it then – Christianity at Bywell in 803. Did the Papal net ensnare the folk of Micelee? That was the purpose of all these churches – total conversion of every living soul; it was not difficult, simple people longed for spiritual meaning to their lives.

So the influence of Lindisfarne, the seat of Northumbrian civilisation, at least skirted Micelee when the 12th Bishop was consecrated on that 11th day of June, 803, by the Archbishop of York and the Bishops of Hexham and Whitby. This was a rare gathering of 'cloth'. How did they get there? Possibly by boat, part of the way; by horse or on foot the remainder, up the river valley a mere stone's throw from Micelee. Did we turn out to wave them past, as on future grand occasions? Did the Council forget to sweep the streets, as when the Queen Mum visited in 1987? Such goings-on – can you imagine? Bishops, let alone Archbishops, don't come without pomp; there must have been a rare fuss, and Bywell a-buzz. It was a place of some note, although the churches that we know, remarkable in their close proximity to each other, were not built until two or three hundred years later.

The first, the pretty little St Andrew's, the 'White Church', so called because of its founding by the 'white', PRAEMONSTRATENSTIAN monks of Blanchland, was not built until 1037. Imagine being asked your occupation and having to say, or worse still write, "I'm a Praemonstratenstian Monk"! The chancel of the larger St Peter's, the 'Black' church

THE TWIN CHURCHES OF BYWELL

ST ANDREWS

of the BENEDICTINE order of Durham, was not built until 1195, after the Normans.

The conversion process got a nasty setback when the warm glow of settled Christianity was struck from the north by the icy blast of Viking terror.

THE TWIN CHURCHES OF BYWELL
ST PETERS

This great occasion at Bywell came only ten years after the first, ghastly, Viking raid on Lindisfarne sickened the souls and struck fear into the hearts of decent people everywhere. Their bloody repulse at Jarrow the next year, 794, merely delayed the sacking of the land by forty years and perhaps caused some complacency, but might also have instigated in Christians a policy of Clerical dispersal. Bishops scattered about the country might have a better chance of surviving – some of them – than clusters of them in treasure-houses almost designed to attract these highly mobile raiders. I cannot understand why a Bishop of Lindisfarne would be ordained at Bywell – unless they just didn't want the Vikings to know.

By 835 raids were widespread, and by 865 no one in what had become a 'decadent' Saxon England was safe from these vicious predators. Christianity was no shield against the ravaging hordes of ruthless and cunning invaders who descended on these shores; killing for killing's sake, treachery and the most sordid depravity were their stock-in-trade. Their speedy, shallow-draught boats, ideal for the flat, easy rivers of the south, made possible even the unruly northern watercourses, in the right conditions even the Tyne as far as Hexham. Here was loot to be had.

At other times, landing any-old-where – Bywell, for instance, or in the valley below Micelee – the raiders grabbed the local cuddies (horses) and overlanded at speed. Everything was fast, commando style – quick in, quick out; these fellows didn't wait for retaliation to gather. They might easily have seized the Bishops at Bywell – and their valuables. Perhaps they were preoccupied elsewhere, or maybe their intelligence system wasn't up to standard. Bishops and all things civilised were the targets of these warrior thugs. The pathetic tale of the wanderings of the surviving monks from the sacking of Lindisfarne, the centre of the religious, cultural, scholastic and artistic world, typified the situation. Not until Durham Cathedral was built around the end of the century did they find a safe resting-place for the bones of their beloved Saint Cuthbert. They must surely have been glad of the dense woods for hiding in.

Micelee would hardly interest the Vikings – too poor to be worth the climb up the hill. Later, like the Saxons themselves, they were seduced by the prospects of an easier life, and the will to slaughter and pillage gave way to a desire for peace and comfort. Their lack of farming expertise would be

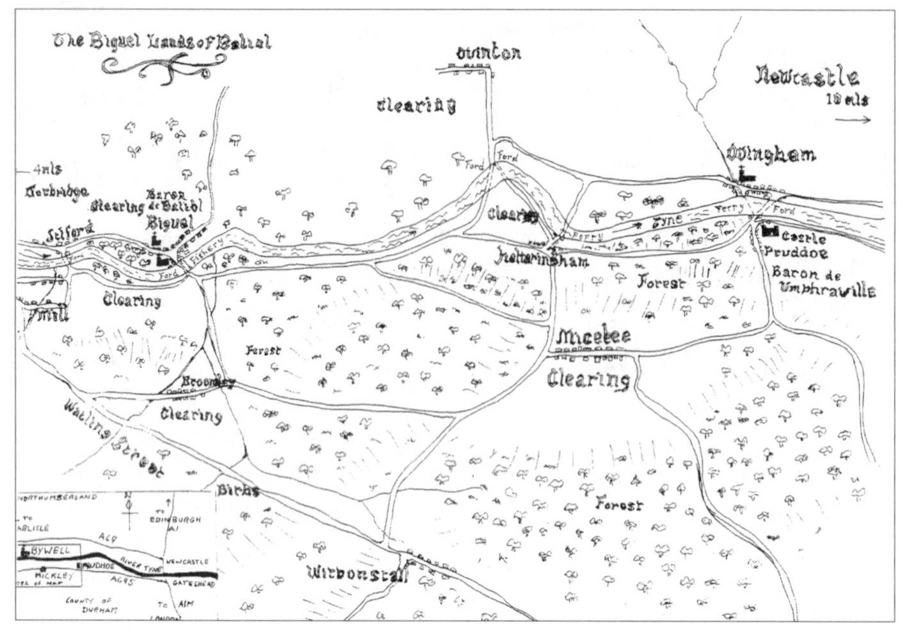

balanced by sound Saxon husbandry – thus do erstwhile enemies become friends; there's nothing like practical necessity for improving neighbourly relations. However, there is no evidence of settled Viking life at Micelee – but they did pass by; Hexham was a better 'shopping' place.

With intermissions during the glorious times of Alfred the Great and Canute, there was mayhem in the land for well-nigh 400 years – as long as the Roman era. Viking depredations were the main trouble, but internecine warring between internal groups played a part – rather like Yugoslavia in the 1990s. The world changes but man remains essentially savage.

Instability followed the decline of the Wessex dynasty of Alfred the Great. This brought what he had forged – a United States of England (allowing that wild Northumbria has never been much united with anywhere) into a state of ripeness for the picking by yet another wave of covetous Continentals – will they never stop! This time Modified Vikings, with most of their old vices and doubtless a few more picked up in their hundred years or so in France after they ceased their roving – but also with some good qualities, which were to manifest themselves in this conquered island through the years, superimposed on the several layers of characteristics of previous peoples.

These conquering Normans certainly influenced Micelee – they integrated it into their New Order of systematic government – through the Baliols of Bywell. They made the people of England subservient to the Lord and King, no longer 'free' as were those of the distant past. Freedom as enjoyed – or suffered – by the Britons was gone for ever, and the kind we know a long time coming.

Early refusal to submit to William brought what might today be termed 'genocide' to Northumbria, and survivors of the vengeance would live miserable, desolate lives in woods and hills. Perhaps the isolation and insignificance of Micelee saved its occupants; perhaps they once again melted into the woods, to sneak out when the flood-tide of pogrom had passed. Possibly it lay deserted and uncultivated until the gradual swell of French, Breton and Norman settlers came north and filled the vacant places. We know that it was settled in 1292, because 'Robert, son of Thomas of Eltringham, was cutting down a tree in the wood of Micelee …'

The Clearing

'Robert, son of Thomas of Eltringham, was cutting down a tree in the wood of Micelee when it fell on him and it crushed him so that he died three weeks afterwards. Verdict – Misfortune. Deodant on the tree – 5d.'.

This according to the Assize Report of 1292, in the reign of Edward I. A deodant was a charge, forfeited to the Crown (acting on behalf of God!), made against anything having caused a human death, to be used in alms, possibly and hopefully to alleviate the suffering of the deceased's family. How much alleviation 5d. would buy in those days is anybody's guess.

With no National Health Service, the nearest soothsayer or herbalist a long walk away in Corbridge (8 miles), or Newcastle (12 miles), and not of much help anyway, poor Robert must have had an uncomfortable three weeks a-dying on his bed of straw or heather. With a bit of luck there might have been someone nearby, an old crone or witch who knew enough about wild plants to mix him a soothing concoction; otherwise he would just have to pray. Praying was fashionable, it comforted the dying and gave hope to the hopeless.

This same Assize Report recorded that:

'Thomas Strangale, called Clayport, struck Edmund of Micelee with a shovel on the head so that he died the third day and Thomas immediately fled and is found guilty. His chattels are worth 16s. 6d., for which the ville of Micelee must account.'

It is interesting to note that the village was held accountable for the misdemeanours of its inhabitants – now

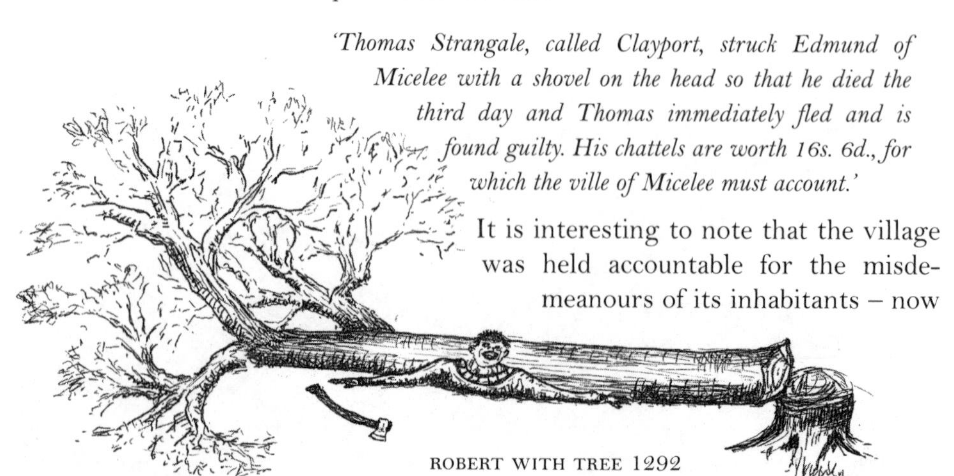

ROBERT WITH TREE 1292

there's a thought for today!

Although England boasts more than one Mickley, it is probable that these Assize Reports of the thirteenth century refer to the hilltop Anglo-Saxon 'Clearing in the Forest' and forerunner of today's High Mickley. It was part of the Barony of Bywell, which in turn was part of the Norman system of strict order and control, devolving down from the King, which ensured that accurate records were kept for purposes of taxation, mustering soldiers, and 'keeping the King's peace'. So that, although these records were of limited scope regarding such an inconsequential place as Micelee, they give us some idea of the kind of place it was and of how the people lived all those years ago.

Simplicity was the keynote – subsistence agriculture, still within but beginning to emerge from, the feudal system in which the King (deputising for God), owned all men and all things. He ruled through, and could be (but wasn't necessarily) guided by his chosen men – his Council of Advisers, mostly Barons beholden to him. These were all-powerful in their own areas so long as they paid their dues and respects, produced a Knight or two and mustered a few troops when the needs of war arose. Kings, Barons and lowly ones alike, all came under the supreme dominance of Roman Catholic Christianity. Normans were dedicated Christians – look at their churches and cathedrals.

Northumberland, a fragment of the broken Northumbria, was a long way from the seat of power and still wild – to the extent of not having been considered worth including in the Domesday Book of 1086. The Baliols and the Umphravilles could not have been particular favourites at court, to be 'rewarded' with such unpromising possessions – unless they were considered the right kind of roughnecks for the job of taming the 'Badlands'.

The floods of strife between the English and Scots ebbed and flowed over Northumberland for centuries and few were safe, except perhaps the likes of Mr De Umphraville in his castle down the hill from Micelee, at Prudhoe. Although more than a hundred years before our first mention of Micelee in the Assize Reports, the new wooden castle at Prudhoe withstood siege by William, the Scottish Lion, in 1173–74. It is unlikely that the folk of Micelee were left unscathed; rampaging Scots had rare appetites and little in the way of victuals would survive their passing during their several months in residence, just two miles down the hill.

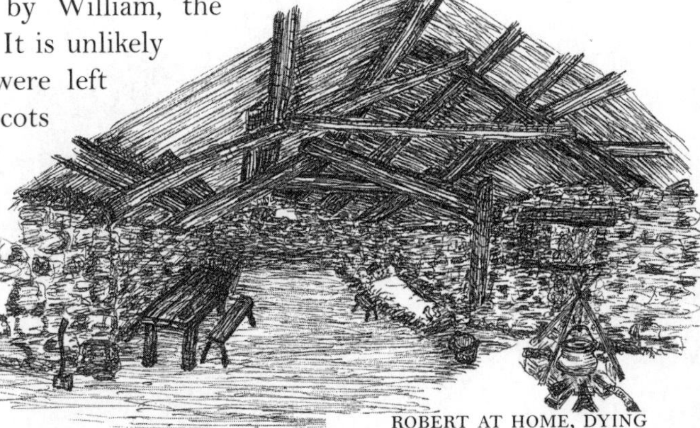

ROBERT AT HOME, DYING

But perhaps no one

lived at Micelee at the time. Lack of firm evidence makes for speculation and conjecture but, as the name indicates, this was an Anglo-Saxon settlement and Prudhoe castle was part of the Norman attempt to subjugate the fiercely independent and stubborn natives of this unruly northern land.

It was likely that any villagers still about kept their distance, or even joined forces with the Scots in common cause against the hated intruders. Any Norman settlers would take refuge with the 'boss' at his castle, or melt into the woods like the natives, to re-emerge when the coast was clear, to resume the business of 'integration'.

The Coming of the Baliols

The Baliols probably came to England in a later wave of Norman invaders. In 1090 William Rufus, the Red Prince, gave Biguel (Bywell), and other lands, to Guy de Baliol for 'services to his king'. He came from Picardy, where the family, Bailliol, or Balliol, were wealthy and powerful.

Baliols had no stone castle at Bywell, but plenty of good oak – Bywell grew the very best – so they and their Normans could be safe in a wooden fort. Or were they absentee landlords? More than likely, for Bernard built 'Barnard' castle, a grand stone affair on the Tees, and I cannot see them dallying over long at Bywell when they had such secure, even comfortable, accommodation further south – except maybe for summer holidays, and a bit of deer-chasing.

The village itself was defensible against marauders, being built in Saxon style, of parallel rows of houses between which stock could be kept safe at night and in time of danger, by closing off and defending the ends of the street. This was standard village practice, but not of much avail against a major Scottish onslaught, although the Baliols were on good terms with the Scots – most of the time. It didn't stop Cumen, Chancellor of Scotland, plundering Bywell in 1140 – in which case Micelee would have been included. It was in an invidious position, two miles from Bywell, and only two from Prudhoe, which William the Lion of Scotland had sworn to destroy. There was no love lost 'twixt Scots and Umphravilles. Poor old Micelee; although it too would be built on the Saxon principle of a defensible street, the defence was more likely to have been against thieves than against serious swordsmen. Living in an outlying ville like Micelee, at a distance from the protection of the Master in his wooden fort, must have been a tricky business indeed.

In the main, the various Baliols seem to have been pretty adept at walking the tightrope of power and possession, and kept Kingly favour, betimes against Church and Barons. The first Bernard gained the favour of King David of Scotland and was rewarded with the gift of more land. Bernard the Second helped and gained some glory, in the relief of Alnwick in 1174, and the defeat of William the Lion. He kept in favour with the monks of Durham by confirming the gift of St Peter's at Bywell. Hugh stayed on good terms with King John and supported him against the Barons at the time of Magna Carta – a bit of a creep, I would say; but then, that was the way of the world, if a hold was to be kept on one's land – and head.

John Baliol inherited in 1228 and was worth 30 Knight's fees – his dad had crept to some effect! John had to bow the knee and pay a heavy fine to regain the King's favour after putting the foot wrong during his period as Regent of Scotland, when Henry's child daughter became Queen to King Alexander the Third. Oh, the machinations: but John gave sterling support to the King in his war with the Barons in 1258–65 and was held in the highest regard – on equal terms with Simon de Montford. He married Devorguil, daughter and sole heir to the Lord of Galloway, Constable of Scotland, direct descendant of King David – and heir to the throne of Scotland. Thus did he unwittingly condemn the Baliols of Bywell.

How is this for a tale of devotion? When John died in 1268 his wife had his heart embalmed in a casket which she kept by her at all times, and had it interred with her in 1290 – resting on her heart – in Sweetheart Abbey, which she had founded in Galloway. She followed her John's devotion to education by completing the college he founded in Oxford – Baliol College. Let those who think those distant times grim and horrid, match that for a story of romance and beauty – in the context of the quick-fix marriages of this age.

Son Hugh died in 1272 and all his possessions were valued. Alexander succeeded and died in 1278, and was succeeded by his youngest brother John, who inherited considerable and widespread lands. Apart from Bywell and Barnard Castle he had Hichin, Driffield, Kempston and Fotheringay – and land in Scotland assessed at £3,289.14s. 1½d, a huge amount. In addition to all of this, and sadly for a man who was scholarly rather than warlike, he was heir-presumptive to the throne of Scotland ... John might have lived quite comfortably and kept the Baliols at Bywell to this day, like the Percys at Alnwick, had he not naively accepted the support of Edward the First in his (rightful) claim to the throne. This against John de Hastings and Robert de Bruce, for a country hardly worth the squabbling over – divided, brutal, uncouth, even by the standards of the times, and impoverished. Why would anyone want it? Only, I suspect, in the case of the English kings, to put an end to the plundering incursions over the border, especially those in support of France, the implacable foe of England.

Whatever the politics, John gave the power-hungry, land-grabbing Bishop Beck of Durham parts of Tynedale – Wark and Symundburn – in return for his help in gaining the throne. He came to be king for a while, crowned at Scone on St, Andrew's Day, 1292. A fateful year – it did little for our Robert at Micelee either. Although ostensibly a mere puppet of Edward, and seen and resented as such by the Scots, John had the will to resist being pushed around but he made the fatal mistake of entering into an alliance of mutual support with the French. This resulted, when Edward invaded Gascony in 1296, in the Scots ravaging Northumberland. They burnt the nunnery at Lambley, destroyed the Abbey at Hexham, and burnt the school – including, so it is said, the scholars.

This unseemly behaviour was unacceptable, even in those days, and Edward's retribution was swift and devastating, to the point of John surrendering Scotland to him. John Baliol of Bywell, King of Scotland, went to the Tower until 1299, then was released and ended his days in 1314, on his estates in France. His English estates, including Micelee, were seized by the Crown in 1293.

John's son Edward was brought back from Picardy by Edward the Third. in another attempt at setting-up a puppet King in Scotland, and he was crowned at Scone in 1332. But the arrangement was never comfortable and though he reigned for 24 years, in 1356 Edward handed the country back to Edward. Like his gentle and scholarly father, neither brutal nor warlike, he was out of place as ruler of a wild and disorderly country, shuttle-cocked between scheming kings of England and France. The unhappy history of England and Scotland might well have taken a smoother, happier path under the influence of the Baliols. They were liberal and forward-looking in running their estates and in the forefront of the movement out of serfdom, towards freedom and happier lives for the peasants.

As it was, Edward Baliol died near Doncaster in 1363, having no apparent connection with the Bywell estates. Thus ended the distinguished line of the Baliols – warriors, nobles, kings and scholars, and erstwhile masters of the Township of Micelee; now remembered only, but honourably, in Baliol College, Oxford.

An interesting aspect of this story of Micelee is the manner of its changing ownership through the centuries – unlike Prudhoe, which has remained in the same ownership throughout its nine hundred year history, although it could be argued that the Umphraville link with the Percys is by now a pretty tenuous one. The widow of the last Umphraville, Gilbert, who died in 1381, married Henry Percy, fourth Lord of Alnwick, and took with her all of the possessions of the de Umphravilles. Bywell was handed around among those in favour, when those in possession put the foot wrong.

In early times land was anyone's who was strong enough to grab it and hang on: then it all belonged to the King, who was strong enough (with God's backing, and an army or two) to seize and hold it all; he doled it out as favours and took it back if so disposed. Status and power became based on land ownership – in close combination with the sword.

The Baliols had the land, and the power – but were still obliged to their King. For Micelee, in 1242, John was obliged to the tune of 'half a Knight's fee'. How much was a Knight worth? I suppose it depended on how good he was at his job (and what position he played in?).

In return the Baron gained the income from the ville in the form of some crops, some labour, and some cash but not a lot as coins had not yet replaced barter in the lower orders. Men were just beginning to emerge from serfdom and pay rent and for goods with their services and crops. All men, serf and lord alike, were still obliged to serve their King when the need arose – except that the Lord could buy his way out. At about 100 shillings for a Knight, 30 would cost a Baliol a tidy sum. This involved keeping records, so that Kings knew how they stood, and kept tabs on cheating. These records – pipe rolls – give us our window onto life long ago ...

The records show that, when John de Baliol died in 1268 the extent of that part of the Barony known as Micelee was:

- In Demesne (one's possessions or domain): 105 acres, value 6d. per acre – 52s. 6d.
- Meadow, 4 acres at 16d. – 5s. 4d.
- Also: 9 Villeins (serfs) each holding 24 acres, paying 6s. yearly – 54s.
- Also: 5 Cottars each holding a cottage with curtilage (plot), paying 6s. 6d. yearly.
- Also: From the mill for multure (toll of grain or flour paid to the miller) 11s. yearly.

Freeholders were:

- Adam of Micelee (surnames were not yet in general use) holds 1 carucate (as much as a team – oxen, not footballers – could plough in a year) and pays yearly 1lb. pepper, value 8d. Also one toft (homestead) in increase of his holding and pays 1lb. cumin, value 1½d. He also holds 1 ploughland of 6 acres by himself (on his own account) – 12d.
- Henry of Halton holds 1 carucate for 1lb. cumin – 1½d.
- William, son of Adam, holds 40 acres, pays 2lbs. pepper, value 16d., per annum.
- Henry of the buttery (buteiller – wine store) holds 24 acres for 1lb cumin – 1½d.
- William, son of Michael, holds 12 acres and pays 1lb pepper at 8d.
- Edmund of Byrtely holds 12 acres and pays 1lb. pepper at 8d.

Notice the Norman names – Micelee was by now fully 'integrated'.

And that is it! Not a lot to it, one might say, and difficult to value by our standards; but in the context of the times, when the entire population of England amounted to no more than the present population of, say, Tyneside, and industry as we know it didn't exist, this was an active agricultural community. The clearing had indeed become 'large'; not necessarily thriving though – in a wet year the rent would be hard to find, and every winter a trial. But at least at times there was relative peace in the land, so that a man could enjoy the fruits of his labours and the simple pleasures of the times, without fear of brutal Scottish raiders or of being hacked to pieces on some distant battlefield in the service of the King. Although serfdom was passing, links of duty and responsibility still tied all men together.

Did I say life was simple? – more likely primitive, little improved on Roman times, even for the wealthy.

Bend your imagination to life without electricity and all its concomitants; without gas, matches or lights other than flickering rush lamps. These were made (try it!) by peeling all but a narrow strip of the outer skin of the rush, exposing the pith, to make a wick, then dipping it in animal fat. Imagine the smell as it burned its dim half-hour life away. Without things mechanical, or musical except simple whistles and no way of passing-on tunes, and tales, except by ear. Only the gentry – and by no means all of them – scribes and men of religion, could read.

Fires had to be worked for; only fallen branches and twigs from the still abundant forests were free – and might have to be carried some distance. Cutting tools were often poor and it must have been very true at the time that logs warm in three ways – by carrying, cutting and burning. The fire was all-important, the focal point of life, provider of light as well as heat; comforter and companion; living, dancing, dangerous, smoky (was there lung cancer?) – the means of making rough, often tough, food palatable – old animals are easier to catch, and tastier than the young and tender.

The main utensils of cooking were hot stones for baking, and the cauldron, hung over the fire and ever ready – anything edible found its way into this stewing pot and came out hot and tasty whenever needed.

Some meats – hedgehogs for example, were encased in clay and baked in the fire's embers. Gypsies might still use this method of cooking hedgehogs but there are few real Romanies about now – and few hedgehogs – and 'Travellers' live on Social Security, are probably vegetarian, and couldn't catch anything to eat except possibly a noodle! Cooking hedgehogs must have posed a problem in sandy places, but Micelee was not short of clay so they would definitely be on the menu – plentiful, tasty, nourishing – and free. Wild meat was good as well as free, its abundance an inducement that brought foreigners flocking to this land through the ages. But the humble didn't eat the Lord's deer – not when he was looking anyway.

EARLY HEARTH

Coarsely milled flour, or in

Micelee often oatmeal, was baked on hot stones or, in better homes, under earthenware covers; pretty rough stuff and not conducive to diverticulitis – makers of indigestion and constipation remedies would have had a pretty thin time, had they been about. This bread, if it was bread and not oat cakes, would be much like that burned by King Alfred (did he burn it deliberately, so as not to have to eat it?) except that wheat grown in Micelee would make even more solid stuff, Northern wheat was never the best for bread-making. There would be no need for fluoride in the toothpaste – jaws and teeth must have been like stone-crushers.

The fire sat upon the earth, or on a flat stone hearth, and the smoke went out, with a bit of luck, through a hole in the roof – or any other gaps.

Roofs were difficult for peasants; the Roman skills of building went with them and only when the Saxons brought their knowledge of lime mortar was building in stone revived – but mostly for religious work. The Vikings were more concerned with knocking down than putting up, so it was only when the Normans took over that building in stone really began in earnest. Again, priority lay in churches, castles and strong houses for the wealthy – for the humble, wood was the stuff of home, and nothing wrong with that. Free or cheap, readily available, and not calling for a lot of skill in the fashioning of a simple cottage.

The very poor lived in hovels – the British equivalent of the Eskimo igloo. Used from the earliest times, still known in Mickley in the eighteenth century, it cost nothing to make (needed no planning permission) and gave shelter from the worst of the weather. Hovels varied with the skill of the builder and the materials on hand. Unlike the men of such places as Corbridge, who could filch nice squared stones from Roman ruins, Micelee builders had only the rough, uneven stones from the fields, which were difficult to build without mortar into straight walls, let alone the square corners necessary for oblong or 'lean-to' hovels that were fairly easy to roof and cover with turves or thatch. So round walls of turf were as likely as stone where skills or stones were lacking – hence now no trace of their existence. Thickly stacked turves or stones, low for stability, formed rough walls with only a hole for an entrance and as like as not no window. The roof was of branches, in the round version crossed at the top like an Indian tepee, interlaced with hazel rods to form a base for turf or thatch of free for the gathering, abundant heather. Hazel has been throughout history one of the most useful and versatile of trees, providing valuable food, fencing, windbreaks, firewood, pegs, rods, wattle walls, foundations for roads and railways over wet land – and walking-sticks for the infirm. Heather made a thatch that was coarse and untidy-looking compared to the neat reed or straw of southern areas, but it was waterproof if laid well and thickly enough on a roof of steep enough pitch; warm and very durable in this harsh climate. It was still in use locally in the eighteenth century but today's thatcher would have to travel some distance for his material – the frontiers of agriculture have pushed heather a long way from Micelee in 700 years. In its day heather must have been supremely useful to the folk of Micelee; apart from providing roofing, it made quick, hot fuel, winter stock-feed and it purpled the land in autumn, as it does now the moors, with flowers that with the help of bees produced sweetening – the only available – fit for the gods – and the brave of heart! It tinted the roofs with a subtle glow of rich, warm colour, and perhaps even made a 'spring-interior' mattress for Robert's deathbed.

The reference, when John Baliol died in 1268, to 'cottars' indicates something better than turf hovels for the recorded people of the ville, but they would be pretty simple for all that. In the absence of mortar, stone cottages would be little better than rectangular hovels. Perhaps they were of wood – timber framed, with hazel wattle, mud daubed walls such as were common in the softer climate of the South; but they would hardly be durable this far north, unless lime could be mixed with the mud and ox-dung daub. So until sawn wooden boards, or lime mortar and quarried stone became available, together with the skills to use them, and cheap enough for common use, there was no choice – the cottage would be of turf, rubble, or wattle hung with heather – the materials to hand. At least no planning approval was needed, and I'll warrant the end-product of the builders' efforts in 1290 were infinitely more aesthetically pleasing, with their purple-tinged, grey and green lichen encrusted walls and roofs, than the technologically-packed masterpieces of design that afflict our senses today. Aesthetically more pleasing maybe – but jolly uncomfortable inside: still with the hole in the roof for the smoke.

Furniture would be of the simplest – table and stools or benches and rough wooden frames, straw or heather covered, for beds – for some not even the wooden frame to raise them off the earthen floor, just the heather with its natural springing and aura of the wild moors. Rough blankets of coarse, homespun wool. Not much inducement to lie late, even in the long winter nights, when there was not much else to do. There would of course be, as ever, the aspiration to 'a better life'.

STONE AND TURF HOVEL

Comfort depended greatly on location, shelter being important up there on the hilltop, but trees aplenty helped. Dampness, though, must have been a vexed problem in the absence of a 'waterproof membrane'. Away from the quick-draining glacial sand and gravel deposits in the river valley, the land hereabouts is largely of a clay nature, good for baking hedgehogs and potentially very fertile – great with a bit of manure and a lot of hard work for growing the classic Geordie 'show leek'; but damp for lying on, although not liable to flood – a good place for the early establishment of agriculture. Three good springs of water would also be a great attraction at this distance from the river; no one in old Micelee had far to carry water – and it would be of good quality.

Wood was the raw ingredient of home. With little in the way of tools except a knife and axe, even the least skilled of peasants could fashion some household items – spoons, platters, even bowls, and make simple beds and benches – skills were developing by the end of the 13th century. Whittling was for winter nights by the fire. Some material could be bought in – good timber from the Lord down at Bywell, and ironwork from the forges there.

More difficult items would be bartered for, although coinage was circulating more freely, so that things like iron and copper implements or utensils that were made elsewhere could be bought from peddlers, who hawked their wares around remote dwellings, on foot or with the aid of pack-animals. Coinage greatly helped the acquisition of special items that could only be bought at the weekly markets at Ovingham or Corbridge, or, in the case of very unusual or rare things, at the great occasional, special, and annual fairs. No popping round to the village shop or along to M&S's for the every need; but the day out at the market or fair with a few pennies in the purse, or something to sell, would be one of life's highlights. The fine weather, early morning walk through two (to Ovingham) or five (Corbridge) quiet country miles in the company of wife (to share the load, as well as the pleasure) and children must have given a gentle joy of a kind difficult to imagine in today's fevered, frantic world. The children had no need of education other than at the knee of life; there was none to be had for the poor anyway, and every day was a holiday – when the work was done.

'Window shopping', before shops, and centuries before sheet-glass for windows, was an active, intimate matter, rather like the Eastern bazaar – full of noise and smells and bustle and strange goings-on, even in places like Ovingham where the thirteenth-century market was somewhat limited but would be the most likely one for Micelee folk – if the river was in a fit state to be crossed.

Strict laws controlled markets, where they could be held and on what days; Sunday was common – when it didn't call for a day off work. The local boss-man, Lord or Baron ('The Council' incarnate!) took his toll from the traders. It seems a bit odd that the Umphravilles of Prudhoe, the Barony of which owed service to the King of nine and three-quarters Knight's fees, controlled Ovingham market, which dated from Saxon times, yet had no market in Prudhoe, which seems to have been a place of not much consequence, apart from its castle; in fact the south side of the river seems to have been pretty poorly served in all manner of ways.

Ovingham was the place for Sunday shopping; there could be had ironware, dried fish (with a teeming river on hand?), salt, millstones. It seems somewhat restricted – and it would need a pretty hefty wife to get a millstone up that hill to Micelee; Corbridge would be the place for 'supermarket' things; it had long been one of the principal towns in Northumberland, vying with Bamburgh as capital, and was still a considerable market town. There could be bought grain, animals, meat, salmon, sheepskins, goatskins, wine, honey, cloth, onions, garlic, herring and other sea fish, salt, cheese, butter, brushwood, stock fish and 'Aberdeens', oil, turves, hides, potash, wool, iron, lead, bark, wood, boards, charcoal, nails, horseshoes, 'cart-clouts' (nails), steel, lard and grease, alum and copperas, copper, griddles, cooking pots, cauldrons and faggots. Corbridge is not what it was.

For exotics there was a three or four hour walk to Newcastle (a horse was a help but few in Micelee had one) and a long carry back, uphill all the way, but there those with money could buy pepper (that's odd – some paid the rent with it in Micelee), almonds, cinnamon, figs, raisins and sea-coal; luxury stuff.

Newcastle was big, and important for the shipment of wool and hides – the only sizeable port in the North after the English destroyed Berwick. Wool here was of poor quality compared to that of the great wealth-creating southern sheep, and was never a major export compared to leather, for which the area was renowned and Newcastle the principal port in England for its export. The earliest craft guilds were skinners, tanners, saddlers and cordwainers (shoemakers). Ships going out laden did not come back empty, so people living within reasonable distance of the port had the benefit of imported food and goods from distant places. Whether the folk of Micelee could afford such luxuries is doubtful – perhaps on a special occasion, in a good year?

Production of hide animals in the country around Newcastle would be profitable, and the gathering of oak-bark for tanning a money-spinner for those with the coppicing rights in the Baliol woods. There is no mention of this in the local rolls or registers but barking certainly went on in the woods of Mickley until the end of the nineteenth century, if not later. There is still a trade in oak bark for high-class tanning, and bark for the gathering in High Close Wood, where I sit writing this. Maybe I would be better – and more profitably – engaged in its gathering!

A Bit of Taxation

By the time Edward I decided to sort out the Welsh, the Scots and the French, methods of raising the revenue needed for waging war, even in those days, were well developed; the tentacles of the tax-collector reached to the remotest corners of the country – even to little Micelee.

Parliament was well enough established for its approval to be needed by the King before he could raise money by taxation; it had to be for a specific purpose, such as a campaign against the French – always good for a tussle – and by a specific means. It is interesting to note, in these perhaps more tolerant times, that Parliament approved the tax of 1290 in thanks for the Royal expulsion of the Jews from England.

Taxes were based on the value of the possessions of all householders, exceeding a small amount determined by a local jury. They, aided by the reeve (chief magistrate of the district) and four men of the ville, also assessed the value of the goods. These assessments were also checked for accuracy and fairness by Assessors and Collectors appointed by the King's Council, who could call on the Sheriff of the County for enforcement. He was the King's direct representative, and very powerful. In 1296 the Sheriff of Northumberland appointed a bailiff in each of 8 wards – one for Tynedale. Bailiffs were responsible for the delivery of legal writs and mandates. There were four coroners, outside the Administration, seeing that there was no abuse of the system – even by Sheriffs or Bailiffs. The system worked fairly well, so long as taxes were just and reasonable. The injustice of the Poll Tax of 1372 provoked the Peasants Revolt.

The assessments were recorded as the Lay Subsidy Roll and give us our insight into life in 13th and 14th century Northumberland.

All this may seem unwieldy but remember that the entire population of England was then only about 3 to 4 million, and although communications were on the slow side, it was quite easy for 'authority' to keep an eye on everyone. The whole set-up was the basis of our present system of ordered, law-abiding, taxpaying society.

To prevent undue hardship, poor people were exempt on clothing and household essentials, food in the larder, ploughs, small carts, rakes and spades. Knights were exempt on armour (tools of the trade?), riding horse, jewels and clothing and vessels of silver and gold. Merchants were exempt on a garment for themselves and their wife, a double bed, a ring, a buckle of gold or silver, a girdle of silk if in daily use (!), and a drinking cup of silver or maple. How stand you on this assessment? "Thank goodness," you say, "for P.A.Y.E." – even if it all goes to provide for politicians and rogues!

The Lay Subsidy Roll of 1296 resulted for Micelee in assessments like these:

> 2 oxen valued at 8s; 2 cows at 6s. 8d; 3 hoggets at 3s; 8 ewes at 8s; 2 quarters of wheat at 6s; 5 quarters of oats at 5s. Total Liability 36s. 8d.

The County Commissioners (yes, we still have them!) duplicated these rolls – without duplicators or computers, kept a copy and sent the other to the King's exchequer, with the taxes.

The Society of Antiquaries of Newcastle are the custodians of these rolls for Northumberland.

The tax rate was set, in 1294, at one tenth for country folk and one sixth for townsfolk. Now there's a thought for today's Chancellors, with V.A.T. on fuel and country folk feeling the cold.

The system was in the manner of today's Local Taxation, assessed and collected village by village, town by town – but the money went south for spending.

To give an idea of the relative size, population and value of various places in this area:

> Newcastle's assessment was in the region of £900, paid by about 300 householders, compared with the Northern capital, York, at about £1,500, paid by about 800.
>
> Hexham, being an ecclesiastical borough, was exempted from the tax system – good for Hexham, except that it is doubtful if the Church was any less severe a tax-master than the King. No doubt the folk of Hexham paid their dues – or there would have been mass migration from Micelee.
>
> Corbridge was assessed at £159 on 77 householders.
>
> Newcastle, Bamburgh and Corbridge, being boroughs, each sent 2 representatives to Parliament – chosen by their peers of course, not elected.
>
> The average assessment for Northumberland towns and villages in 1296 was £31 and these are the Ward totals, with Glendale and Coquetdale the wealthiest places:
>
> West Tynedale, £553.10s. 2d.; East Tynedale, £1,430.2s. 1d.; The Boroughs

(Newcastle, Corbridge, Bamburgh), £1,109.18s. 0½d.; Tyne and Wansbeck, £885.3s. 8½d.; West Coquetdale, £956.2s. 0d.; Glendale, £1,180.17s. 2d. Ha'pennies were treated with respect!

These local assessments for East Tynedale make interesting reading:

Prodow (Prudhoe).

Barony held by Sir Gilbert de Umphraville, Earl of Angus, owing service of 9 Knight's fees. The demesne (in ownership) covered 120 acres arable and wood. 40 bondages of 18 acres, 16 cottages, several free tenants and tenants at will; 2 water mills and a Tyne fishery.

G. de Umphraville, £10. 2s. 4d.; Ten others, including Gilbert the Fool, £1.0s. 9d. (taxed at a tenth of a tenth of the other, Lordly, Gilbert, the Fool was no fool). Total assessment, £23.15s. 7d.; Tax due £2.3s. 3d.

It would appear that Prudhoe hardly counted or there was a bit of tax fiddling going on!

Heltringham (Eltringham).

In the Barony of Baliol of Bywell.

Held in 1271 by Adam of Heltringham by drenage (work equivalent) service worth £2.4s. 9d.

Assessments were : Adam of Heltringham, £1.18s.; Adam, son of Alan, 11s. 9d.; Ranulph of Heltringham, £1.0s. 9d. Total assessment, £3.10s. 6d. Tax due, 6s. 4½. Half the total tax was on one household.

The original Heltringham disappeared when 'the householder' cleared dependants from around his house. The same happened at Apperley and Healey. The local boss liked his privacy, just as much as did the Lord.

Apperley

In the Barony of Baliol of Bywell. Held by Adam of Newcastle, grandson of Adam, clerk of Newcastle town court.

Adam of Newcastle, £18.3s. 4d.; Denise of Micelee, £1.13s. 6d. Total assessment, £19.16s. 10d. Tax due £1.16s. 1d.

Biguel (Bywell)

The Barony of Baliol. In demesne, 180 acres arable, 16 meadow; 3 free tenants, 2 bondagers, 19 cottars, a water mill and a fishery. Total assessment £18.13s. 4d. Tax due £1 3s. 11½d.

Owyngham (Ovingham)

In the Barony of Prudhoe. Held in demesne by de Umphraville. A parish. The Rectory valued at £96.4s. 10½d; A portion of the Priory of Tynemouth, £3.0s. 10d; Thomas of Nafferton, £17.0s. 6d; Roger, son of Vyup, £3.13s. 6d;

Roger of Higham, £4.1s. Total assessment £8.12s. Tax due 15s. 7½. Roger Higham was a merchant and Bailiff of Newcastle, also held property at Whittonstall and Apperly. Did he 'commute', or was he an absent landlord?

Owynton (Ovington)

In the Barony of Bywell, held in one twelfth of a Knight's fee.

Eleven assessed, the highest £5.8s. 4d. (a widow). Total assessment £26. 19s. 5d. Tax due £2. 9s. ½.

Micelee

Part of the Barony of Bywell, held in the service of half a Knight's fee. The assessments were:

> Roger Conil, £1.15s. 9d; William, son of Michael, 17s. 6d.; Thomas, son of Roger, 19s. 3d.; Adam, son of Roger Conil, £1. 12s. 10d; Richard the smith, £2. 3s; William of Gainford, 13s; Walter the Reeve, £2. 0s; Adam of Birkenside £1. 3s; Isabella the widow, 13s; Adam of Micelee, £3. 16s. Total assessment £15.13s. 4d. Tax due £1. 8s. 6d.

So Micelee had a higher tax value than Prudhoe, discounting the Baron; higher than Ovingham, and almost as high as Bywell, which boasted the added assets of the water-mill and fishery. Although Ovington was worth only a twelfth of a Knight's fee, compared to a half for Micelee, it appears to have been a better-off place in that eleven households were assessed at a total of £27, compared to ten at Micelee worth less than £16. Which seems to belie the saying, of more recent times, that Ovington lies on the sunny side of the river and Mickley on the 'Money' side. Perhaps the difference then lay in the more favoured location agriculturally, sunny and less exposed, with easier access to markets and no difficult river crossing.

Names Skills and Status

Micelee's tax returns showed the trend towards 'surnames' – identifying people by what they did rather than whence they came or who their father was. There is Richard the smith – Richard Smith; and Walter the reeve – Walter Reeve. Indicating that the ville boasted not only a blacksmith, but a man of consequence; that is if the Reeve lived in the ville and did not just own property there. There must have been at least one decent house.

There was also a mill, so, potentially, a Mr Miller. Up there on the windy hilltop it was likely to be a windmill – but possibly an ox-driven 'ginge', which would be easier and cheaper to build and independent of the weather; but the wind came free – oxen had to be fed.

There was a 'buttery'. This puzzles – not for making butter, as might be expected, but BUTEILLER – wine store. Wine in Micelee seven hundred years ago? Hard to believe, but there it is, and a keg of wine by ship to Newcastle then twelve miles by oxcart on virtually non-existent roads, would be a welcome luxury to people used to water or home-brewed ale of variable and mostly pretty vile quality. Perhaps it came upriver by shallow-draught boat – Romans, Vikings and probably other oarsmen have made better use of the river than we who are spoilt for choice of transport. Either way, it is to be hoped it was a wine that travelled well.

The 'Micelee' of Saxon times, and the French 'buteiller' indicate movement of language, continued over centuries, that embraced British, Roman, Celtic, Saxon, Danish and French and moulded what came to be known as 'English' by the time of Chaucer. The language of Micelee in the days of Robert of the tree would be mongrel, but predominantly French. Latin remained the word of the Church and scholars, but Micelee was too far from churches, and short on educational aspirations in the peasant classes, to be unduly bothered about Latin. Normans, and their language, would be dominant.

The latent abilities of simple people were more inclined towards the development of craftsmanship, driven by the needs of agriculture and hopes of an easier life. The methods and tools of agriculture (which dominated – getting enough food was the principal occupation) changed only slowly in almost 2,000 years until the eighteenth century. Tools improved as better materials became available, but the sickle of today is essentially that of 1296 and earlier.

Mr Smith was the man in whose hands the developing skills of metal working were carried inexorably towards the Industrial Revolution; and here we are in 1296 with a Smith in Micelee, probably using iron made at Crawcrook, where there was early forging, providing for the agricultural and domestic needs of the ville – but never developing beyond this, unlike the smiths of Bywell, who became renowned for the making of iron goods, especially fittings for horse harness. Micelee Smith probably learned his skills at Bywell.

And here we are, seven hundred years later, still with a Smithy in Mickley – but sadly in name only. It ceased to work in 1928, when the last remnants of the old Baliol estate, of which it was a part, were sold; it is now a dwelling-house.

Life and Death

The simple, indeed primitive, lifestyle enjoyed by the peasants of Micelee was not much different from that of the nobility – except for the trappings. Perhaps the Baliols and Umphravilles were less likely to go hungry, although not necessarily so – in times of famine a peasant had as much chance as a Lord of catching a fleet-footed rabbit. Lordly clothes would be fancier but not necessarily warmer for withstanding the rigours of draughty castles, which would be no warmer, perhaps colder, than a cosy cotte or hovel – and just as smoke-filled. The big difference, and it made all the difference, was in the unremitting toil that was the peasant's lot, in trying to eke a precarious existence from the land, with everything done by hand or at best ox-driven. There was the horror and fear of quagmire, drought, failed harvest and short, cruel, bitter winter days spent gathering ivy, twigs and gorse (for pummelling into a state fit for animals to eat) to sustain the few animals that could be over-wintered and on which depended tomorrow's spring, when yesterday's summer had given Micelee a miss. The grimness would be balanced, to some extent no doubt, by the joy and satisfaction of springs glorious, summers fruitful, and autumns rewarding – but all jolly hard work. This was the lot of the simple man and his family – some joy, a lot of misery. It helped if order and peace reigned in the land – sometimes it did.

The Lord did no toil, but from Roman times to Victorian he knew not the pleasures of central-heating, plumbing or sanitation; he was as likely to die by the sword as his villeins and by jove he had to look to his loyalties. Today's boss-man, if he jumps the wrong way, might lose his job and the company car; yesterday's noble, backing the wrong royal (or usurper) stood to lose everything – including his head and his entrails.

The noble's wife's biggest problem, apart from keeping his head on his shoulders, was bearing children – just like the peasant's wife; there was no escape, it was their lot, from puberty to menopause or death (which often came first), at the rate of perhaps one a year. The remarkable thing is that population growth was slow. As in wildlife, mortality was high, especially in childbirth and infancy, and in wars. Neither did it help to have trees falling on a fellow.

Death, being ever at hand, was accepted as just another part of life.

It may be that total acceptance of Christian beliefs, firmly rooted as they were in Northumberland, gave a comforting salve to the bereaved, but just as important were the practical necessities of 'getting on with it', rather as in time of war. There was no time to mope. Today's death is often at a remove and almost unreal – not on a pile of heather in a corner of a dark, dank, smoke-filled room, with life, of necessity, continuing all around. Bodies were best buried nearby, cemeteries did not become really popular (!) until Victorian times, and who could afford fancy headstones? Knights seemed to manage stone coffins, with decorated lids, and some of them are still to be seen, often built into church walls and floors; but Micelee boasts nothing of this so we are left wondering what happened to all of those half Knights? We are denied the wealth of information that burial places have provided for archaeologists and historians through the years; and have nothing to show where Robert and Edmund lie; nor all the other good, and not so good folk of Micelee. It is a long carry with a body to Ovingham or Bywell for a church service (and what if the river is impassable), and probably room there only for Knights and their ilk anyway. So did it matter if a tree or shovel-smitten cottar of the ville, or his new born babe, had consecrated ground to lie in? His rest is doubtless no less comfortable for not being in a stone or even wooden coffin, nor even satin-lined chipboard. We shall never know – there is no known burial ground at Micelee, until modern times. Perhaps anywhere would do for a burial; few would notice the passing of a peasant, or where he was laid to rest, but should we, one day, unearth at Mickley a pile of old bones, we might know if they were Robert's, by the crushed bones, or Edmund's, by the stoved-in head.

The Nevilles

Bywell in the hands of the Crown was awarded to the nephew of King Edward I, John of Brittany, Duke of Richmond, in 1299. Alianor, widow of Alexander Baliol, remarried but retained the salmon fishery at Bywell and one acre of land, although she played no further part in the story of the Barony. Richmond gave Bywell to his niece, the Countess of Pembroke, in 1331, and on her death in 1376 it reverted to the King, who granted it to Ralph de Neville, Lord of Raby, in return for 'services rendered'.

The period between the Baliols and the Nevilles was a pretty messy one for the Bywell area. It was pillaged (again) by the Scots in Richmond's time; they camped at Bywell in 1346 on their way to being trounced at Neville's Cross, where the young King David, son of Robert Bruce, Saviour of Scotland, was captured. Imprisoned for 11 years, he was eventually ransomed, to the great impoverishment of his country – another unhappy result of the Scot's continued dallying with the French. David was succeeded by Robert The High Steward – the first of the Stuarts. He inherited a still very much divided country – was it ever otherwise? The Scots again plundered Bywell in 1347.

As a result of this lack of order and control and protection from the Scots, the Bywell estates, including Micelee, fell into poor condition; the Manor was worth only £26.13s.4d. Nearly 6,000 oak trees were felled in sixty years up to 1335. Bywell was renowned for its oaks and their despoliation, on all sorts of pretexts (500 supposedly for the repair of the millpond and mill) must have been a tragedy akin to our present- day destruction of the rain-forests, and for the same reason – greed, lust for money. Good oak was valuable, in an age still heavily dependent on timber for many of its needs.

MIGHTY BYWELL OAK

It was possibly at the hands of one of these oaks that Robert, son of Thomas of Eltringham, met his untimely end in 1292. If it happened on St Andrew's Day the locals must not have had a day off for the crowning of their Lord as King of Scotland. Or perhaps Robert was doing a bit of 'moonlighting' while the boss was away ... We do not know who pocketed the cash for all those trees, nor who paid the deodand of 5d. on the one that did for Robert.

Near anarchy prevailed on John's estates while he was away on Kingly duties, presumably attended by his most able, trustworthy vassals; one thing is certain – a lot of cheating went on. The way of life may have changed in 700 years but the principles remain the same – when the boss turns his back there's no end of bother!

Backing the wrong horse not only put paid to the Baliols – it didn't do much for their successors the Nevilles either, nor, you may recall, for their neighbours the Derwentwaters along the road at Dilston. Only by hedging their bets, one brother backing the loser, the other the winner – did the Percys at Alnwick ensure a future for their dynasty. They are still there.

The Nevilles began their sojourn at Bywell in 1376. They were formidable warriors: Ralph, first Earl of Westmorland, fought at Agincourt, Lord John died at St Albans in 1451, Sir John got himself killed at Towton in 1461. Perhaps they were not so formidable after all!

Ralph, the second Earl of Westmorland, succeeded his grandfather in 1426 and set about constructing a 'proper' castle at Bywell, stones and all; but it got little further than the tower, which still stands. It certainly could not be described as 'grand', but in 1464 the pathetic King Henry VI, after his defeat at Hexham, found his way there – and left behind his Kingly trappings when he had to skip hastily on.

Charles Neville became the sixth and last Earl of Westmorland in 1564, and with Thomas, Earl of Northumberland, led the Northern Catholic resistance to church reform, and the Rising of the North, against Queen Elizabeth, in 1568. The promised support, from the south and from Spain, failed to materialise and the sad and inevitable outcome was that Thomas, like Derwentwater, lost his head – betrayed for £2,000. His estates went to his loyal brother, Sir Henry Percy. Charles lost his estates, including Bywell, but hung on to his head by skipping to France, by way of Scotland, and died there in 1601.

Retribution on the heads of the rebels, great and small, rested in the hands of Sir John Foster, Lord Warden; it was swift, thorough and bloody. Examples were made in every town and village involved. Peasants followed their Masters – duty bound. Bywell mustered 60 horsemen, who would almost certainly include any battleworthy owners of horses in Micelee. If so, and although the settling-up in Northumberland does not appear to have been recorded, it is more than likely that some hapless soul from the village met a fate designed to deter anyone else from following his bad example in following the bad example of his Lord.

The Reiver Factor

Overlying the history of Northumberland for about 300 years, up until Henry VIII's time, were the 'Reivers'. The 'Wild Frontier', 'Borders', or, for the purpose of supposed control and government, the 'Marches', included Mickelee, but only just. It lay at the south-eastern edge of the Middle March which included the prime Reiver centres of Tynedale and Redesdale, and was kept in a kind of order by Wardens appointed by the Sovereign. Wardens were themselves usually little more than successful reivers wearing sometimes rather thin and tatty clothes of respectability. Sir John Foster was one of them, and rather more successful than most; he was a noted, or should we say notorious, Warden of the Middle March.

The rough and desolate, forbidding area of 'no man's land' betwixt England and Scotland forms a natural barrier against incursions from either side – except in the coastal plains, where rivers play their part – unlike the Tyne-Solway 'narrow neck' favoured by the Romans on grounds of shortness, for building their wall. The length of this natural frontier, being diagonal as well as rugged, and a long way from the seats of power, made it costly and difficult to police; oh yes, cost counted, even in those days, when it came to law and order. But, worst of all, the country by its very nature bred a race of people apart from normal Scots and English, tough as tempered steel, resilient as oak, and as free-spirited as the very Cheviot winds. Merely to exist in this wilderness called for exceptional qualities – the Reivers possessed them.

Cast these people as 'pig in the middle', to be used, fought over, devastated, cheated, by successive Kings and Governments in London and Edinburgh who consistently failed to apply justice and order to an area which counted for little except in times of war, and what came forth? – Reivers!

It is not my purpose here to write at length about Reivers, they have been well enough written about, and enthrallingly. I make mention of them only as I think they may have affected Mickelee, lying as it did on the 'softer' southern edge of the English Middle March, certainly not a seat of reiving, but perhaps a victim of it. Reivers were a product of a hard life and lawlessness, they battened on each other and any eligible victim of murder, robbery, arson, pillage, blackmail – even coined the word, amongst others – ransom, treachery of every kind. Rob or be robbed; the survival of the fittest – or the most vile – in a primitive and most ghastly form (were they cousins of the Vikings?). Civilisation, even in the style of the times, fell apart in the Borders in the time of the Reivers.

This unhappy chapter in the story of the noble land of Northumbria climaxed in the reign of Queen Elizabeth and only came to an end, an extremely bloody and traumatic end, it must be said, with the Union of the Crowns. The two countries then combined in draconian measures against the Borderers, who could no longer seek refuge 'on the other side'. Many had to flee their native land.

Most of the reiver activity was cross-border, and much of it clan or 'surname' oriented – feuding was a popular pastime, groups were based on family units. But when the border was too 'hot' or the usual victims too strong or alert (or just picked clean), and the pot empty, the womenfolk, as was their wont, would drive them forth on a 'rode' in search of pickings. A Charlton, Robson, Milburn, Forster or Fenwick would do – if he could be sneaked-up-on asleep. The chances of that were never good, amongst the tougher nuts of Tynedale, where resided in their hovels of turf and heather that could be rebuilt in a few hours after burning, as tough a set of nuts as ever tormented the land. So how stood the less tough nuts down the valley?

Large scale 'rodes' of one or two hundred armed-to-the-teeth villains on their incredibly tough, fast, silent mounts (unshod for soft bog and heather ways) were made on special occasions over considerable distances, even as far as Yorkshire. But the ordinary, run-of-the-mill foray was a family-sized commando style raid – quick in, quick out, after the style of the Vikings. These lads knew a thing or two about military techniques, and never a Cranwell in sight. The idea was to grab some loot, cause a bit of mayhem, and make haste for home. The wild moors, bogs and gullies of the Borders lent themselves to this technique and were in fact its *raison d'être*; but the dense woods of Mickelee were a different matter. The inhabitants, given warning, could take their bits and pieces and animals and 'melt' – this their best and only line of defence, as people of the land, rather than bloodthirsty robbers. A Smith or a Miller was no match for a Charlton or a Fenwick.

Another problem for these brigands was that, although Mickelee itself was probably indefensible, in better times both Bywell and Prudhoe would be garrisoned. This would make it possible to mount a 'hot trod' (a burning turf, mounted on the end of a lance, gave pursuers unrestricted right to follow) and so retreat to the hills a bit tricky. So the plight of Mickelee was perhaps not as desperate as that of places 'out by'; but it still warranted a watch to be kept every night. Two men were posted out of Bywell, which always included Mickelee in such matters, and a roster kept. Bonfires were lit to warn of impending danger and I shouldn't wonder if raiders preferred wet nights, when lighting a damp bonfire in the rain, with flint and tinder, could not have been other than slow and uncertain.

However, all in all, Mickelee would get off pretty lightly in the reiving business. It was more likely to suffer from the incessant to-ing and fro-ing of successive Scottish and English armies, up and down, and round about, seeking provender wherever it could be grabbed. These armies often marched on pretty empty stomachs and would never pass the chance of a slow-footed Mickelee cow or a sheep or two; nothing was ever safe.

During the internecine struggles for power between Kings, Church, Parliament and People, Northumberland was, with the Percys of Alnwick calling the shots, the bastion of England against the Scots – and suffered for it. For long periods the area was excused taxes in recompense for the troubles and losses. But at least, by the end of the reiving age there would be stout stone walls and solid doors with bolts to keep out the less determined villains.

Post-Reiver Changes

Micelee men would have gone to war with the Baliols and the Nevilles, they would have been at Agincourt. The Percys, who had some affinity with the Nevilles, and fancied themselves as power-brokers, trawled the countryside for troops, so there would probably be Micelee men at the 'small' battle of Shrewsbury in 1403, where the mighty Hotspur met his end. It could not have been so small for him. Henry Percy had fallen out with Henry IV when the King refused a demand for cash towards the cost of all the warring; he was too hard-up, or so he said (was that why he was BolinBROKE?), so Hotspur, in his arrogance, went to war against his Sovereign. Not a wise move.

There would be Micelee men at Bannockburn, when the prime of English manhood was slaughtered by Robert Bruce, grandson of John Baliol's rival to the Scottish throne.

So, never-ending demands were made on the populace, by war, when peasants with billhooks ('bring your own') and pikes were the infantry; by falling trees, by the incursions of reivers, and by the frightful ravages of the Black Death, which scourged fourteenth-century England. Only the need for a well-trained, professional army, built around the redoubtable, world-beating Welsh longbow, gave some relief to peasants, to allow them to bend their efforts to rebuilding the population, which they no doubt did with some relish; but it was a slow business, and the country suffered serious labour shortages, especially after the Black Death. These shortages began the processes that led, slowly but inexorably, to the emancipation of working men and the industrialisation of the country.

It became no longer easy to raise armies, except by making it worthwhile – for the Indians as well as the Chiefs – although attempts were still being made as late as 1595 to find men for fighting by 'mustering'. They could be somewhat elusive. At Stagshaw, of 76 'light horsemen' from Bywell, 74 had their horses disallowed (they wouldn't bring their first string, would they?). Another 83 failed to turn up. They were needed at home.

The Village in 1526

'At home' was the village. The rent returns for Mickelee show it as having much the same population as in 1268, having recovered from the intervening strife and plague. Maybe some overtime had been worked at population rebuilding.

The main noticeable differences are that now everyone had a surname and paid their landlords, the Nevilles at Bywell, in cash – except Thomas Fenwick, who still paid with 1lb. of pepper. Pepper and cumin had paid the rent in Micelee for hundreds of years, it was easier to carry than a sack of barley, I suppose: not any longer; pepper now grows in glasshouses and is eaten green, red or yellow in salads, or comes powdered, black or white, in little boxes. Where is the farm that grows cumin? It is an annual plant with bitter seeds that are carminative (anti-wind, to save you looking it up) and it too is bought in shops. It must have been valued and in demand in the halls of the gluttons.

George Fenwick paid 1s. rent; George Horsely only 1½d.; the Earl of Northumberland paid 8d. for land at Edgewell – you would have thought he'd have enough of his own. Six 'free' tenants paid not very much. The five 'tenants at will' paid much more; the widow of Edward Eltringham, a familiar name, paid 17s. 9d.; Robert Brown 5s. 8d.; and the whole township paid 7s. for a parcel of the Lord's 'waste, lately enclosed'. We see the movement towards enclosure, and the lot of poorer people improving.

By this time Bywell sported about fifteen shops and was a right busy place. Micelee still sat under its wing and there is no evidence of shops there, but it had nearly as many farmers, still farming in the manner of past ages; small scale, ox-driven, but with more horses (even if unfit for military service) – and more autonomy – the boss was losing his grip.

Wool and England

The fifteenth century saw, in the midst of and in spite of, almost continuous strife and periods of widespread disorder, a great development of 'Englishness'. French was largely replaced in common use by the language we know as that of Chaucer, of the Midlands, if you like – still recognisable and readable today. Anti-foreign attitudes grew, education developed, not only in substance but in scale and scope – far beyond the narrow confines of Church and Aristocracy. And, perhaps above all else, shaping and motivating the Island race, came the stirrings of their great inventive and commercial skills and instincts. Shafts of light pierced the grey, sometimes black, aura of medieval feudalism.

Perhaps the great trading, industrial and educational movements taking place in the south were hesitant to impinge on the 'backward' north, but the sunshine of a period of peace and calm, shining on the 'Clearing in the Forest' must have been welcome indeed.

The economy of England, when it first could be said to have one, was based on wool, the best in Europe, but the trade initially was only in wool – we had not yet learned the value of 'added value'.

After the invention, in 1185, of the 'fulling mill', worked by water-driven trip-hammers, mechanised wool processing, England never looked back. Wool from the sheep is filthy stuff, it has to be cleaned by having 'fullers earth' (a pulverised clay) trodden into it, then washed out in running water. Both the clay and the water were to be found in abundance in the Cotswolds, in close company with sheep bearing the very finest of fleeces – an unbeatable combination. The natural consequence of this happy situation was the growth of cloth making, and the industrial processes accompanying it. This in turn moved labour out of the stranglehold of the old Guilds and the iron grip of the Lord of the Manor.

In spite of war and plague the labour force increased steadily, and became entirely 'paid', changing the structure of society – in the south. Up here change was slow and the economy still, at the end of the fifteenth century, of a 'Third World' nature.

No 'Midland' English here; the language was an odd mixture all of its own, perhaps unintelligible to the Southerner (much as now, some might say) but it is possible, looking through 'Geordie' eyes, to see the link between medieval and twentieth century dialect. Did the present-day exhortations that reverberate through Newcastle on winter Saturday afternoons spring from the jousting lists, where Knightly chaps amused themselves by knocking each other off their horses? Did excited spectators encourage their favourites with the call, "Howay you Knight, Ted" (Howay United), and "Howay the Lords" (Howay the Lads)?. 'Howay', meaning 'Come on – get on with it', hasn't changed, BBC or not.

What has all this to do with Mickelee? Well, Chaucer's English became national very much as the result of the efforts of one man, himself the product of the wool trade that I've been going-on about. He was William Caxton, whose influence greatly affected Mickelee 300 years later, through one Thomas Bewick.

This country probably owes more to William Caxton than to any great warrior or statesman. He brought to us possibly man's greatest creation – books. Ah yes, I know about Lindisfarne and manuscripts; but I mean books, the books that you and I can read, and afford to buy, or borrow from a library, or even write and get published, with a lot of luck. The books that are the basis of education.

Imagine, if you will, the world of Robert, son of Thomas of Eltringham (where Bewick eventually made his mark), before he was crushed by his wayward tree. He had the light of day to see by, and at night rush lights and firelight glow – but never a book to read to while away the time, enlighten his mind, broaden his horizons and pleasure his imagination. Caxton changed all that.

A good product sells itself, so it is said, but it needs salesmen, so the commercial structure for selling wool abroad developed, and with it a thriving English community in Bruges, the centre of the continental cloth trade.

The young Caxton, who was born in 1421, had not completed his mercer's apprenticeship, learning about cloth, when his master died, leaving him the generous sum of £13. This was a year's income at that time, for a minor squire, and enabled Caxton to travel to Bruges, to complete his apprenticeship, which was a serious business – nothing slaphappy about it; Caxton learned his trade. It paid off, he stayed on in Bruges and did so well that he was able to 'take early retirement' from mercering while still in his fifties, with a pocket-full of money, and take up a new trade – printing.

At about this time, in Germany, a fellow called Johannes Gutenberg – he too deserves a touch of our cap – devised a simple printing press, in Mainz, and made commercial printing viable. He printed the great 42 line Bible and soon there were presses in about 20 other European towns – but not in England.

So Caxton returned in 1476, to London, bringing his press with him. Here he devoted himself to publishing books in English, in a form that made them intelligible. He translated from Latin, the standard language of books; but, more difficult, he unravelled and printed the strange assortment of spoken words used by the various descendants of the 'all sorts' of people who had dropped in on this isle throughout its chequered history.

Recorded by the quill pens of none too reliable scribes, on pretty rough paper, these words, even if no more difficult and obtuse than modern 'Geordie', must have posed monumental problems. That he succeeded in rationalising this jumble into English is to his everlasting credit.

In the years from 1477, when he printed the first book published in English, to his death in 1491, he published more than 90 books, 72 in English. Among them was the first *Aesop's Fables* – which was to become the subject of the last of Thomas Bewick's engraving masterpieces, when printing had moved on somewhat and books become illustrated.

What, I wonder, would Caxton say, could he see the outcome of his work, when today the humblest, poorest person in the land has access, for the asking, to millions of books from all over the world, on any subject the mind can conjure.

This link, through the centuries, between William Caxton and Thomas Bewick of Eltringham, in the township of Mickelee, illustrates, I believe, the progress of civilisation in the land, and the movement towards 'Englishness'. The fifteenth century was not an easy time, but the country made great strides forward – while in Mickelee the clearing grew bigger.

EARLY WOODEN PRINTING PRESS

Iron, Steel and a Bit of Art

By the 16th century iron – and steel, were playing a much bigger role in life, spurred on by the wool trade. Improved tools, on the land, in workshops and in homes, not only made life a mite easier, they speeded up the processes. The well designed and made iron plough and other horse-drawn implements such as harrows, with improved techniques and crops, raised farm output, for feeding the increasing proportion of the populace no longer working on the land. People worked, and lived, in centres of trade and industry to which food had to be transported. More horses and horseshoes and nails, more carts, better roads. More work for smiths, carpenters and stone-breakers (captured rogues?). At least it was downhill all the way for Mickelee horses taking food to urban workers; but I don't suppose they came home empty-carted, there might still be the odd keg of wine, or a millstone, or some exotic food from afar – or some iron ... Ironwork was the speciality of Bywell. It is reasonable to assume that the skills of Bywell were not wasted on the Smith of Mickelee; but iron doesn't grow on trees, so those poor horses must have had to haul the stuff up the hill – from where?

Iron ore – and coal – had been mined from early times near Whittonstall and may have been used by the renowned sword-makers of Shotley. Some of it found its way down to Wheelbirks, in the Township of Mickelee, where the remains of an old forge were found in 1884; and no doubt farther down, to Bywell. Downhill was best for iron. It was not the easiest of materials to handle, and I mean handle, in the absence of mechanical aids. It produced a breed of men, the iron masters (and their wives, who usually worked with them, a form of 'women's lib', I suppose), in strength above all others – maybe a bit short-lived.

The crude ore had first to be washed, roasted to remove some of the impurities, pulverised and sieved; then heated molten white in the 'bloom hearth', where more impurities drained through the slag hole; then mixed with charcoal to harden. The 'bloom' would weigh perhaps 2 cwt and, as can be imagined, was extremely hot and smoky to handle – without much in the way of protective clothing. This heavy mass had to be removed to the 'string' hearth, where it was forged, reduced and improved still further; not work for the faint-hearted. The addition of further carbon (charcoal) was needed for refining the metal and so the demand for wood for charcoal became immense. The countryside swarmed with charcoal-burners, and the woods were decimated.

There is a mention in *England in the Time of Caxton* of iron-making at West Crawcrook, near Ryton. This iron could have found its way to Mickelee but it was still a tidy haul, so which iron was used, Crawcrook or Whittonstall, probably came down to the individual preference of the smith, and its suitability for the job in hand, and of course the price.

The ever increasing demand for iron and steel kept every furnace in the land going 'full blast' (how these terms become fixed in the language), and the skies in the iron-making areas darkened with smoke, causing distress and anger. Iron masters and smiths became amongst the most important and wealthiest of men, indispensable to the functioning of most activities and the hub around which the skills of craftsmanship, and artistry, developed.

No smith worthy of the name would make even the simplest of household or agricultural implements without applying some adornment, for his own satisfaction, the notice and pleasure of the customer, and a jolly good advertisement of his prowess. And not an Art College in sight. This was a great area of exploration in skill and artistry by simple people. Just look at the functional beauty of some of the surviving pieces of work from these distant times and marvel at the inspiration that guided the gnarled, horny hands of the village smith.

But this was the time of Renaissance, the new blossoming of art, culture and inspired thinking that had withered with the civilisations of Greece, Rome, and in its own small way, Northumbria. Mickelee was not to be left untouched.

Tudors and their Times

Mickelee and such inconsequential places were too busy going about their homely affairs to notice the cultural revolution going on in Europe and spreading to England. The sound policy of Henry VII in marrying his daughter, Princess Margaret, to James IV of Scotland on 8 August 1503 brought a period of calm to cross-border relations, and enabled the folk of this area to go about their lot unhindered by the distractions of war.

Better implements and improving agricultural methods pulled rural dwellers slowly out of the doldrums of neglect and despair that had beset them in the 'bad times'. Henry VIII caused a setback when he sought adventure in France, resulting in the old Scottish-French alliance again being invoked, bringing claymores and schildrons once more to Northumberland. At Flodden Field the power of English disciplined, controlled archery, with a force and rate of fire unsurpassed until the days of the Winchester rifle, laid low the flower and glory of Scotland and put an end to Scottish dreams of dominance by force of arms, to the – temporary – comfort of Mickelee.

Whatever the judgement of history on Henry VIII, he reigned long and, all in all, he reigned well – in a way. Above all, he grasped the nettle of church reform, albeit for perhaps dubious reasons. Remember, these were still the days of the supreme power of Sovereigns; Parliament was there, certainly, and Magna Carta, but both could be manipulated by despots. Tudors could not only compose tunes – they could call them. But then, as now, there was in the English a feeling for what is right and a wish for firm control of the nation's affairs. They got it from the Tudors.

The spirit of adventure that still burned in the island race had plenty of scope in charting the oceans of this spherical world, settling new, far-distant lands and developing outlets for the products of their skills and inventiveness. The English no longer had real need for war with France – for a time, anyway. Spain, however, was a different matter.

The personal affairs of Henry that brought about the rift with Spain and yet more war, were also instrumental in developing English sea power, and colonial aspirations. But the domestic outcome of these affairs was what previous monarchs had aimed tentatively at without any noticeable effect –

the removal of the nation's affairs from Papal control, and the removal from the Church of its over-great powers of wealth-gathering (So here we are, 400 years on, relinquishing these powers to European control without a head rolling or a shot being fired!). That the outcome was also the end of the Neville dynasty at Bywell was coincidental, but cogent and relevant; they backed the wrong (Catholic) horse – for the last time.

There was a need to be nimble-footed in the fifteen-hundreds to avoid being burned entire, at the stake, or just in part – the bowels, before your eyes. Or there might be a choice of how to die – the 'nice' way, if noble and favoured like Anne Boleyn, of decapitation on the block by a sharp, accurate sword. Not quite so noble, for the likes of the hapless Derwentwater, and it would most likely be by a number of strokes of a rusty old axe.

This was the age of ingenuity in methods of torture and murder in the cause of religion. Heresy was the fashionable crime and those who knew what it was and leaped adroitly enough from side to side could avoid, for instance, being pressed on the floor beneath a door loaded with boulders, like the pressed flowers in the books of our childhood. Slow enough, this one, to give time to reflect on the sin of being Catholic, or Reformer, in the wrong reign. It was all a question of timing.

The Northern Gentry, presumably carrying their followers along, stuck pretty staunchly to their beliefs in the old tradition of Catholicism. Some Percys (some were nimble) and the sad and gentle Radcliffe, Earl of Derwentwater, paid the price. Charles, the last Neville, Earl of Westmorland, was attainted after throwing in his lot with Mary, Queen of Scots, and although he was agile enough to keep his head he lost his estates in England, including Bywell, and spent the last 30 years of his life in exile. Shades of Baliol.

It looks as though Charles took half the population of Mickelee with him. In 1538 the Muster Roll shows two entries under Myckle and Mikel (permutations on the spelling of our favourite village are endless). They showed a total of 57 men, able, with horse and harness, and 186 with neither. Even divided with the other 'clearing in the forest' in Yorkshire, this is a fair turnout for a little village. By 1595 the whole of the Bywell Lordship could only attempt to raise 150 horsemen, and half of these were absent and no horses fit for duty. By 1608 there were only 5 freeholders, most of them Newtons, in Mickelee, doing 'suit and service' for Bywell, and total rents were only £11.10s. 5d. Where had all the ploughers gone? (My apologies to the singer, Marlene!)

Bywell after the Nevilles was tossed about between various owners. In 1625 Charles I gave it to the London merchants from whom his rash and impoverished father, James I, had borrowed money (to buy brogues?). At that time the rent for the 'Manor of Mickelee' was £21.11s.10d.; it doubled in seventy years. The population was rebuilding and inflation was rife. The money-hungry London landlords needed their rent, and as usual, the peasants suffered. It was a bad time for peasants.

These London businessmen, absentee landlords, sold Bywell, including Mickelee, to the Fenwicks of Wallington (the reivers had come out of the hills and donned cloaks of respectability) who kept it until the death of William in 1719, when his estates were divided between his two daughters. Mickley and Cherryburn went to Isabella, wife of William Wrightson, MP for Newcastle but of a Yorkshire family from Cusworth, near Doncaster.

In 1663 the taxpayers of Mickelee were: William Fenwick, £80; Edmund Newton, £3; Stephen Thompson, £4; Margaret Lumley, £4; Mr Boutfellow, £1 (why was he 'Mr' when he only paid a pound?). Money now came more in pounds than in pennies – or rather, I expect, it came in pennies and went in pounds; the inexorable process of currency-devaluation was under way.

Sheep, Trees and Taxes

It might be said that England in the 16th–17th centuries rode to power on the backs of sheep, riding roughshod over the wretched peasant farmers, whose arable plots were grassed for grazing, and the common land enclosed. The agricultural revolution created the New Rich – merchants, industrialists, businessmen, bankers. This was the time of the emergence of the power of currency, cash mightier than the sword; wool was the catalyst. But it dealt despair, starvation and death to many of the lower orders for whom there was no alternative to arable farming as a means of existence.

Fortunately for Mickelee, it was insulated from the worst effects of the changes by being in an area which still produced coarse quality wool. Here leather remained the important rural export and the products of the forest a major resource – oak bark for tanning, charcoal for steel making, and timber, especially oak, for building, particularly shipbuilding. This was one of the fastest growing industries of Tudor and later times, and oak the key to English power at sea.

Great inroads were made into the remaining forests, and those of Mickelee were virtually destroyed, so the name became a misnomer, for there can be no 'clearing in the forest' if there be no forest. Timber became too valuable for burning and coal increasingly showed its sooty presence; oak became too good for any except the best of buildings and furniture. Lime-mortar came downmarket to the homes of cottagers.

Historians make passing mention of the clearing of forests and the bringing of great areas under the plough and into grassing for sheep, but what of the actual job of clearing? Felling the tree was relatively simple, (so long as it didn't fall on the feller.). Improved iron made for better axes and faster, easier saws, although using them was still men's work. Felling a tough old oak of four, five or even six feet diameter, with none too keen an axe would have been perhaps two or more days' sweaty toil; with a good saw and a man on both ends (and a smith on hand to keep it sharp), perhaps a few hours. Not quite chain-saw standards, but fast enough for the times, when nobody was in much of a hurry anyway, and it certainly got the forests cleared. Bark-strippers and charcoal-burners would see off the small stuff.

What then, of the stumps? We hear little of stumps; but I can tell you, from personal experience, that stumps aren't funny, not without bulldozers and the like, which make a mess of the land anyway. The trouble with stumps is that, apart from being buried, they have long, thick rooty appendages for anchors, the size of the treetops. These have to be dug around (with wooden spades?), cut through and removed in sections, to sufficient depth to undermine the main bulk; the tree with a taproot is the very devil. Then the knobbly stump has to be got out of the hole; a team of oxen would help, but in their absence it is a slow, hard task. I have spent as long as two weeks removing a single old oak stump from the woods of Mickley. Then there remained a hole the size of a modern bomb crater and not a lot to fill it with, in the absence of the mountains of household rubbish we nowadays have difficulty in finding holes for. It is surprising that we read of people being killed by falling trees, but no mention of backache.

The big advantage of trees over sheep as money-spinners on the Bywell estates was that marauding Scots, who seemed to be blamed for just about everything, couldn't easily carry them off – athough it must have seemed at times as though the trees grew legs and walked away on their own. Unfortunately, the profit from trees went into the pockets of landowners, unless perhaps they lived in London and the Reeve was as crooked as a reiver. So the poor peasants continued to hang on a kind of clothesline of subsistence agriculture, supported on posts of Baronial munificence, where such existed – as had been their lot for centuries.

Even peasant pleasures in these times were constrained by edicts from on high. Fortunately, the lads and lasses of Mickelee were too far from Bywell and Ovingham to be punished for hanging about the churchyard on Sundays 'engaging in conversation of a non-religious nature'. More likely, up there on the hilltop, they would incur the wrath of the law-enforcers by playing some 'unholy game' such as 'piping and dancing', 'wakes', 'May games', rush bearings, bear-baits, bonfires, and 'all manner of unlawful gaming'! When else could they have a spot of innocent (well …!) fun, Sunday being the only day off? It had been ordained by Cranmer, in Edward VI's time (1547), as a result of concern at Sunday 'idleness, pride, drunkenness, brawling and a lack of honouring God', that Sundays be kept for religion, 'being friendly to neighbours', 'visiting the sick and poor' – and 'Godly conversation'. Worth a thought, is it not?

Through all the trauma of religious infighting that rocked the land through the years, and regardless of the consequences to their noble Lords, to whose coat tails they were firmly fixed, ordinary folk had deeply instilled religious feelings. These were rooted, in the North, in the Catholic Church; Durham Cathedral was still a seat of Popery until about 1700. So, even if Mickelee folk skipped church when the river was in flood, the snow too deep, or the games too enticing, they would not wish, should they dare, to stray too far from the dictates of church and conscience.

The infiltration of fresh thinking from the south, increasingly in the form of printed pamphlets and even books for those few who could read, stirred, even in humble people, a new thirst – a yearning for knowledge. This was not only in religious matters wherein had run in the past the mainstream of philosophical thinking, but in science and the arts.

In a world that was now big – very big – and horizons distant, Newton watched his apple fall, Harvey postulated his theory of blood circulation – literature flourished; Pepys wrote his diary, Pope his poems, Shakespeare his plays. Turner, Constable and Gainsborough brushed their masterly canvasses, and, on a more practical level, Wren built his churches and Chippendale his chairs. At last, good white paper was being made in England, so all this new-found knowledge and culture could be disseminated, courtesy of Caxton and his printing press. Education and enlightenment were very much on the move by 1700 – but perhaps only stirring in Mickley.

Taxes, as well as rules of behaviour, weighed pretty heavily on everyone in the land; Governments, now that they had got the hang of it, were not slow at inventing new methods of raising taxes. Although Mickelee, along with the rest of Northumberland, had been excused taxes in the 'bad times', times were now better – and chimneys had been discovered. They reached up to the heavens, proclaiming the presence of the hearths of even the lower orders. Here was a source of ready, collectable revenue – chimneys couldn't hide from the tax assessors. So, for the 'Hearth Tax' of 1664–5, in Mickelee, Edward Newton and Richard Newton paid on two hearths each and eleven others paid on one each. Six others were too poor to pay, so there was means-testing and 'low income relief'.

We see that there were two houses big enough and prosperous enough to have two fireplaces. What, I wonder, did the Newtons do, that lifted them up the income ladder? Was there a separate kitchen, or, luxury of luxuries, a fire in the bedroom? The others, with only one hearth, perhaps still had only one room, possibly with a bedroom upstairs, with the livestock below providing 'under-floor heating'. Walls were by now largely of lime-built stone, with secure doors of sawn wood; furniture was good but still simple – the skills and artistry of the carpenter had advanced in parallel with those of the smith.

The nature of the village remained agricultural, but on a larger scale; the clearing continued to extend. But the rate of change was still slow – at about the speed of oxen and comfortable for men to keep up with.

A Different Kind of War

The heavy taxation of the 16th and 17th centuries had to be raised for the usual reasons of waging war and supporting extravagant kings. War sometimes brought profit and benefit but extravagant kings brought only resentment and anger to the people. James I was a prime example, who with his Scottish henchmen milked England dry; the Stuarts were an extravagant lot – and Catholics to boot!

There were, however, two benefits from James's reign, in addition to the obvious one of a (nominal) bringing together of the ancient adversaries. James was responsible for the definitive publication of the Holy Bible – the world's continuing best-seller and pillar of the British Empire. The other, probably a legend, and perhaps of dubious benefit: he was supposedly responsible for the creation of the Geordie race! The story has it that, when James arrived in London, he was so appalled at the state of his courtiers' footwear that he sent post-haste to Scotland for two thousand pairs of brogues. Unfortunately, what with the state of communications in those days, the message became a bit garbled on its way and it was not until they reached the Tyne on the way south that the mistake was realised and the 2,000 pairs of ROGUES were stopped there – with the consequences we all know.

On a more serious note, his son Charles was responsible for, amongst other foolish things, the murder of Sir Walter Raleigh – one of the great Englishmen – and the alienation of his Scottish kinsmen and the subsequent ravaging, yet again, of Northumberland.

The large Scottish army which frightened the rabble of an English army to flight at Newburn in 1644, then took Newcastle, would have needed every grain of corn, every sheep and cow they could grab from the hapless folk of Mickelee and hereabouts. By now there was not enough dense forest left for them to hide in, as had their forebears, and there were more of them to 'melt'.

Charles was also blamed for the Civil War but the root of the trouble from which grew the passion and fervour of that unhappy business was, as well as that old festering sore of religious intolerance, the emergence of the 'will of the people'. Could it be called 'Democracy'?

Those days saw the dying throes of the absolute rule of kings. They died slowly, in their despotic role, and it took a long time for Parliament to get its act(s) together. It might be said that it has not yet succeeded, but it set itself on the road, in Charles's time to become the 'Mother of Parliaments'. In the meantime, the peasants of Mickelee suffered their privations, paid their taxes, and amused themselves as best they could, in the face of civil war and the religious convulsions that plagued, along with the Plague, not only England but the whole of Europe. From early Christianity pure (!) and simple, men and women moved slowly through the processes of enlightenment that brought not only longbows and gunpowder into the repertoire of civilisation; they also began to develop some freedom of religious thought, albeit still within the strict parameters of the times. They were, in theory, still bound to attend church on Sundays, but whether thoughts were Catholic or Protestant was no longer clear-cut, although there were still plenty of people prepared to prevent others from going their own religious way. The close cousins, heresy and witchcraft, were greatly searched out and sorted out; there was nothing like a good roasting at the stake for drying-up free thought. Witch-hunting was a great sport and if someone had a grudge against you it was a mite more difficult to prove innocence than guilt. All they had to do was toss the accused in the river – floating proved guilt, sinking proved innocence. 'Heads you lose, tails I win'.

As late as 1673 a notorious witch-hunter – it was a profession, like Wild West bounty hunting – name of Anne Armstrong (another reformed reiver?) of Birches Nook, accused four women, from Morpeth, Stocksfield and Prudhoe, and Lucy Thompson of Mickelee, of practising

OLD BIRCHES NOOK

witchcraft at Riding Mill. This was probably in what is now the Wellington hotel. By then 'proper' trials were required and guilt without real evidence more difficult to prove, so these poor women were acquitted. But ugly superstitions were so deep-rooted in simple folk that it is doubtful if anyone accused of witchcraft would ever be other than guilty in the eyes of their neighbours and would more than likely be driven from the area. However, the seeds of fresh thinking were falling on fertile ground and the worst excesses of bigotry and prejudice beginning to be questioned.

All the turmoil of the Civil War had less impact on Mickelee and Northumberland than on the south where most of the fighting was done for a change, and there was some concern to save the emerging coal trade. COAL – now there was a new thought: Northumberland might at last have a role other than as a buffer against the Scots.

Great England

One of the most exasperating puzzles to the student of mankind is what brings forth greatness in particular individuals, what combination of factors sparks off genius at a particular time, in a particular field? Perhaps it's a question for anthropologists.

Names pepper the history books; from Greece there are Hector and Homer; Rome there are Caesar, Michaelangelo, Da Vinci; Europe – Charlemagne, Louis XIV, Napoleon Bonaparte, Rubens, Hitler (like it or not); in Northumbria – Edwin, Bede, and Lindisfarne, the collective name for the anonymous greats who produced the Gospels. And England, what of England? Throughout its history we see an 'outstander' here and there, mostly when occasion demanded, mostly kings and warriors – showing a spot of culture here and there, even in the dark days of strife and savagery. But what price culture in the Borders while London's Globe staged the works of Will the Bard?

Then suddenly, for no apparent reason, there came upon the land a great and glorious outburst of good things, like spring sunshine through the dismal clouds of winter. The Stuart dynasty played some part, but the main force was spontaneous, sparked in the 17th century and spread over perhaps 200 years, reaching its zenith in the short but wonderful years of the last of the Stuarts – Queen Anne (of the shapely legs?).

I suppose peace and goodness brings forth culture; danger brings forth courage and Churchills. England, after the coming together with Scotland, and the putting aside of internal strife, leapt mightily to the pinnacle of world power and eminence in every field. The names of Pitt, Marlborough, Clive, command the heights; on a different plane there are Constable, Gainsborough, Turner – Wren, Adams, Pope, Defoe, Swift; 'practical' artists like Sheraton and Chippendale – and 'Capability' Brown from Northumberland, gracing southern gardens with new ideas. Most important, driven by an insatiable thirst for knowledge and the burgeoning industrial revolution, scientists emerged such as Isaac Newton and Michael Faraday and veritable hosts of others, in every sphere of human activity, down to the dirt and grime of Telfer and MacAdam and their road making. Watt watched his kettle boil (so they say); coal miners got down to serious business ...

Bewick mined coal – at Mickley.

Which brings me to the boy Bewick. Why should young Thomas, son of a small farmer (Cherryburn was small even by the standards of the time) and miner, living in the backwoods of Northumberland, have this remarkable propensity, from his early days, for drawing? Not just drawing, but drawing of a quality to fit him for company with the very best – one of the great artists. To say nothing of his stature as an ornithologist and his no little ability as an author. Why him? Why should this come about in Mickley, where there was no precedent, no example to follow?

A Little Bit of Coal

Let us go back a bit – like a few million years, before Micelee was even a twinkle in the eye of history ... Wet was the world, or this part of it anyway; wet, mild and luxuriant, densely forested with trees the like of which we can hardly imagine – giant, fast-growing, fast decaying into boggy sludge. A bit like a giant version of the spaghnum-moss beds on our wet moorlands, that turn eventually into peat.

This growth made coal, not peat. The rotting vegetation sank to the bottom of the water and was slowly covered with layers of gravel, sand and silt, building layer upon layer, as each growth of forest lived, died, and was covered and compressed by successive courses of growth and sediment. It is difficult to imagine that solid coal dug from a seam six feet thick, a thousand feet underground, was once a forest, growing on the surface, but there it is – that's my potted version of how it happened: it took some time, these things can't be rushed – but their undoing can.

It just so happened that some of these layers of 'coal' thus laid down, rested under this old Kingdom of Northumbria; most significantly for Mickley they sloped upwards from their deepest parts under the coastal areas, some surfacing or 'outcropped' on the north-facing slopes arising from the river Tyne west of Prudhoe.

Early man, when he mastered the art of making and controlling fire, had no need for coal – there was plenty of wood, so why bother? It must have been a pretty rotten experience when he first set alight to the 'black earth' and it gave off the most noxious, noisome smoke – from the very Devil. There must have been a rare panic to put it out. Even the clever Romans thought not a lot of it and only when monks came along and saw some merit in the filthy stuff did exploitation begin, in a very small way. Little did

LAYING DOWN THE COAL LAYERS

NEWCASTLE IN THE REIGN OF QUEEN VICTORIA

early man realise how much warmth and potential comfort lay beneath his feet.

There were no monks in Mickelee, although there is a suggestion that part of the west wall of Eltringham House, down by the river, may have been of religious origin. I doubt it – there would have been mention in the records of Bywell or Ovingham. It is possible, I suppose, that a 'hostel' type place, on the south side of the river between the two seats of religion would have been useful for travellers blocked on their way by an angry Tyne, or it would have been a useful place for a nunnery! No, it was more likely to have been a Manor House.

There is, I believe, some evidence of monks mining to the west, between Bywell and Broomley. Bywell would have a use for coal when the wood ran short, for the iron-working activities. The destruction of the forests focused attention on alternative sources of heat, and there was little choice, so smoky coal became increasingly acceptable, although there was at times great outcry against the 'dark clouds of sulphurous smoke' which hid the sun in the iron producing parts of England. Laws were passed against its burning; Parliament petitioned Edward I in 1306 to ban the burning of 'coale' in London because of the filth and smoke. Twenty years later it was in general use. Queen Anne ruled that coal should not be burned in royal households; although cinders (coke) were generally acceptable – no soot, but my goodness, the fumes. There is little chance, these days, to sample coke fumes, but I can assure you that a good lungful would keep you wheezing for a day. Coke fumes could be breathed until recently from coke-fired boilers and the braziers much favoured by night watchmen on building sites, and were a major ingredient of 'smog'.

Progress, it is said, is irresistible, and by 1700 coal was driving the nation, and especially Tyneside, inexorably towards prosperity, albeit a sooty one.

The Newcastle coal measures were close by the river, but deep, difficult and dangerous to work; nor was the Tyne the easiest of rivers for sailing ships carrying the coal away. However, spurred on by fortunes to be made, the dangers of mining and sailing were faced and overcome, although not by the fellows making the fortunes. The trade was quite brisk by 1615, when there were about 400 ships out of the Tyne and about 14,000 tons carried. When the Scots took Newcastle in 1644, after the battle of Newburn, there was great hardship in London because of coal shortage; but it was not until the end of the century that the trade really bourgeoned. By 1700 exports from Newcastle were about 200,000 chaldrons; by 1775, about 380,000 (260,000 to London); by 1800, 520,000; and 1828, 800,000. That's a strange word – chaldron, not much heard these days; it was the standard unit of measure for coal in those distant times and amounted to 53 cwt., Newcastle measure. At 20 cwt. to the ton that's more than two-and-a-half tons (If you want it in tonnes you will have to do it yourself). In 1839 the cost of coal on ship in Newcastle was 10s. 6d. per ton; in London £1.12s. 6d. So where was the profit for the fellow with the pick? There were by then 5,000 of them and 3,500 boys, working underground, with another 4,000 men and boys above, at Tyneside mines.

This was 'boom' time indeed; the Tyne became 'Coaly' and London sooty, but warm – except when war, or awkward Geordies, held up the supplies. The development of the coal trade transformed the area from being a pretty poverty-stricken, 'third world' buffer-zone between warring nations, into a

COAL STAITHES

prosperous, bustling hive of industrial activity and great importance; and not a little culture thrown in. But it all depended on water transport, horses couldn't cope with the quantities involved, except to move the coals the short distances to the loading places (staithes) on the river – and even that with increasing difficulty. The river was tidal and therefore navigable, only as far as Newburn, so the ships stopped there. Not so the coal seams, they went on up the valley, too far for the ships to reach; Wylam was the limit. Its coals could be moved economically to staithes at Lemington – but only just. Wylam was a 'flash-point' in industrial development and it became a nasty, smelly, slummy place, with blast-furnaces as well as mines, because there was iron handy and iron and coal were by now inseparable associates.

Four miles up the valley, Mickley maintained its rural status – its coal couldn't reach the ships, so mining here was small scale, mostly for domestic use and little changed in method from the days of monks with their wooden shovels.

Ralph Bewick could not have made much of a living from his 8 acres at Cherryburn, and progressive enclosure of the Commons didn't help in the struggle to feed a fair sized family. I don't suppose he had heard of 'diversification', but he diversified – into mining; or perhaps he was a miner already and took up farming part-time. Either way, in the early 18th century he kept a cow or two, and a pig and a horse, a few hens and geese: self-sufficiency I suppose – and he didn't need to eat porridge and jump up and down to keep warm, he had two fires in his house and his own coal. He paid rent of £60 per year for 'landsale' (local use) collieries on Eltringham common and Mickley 'West Wantes' and rented Cherryburn for £50 p.a., until 1791, when he bought it in a sale of farms by Christies the auctioneers. Land by now was available to anyone with the money to buy – neither sword nor Royal favour counted any more. The house was not very grand; as Coal Owners the Bewicks did not amount to much. They mined coal here, there and everywhere around Mickley and Eltringham for about 200 years, but they were very limited operations and never employed more than a handful of men. Little trace remains of their activities – like the monks' workings, they were so small that Nature's cloak soon masked them.

Their mining methods were little improved on those of the monks either, not much more than 'hole in the ground' mining. The coal would be shovelled into wickerwork baskets or 'corfes' and either dragged to the surface along a sloping tunnel or 'drift', or lifted up the not very deep shaft by means of a simple ox or horse-driven winding mechanism or 'ginge'; then by cart or pack animal to house or smithy. No industrial use hereabouts, but a steady demand for the needs of a growing population, which more or less doubled, nationally, in the 18th century, to about twelve million.

The principle Bewick pit was at Mickley Bank Farm and I can show you where that was, because they were still working it (from when Thomas was a lad) when the farm was sold in 1928 on the final break-up of the old Baliol estates. Traces survive, on the hillside where Stoneygate Bank joins the A695. (have you noticed how the nomenclature of roads reflects the changing times? From a descriptive old name, indicating the nature of the place, to a sterile, soulless number). In its heyday Mickley Bank Colliery boasted a couple of coke ovens, across the road where now stands 'Bob's Body Shop', where presumably, a body can be bought! (I believe he fixes car bodies). What the coke was used for I know not but in the absence of local industry and a close-by railway I can only assume it to be used for domestic boilers or for heating glass houses, which were both in vogue by about that time – late in the 19th century.

The whole of the escarpment that forms Mickley Bank Farm and runs east to West Mickley has been riddled, through the years, with small pits working coal outcrops. When the Bewicks gave up in about 1960, there came to an end more than two hundred years of this form of mining – by one family – when the coal finally ran out.

Fenwicks and Humbles

Changes in land ownership characterised 18th century Mickley, while Newcastle fuelled itself and England into the age of industry and invention.

It is worth a quiet smile when we read that a branch of the Fenwicks, foremost among the thieving rogues of reiving times, should pay honest money for Bywell, including Mickley; a bit like Al Capone becoming US President. No offence to my good friends the Fenwicks who still live hereabouts (are they related? – they don't own Bywell, and only a tiny part of Mickley. "Ah me," they say, "what went wrong?" And – "Heyho for a bit of reiving!").

William, the last of the Bywell Fenwicks, had only two daughters and when he died the estates were divided between them. Mickley went to Isabel, wife of William Wrightson of Cusworth in Yorkshire. She had only one child, a daughter, who married John Battie of Warmsworth in Yorkshire in 1748. In 1761 the Batties inherited her property and assumed the name Wrightson. William, her son, succeeded in 1784. His two sons left no children and the estate descended by will to their great-nephew, William Thomas, grandson of their sister, Harriet. He assumed the name of

OLD ELTRINGHAM

Battie-Wrightson on succeeding in 1891. There's convolution if you like! The owner when the lands were sold in 1928 was his son Robert Cecil Battie-Wrightson.

William Fenwick's widow re-married – the Reverend Septimus Hodson. They sold Eltringham Farm to Thomas Humble in 1802 and Bywell to the forebears of the present owner – T. Wentworth Beaumont, Lord Allendale, for the sum of £132,000. So came the division of the Bywell estates of Baliol, separating Mickley from the Lordship, after five hundred years.

Eltringham was a kind of riverside suburb of Micelee, (which was in its day a fair-sized 'township'); it didn't amount to much, just the House and farm, a few cottages and one or two small farms like Cherryburn, and the pub-ferry house. It is said that the owner of the house disliked the close proximity of his tenants in the cottages and 'got rid of them' (arsenic?), effectively destroying the Eltringham of old. The names of the previous occupants of Eltringham House are not recorded, but they would have been tenants (of Bywell), not owners.

It was a son of Thomas of Eltringham who had the tussle with the tree, and there were 'Eltringhams' in the area for hundreds of years, some at least, I'm sure, of consequence. Whether they were named after the place or the place after them, it seems more than likely they had a foot or two in the door of Eltringham House in the course of the centuries.

Land taxes paid in Mickley for the year 1763 were :

> Stephen Thompson paid 11s. 2d.; John Lumley, 11s. 2d.; Thomas Newton, 2s. 10d.; John Newton, 8s. 4d.; Cath Ridley, £1.2s. 4d.; John Browell, £1.2s. 4d.; Geo. Eltringham, £1.2s. 4d.; William Forester, £1.13s. 4½d.; Charles Browell, £1.13s. 4½d.; Wm. Eltringham, £1.7s. 11½d.; John Eltringham, £1.7s. 11½d., and John Bewick, 8s. 8d. The Newtons were still around, we will hear more of the Eltringhams, there is a new name – Browell; but what had happened to the Fenwicks?

Although by no means grand, Eltringham house is the only house of substance and interest in Mickley, of which Old Eltringham is now considered to be a part; all the others are at best farmhouses. This house is different; not a farmhouse, for a start; it stands alongside Eltringham Farm house – just to confuse the delivery men, but it is not part of the original farm. There is a cellar, with a well for a safe and comfortable water supply. This perhaps points to its having been secure or fortified. The old 'riven' wooden lintel high up in the west wall suggests some antiquity – possibly the 17th century or earlier, when timber was split lengthways with wedges, rather than sawn. The main part of the house is Victorian I believe, but I'm no expert.

The Humbles were a Prudhoe family; Thomas, who bought Eltringham in 1802 was the son of Anthony, of Prudhoe House. A man of some note, with cash and time to spare for dedicated fox-hunting, he maintained the Prudhoe pack of foxhounds for fifty years. Thomas, who lived from 1768 to 1841, maintained the family interest in hunting and kept the hounds at Eltringham farm, as did his son, also Thomas, even after the hunt became the Braes of Derwent, under the Priestmans of Slaley and the Cowans of Apperly.

Thomas the younger had one son, Joseph (1854–1922), known locally as 'Squire Humble' – whether from respect or, I suspect, more likely the product of sly Geordie miner's humour. Whatever the reason, he earned their hearty dislike – probably just because he was the land owner. He cut a fine figure on his hunter, following the Braes – and the gates were painted white. His life virtually spanned the era of industrial activity in Mickley.

Only one of his four children, Lillian, survived – death in Mickley was no respecter of wealth or status – and she too cut a fine figure with the hunt, side-saddle, with her buttonhole of violets and later, in harder times, tagging along in her pony and trap. She died in 1949, when the farm no longer had either a hunting connection or an industrial aspect.

On Joseph's death in 1922, there being no direct heir, the estate passed to Riddle Bell, son of Mary Humble of Prudhoe who had married a Bell of Harlow Hill. He changed his name to Humble, as did his brother Thomas when he inherited in 1948 – after the manner of the Battie-Wrightsons, it seems to have been a common practice. He died in 1992, but there is yet another Thomas coming along, his grandson; with no Hunt connection, just a straightforward working farmer, one of the only two now left in Mickley. The other farms have all been transformed into 'residential units', and not a rat in sight – although there could be an odd bug or two lurking under the plaster.

Building in Mickley

Old, interesting buildings survive at Eltringham Farm; stables, byres and the like, and especially the granary with its lovely chimney, complete with tree growing from the masonry. I believe that barley was malted here for Ovington brewery in the 'good old days' when beer was still brewed locally. The beer made over the river was, I understand, like, and referred to locally as, 'Guinness'. The barley was taken by cart to the western end of the farm and across the river by ford directly below Ovington. It would take two or three good horses a fair effort to get a cart load of barley up that hill – I hope the beer was worth it!

Let us not forget that this Mickley was always a farming place, and still pretty simple farming when the Humbles arrived, with the work being done by hand and horse. Dues were no longer paid in cumin and pepper and there is never a hint of these now. Would cumin be a good 'diversification', in these days of gluttony? Roots such as turnips were by now well established in sound rotational systems and took a lot of the terror out of over-wintering stock – but not all of it.

Lime mortar was the key to permanence in building, it filled gaps and 'bedded' stones firmly. The Romans built with it, the Saxons had the know-how but made little use of it; the Normans used it widely and with great skill, but its use for ordinary building was long restricted by its local availability and the limitations of transport. Mickley had no limestone, but sandstone enough, sand and gravel aplenty in the alluvial valley, and no shortage of timber. Good permanent buildings would have been possible – but not without lime. When I built my house of stone and lime in the 1950s the nearest source of kiln lime for slaking was about twelve miles away at Fourstones, west of Hexham. There had been lime near Corbridge but this was still a long cart-haul away from Mickley, which explains why there are so few buildings predating the 19th century.

Mickley's earliest extant examples of building in stone are parts of Eltringham House and farm, the original Cherryburn, and the old school on the hilltop, whose Master bothered Thomas, the boy Bewick, into truanting more than learning.

Cherryburn is a good example of rough lime-rubble construction that has

GRANARY AT ELTRINGHAM FARM

stood the test of time, nearly 200 years since Bewick regretted the dilapidated state of his old home and it is still going strong. Slate has long since replaced heather thatch, and recent renovations have given it a new lease of life.

A school at Mickley 200 years ago really was something. Fee-paying of course – and tyrannical. Farmers who were sufficiently far-sighted to spend hard-earned money on schooling for their children expected results, and they were achieved in those days as much through the posterior as through the head. This did not do much for young Thomas, who thought 'draw draw' better than 'war war'. His father agreed and put him with the vicar of Ovingham – there was a family connection – where he not only continued his artistic development, on the church porch flagstones, but acquired the literary skills that led to the Memoir and its written evidence of local life in his day.

The old school on the hilltop, with its roof of stone, continued in use until the Education Act of 1870 made education compulsory, and industrial development down the hill called for modern schools. It is still there, the old school, but heavily disguised as a house, as is the nearby old smithy, which was in use well into the 20th century, as was the 'Commercial Inn', one of the two inns that the old village boasted and that are no more.

Continuing Progress

The link between rural and industrial life was the smith, backed up by the iron master and the carpenter. Micelee never had an iron master, its iron was brought in, but smiths used coal for their furnaces from early times and pushed the search for it – there wasn't far to search at Mickley. The Bewick family, in their mining role, almost certainly supplied coal to local smiths in the 18th–19th centuries.

The smith and the carpenter between them fashioned most of the artefacts of life, from the plough and the cart to the candlestick and the poker, the door and its hinges. There are still some smith-made hinges about in the village, but alas when I tried to have some copied, the fellow who passed as our local smith made a most awful mess of them. "You can buy them in the hardware shop," he said! By 1910 the Mickley smith was not a Smith but a William Ward, and he did little more than shoe horses; by then everything was being made in factories.

Factories ('manufactories') lived cheek-by-jowl with coal mines and steel works, they needed each other.

By the time the young Bewick left his idyllic country patch to serve his apprenticeship with the Beilbys, the Newcastle engravers renowned for their glasswork, factories were well in vogue. Pretty horrid most of them were, too, all jumbled up with the remains of the medieval town and a lot of filth and disease; but the town was a-buzz with activity and the country lad must have found it tremendously exciting – within the strict controls then exercised on apprentices.

Being the nub of the world's coal trade, Newcastle waxed prosperous, and there was a good social life; arts, crafts and the sciences flourished. The world seemed to be centred on the very streets where the young man walked to the coffee houses that were the meeting places of the sober Wesley and his Methodists, then busily engaged in fighting the good fight against the evils of drink – not knowing that coffee was nearly as bad; well, not quite. There this country boy engaged in earnest, erudite coffee-house conversations, though when he was older he equally enjoyed pub talk and a pint.

The talk was of discovery and faraway places, of politics and war, revolutions in America and France but not at home, where Cromwell was long gone although still too close for contemplation of more of his kind. Where Bonnie Prince Charlie and romantic Scottish dreams were finally laid to rest. The world was in a hubbub of change and the news of it. A new word, news – spread by pamphlets, news-sheets and early newspapers – good old Caxton! The *Newcastle Courant* had started publication in 1710, at 2d. per weekly issue.

At work in his engraving apprenticeship, Thomas Bewick was part of the thriving world of book publishing, which also increased his awareness of the wider world around him – from which Mickley was still fairly insulated. So at weekends he walked the long twelve miles home and disseminated the 'town talk' among friends and family and local hostelries, notably the Hare and Hounds, on the river bank by the ferry crossing, only a young man's stone's throw down the hill from Cherryburn. He did his bit in the process of informing and enlightening his village friends, and a right popular figure he would be with his ready yarns, and his news-sheets for those who could read. To say nothing of the song sheets – anyone could sing. Though I doubt if his mother and sisters much approved of the bawdy nature of most of the songs being sold around the streets of Newcastle at that time!

A powerful new stratum was now developing in the social structure of England – the 'Middle Class'. There was quite a lot of it about, pulling itself up on the backs of the proletariat, who wallowed in the quagmire of urban industrialisation. A different kind of serfdom now accompanied a new kind of master, often more brutal and uncaring than the old nobility. Who can say, these years on, which was worse, rural serfdom or industrial slavery? For the young Bewick the bird song, the butterflies, the good country air, were infinitely preferable to anything that town could offer, but town was where the work was and he had to make do with the refreshment of weekend visits. He was fortunate.

It is probable that what saved England at this time from bloody revolution of the French kind was the emergence of religious fervour. Led by John Wesley, it swept the country and gave the struggling masses something to think about other than their misery. If they played their cards right (except that cards were sinful) there might be something better for them in the here-after; this life held little prospect of anything special.

He got about, did John Wesley, and neighbouring Prudhoe boasts a plaque where he preached in 1757 at the home of Anthony Humble. Thomas Bewick was then four years old. Prudhoe also boasts, in a tourist brochure from between the wars (tourism in Prudhoe in 1930? – someone was being mighty optimistic), of being the place where Wesley caught the cold from which he died!

While the Beilbys and Bewick created their masterpieces in Newcastle, and Constable and Co. theirs in the south, the horrid French reared their heads again. They thought, no doubt, the English ripe for revolution, when

BEWICK ENGRAVING

in fact they were just enjoying a bit of old-fashioned decadence – as now. They got their come-uppance at the hands of Wellington and Nelson, did the French, and Nelson got a column to himself in London, from a grateful nation. Wellington got the boot! (do forgive me).

This twenty year Napoleonic business had a marked, if obtuse and convoluted effect on Mickley. Apart, that is, from the possibility that it lost a son or two in the 'glorious' battles; the Northumbrians, now shoulder to shoulder with their erstwhile protagonists from over the border, were ever in the thick of it.

War had changed a lot since the days of Mickelee men mustering with their unfit horses and makeshift weapons; gunpowder was in vogue. Bewick, in one of his engravings of Ovingham shows a soldier, minus a leg which he had left behind at the battle of Minden in 1758 in a previous war. We were ever at it with the French.

We don't hear much of Minden, where 20,000 English fought under Ferdinand of Brunswick, who mustered 40,000 troops against the French 50,000. Six English regiments mistook their orders, what with the language problem and all – not much changes in the army, does it? They advanced on the French, these mistaken squaddies, in ordered line, ignoring artillery fire from their flanks, and 'tumbled charge after charge' with their disciplined musketry volleys. This was one of the greatest examples of coolness under fire in the history of war. The French were completely broken, said their General – "I have seen what I thought impossible – a single line of infantry break through three lines of cavalry, ranked in order of battle, and tumble them to ruin."

This fellow in Ovingham had returned from Minden. Did a grateful nation give him a handsome pension? – or only a wooden peg of a leg and a crutch to help him home? An interesting sequel to this story (being a romantic, I like to think it so), arose just a few years ago, when a friend of mine who made Northumbrian pipes, called on a cobbler, name of Pigg, who made leather bags for his pipes, in Ovington, along the road from Ovingham. He showed my friend an old sword that had been discovered behind a chimney-breast. Did it belong to our one-legged hero of Minden? I like to think so, that it had been lying there for nearly 250 years.

Bewick the Artist

Our view of the times is enlightened by many such engravings by Bewick as the wounded hero of Minden, which are characterised by his keen observation of life around him. This man of genius deserves more than a passing mention in the story of Mickley, neglected as he is in public esteem compared with the Big Boys of fashionable art, and even John Martin from upriver Haydon Bridge. Martin could command a wall or a hall with one painting, Bewick has to be searched for, and if the eyes are below par, needs a magnifying glass.

Book illustration, before the days of lithography and photography, depended on engraving – forming pictures by scratching fine lines on blocks of wood or copper (we are here concerned with wood), applying ink to the surface and pressing it on to paper. There's simplification if you like! To see how it's done a visit to Cherryburn is well worthwhile. The results were often pretty poor and very limited in size by the available material – box-wood. This is not, as might be thought, wood for making boxes, but the wood of the Box tree, a small, very slow-growing bush which those interested in gardening will know as an attractive hedging plant. It produces a hard, fine-grained wood, very stable when seasoned, but only of small diameter. Great for rulers (scholarly, not kingly) if they are not now all of plastic; I remember them from schooldays, and joiner's folding 3 ft. rules: but very limited in size for drawing on, as only the 'end grain' can be used in engraving – not usually more than about four inches across. Hence the miniature nature of the art, the rarity of artist wood engravers, and the need to look closely.

Many artists have been capable of producing big masterpieces in oils, or not so big in water colours; Bewick himself was no mean water colourist, probably about as good as they come. Very, very few could produce his tiny, inspired engraved masterpieces. That his work, by its very nature, should be limited to book illustration is regrettable. More so that it was confined to a short period in printing history prior to Fox-Talbot's invention of the camera in 1839 and development of the means to print photographs. Bewick's work could never be drawing-room favourites, nor his name a household word; but he must rank amongst the great in the world of art. And he was made in Mickley.

A keen eye and a steady hand are the physical attributes that come to mind in assessing the qualities of a good engraver. In Bewick these were combined with infinite patience, an acute sense of observation and feeling for the subject, a well developed sense of humour – bawdy, in keeping with the times – and, perhaps above all, an early life spent at Cherryburn in close contact and sympathy with country life and all things wild and natural. Wild and unruly himself, happier truanting with the foxes on the Common and the birds of the 'Close' woods than absorbing the educational pummelling of Mr 'Shabby Rowns' at Mickley school or the more persuasive Latin and arithmetic of his gentler (perhaps!) mentor, the Revd Gregson, at Ovingham Church. He early learned to wonder at the beauty of the blue jay feather, the shimmering, flashing trout in his water world of Tyne, and the trees, oh yes, the trees, which dominated his entire artistic life. Most of his engravings show at least one tree. Sighing, moaning, lashing, clutching monsters; tossing, dancing, gentle green and golden fairies; ice encrusted, snow bedecked, ever changing, ever present trees – distilling the very essence of rural life, cast on the air for the young Bewick to absorb into his soul and by some strange and wonderful alchemy pass out through fingers on to wood and paper to gladden our lives two hundred years on.

Not intending to adorn wealthy ladies' drawing-room walls nor to empty wealthy gentlemen's pockets, Bewick could and did indulge in a freedom to depict life as he saw it, warts and all, seldom seen in the top echelons of art of his time. The contrast of his crafting of the very finest detail of birds feathers and the stark realities of life in the 18th century is superb and unique. All done, remember, without a whiff of technology – only candles to light his way, and not a match to light them. Go and see, and wonder at his work; go to Cherryburn. Cherries still grow there, alas no longer by the chuckling burn which has long been dry, sucked below into mining caverns. The place has been prettied up for tourists and lacks the feeling of life gone by, but it tries hard and is interesting. A quiet corner may be found with a tree to sit beneath, where the magic of Mickley past might be savoured, and, who knows, a fox could pass by – they are still about – and the jays – descended, no doubt, from Bewick's companions.

Steam and Railways

If coal powered the Industrial Revolution, the steam-engine drove it. What went before – water-powered industry, was chicken-feed compared with what was to come; but the incentive that cleaned up the streets and made a lot of horsey people redundant, was war. This was when Napoleon unwittingly changed the course of Mickley history ...

Without horses Englishmen couldn't dash about Europe killing Frenchmen – or they couldn't in Wellington's day. Apart from hordes of cavalry, he needed horses for transport and for dragging guns about – bows and arrows were out by now. An army of 50,000 takes some supplying by horse and cart – and the horses need feeding. Horses have the advantage over lorries and tanks in being able to reproduce themselves, although it takes two to get a third and they need to be of the right gender. But they can't be rushed, nature has to take its course – no production-line stuff here. By the time war had gone on for twenty years, and as ever, war needs came first, the shortage of horses at home became acute, and, in a bad year, so did the shortage of feeding-stuff.

So, towards the end of Bewick's life, talk in the coffee-shops was of crisis in transport – not enough horses, not enough food for them. Canals were the answer in some places; a scheme was mooted for one from Newcastle to Carlisle. Coal had to be moved, the nation had become dependent on it; a lot of thinking went on, it was a great time for thinking ... Perhaps the by now successful steam engine, given legs, could solve the transport problem? Laughable though it may seem, mechanical legs were tried!

Collieries such as Wylam, at a distance from staithes on the river, were most seriously affected by the horse shortage and some devised ingenious ways of moving the coal – tubs running downhill on ropes, pulling the empties up, that sort of thing; but this was unsuitable for Wylam, five miles from the nearest staithes at Lemington, with not much of a slope between. The situation became so bad that there was a threat of the mine closing. Fortunately the owner, Christopher Blackett, gave his manager, Thomas Hedley, every support in his search for a solution.

Several men at this time were attempting to get steam mobile; Trevithick, down in Cornwall, where there were similar transport problems, led the way but missed the fame by failing to develop his early advantage. The Stephensons stole the glory. George was born at Wylam but soon moved and spent most of his life elsewhere and doesn't seem to have been much associated with the place, unless in filching Timothy Hackworth's ideas (I've just trodden on the toe of a sacred cow!). Wylam basks in Stephenson sunshine, but it probably has better claim to fame in Hackworth and Hedley – and Blackett, who backed them. Let no one detract from Stephenson's achievements in the development of the railways, but the work (and the ideas), that made all the rest possible, was done at Wylam by Timothy Hackworth and Thomas Hedley. It was Hedley's insistence that smooth iron wheels would drive on smooth iron rails, albeit with the help of sand and gradients not too steep, that made feasible the use of steam powered transport. The rest, as they say, is history.

Steam engines were extremely heavy; all that iron and water and coal on iron wheels, was insupportable on clarty (muddy) roads. Only when the efforts of Telfer and MacAdam bore fruit in the shape of smooth, firm roads and bridges did steam traction on roads become feasible. That is another story, not mine to tell – this is about steam on rails. Cast iron superseded wooden rails in pits in about 1777, and although expensive, lasted well, until steam locomotives weighing several tons were run on them. They cracked and needed continual expensive replacement; but steel rails in long lengths, made possible by tremendous advances in steel-making techniques and the development of the rolling mill, provided the platform from which the railway systems of the world developed.

The Newcastle-Carlisle canal idea was dropped (but has just been revived after 200 years!). Costing favoured a railway, which by 1825 had become a feasible proposition, and hordes of navvies were soon disturbing the quiet of the Tyne valley, building a RAILWAY to Carlisle – by way of Mickley. Go, if you will, and take a look at the 'quay wall' that holds the track above the Tyne as it sweeps against the escarpment between Prudhoe station and Mickley level crossing. Ponder the magnitude of the task and the dedication of the railway pioneers who took this sort of thing in their stride. No Wild West or Rocky Mountain adventure – just an ordinary bit of railway engineering; it hadn't been done before, it had to be right, it had to last; railways were for ever, or so they thought. It is still there, this Quay Wall, doing its job, after 160 years.

The stone for this wall could be brought on the completed section of line at least part of the way to the site, on wagons pulled by horses; thereafter everything had

PUFFING BILLY

to be done by hand. All the work of digging out the shelf on the hillside and building the beautifully curved wall that supports it and protects it from the river, was done by men, with picks, shovels, barrows and tripods. This was the age of the Irish 'navvy', who 'navigated' across the country not only canals but railways too. Fugitives from the privations of their native land, lonely and ill-done-by, but as tough as the rails they laid, they swept across the land, trailing behind them an orderly double row of railway lines. The stone blocks initially used to form the even bed to take the rails, cracked, and tended to move out of gauge and were soon superseded by heavy baulks of creosoted timber 'sleepers', which were flexible and lasted for years, then made robust garden sheds and permanent 'raised bed' leek trenches. Recycling of a high order!

These 'navvies', who weren't all Irish, moved with the railway, lived rough and were sustained, more or less, by the railway company. They worked hard, almost like slaves, and drank even harder when opportunity arose. The inns of Ovingham, and the Hare and Hounds, on the river bank by the ferry below Cherryburn, right on the line of the track, must have been no place, during the coming of the railway, for quiet country lads; and quiet country parents would be constrained to keep their quiet country daughters well-wrapped secrets! Strangers from afar, with odd accents, wild ways and (some) money to spend, these workers must have been to Mickley what later wartime American airmen were to East-Anglian villages; except that Mickley had no facilities for receiving their money – no shops or places of entertainment, only the inn, which no doubt made a killing while it lasted.

They soon passed, this army of workers – railways were built fast, especially this 'quay wall', rising from the river bed (hence the 'quay'), which could only be worked on when water levels were low and placid: no quick-set 'ready-mix' cement then to speed the work. The Mickley end of the wall, above water level, so perhaps considered less vulnerable (or maybe the pub was too close), collapsed in 1919, and as a result the track had to be realigned and the station closed. It was not built as, nor intended to be, a permanent station, but for all that, was quite well used for well nigh a hundred years. The level crossing, signal box and twelve cottages for railway workers came to be known as Mickley Junction, another misnomer – no junction, only sidings. It was listed in the timetables as Eltringham Station.

The navvies went on their way and the line from Blaydon to Hexham was opened in 1835, and from Gateshead to Carlisle, officially, in 1838 – in a funny old way. The participants would need a sense of humour! Neither engines nor weather were especially reliable. There was, as could be expected, a lot of Victorian pomp and circumstance; and a good soaking for two mayors, their hangers-on, and 3,500 passengers, on the seventeen hour, thirteen train, 'memorable occasion'. You can bet it was! The coaches were

THE 'QUAY WALL AND BATHING BEACH'

HARE AND HOUNDS INN
WALTER ACKROYD
LICENSED TO SELL ALES, WINE AND SPIRITS ON OR OFF THE PREMISES

little better than open coal wagons – railways were intended for carrying coal, passengers were an afterthought.

What would Thomas Bewick have made of the despoliation of his beloved countryside? He died, perhaps fortunately, in 1828 and had heard only talk of things to come; he never saw the rumpus. But he applauded anything designed to make the lot of man, and animals, easier; detested squalor and cruelty, in what were still pretty cruel times. Fears, commonly held, of panicking country animals beset by these fiery monsters on wheels would have disturbed him, as factory farming disturbs people of compassion today, although he would have been pleased by the way these newfangled 'roads' settled into the rural scene. The birds hardly blinked an eye (if larks could soar singing over Passchendaele what price a chugging train or two?), cows stared incredulously – what would silly man get up to next? (what indeed). Only the fleet footed horses nipped off to a safe distance but not for long, they quickly adjusted.

Landowners took longer; some held out against the 'march of progress' and delayed the building for a while, but their worst fears did not materialise and in any case were quickly assuaged by the obvious benefits of better communications. A scent of money hung in the air!

Worst affected were, of course, those who lived close by the line; Eltringham House and farmhouse were within easy view and hearing and the 'Squire' had serious misgivings. However, wayleave payments, a screen of trees (shades of motorways to come), quick and comfortable (?) rides to Newcastle; and – a prospect of exploiting the rich abundance of high quality coal sitting untouched under Mickley. These 'planning gains' easily balanced a bit of unaccustomed noise and 'visual intrusion'; Squire Humble was persuaded! His tenants had no choice; but it was fun to 'watch the trains go by' – a new pastime for country children and they could make daisy-chains while they waited on the railway bank.

The noise was hardly noticed after a time, even by those sleeping within a few feet of the line, such as mine host at the Hare and Hounds, the workers in the cottages across the line, and even the Stationmaster at high-class Stocksfield station. If he lived by the railway he had to live by it. The 'earth shook' most nights, once the heavy goods trains got going; shunting was a noisy business. Shunting was not long delayed at Mickley and Thomas Humble had no objections – it shunted Mickley coal and coke away.

Not much of the noise impinged on Cherryburn. A few years earlier and the railway would have saved Thomas Bewick and his brother John, who went to work with him at engraving, the long, sometimes hazardous trek home from Newcastle. Footpads and highwaymen were still about, and even the death penalty for robbery failed to keep the roads safe for wayfarers, a thousand years after 'a woman and her child could walk the breadth of the country in safety'. The advent of street lighting and Robert Peels 'Peelers',

MICKLEY 'JUNCTION'. ROAD TO FERRY. SALMON NETS, SIGNAL BOX ON RIGHT, HARE AND HOUNDS IN THE CENTRE DISTANCE

or 'Bobbies' eventually improved the lot of travellers but in the meantime passenger trains helped. Mind you, Bewick was a big fellow, and carried a big stick; he was accustomed to getting wet and liked to take his time and look at things – enjoyed the walk; so perhaps he would have preferred the railway to have given Mickley a miss.

Neither did the railway much affect the mining Bewicks, Mickley Bank pit was much too small to aspire to distant markets; it just kept going, on and on, in its own quiet way. Thomas's other brother, William, kept it and the farm going while he, and John, went off to the cushy life of art and publishing. Neither of them made fortunes, but they were comfortable. Cherryburn did well enough to have a 'round' cast-iron oven; this was quite an advance in baking for 'ordinary' homes. The fire was separate, and hot air was drawn by way of flues round the oven, which was like a big iron pipe built on its side into the stone, or brickwork. One end was closed, making the back, and the other had a round, 'drop down' door, hinged at the bottom to make a shelf when open. There was, in the smaller versions, only one shelf. These simple ovens gave a degree of control previously unknown and in the hands of experts performed miracles of culinary delights. Round ovens were still 'around' well into the 20th century and the recently restored 'Bewick Birthplace' (Cherryburn) now has one that replaces the long-lost original; it was taken from the basement of Rosedale, my former home in the village, when it was recently altered, having been built, with its round oven, in about 1900.

The booming Bewick coal trade, still of a local nature, financed the building of a replacement for the old Cherryburn farmhouse, but like the railway, it came after Thomas's death, too late to please him with its sound, spacious, but by no means grand, Victorian style. There was a fireplace in every room and a fine iron cooking range in the roomy kitchen – why not, the coal was still free, and there was no tax on fireplaces. The house is as good as new, and the range capable of making a rice pudding or a baking of bread, if someone can do it.

ROUND OVEN

The Queen Mother, after she opened the place as a museum, sent back a courier for a loaf baked in the coal-fired oven by Anne Benbow, the warden's wife. She remembered the same kind of range from her own childhood – and blackened her royal glove touching with affection the newly black-leaded iron kettle.

By the time of the new Cherryburn, the Common had gone, much to Bewick's anger – grabbed by the greedy, who already had enough land. With the common went the last of the hovel dwellers, a man of Bewick's acquaintance. He had 'squatted' in a self-sufficient, self-reliant kind of way, bothering no one, growing a few vegetables, catching rabbits (and fish no doubt) – and hiding his bee skeps in the still dense 'whins'. Honey was his cash-making equivalent of Bewick coal, but he lost out with the Enclosures, while the Bewicks lived on.

When the tithes of Mickley were commuted in 1839 the lands were in the hands of:

Battie Wrightson, 822 acres; The Duke of Northumberland, 110 acres; Joseph Humble, 134 acres; Bewick, 8 acres; Thomas Thompson, 1 acre; John Johnson, 24 perches; Joseph Lowes, 22 perches (who now knows what a perch is?).

A hundred years later the pitmen of Mickley still referred to the 'Common' and walked their whippets on it. The Bewicks still dug coal from Mickley Bank until after the final link with Feudal England was severed in 1928 upon the break-up and sale of the last remnants of the old Baliol estate, where Robert, son of Thomas of Eltringham set about felling a tree ...

IRON RANGE

Section Two

The Second Part

The Second Part

At first the coal-powered flood-tide of Victorian industry barely wetted the toes of Mickley. The hilltop settlement of the Adams, Edmunds, Williams and Henrys, now soundly built of stone, with chimneys (untaxed) for coaly smoke, remained an epitome of agricultural England – slow, horse-drawn, still with an ox or two, still pretty primitive – but coal-warmed, the Bewicks saw to that. The impact of industry was manifested only in better tools, farm implements and domestic equipment such as iron ovens, round for the poor, ranges for the better off.

When Bewick died in 1828 anyone wanting to read one of his books or a newspaper after dark had to do so by candlelight. At least it was an advance on rush-lights, but it was not until 1854 that the first paraffin lamp was made and that in faraway New York. Sulphur matches ('Lucifers') to light either candle or lamp were not made until 1854, in neighbouring County Durham, so in the meantime fire, pipe or candle had to be lit by the time-honoured method of striking steel on flint to make a spark to ignite 'tinder'. This was fine dry powder made from charred cloth, fungi, or decayed wood. Tinderboxes are still to be found, and many beautifully made and ingenious devices for striking steel on flint. Later versions, made in millions in the form of 'cigarette lighters' substituted petrol for tinder; and my, how the little serrated wheel that scraped the flint into a spark, made the thumb sore on a windy day! The modern version, cheap and nasty but practical, 'throwaway', uses gas.

Lots of interesting things were going on at this time, apart from trains. The first Ordnance Survey was made in 1801, so Mickley found itself on the map. Bewick, had he lived in Philadelphia, could have indulged in soft drinks in 1807 – he did not approve of drunkenness. He might have kept himself dry with a coat made by Charles Macintosh, or had his trousers stitched with fine cotton thread made in a Paisley factory. Cotton was supplanting wool, and rubbing shoulders with coal and steel on the road to wealth that led Britain to being 'Great'. Michael Faraday's 1831 dynamo, putting electricity to work and heralding the technology of the 20th century, came too late for Bewick to marvel at and he never was able to applaud the McCormack reaper of 1834 which began the mechanisation of farming; he really would have liked that, having lived closely with farm drudgery. It took 150 years but this process of mechanisation was to almost dispense with labour on the farm.

Mass-production of cheap sheet glass was one of the great developments of this time; it enabled the tall Georgian windows that graced the burgeoning architecture of town centres to be glazed with large-sized pieces of glass that could not only be seen through, they let in lots of light – unlike 'bulls eye' panes that were limited in size by the previous simple production methods. About eleven inches by eight is the size of the old piece in my back door; it lets in some light, is difficult to see through (but stops peering in) and has great charm, but must have made it difficult to see the goods in old shop windows. It also acts as a magnifying glass in focusing the sun's rays, scorching paint work and probably the goods.

Sheet glass not only enabled Grainger, Dobson and Clayton to lighten their magnificent, visionary redevelopment of Medieval Newcastle with streets lined with almost continuous glass-fronted shops; it allowed the Humbles and Bewicks their fine Georgian style box-windows – making work for the now highly skilled local craftsman-joiner. It also enabled poor people to have light in their lives other than by candles and John Wesley. Gone were the days when only the wealthy could afford glass, and took it with them when they went on holiday! Governments being what they are, and windows becoming popular and numerous, for a time there was a tax on them. It was bad enough people having fireplaces, but *windows* – whatever next! A foolish and iniquitous tax, it didn't last long, but the consequences are still to be seen in built-in windows in old houses. Not in Mickley – few houses had several windows, and their owners could probably afford to pay the taxes.

Having the raw materials to hand, Newcastle naturally became a centre of glass-making, but conveying window-size sheets to Mickley must have been somewhat tricky. Even after the advent of trains it would have to be got up that hill by horse and cart on rough roads that in Mickley had not yet felt the smoothing touch of 'Tar-MacAdam'.

Light in homes, newspapers and books to read, a village school – all of these brought refreshment to the minds of country folk with a thirst for knowledge. On the wider scene, the realisation was dawning on employers and politicians that workers in modern industry were the better for being able at least to read and write, possibly even think – although that might be dangerous. Workers realised that these new skills gave them a modicum of power – with more to come, lots more. It was the Reform Bill of 1832 that opened the gates which eventually led to the 'Common Man' gaining control of his own destiny – in theory; he would at least have a vote in it.

The following year slavery was abolished in the British Empire; but young boys still worked down mines in Northumberland.

Beneath our bit of Northumberland the coal measures lay undisturbed, apart from the scratchings of ancient monks and the Bewicks. The Low Main seam, the shallowest, had long since been taken out, but there remained the Hodge, up to 2ft thick; The Tilley, up to 2ft; the 5/4, 3 to 4ft; the 6/4, 3 to 4ft; the Yard, 2ft. 9ins. to 3ft; and the Brockwell, which was really three bands of coal, 2ft. 6 ins., 6 ins. to 2ft., and 1ft, making it 5ft in places.

A lot of coal, but not in very thick layers, and about 15 to 35ft strata between each. The enticing thing about Mickley coal was that it was of very high quality – and near the surface, relatively speaking, on the north-facing slope that forms the south side of the Tyne Valley from Prudhoe in the east, to Mickley, then sweeps south beyond the steepest part of the hillside, where stands Mickley Bank Farm. Eltringham Farm sits at the base, on the valley floor.

The advent of the railway set minds racing, and in 1840 Messrs. Clark, Anderson and Humble the landowner, got together and set about exploiting the potential of this coal; it was not difficult to see the possibilities. They just had to look at Newcastle!

Let us glance again, for a moment, at the story of coal on the Tyne from about 1306, when Edward I, under pressure from Parliament, banned the burning of coal, except by smiths, because of the smoke and fumes. But you can't halt progress, and by 1330 coal was in normal use in the Royal households. From then on the inexorable march of 'King Coal' carried Newcastle into a position of pre-eminence in the world of industry, shipping and commerce. The attendant social and domestic 'infrastructure' made for a good life in Newcastle – for those with fingers in the pie.

In 1600 there were 400 ships out of the Tyne, in the coasting trade. In 1620 about 14,500 tons were shipped. From 1704 to 1710, 180,000 chaldrons (a chaldron, Newcastle measure, was 53cwt.). In 1770–76, 380,000 chaldrons were shipped; in 1791–99, 480,000 chlds. In 1800, 52,000 chlds; in 1828, 80,000 chlds.

Men employed at Tyneside pits about that time numbered around 5,000 underground, and 3,500 boys, with 3,000 men and 700 boys above ground.

In 1840, when work first started on Mickley pit, the cost of coal on ship in the Tyne was 10s. 6d. per chaldron and in London £1.12s. 6d.

In 1782 John Bewick agreed to pay his pitmen 1s. 1d. per score (20 corfes, the hazel wickerwork basket used for moving coal underground, holding 6 bushels. A bushel was the measure of bulk equal to four 2 gallon buckets.). By 1841 Bewick was paying 3s. 6d. per score; so if a man dug twenty corfes a day his weekly pay was £1.1s., when rent for a year for a cottage and garden was £3.10s.

As is usually the way, these men and boys at the bottom of the pile (pit-heap?) got little for their efforts except sore backs, a-crushing, a-gassing and a-burning. The landowners, the 'coal owners' and the investors did quite nicely thank you, although in fairness, they too had their bad times and their problems; some of them came a cropper. It was a time of high adventure and not a little risk-taking.

The smoke and grime from all this activity drifted mostly eastwards towards the sea, darkening the skies and settling on the way a sediment of soot on buildings and people and into their lungs. Wallsend became one of the worst places in the country for the industrial-age diseases, tuberculosis and rickets. But hardly a whiff of this disturbed the nostrils of the country folk of Mickley when Messrs. Cookson, Cuthbert and Liddell formed Mickley Coal Company and set about in earnest the task of cutting a slice of the industrial cake of Tyneside from under their feet.

Messrs Clark and Anderson had disappeared from the scene; the Humbles stayed on but strangely, took no direct part in the forthcoming operations, other than drawing the wayleaves. They certainly didn't wax wealthy on the coal from under their land. Perhaps they took bad advice, or their accountant wasn't up to his job – or did them down; there was a lot of cheating about, and farmers were perhaps easy prey for city-slickers.

This 'shallow' coal had the advantage of needing no difficult, dangerous and expensive shaft, it could be 'walked' out on little railways. It was of a quality good enough for coking, having a carbon content of 80%, 19% gaseous matter and only 1% ash – none better. Although by this time 'cinders' (coke') was no longer the preferred fuel for locomotives, the demand for coke in industry was huge and increasing, especially after 1856, when Henry Bessamer transformed and cheapened steel making with his new type of coke-burning furnace.

There was also of course the shiny new railway, a mere few yards from the site chosen for the pit entrance at the base of the hillside. Water, too, was at hand in the river, which, although not tidal or navigable, was useful, with the help of by now well established, steam-driven pumps, for cooling and washing coke. There was also the advantage, for Mickley Coal Company, of coming late to the scene, so that lessons hard-learned in other pits could be heeded and new techniques and equipment utilised. The corfe, for instance, had been used since times forgotten for conveying coal; it was just a 'Jumbo' sized shopping basket, with wooden slides on the bottom for dragging along tunnels and a hoop across the top for lifting by rope up shafts. The two Bewick pits were good examples of how the corfe was used: at Mickley Bank – a tunnel, or 'drift' dug into the hillside – the corfes were dragged out on little wheeled trolleys. At Eltringham Common – a shallow shaft – they were lifted on ropes worked by horse – or ox – ginge (windlass).

Iron began to be used in mining in 1795, at Walker, on the Tyne, and by about 1844 corfes were replaced by 'tubs', or small wagons of wood and iron, on wheels, pulled on rails by ponies. Ponies, some of them 'midget' where seams were low, took over the work of pushing and pulling corfes and tubs when women, and boys under the age of ten, were banned from working underground in 1842 – against, believe it or not, intense resistance, not so much from the bosses, as would be expected, but from the workers themselves – they needed the money! Women never worked underground in Mickley pit.

CORFE AND TROLLEY

Change has strange ramifications; wooden tubs and the demise of the corfe brought a disastrous fall in the price of hazel-nuts. That was, to hazelnut sellers! Hazel is a most useful tree, or bush, really, capable of being 'coppiced' over many years. Coppicing is cutting down, allowing new shoots to grow for perhaps five to eight years, depending on the purpose of the rods, then cutting down again, over and over. Coppiced hazel grows fast and straight, is easily split and pliable; it was used to lay foundations for Roman roads over bogs and even as recently as the 1950s was used in this way in the building of much of the Spadeadam Rocket Testing Site. Hazel was used for the walls of early, and not so early but cheap, houses "of clay and wattle made"; for woven fencing and hurdle shelters for sheep; and still, nowadays, to stop snow from blowing on to exposed roads. It makes baskets but no longer makes corfes; it makes, but they are sadly out of fashion, rods for chastising wayward boys; and excellent walking sticks for the aged and infirm and for farmers to lean on when there isn't a gate about. Some farmers, especially of the shepherding kind, have become very skilled at carving horn handles for these sticks, which tend to become works of art for exhibiting at agricultural shows, and can be quite superb, but far too fancy for catching sheep by the neck, which is another function for farmer's sticks, besides leaning on.

This wonder tree also produces food, for man, squirrels, birds, mice and even farm animals – but only when left uncoppiced. The woods for miles around mining areas were extensively coppiced during the heyday of the corfe and nuts were correspondingly scarce, and expensive. No doubt some enterprising woodland owners kept their hazels just for nut production. There was a lot of woodland about Mickley then, and all the hazel would be coppiced; now only the Close woods, High and Low, Common Wood and bits around the old pit workings still carry the offspring of those old hazels. Few, except red squirrels and mice now harvest the nuts; I doubt if small boys would know what to do with them and anyway, "Don't do that dear, you might break your teeth," would soon put a stop to any nut-cracking venture! Within ten years of iron and wood tubs ousting the corfe there were so many nuts that the market was flooded, the price slumped and they were hardly worth the gathering – so much for keeping your woodland just for nuts! – and the corfe makers were out of a job.

Pitmen and their housing

Coals can't be dug without people, and there weren't all that many around Mickley (maybe a few spare corfe makers), and they were mostly employed in farming except for a few in the Bewick pits – who now got better pay to keep them there. Perhaps farm workers also got a better deal, to sway them from the temptations of 'free' coal and a better house. But I cannot see many deserting the outdoor life, rubbing shoulders with raw nature, to work in stygian holes in the ground. Their sons though, might, as ever, be tempted by promise of a somewhat better life – and thus began the steady movement of people from the land, accelerating through two hundred years until today machines seem to run the farms themselves and ne'er a man in sight – nor even an animal, on many farms – they're all 'cell-packed'!

So where did all the 'new' miners of Mickley come from? Farmers' boys were all very well for herding cows and turning a turf or two, but opening up a pit? Specialist 'sinkers' (the men who sank the shafts) and their drift-mine equivalents, were needed. They came from elsewhere, and had to be enticed from established pits, so perhaps they were better off than some. Possibly living in the country was an added lure, compared to dismal places like Walker and Wallsend, but I doubt it – there wasn't even a shop in Mickley.

In addition to a rapidly growing population, two sources of labour – cheap labour – were available in 19th century England. Ireland, without an Industrial Revolution of its own, was one. In 1845–6 the appalling tragedy of the great potato famine decimated a population which could only just sustain itself in a good year on the staple diet of potatoes. The entire crop was destroyed in two successive years by 'potato blight', a fungus disease easily controlled with copper-sulphate; but they didn't know and didn't have the means to apply it. Over one million people (no one really knows how many) died of starvation and associated diseases in the resulting famine. Many sought escape in the bright New World and found a short-cut to Paradise on the journey, in ships no better than the 'slavers' so recently abolished.

Others took the shorter, less hazardous step across to England for sustenance – they had to work for it. They built railways and canals and roads and whatever came to hand; or they could work in pits failing a job in the good clean air.

Scots too – the Great Settlers – were still leaving their native heath in search of something better. Georgian pogroms and harsh repression following 'Bonnie Charlie's last escapade depopulated the country, apart from where their own Industrial Revolution saved the 'coaly' parts. But Scots could walk to England and many did; it is easier, and less bloody, they learned, to conquer by being friendly!

So Scottish and Irish names came to join the old Anglo-Saxons and Normans of Mickley – and perhaps one or two from Cornwall, from whence mining know-how was disseminated throughout the country, and not a little of the world. But the old stock survived and still dominated. The Eltringhams were still around into the twentieth century, when George was secretary, then manager of West Mickley Coal Company; he lived, believe it or not, at Eltringham! After many hundreds of years there are no Eltringhams here today – the nearest is fifteen miles away and there are only a handful in the whole of Northumberland.

As good seams were found and the coal began to flow, the metamorphosis of pretty-country-butterfly agricultural Mickley and Eltringham into ugly-industrial-moth Mickley Square took place apace. The centre of gravity of life rolled down the hill, leaving the old hilltop 'ville' to go quietly about its peaceful ways, while a fever of activity broke out in the valley below.

People need houses. Irish navvies can live in 'mobile homes' (tents and huts) and move on with the railway but miners stay put (putt?) and need houses. In the days before Planning Controls, able men like Clayton, Dobson and Grainger built such places as Grey Street, in Newcastle; they had ideas and skills, confidence in the future (why not, there was everything to play for, the whole world was astir), and plenty of money. They built to the needs of the times, but with flair and imagination and due regard for the future. On the other hand a little fellow in the country needing somewhere to live built his house – he had moved on from hovels – where he wanted it, according to his needs and means and the willingness of the landowner to sell a plot. The results grace the fair face of the land to this day and exercise the minds of planners no end in 'conservation'.

Mine-owners, mines and miners posed different problems. The very act of digging coal was a messy, dirty business, and, being labour intensive, called for a heavy concentration of houses as close as possible to the grimy hole on the ground and its associated grimy ancillary activities – energy was better expended on digging coal than on walking long distances to work. All this was difficult to hide, and nobody really bothered, so the mining villages which sprang up all over the North East of England were largely responsible for its reputation for dismal filth.

Whether Messrs. Cookson, Cuthbert and Liddle dwelt much on these matters is doubtful; they would certainly be constrained more by geological and topographical factors than by concern with environmental issues, and money played its part – planning doesn't come cheap.

Coal could only be dug where it happened to be, and the nearer to the railway it could be surfaced, the better. The only environmental consideration would be whether the landowner could see the goings-on from his windows. As the old hamlet of Eltringham was depopulated and died because of its too close proximity to Eltringham House, it is doubtful if 'Squire' Humble relished the prospect of a messy great mine and its village on his doorstep – to say nothing of the pitmen.

By a fortunate coincidence the 'drift' entrance and its associated buildings fitted very comfortably, almost out of sight, into a lovely hollow where a little burn drops down in 'Riding Dene' on to the fertile riverside farmland. The rough area of the Common lay above and west of this and had recently been handed on a platter to the Battie-Wrightsons and Humbles under the Enclosures Act of 1812. Thomas Bewick had been incensed by the injustice of this, which was done in the name of 'improved land use' and 'more efficient farming' (familiar 20th century words), but in fact deprived country folk of their ancient rights, to build a hovel, nurture their garth (plot), keep their beehives and graze their black faced, long-legged sheep. Sheep with a flavour – whose company Bewick preferred, on the hoof and on the plate, to that of London high-society and the new breed of 'fattening' sheep whose flavour he likened to that of blubber (what would he have to say of what we eat today?). According to him, these simple folk of the Common lived very healthy lives on a diet of not much more than potatoes, oats and milk, and what they could catch. Sounds pretty good to me, and oh, the flavours! Now it became a question of, "You'll just have to get a real job in the pit, and you'll be a lot better off, with a proper roof over your head." So came to an end the last trace of Mediaeval Micelee.

The practice of building miners' houses cheek-by-jowl with the pit was followed in building the first of Mickley's new generation of workers' houses, on the rise overlooking the site of the drift entrance. Housing the first of the workers opening up the pit, they numbered only eight, in a street of four, if you can understand that: back-to-back was the style – but more of that later.

For the anticipated influx of at least one, possibly two, hundred workers, consideration would have been given, for closeness to

THE DRIFT

work, to building houses for them on land to the east, between the pit and the 'ferry road', which, with the advent of the railway, became known as Station Bank. The Company offices were actually built on this road, just above Cherryburn, in isolation from both pit and village, suggesting that this had been the most likely place for the housing. Whether Squire Humble intervened cannot be said, but this rash of houses would have been awfully close to the 'Big Hoose' and looking down on it. Village boys could almost have cast stones into the garden; and this not long after pitmen had been likened by Bewick to 'tribes of Cherokees and Mohawks but more wicked – demi-barbarians'!

So the 'Square' was built, with good enough reason, at a remove, not on Humble's land as would be expected, but on land leased from Battie-Wrightsons (perhaps the terms were more favourable) up the hill at the intersection of Station Bank and the Gateshead-Hexham turnpike. The workers would have to 'commute' to work – a quarter of a mile instead of a few yards; anyway you can be too close to your work …

The 'Raas' and Living in Them

Housing for workers called for no extravagances – four walls and a roof was about it, with a simple fireplace and a little window – with glass. After all, they were not all that long emerged from a form of serfdom and it was such a pity that coal-owners had to go to all that trouble and expense just in order to get them to come and dig their coal!

Expense? Not a lot, really, although it was investment without immediate cash return, until the pit got going. This was 'affordable', 'high density' housing supreme – the back-to-back street without frills; not even a bit of landscaping. Each house boasted only one outside wall, about sixteen feet long by ten feet high, except the end houses in each section, which had an extra, and higher, wall, it being the gable. One room at ground level and a garret in the roof, reached by stairs little better than a ladder; one door, opening directly on to the street, with a window alongside, and a tiny dormer upstairs. Some, where the wall was a bit higher, had the bedroom window in the wall – at floor level. The larder was a little extension, jutting out into the street, with a tiny lattice grid ventilator to let the flies in – except that it was too dark for flies to find their way, so flies in the larder were never much of a problem; which was fortunate, because you never knew where they'd been!

Flies in the living room, for this is what the house downstairs became, had a better time. At least they were warm and could see where they were going; not that that prevented them from getting stuck on those hanging sticky fly-traps that every house in summer eventually boasted before the much more subtle and deadly D.D.T. came along. These 'fly-papers' were intriguing little monsters; they came in small cardboard tubes: pulling a tag on the end drew out the length of 'claggy' (sticky) paper which was then fixed to the ceiling with a pin, without – hopefully – getting it stuck to the person. They were supposed, the early ones anyway, to contain arsenic in the sticky and I remember, when very young, being greatly intrigued by the tale of someone who supposedly poisoned his wife by this means. How to administer it must have been a problem, and my youthful imagination ran riot! I never knew if the flies ate the arsenic, but I do know that if they stuck by the feet and not the wings, they buzzed for a very long time; ten or so a-buzzing made quite a buzz! At least they didn't fall, like the DDT victims in their dying throes, into the sugar bowl or cup of tea.

Well now, this doesn't get the houses built – and the pit needed its workers …

The great luxury of these houses, compared to hovels, was the fire: apart from its being raised from the hearth, and kept behind bars, it fed heat by way of simple flues to an oven, albeit a round one, on one side and a 'setpot' on the other – a means of heating water other than by kettle or pan. What wanton extravagance!

Ah yes – water; second in life's essentials only to oxygen, more immediately important than food, useful for cleaning clothes and, for those inclined that way, for having a wash. Now, those who devised the 'New Town' of Mickley were no Graingers or Claytons, nor even architects or 'planners'; they thought only of getting roofs over heads as quickly and cheaply as possible. They gave no thought to 'planning gain', to belts of trees or grassy bits – the countryside was full of them – or to paved streets, although MacAdam was working on those. Nor to toilet facilities. Nor to WATER! It must have established planning criteria for all time; first put up the buildings, then try to sort out the consequences.

Water in those days came in buckets, just as in the days of our Robert, from the nearest spring, stream or well; it was not even passed by a local Health Inspector. The great cholera epidemics that ravaged the crowded, insanitary Victorian towns – like Newcastle in 1832 – initiated waste-disposal systems and clean water supplies in pipes, but not in villages like Mickley in the 1840s. Housewives in far distant New York could buy the newfangled washing powder – those of New Mickley would have to walk nearly that far for water to put it in. Mind you, buckets were improved on the old leather or wooden ones – industrial advances impinged on even the simplest things;

LIVING ROOM IN THE 'RAAS'

galvanised sheet steel buckets, or white enamelled ones for drinking water, were light to carry – but not the contents. A two gallon bucket of water weighs over 20 pounds; one in each hand, 40. How many gallons for the daily needs of a family of four, six, ten? – and one – more when the boys grew up, coming home encrusted, clothes and self, in a grime of coal dust and sweat.

Micelee on the hilltop had three springs for only a handful of houses, one at each end and Cuddy's Well in the middle: the well is still there. A cuddy is a horse hereabouts. The Square had only one source of spring water for two hundred houses – neither was it on the doorstep. There was of course the river half a mile down the hill – and what a hill! It was UP the hill when the buckets were full, and the water not always fit for washing even pit clothes.

The spring must have been that which waters Riding Dene and rises away up the hill towards old Micelee, just below where now stands the Vicarage on Eastgate Bank. This was not as far as the river, and uphill empty; downhill full, and in times of good flow, water could be caught from the stream, a mere hundred yards or so from the nearest houses. I have never known this stream to run completely dry, but in times of drought it can become a mere trickle and would be hard-pressed to fill even two hundred buckets, one per house, in a day. To be sure of a full bucket, it would be up the hill to the source to join the queue of perhaps a hundred women and children, to fill the trickling hours from perhaps four in the morning, with bickering and moaning, in order to ensure enough water for a wash and drink for the homecoming workers. This was 'woman's work', but children, with no school to go to, were fair game, so there was quite a bit of bucket-toting by under-tens. The overs-tens, boys anyway, were down the pit with their dads, looking forward to a good wash when they got home.

When wives and children got the water home, the kettle – big, black, cast-iron, heavy even empty – would be filled, boiled on the hot coals and lifted aside to 'sotter' – boil gently – until needed for tea, or to supplement the bath water if the setpot hadn't warmed enough. The 'lifting aside' was done with a 'kettle holder'; usually a square of double, thick knitting, practice for learners, with a loop at one corner for hanging, ever at hand, from the end of the mantlepiece. Handles got hot on open fires. The rest of the water from the buckets fed the 6 to 8 gallon setpot and if it was empty or low, another trip to the spring would be called for – and another for the two buckets to have 'on hand'. Water, hot or cold, was never wasted, not a drop when the spring ran low.

We certainly take our water far too much for granted.

Miners and their families wasted little, they had little to waste. I wonder how this kettle water was used in the early days in Mickley Square, not so very long after the Boston Tea Party set America on the road to independence. Tea then came from Clive's India in wind-powered 'clippers' and was kept locked in fancy Georgian caskets, now 'very collectable', by gentry who ceremoniously and graciously enjoyed the first brew from fine china teacups. The servants perhaps got the second – and third – brew, then used the leaves for cleaning the carpets.

This kind of economical use of tea reminds me of the anarchical tale I tell, of the hard-up, or mean, pipe smoker of my ken who used his tea-bag – this was after leaves went out of fashion – for three days, dried it, then smoked it in his pipe. A problem arose when the corners of the bag, which overhung the bowl, fell burning to the ground, singeing the carpet. So he wrote to Mr Tetley, who responded with that marvel of technology and advanced thinking – the ROUND tea bag, which fits the pipe bowl perfectly. It's true, I swear! At least miners had no worries about carpets, and by the mid-nineteenth century, tea was in better supply, less heavily taxed, and perhaps within the prudent miner's pocket. He certainly couldn't splash it about, and water was the drink for underground, carried in tin, cork-stoppered bottles. The days of the home, or village brewed rough ale as the staple drink, were gone – that was for country folk, not industrial workers.

Tea, even when it reached the lower ranks, was still treated with respect. It was kept in the poor man's equivalent of the Georgian tea casket – pretty, painted tin boxes called caddies which stood on the mantle shelf, itself made attractive with a velvet, tasselled fringe, and underhung with a long brass rail for drying and airing clothes and towels.

The mantelpiece surmounted every fireplace and was the repository for all of the immediate small necessities of life. A man could lay hands on his clay pipe there, and 'spills' – thin slivers of wood, made with a knife in idle moments on long winter nights – to light pipe, candles and the later paraffin lamps, from the ever-burning fire. There might be spectacles for those few who needed, and could afford them; a box with pencils and possibly a penknife. The kettle-holder at one end, and a pincushion at the other, hung by their loops and were similar, except that the pincushion was stuffed with sawdust or the better ones with hair, like a chair. Sometimes an ornament or two – a china dog at each end (popular wedding presents, and they had to be displayed – there was no knowing who might call), and perhaps a clock in the middle. In many households there hung from this mantelpiece the symbol of parental authority – the strap, or belt; always to hand, seldom used – its very presence enough. It was preferable to the belt holding up the trousers – there is nothing more undignified or destructive of authority than a man's trousers falling down in the course of chastising a wayward son.

The ever-present fire, that lit the spills, boiled the kettle, heated water and oven, also provided warmth, lovely warmth, for the whole of the house. With coals aplenty, fire up the chimney never out, the very walls, two feet thick solid stone, became giant heat-storage units that kept these homes as cosy as pie – so long as you were quick about getting the door shut. Otherwise the

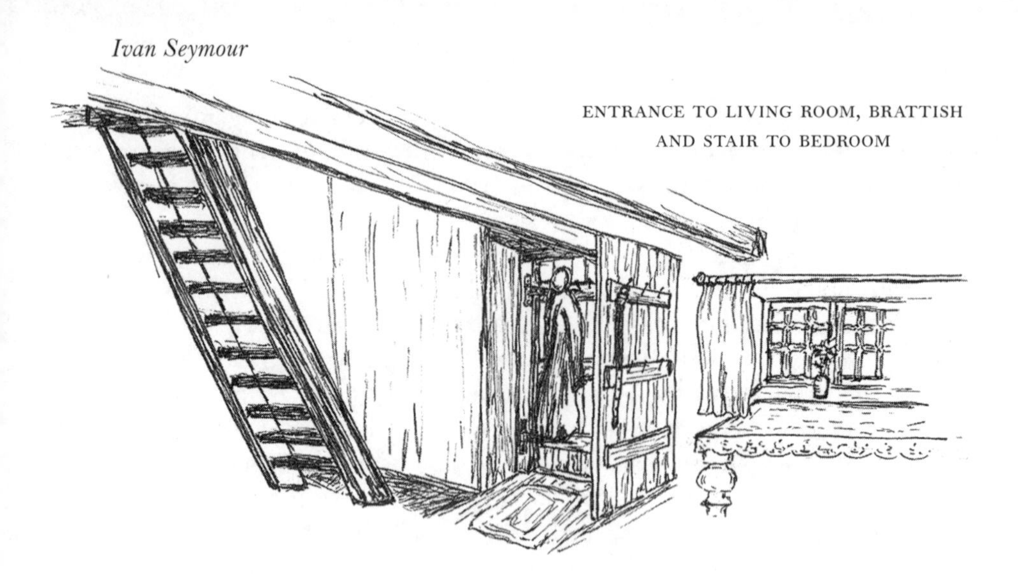

ENTRANCE TO LIVING ROOM, BRATTISH AND STAIR TO BEDROOM

elements galloped in behind, straight into the room. They could also sneak in, even with the door shut. It was only a simple 'batten' door of boards, not always a good fit, and in the absence of 'draught excluders' there had to be recourse to coats and hanging blankets to repel the wintry blasts.

Most houses in the course of time developed a 'brattish' in defence against the blast. Miners were not renowned for their woodworking skills and seldom possessed tools, but the pit joiner – who, with the smith, retained his place in the hierarchy of skills – was usually prepared to help out for a bob or two. He could not be expected to turn out a fancy sideboard or build a noble staircase – but he was good at brattishes – he had experience. Being a vital part of the underground ventilation system in pits, there were a lot of brattishes about; they were merely wooden partitions or screens for deflecting currents of air to create efficient circulation through the workings. In domestic application this screen jutted out from the wall on the 'room' side of the door, to deflect the draught into a more circuitous path from its most favoured route to the fireplace by way of the table and anyone sitting by the fire. Fortunately for the well-being of the occupants it failed to eliminate the movement of air between door and chimney, which helped save country dwellers from the worst of the tuberculosis scourge which greatly afflicted town dwellers, where the outside air was as bad as inside.

Upstairs needed no brattish. It had no door, hardly a window, and precious little air; what there was came up the same hole in the floor as the ladder, and was warm from the living room – some help in the winter when the only protection from the elements was a layer of slates, not renowned for their insulating properties. Recourse was often made to 'hooky' or 'clippy' mats on the bed for warmth on the worst of winter nights. Eight children in a bed helped!

In summer, quite the other way, with the sun on the hot slate roof, only a tiny window to open and the non-stop fire below in the room without ventilation other than the door, the whole house became as hot as the oven. The bedroom, where the night shift miner was supposed to sleep, was airless, tropical – and heaven help the boy who made street noises when the window was open!

Furniture in these homes was surprisingly good, still pretty simple but well made, robust and some of it very attractive – the 19th century was the age of sound furniture making. The main item, the table, was usually about four feet square, with thick, turned legs and a scrubbable, boarded top, in later times covered with 'easy-wipe' oilcloth with pretty patterns and sometimes scalloped edges. Between work, it might be covered with a chenille cloth, tassel-edged to match the mantel-frill. Sunday tea being special, called for a clean white, often embroidered, lace-edged cloth, made sometimes by a gifted daughter of the house. But this table was a workbench as well as eating-board. Clothes were scrubbed on it and ironed, baking was done on it – and what baking! If there was a paraffin lamp, it sat in the middle on winter nights, giving off its mellow, warm light and a slight, not unpleasant smell of burning oil, while those who could, sat around reading, or making mats.

Candles preceded paraffin lamps as the main light source and continued as ancillary lights until the advent of electricity, but not usually in the brass candlesticks that were for 'show-off' ornaments on the mantelpiece. Workaday candles did their jobs securely and safely in flat, painted tin holders that could not be knocked over, held the molten grease and a box of matches, and had a finger-ring on the side for carrying upstairs. The atmosphere of life with the candle is evoked in the first rhyme I ever learned:

In winter, I get up at night,
And dress by yellow candlelight;
In summer, quite the other way,
I have to go to bed by day.

They caused an awful lot of fires in homes, did candles.

There were no carpets, nor even strewn rushes on the floor, which was of earthenware flags of kiln-baked clay, eighteen inches square and laid directly on the bare earth. 'Damp-proof membrane' had no place in these houses and where the earth below was damp, the folk above were also damp. Good thick, free for the making, 'clippy' or 'hooky' mats had their heyday in keeping out the worst of the damp and cold from below; classic recycling, this. All you needed was a disused hessian sack – almost everything came and went in sacks – cut open, and a pile of worn-out clothes. No clothes were discarded until completely worn out, many passing from generation to generation or house to house. When they could no longer be patched or mended they were cut into narrow strips about 1 inch wide and used in lengths for 'hookies', pushed through holes made with a 'progger' in the hessian weave, to form little loops. The result was a flat, woven effect mat, hard wearing and perhaps marginally easier to keep clean than the 'clippy'. For the 'clippy' the cloth strips were cut again, into two or three inch lengths, and each end pushed through close-together holes and pulled tight to form a 'pile'. 'Clippies' were harder on scissor fingers. The more artistic mat makers created sometimes quite elaborate and atractive patterns, although a familiar old coat or pair of trousers might still be recognized. Eventually it was possible to buy cut to size and ready printed hessian, although the heavyweight stuff of some sacks was by far the best – and a mat was only as good as its hessian.

The 'progger' for making the holes and pushing the cloth through, could be bought ready made, of pointed steel, with a knob on the end to save the palm; or it could be just a piece of pointed wood. Every household needed a progger or two; we still have two, made by my father in oak, shiny from years of progging ...

Mats could be made, on winter nights across knees (several, if there were idle hands), or on the table, or, fancy of fancies, on a 'mat frame', which was much better and easier and all the family could sit around it. The colliery joiner did a roaring trade in mat frames, which were simple, adjustable wooden frames for holding and stretching taught the mat hessian.

The resultant mats were durable and very warm when pressed into service in their other role as bedclothes on the coldest of nights, but they gathered a lot of coal dust and when 'coal-charged,' were very heavy. The only way to clean them, if you could call it that, was to bang them against a wall – 'dad' them. Dadding was best done at a distance, on a favourable wind; otherwise the coaly dust all came home. It most certainly was not to be done with washing hanging out! Pit trousers were also 'dadded' to rid them of surplus coal, but were lighter and easier than mats. Dadding was 'woman's work', in addition to producing pitmen for the future.

It is difficult for the modern mind to understand the way of life of those times; we recoil from the apparent horror of it. But there was nothing to compare it with and in any case, no choice. The miner and his wife moving into these brand new houses in Mickley probably came from something worse and dreamt of making them better – so long as the coal company thrived and the man did his job. Wives accepted their lot, although not always with docility! In return for a kind of security, and a home, they cared for home and husband with pride and devotion and produced and cared for their children, although far too many died in childbirth. This mutually beneficial, or at least acceptable, arrangement seemed to work; things got done, they had their pleasures, there was little in the way of broken homes and no divorce, and neurosis had never been heard of. It was an ordered, controlled kind of life – everyone knew where they stood, and didn't have much of a choice of places to stand.

So, in the course of time, these four walls with a roof and a fire became housewives' palaces, the epitome of homeliness; full of good smells, good feelings and family – and neighbours next door – very close next door! Of course, there was a black side, coal black, but I believe the good predominated and lasted, indeed developed, over more than a hundred years. I count myself privileged to have seen, heard, smelt and tasted this simple, wholesome way of life at its zenith. Mind you, those housewives had to work at it!

The Daily Round

The daily routine, of water-carrying, cleaning, cooking and so on, circulated round special days: Monday, the horrible day of the week, let's get it over – washday. It began early, with seeing that there was enough hot water, breakfast over, those for work on their way, and those for school in later years – this was the invariable routine for a hundred years. Washing in piles around the floor in order of dirtiness and priority of whiteness. Whiteness was important, as much a matter of prestige as hygiene, when your washing hung to dry on a line across the street. No Persil then, just a block of green, red or yellow 'washing soap'. Not so very long before, people could make their own, or someone in the village did; now there was a law against it and soap came from vile factories where, and in equally noisome glue factories, worked the 'unemployable'.

Should you fancy trying your hand at soap as it was, when nobody's looking, because making it is probably still illegal – here's a recipe:

All you need is some fat and some wood ash. Any fat and any alkali will do (bear in mind that alkali burns), but in days of yore they came from well-fattened animals and any fire before coal came along. You can induce the required liquid alkali from the wood ash in the same way that pre-chemical gardeners got their plant food from sheep droppings – put it in a sack and wet it, but instead of immersing it like manure in a lot of water, just make it moist and add more water every day or two, until you can collect the slow drips of alkaline exudation. Don't rush the job – too much water is no good.

The fat needs to be clean and clear and it and the alkali warm; the skill is in mixing the two together at the right, slow speed until the mixture is thick but still liquid enough to pour into moulds, after adding colouring (and perfume if needed). Caustic soda could be easier than wood ash, and for the extra cleaning of clothes and dairies added borax or ammonia could kill a lot of germs. The ultimate germ killer was carbolic acid, and 'Lifebuoy Carbolic' soap sent most small boys of my time to school germ-free and carbolic scented – albeit with smarting eyes if they failed to keep them tight shut during the washing operation! To this day the word 'Lifebuoy' conjures up the very essence of cleanliness. No longer allowed – carbolic is harmful.

Well, there you are – soap, simple; try it on your face if you dare, and see how you like washing clothes with it.

Back to wash day; water hot in the setpot, cold in buckets, and the 'big pan' boiling on the fire. Some kept this pan just for boiling clothes, most shared its duties with potato boiling and broth making; it was, as the name suggests, pretty awesome as pans go: cast iron, with a capacity of twelve or sixteen pints, and a very long handle, or a small one on either side, it was one of the most dangerous domestic devices ever invented. Full of boiling water to which a few scrapings of soap had been added, and the special items that had to be boiled for extra whiteness, such as 'Sunday' blouse or shirt; or for extra cleanliness, like tea-towels, dish cloths and towels, this frothing, scalding monster had to be carried, two handed, to the poss tub: this was a sawn-off beer barrel which stood outside the door, with the 'mangle', and was used there on reasonably fine days – on others it was trundled indoors. Into it went the steaming contents of the pan, which if necessary was returned to the fire with another load for boiling. The clothes in the barrel, except the 'delicates' which were cooled and squeezed and gently wrung by hand, were thumped until judged clean, with the end of a 'poss' stick, which was made from the trunk of a tree – or must have felt like it to the wielder. Then they were lifted into the tin bath full of warm water, sitting on a chair for easy reaching and lifting; there it was hand rinsed, ready for 'mangling'.

WASHING

WASH DAY IN LOW ROW (LAA RAA SOOTH)

More hot water and soap would be added to the tub and the progressively dirtier, heavier clothes dealt with in the same manner. Exceptionally dirty or stained clothes were laid on the table, well rubbed with the soap block, then hard-scrubbed with a brush of the type used for scrubbing floors and doorsteps. The dirty water was discarded into the street – there was nowhere else, until a drain was laid at the end of the century, when water could be poured down the gully that was provided outside every house door.

This washday possing of clothes was a mighty business, made suds and sweat fly and a great reverberation of thumping around the village. It was this noise, of a hundred or more tubs being thumped in the washing process, that greeted my puzzled ears and gave my first and lasting impression of Mickley when I came to live here, at the age of eleven, in 1936. Possing by then had resounded over Mickley Mondays for well-nigh a hundred years.

Mangling the clothes was no doddle either – for those who had a mangle. Like most machinery of those days, the mangle was big, cast iron and wood, durable – and effective. It was often quite ornate and nicely painted in the way that Victorians had of making even the most mundane of things attractive; although beauty is in the eye of the beholder and I doubt if the belaboured wives of Mickley saw much beauty in the mangle. Times change and the mangles that survive have become 'collectors' items', for painting up and standing on the patio, graced with trailing plants. Could, I wonder, a modern Ms turn a 'screwed down' mangle handle?

The great thing about the mangle, if you could turn it 'screwed down', was that it got the water out, and that's what it was for, whatever you might hear about them being for pressing clothes; perhaps in more splendid homes – not in the 'raas' (rows). Turning a big screw on the top adjusted the space between the wooden rollers, according to the thickness of the item, how dry you hoped to get it, and how strong you were feeling. If you didn't have a mangle, which cost all of £8 in 1860, when a miner might earn no more than about £1 in a good week, you did your best by hand 'wringing' – twisting the sodden, wet clothes in a kind of rope, like 'thick twist' tobacco. They took twice as long to dry, depending on how powerful your twist, and hand wringers developed powerful biceps!

On fine days, drying was on a line in the garden, if it was close at hand, or strung across the street; which meant that sensible people of the horse and cart fraternity kept well clear of the streets on Mondays! Neither off-white sheets nor the state of your underwear (if any) could be hidden from the neighbours' view. But the sight of all this sparkling washing, dancing up the street like row upon row of out of time, but lively chorus girls, was well worth a corner of memory's storage space. So too was the sight of winter-frozen washing being 'broken' over housewives' arms for carrying in. I never heard a woman complain about this, although it must have been agony; they liked their washing, especially whites, to have a good freeze and a good blow in the wind imparted a fresh country smell that today's 'fabric softener' could never hope to emulate.

On wet days the drying came indoors, on to a big 'clothes horse' in front of the fire; the pit joiner did a steady trade in clothes horses as well as mat frames and brattishes – a wonder he got any work done at the pit. The atmosphere hung heavy with the peculiar, dank, soapy smell of wash day. But every effort was made to clear the decks before the man or men came home – anything left over would dry overnight or next day. The men didn't like wet washing about the place.

Even on a good day, when clothes dried as fast as they were hung out, ironing was usually left for the morrow – enough was enough for one day.

Even the dinner on wash day was a scratch affair – 'caad waarmed up' (cold warmed up); the remains of the Sunday dinner, re-heated, and no worse for that. The miner, in good times, ate well, and enjoyed it. The bone and left-overs from the roast formed the basis of the broth on Tuesday and perhaps Wednesday (always better, second day). Steamed pudding, spotted dick or treacle, usually filled any gaps. My, were those puddings good ...

Tuesday was ironing day – a long, slow, tedious, standing job, with only thoughts and perhaps children and neighbours, for company; no 'Mrs Dale's Diary' to while away the time. But a fair bit of concentration was needed. Good ironing was a matter of pride but could easily be ruined by a moment of carelessness. It was the indicator of good housekeeping and not to be skipped.

The pit joiner's skills didn't run to ironing boards, and they hadn't been thought of anyway, so the table took on this other role. The iron, in its true sense, was cast iron, 'flat', and heavy; two of them if you were well off – one in use and the other heating against the fire, but not on it, or it dirtied the clothes. The skill was in getting the iron hot but not too hot for the material being ironed; the test was by spitting on it – just a little spit! – and the rate at which the spit danced and spattered off the iron denoted its temperature. The squeamish or genteel held the iron close to the cheek for testing, but not too close: it was a hazardous method and produced many a charred genteel cheek. There were many variations on the iron – different shapes and sizes for different jobs – but a great improvement was in the form of a outer case into which a hot cast-iron block was placed. This block could be heated directly on the fire, there could be several, so that there was no waiting for the heating, and, most important, the risk of dirtied laundry, the bane of the housewife, was eliminated. Thus did life's little betterments come along.

As each item was ironed it would be hung on the brass rail above the fireplace, or on the clotheshorse, to air for a while then be sorted into piles for 'putting away'. 'Away', for the downstairs stuff, was in the next most important piece of furniture to the table and chairs – the 'press'. Not, strictly speaking, a real butler's press, but similar: a storage unit, with three drawers below and a cupboard above. The cupboard was usually used in its original sense – for cups; the best china, safe for Sunday tea; and for miscellaneous storage. The drawers held tablecloths, tea-towels, towels. Sheets, shirts, dresses and such went upstairs out of sight into an ordinary chest of drawers. Many homes eventually ran to a tall, well made mahogany-veneered chest of drawers that graced the living room and housed just about everything in the way of clothes and bedding, and the shallow top drawer was home for all the little bits and pieces that had no other place. These cottages became pretty well furnished.

There was more cast iron for the beds – all fancy scrolls and floral decorations, except where the money and ostentation ran to brass knobs, which were great for youngsters to screw off and play with on wet days! Beds took up most of the remaining space in the house; one upstairs to begin with then, separated only by a curtain, another for the children; then one downstairs if necessary, and the parents moved down. Children could sleep six in a double bed, head to toe, and often did when families reached ten, twelve, or even sixteen. There is a story of one village boy becoming mislaid and, after much searching, a neighbour, with whose children he had been playing, doing a head (or foot?) count and finding seven instead of six in the bed!

Chairs for comfort were thin on the ground and made of wood, with cushions – upholstery for miners was a thing of the distant future. If there was a comfortable chair the man had it, by the fire; he reckoned he'd earned it. Children sat on what we would call kitchen chairs or wooden dining chairs, 'crackets', or on the little boxes at each end of the fire curb, where dad would sometimes sit to enjoy his clay pipe within easy spitting distance of the fire. Some fastidious wives insisted on a bucket, or even a spittoon!

Baking days could vary a little within the constraints of washing and ironing and the weekly 'cleaning', which was more thorough than the routine daily clean and involved such pursuits as scrubbing and 'whitening' the doorstep, taking out and thoroughly 'dadding' all the mats, brushing and if necessary washing the floor and the messy job of black-leading and polishing all the black iron bits. Kettle, pans, oven door, fire-irons, setpot lid, etc., all got the treatment, and responded with a lovely warm glow, although not quite the sparkle of the showy brass candlesticks on the mantleshelf. Black-lead is another banned, poisonous, substance but it doesn't matter, because there is no longer any cast-iron to put it on, thank goodness, says the housewife. As it was always good to have a spruce house for the weekend, the cleaning usually happened on a Friday, so, almost by default, Thursday was baking day. This day conjures up a different set of pictures, a different set of smells – ah, the smells!

If you walked the road from Mickley to Prudhoe, and you did, because that was how to get there, you walked within four or five feet of the summer-open doors of some of these cottages – 'High Raa Sooth' (High Row South, the Siamese twin of which was High Row North). Parallel and down the hill a bit ran the other principal village street, Low Row North and South – the Laa Raa. At right-angles was West Street, Cross Row, and, much later, East Street, all making up the more-or-less 'Square' which distinguished this village from the old ville of Micelee. If you walked slowly along High Row South you could savour the full force of baking day, the length of the street – about thirty-five houses worth. If, in later days, you walked along the Low Row to the football field, you could have forty-five houses' worth, and another forty-five back the other side!

No shops graced the streets of early Mickley; if a loaf of bread was needed, or a pie, you made it yourself, or a neighbour did it for you. At least there was a reasonably efficient oven, once you got used to it, and plenty of coal for the firing. But where did the flour come from? There was no longer a mill in Mickley.

Although the coming of the railway to Mickley opened up the possibility of shopping in Hexham or Newcastle, it was not exactly 'convenience', and there was still the hill to lug the bag of flour up. So it would seem, after all, that it was a good idea to build the Square by the road, now an 'all weather' affair, properly made, with a reasonable surface. It carried frequent coaches, carriers aplenty and hordes of itinerant traders and hawkers, only too happy to deliver your goods to the door. Poetry again reflects the times:

> I wish I lived in a caravan,
> With a horse to drive,
> Like a peddler man …

Silly little three-pound bags of flour would only mock the appetites of men who did men's work, wives who did men's work and children who played like the very devil. Flour was cheaper in bulk and there to hand when needed, and stored in the earthenware 'crock' or the big tin bin with a 'half-lid', one or other of which stored the finished loaves, safe from the mice which plagued old-style houses.

Bread, in Victorian times, was the 'Staff of Life'; they were good at that sort of saying, religious tracts, and clever verses for autograph books. In truth, workers did lean pretty heavily on bread and potatoes in their staple diet. They could grow their own potatoes, given a garden, and cook a few as needed, but they didn't have the smell of new-baked bread! Not just bread for the week, perhaps a bit dry by next baking day, but 'fadge' and 'stotty cake' for immediate consumption; 'Granny loaf', tea-cakes, with spice only for Easter, not spread along the year; scones, meat pies – especially rabbit, another staple; tarts of the season, mostly apple and blackberry, separately or combined, or just jam. When the pig was killed, 'Singin' Hinnies'.

'Stotty cake' and 'fadge' were a quick form of bread, baked flat and round on the oven shelf, from unrisen or partly risen dough – terrible for the digestive system. But who gave indigestion a thought?

'Singing Hinnies' were, and still are for those who know how, 'state of the art' girdle scones, rolled out thin and cut into rounds, to the size of any suitable cutter – usually a cup or mug before tin cutters became available: but you could use a knife and make them any shape! 'Hinny' is a Tyneside term of address, a form of endearment, like 'Honey', 'Dear', 'Pet' and 'Love' in other – less inventive – places. An odd name for a scone, but they are delicious, best buttered and eaten hot. The 'singing' bit, over which there is some argument amongst those who know no better, comes from the excessive amount of lard in the recipe, which causes the scones to 'sing' – or whistle, according to your ear – but could you have a 'Whistling Hinnie'? – as they cook on the hot iron girdle, hung over the open fire. The extravagant use of lard arose from the need to use up the large amount that came from 'home-killed' pigs, before it went rancid, in the days when a good pig was a fat one and no one worried about 'cholesterol'.

Remember that this way of life was akin to Cobbet's 'Cottage Economy', and although the cottages were stuck together in rows, in big groups, pigs and hens still lingered on in the system and provided important supplements to otherwise frugal diets. With no fridges to keep food beyond its natural life span, food from the pig was shared around – fresh. Black, and white, pudding, sausages and pork, trotters and head; there was no waste. They were only killed when there was an 'R' in the month – the cold time of year. Bacon had to be sent to a farm or butcher's, for salting – in exchange for a share. Miners' cottages had no room for that sort of thing. But there was a rare fever of activity around pig killing time, for all that – and a certain amount of gluttony! Come to think of it, there seemed to be a remarkable lack of coronary thrombosis.

All this talk of food brings to mind another of life's little distant pleasures, now extinct – 'Billy cake'. Another form of scone, I suppose, but mostly for the poor; the wealthy didn't know what they were missing. It was made in a frying pan over the fire – could be a camp fire – especially if you were in a hurry for something hot and tasty. It was only flour, water and a pinch of salt, mixed to a dough and rolled out thin. I don't remember if there was baking powder. There wouldn't be if it was 'Hillbilly' cake. It stayed thin, was browned both sides on the girdle or frying pan, and needed a lot of skill and a sharp knife to slice through the middle for buttering hot, to go with Dutch cheese toasted on a fork at the fire. Just you try toasting Dutch cheese on a fork at the fire – if you can find a fire – and it will all drip off into a splodge on the hearth. Ours – my father was a Master at cheese on a toasting fork – was browned crisp and bobbley, like the surface of a volcano, on the outside, yet still firm but hot in the middle; the perfect complement to Billy and piping hot tea on a winter's day school home-coming. I've got carried away by all this flavoursome nostalgia ... Schools? who had heard of those in 1840s Mickley Square?

LAST BRICK OVEN IN MICKLEY, FLORRIE HOWDON AND HER MOTHER

Time Off

The 'five day working week' didn't ease the life of miners until a hundred years after the Square came into being. On Saturdays, the early, 'fore' shift went to work as usual in the small hours and came home late morning (2–30am. to 10–30.). There was no second shift, so, apart from essential maintenance work, Saturday afternoons and all day Sunday were 'time off' for family matters, a jaunt to Hexham or Newcastle for shopping or pleasure, or for gardening. Gardening was important, it was the means whereby the miner could not only make it possible to live on his meagre pay, but provide variety and even a little luxury in the diet. In addition, and most important, it was an escape from the grinding strain of pit life, and a source of great pleasure.

The eternal, almost primeval joy of tilling the soil, watching and taking part in the miraculous cycle of growth, from seed to harvest; of breathing the good air, feeling the warm sun, even sitting in it in resting moments – which are always allowed in a garden – and smelling the glory of summer rain on sun-warmed earth; all against a background of a working life spent in dank, noisome black holes in the ground. This must have been the nearest to bliss a miner could ever hope to achieve. Could he have sported a sundial, it would surely have had on its plinth the words that graced many a more decorative, less functional garden of the time:

A kiss of the sun for pardon,
The touch of the rain for mirth,
You are nearer God's heart in a garden,
Than anywhere else on earth.

He had his garden, this miner, not through the altruism of the colliery owners, but because of the provisions of the Enclosures Acts, which entitled, and still does, every man to a plot of land on which to grow food for his family. This entitlement is manifest today in 'allotments', which cash-hungry councils sell off as prime building sites – whilst fulfilling their obligations by offering alternative land for gardens at an impossible distance.

The provision was made, in Mickley, by dividing up the hollow of the 'square', and a similar area to the north and south of High and Low rows into 'perch' sized plots, each one allocated to a house. When all of the houses were completed, one hundred and seventy-eight gardens, some a street-width from the door; for the less lucky ones, perhaps fifty yards away.

As the surrounding hawthorn hedges grew a few years high, close trimmed and dense, these gardens became not only private, almost secret places, they developed what today's 'horticulturists' would call a 'micro-climate'. Here crops could be brought to harvest a week or two ahead of exposed sites, and quite exotic flowers could be grown, by rough-hewn men of gnarled hands and earthy speech, to satisfy their inner hunger, born of peasant ancestry, for the delights of nature, and to counterbalance the grim squalor of working life.

A corner of the garden often contained a hen 'cree' or small hut, and a tiny enclosed 'run', where the half-dozen inmates stretched their legs, dust-bathed in dry summers, and recycled garden waste, supplemented with kitchen scraps and a bit of corn, into 'real' eggs. Maximum crop production precluded too much livestock, so it was usually a choice between hens or a pig, which also recycled waste but gave only intermittent 'crops' of meat, whereas well managed hens spread their harvest over the year – except when moulting, and brooding, when 'mum' had a rest from laying to rear her family. This family rearing is worth a word or two, for those who have never and are never likely to, experience its delights …

One of my childhood duties was to collect the eggs, feed the hens, and be sure they were safe from the fox at night; and, as they roamed free over a bit more land than the miner's garden, to watch for the wayward one that 'laid away' under a hedge or in a clump of nettles. This watching was often done swinging on the coal house door, for more height and a wider view, and was a happy way of whiling-away the time. I once found a 'cache' of twenty-seven eggs – mustn't have been doing my job very well – and remember my mother testing them for 'fit to use' by putting each in turn into a bowl of brine. Memory fades, but I think the rotten ones sank. My favourite among hens, a solitary black one amongst White Wyandottes, Leghorns, Light Sussex, Rhode Island Reds and goodness knows what else, disappeared and I mourned her going as fox-food, although I found no feathers. Three weeks later, to my immense joy, she came clucking home (broody hens are known, hereabouts, as 'clockers'), proudly marshalling her family of ten yellow, golf ball-size cheep-cheeping chicks. It's better than watching telly, I can tell you, seeing a mum-hen summoning her family to dinner – a tiny morsel of selected suitable food, pecked smaller if necessary – with high-speed, excited 'clucks'; in contrast to the slow repetition of 'follow me children' normal walkabout clucks. Or watching them tucking under her, into the soft warmth of her under down, in safe shelter from cool breeze, sudden shower, or night-fall. Or perching on her back, basking in summer sunshine … Ah, departed joys.

The broody hen in a miner's garden, rearing replacements and surplus cockerels for the pot or Christmas roast didn't quite enjoy these 'free range' privileges; she was kept in solitary but safe confinement in a separate little 'cree', displaying her maternal instincts as best she could, especially when allowed to wander around the garden in search of pests – and a change of diet when the gardener wasn't looking! At least she had fresh air and sunshine, room to stretch her legs, and good, natural food – just like the miner whose hospitality she enjoyed.

The hen, the pig, and pigeons were valuable sources of fertility for the garden, supplemented by what could be gleaned from the street with a bucket and shovel when a horse passed by – transport emissions were very welcome, and tangible, before fertility came in nice clean bags, from factories. Manure could sometimes be bought by the cart-load from a farm but most farm tenancy agreements forbade the sale of manure off the farm, as being the main means of maintaining land fertility. No self-respecting farmer would sell manure anyway. However, manure from the colliery stables was led, free, to the 'tatie garth' or potato garden and pronounced 'taytee', which was an area of open land, without dividing hedges, beyond the gardens of Low Row North. Here a miner could have a plot of land specifically for growing his potatoes, leaving his garden free for more exotic crops – like leeks. Leeks, whippets and pigeons became, in the course of time, the principle recreational pursuits of the miner – although there were others! However, these pastimes did not become 'organised' until there were places to show monster leeks, organisations for racing pigeons, and meetings for showing or racing whippets.

Manure was vital to gardening. Rotational cropping was by now a well-established agricultural principle, but on small plots there could not easily be a 'fallow' or rest period, or manuring by grazing animals, as on farms. A few hens or a pig helped, but not for everyone, and not enough. So now we come to a rather delicate matter; anyone squeamish should look away.

Waste and Water

Perhaps you have noticed that in the building of this New Town of Mickley, although gardens and a fire were mandatory, there was what we today might consider to be one important omission – somewhere to perform the vital 'calls of nature'. The cholera-driven move towards drains and WC chains did not apply, as yet, to little places in the country; the 'infrastructure' did not exist, even in thinking. Who wants a bathroom, when you can scrub in a tub, in front of a roaring fire?

However, even the Romans had privies – flushaways, at that; and one of Bewick's light-hearted works, in a bawdy way and expurgated for sensitive eyes, depicted a rear view of a man 'at stool' in a rather dilapidated but recognisable closet, or 'netty', in local parlance. They were not entirely unknown in Mickley. So why no rows of 'netties' to match the rows of houses? In a word, if you can believe it – manure. At a time when waste of resources was abhorred ('waste not, want not') and manure precious and essential for crops, human excrement was not to be discarded (sniffed at?). The miners of Mickley did not want privies, they wanted the manure. Neither, I suspect, did the mine owners – they would merely be an additional expense to build, and who would empty them? 'Potties' and buckets were used indoors, and at Prudhoe, where the pit village came later, it is recorded that they were emptied into stinking cess-pits just across the street. There is no record or evidence of these at Mickley, and it would make sense, be easier and less offensive, to carry a daily bucket to the garden, where a 'moving trench' system could be kept for the purpose – a kind of underground compost heap. This would without doubt be more pleasant, or rather, less noxious than the occasional emptying and carrying of the accumulated contents of a vile cess-pit. Life was, indeed, raw.

Not as raw as in the cities, where as many as fifty or sixty people lived in one rat-infested, flea-ridden, lousy house, without water or sanitation, cheek by jowl with slaughter houses from which the waste was cast into the streets for dogs, rats and crows to consume. It took pestilence such as the great cholera epidemics, aided to some extent, in Newcastle, by the fire that destroyed the medieval Quayside area, to bring about the cleaning-up and rebuilding into well-planned and designed, often quite magnificent, towns and cities, with piped water, and sewers – pitching untreated into the rivers, that which had previously been thrown into the streets. You probably know about the consequences of that, which is another story.

Newcastle and Gateshead Water Company was formed in 1845, five years after Mickley Coal Co., and was charged with the duty of supplying clean drinking water to every house in the towns. By 1848 it had built Whittle Dean reservoir and laid a 24 inch pipe to Newcastle, capable of carrying four to five million gallons a day. By 1849 sixty-three thousand people had clean water; the Devil of disease a-riding, fairly caused a hustle!

By 1869 Hexham was fully sewered – directly into the river. There was a move (a 'motion'?) to replace WCs with ash privies because the state of the river was causing such concern.

Meanwhile, Mickley carried its water in buckets – and its sewage. I like to think that they could afford separate buckets. In spite of all these efforts, there was typhus in Newcastle in 1866, and 'fever' in Mickley. No wonder.

The 'Board of Guardians', the body appointed, in the days before elected local government, to keep an eye on health matters, expressed great concern about the lack of 'fever beds' in Mickley. They threatened those responsible – Mr Liddle and Mickley Coal Co., who then fulfilled their obligations by putting aside two houses for the isolation of fever victims; but they did not build privies. Mickley at that time came under Hexham control in these matters, and nobody up there bothered much, except when a problem arose that just could not be ignored.

The 'ash pit' was mostly associated with bigger houses, and was a small outbuilding with a low wall across the front over which ashes from the coal fires were thrown – and there would be a lot, in multi-fired houses. Any waste that could not be recycled by pigs or hens, or fed to cats or dogs, was included; there was not a lot of that.

Dearly beloved brethren
Is it not a sin
When peeling potatoes,
To throw away the skin?
The skins feed the pigs,
The pigs feed us,
Dearly beloved Brethren,
Is it not thus?

So the contents of the ash-pit were mostly ashes and were taken away by cart occasionally, to be tipped into a suitable hollow that needed filling, or spread on heavy clay soil, which it opened up and made more 'workable'. Then someone had the bright idea – he didn't patent it and he isn't named in that excellent book on the subject, *The Specialist*, so we don't know who he was – of combining the ash-pit and the privy and calling it the ash-closet. Mind you, a netty by any other name would smell as sweet! Nevertheless the ash-closet was a great success thoughout the days of coal fires (it wouldn't work on gas!); it tidied the place up, killed two birds with one stone and was tolerably inoffensive, but it required a lot of big holes for filling – and it didn't manure the gardens. So it was a long time before it came to Mickley – more than fifty years after the 'Rows' were built, the farms a bit earlier. The 'double-seater' at Eltringham Farm could be seen until recently, but not in use.

Eventually though, given the prospects of cart-loads of strawy horse manure from the stables, rather than human excrement from bucket or potty, and under the inexorable pressure to get to grips with the dreadful scourge of infectious diseases; with the added inducement of reasonably comfortable, sheltered, private places in which to bare their bottoms (the men had made use of the garden – it saved the carry), even the stubborn, some might say 'pig-headed', miners accepted the march of civilisation and the 'netty' came to the 'Raas'. Not one to a house, though – that would have been luxury beyond reason – but one between two! Not only that – across the street (flies were reckoned to have a limited operational range of about that distance – twixt germs and jam), and in the case of High Row South, the hazard of the main road, now the A695. This was a thirty yard dash even on a good day and it is hardly possible to view with equanimity the prospect of diarrhoea afflicting your neighbour and his eight children on Bank Holiday Monday with the road full of show-bound traffic. Fitting your turn at the netty, even without diarrhoea or road hazards, into a tight schedule could have been no joke.

They were 'semi-detached', these noble edifices – two together, with a low wall between for conversing – or 'not speaking' – over. Built of stone and quite roomy, the ash-pit, which was the working heart of the system, had to hold a week's-worth of ashes and whatever else. Dark inside though; light sneaked in only through chinks in the door and, dependent on how artistic the bent of the pit joiner, through holes – round, diamond, vee-shaped, etc., made in a pattern near the top – see *The Specialist.* In the better lit ones you could just about see to read and miners were used to the dark anyway; otherwise you took a candle. By the time netties arrived so had the school, and miners were on the way to literacy.

THE NETTY

The doors were on the

side farthest from the road and swivelling, cast-iron hatches, low down on the nearer side were used for the weekly emptying by the 'midden men', with long-handled shovels into 'ash-carts', when local councils took over responsibility for such matters. A bucket swung under the rear of the cart, containing a brown powder, presumably a powerful disinfectant, a little of which was cast through the hatch after each emptying. It cannot have done much good but it showed willing and an increasing awareness of the importance of cleanliness. Lister and company were having an impact, even in the 'outback'.

This refuse was disposed of in 'tips' at as far a remove as possible, to avoid the transmission of disease by rats or flies. Mickley refuse, mountains of it, went to the Common Wood area, henceforth known as 'the tip'. Can you imagine the outcry today? In recent times, when the discarded fertility and potential disease has long since washed away, or transformed into nettle beds or banks of luscious blackberries, amateur archaeologists have dug there like miners, in search of miner's artefacts. Apart from broken plates and teapots (for tea was now within reach of all but the poorest, at 3 to 4 shillings per pound, duty 1s., in 1864; a year later duty was down to 6d.) – and Victorian times saw huge production of very attractive, cheap pottery and china – it is amazing what a treasure-house of old bottles and jars these tips are, if you are interested in that sort of thing. Miners had little of value, broken or otherwise, to discard into ash-pits, but even old earthenware ginger-beer bottles now have a value. In about 1865 they were 1s. 3d. per dozen – full!. 'Double syrup' lemonade, 1s. 6d. They were a way of drinking safe water.

The netties remained in active use, one between two families, emptied in the same way but by special lorry, and the contents dumped in the same place, until 1960, by which time the A695 was a fast, motor-laden trunk road, like Show Day every day.

The hazards of the netty were not only of the motor car, and were sometimes amusing – to some.

You tried to avoid 'going' when the ash-cart was due – *they* were pretty regular – but if you had to, made sure you were 'off' before the outside hatch was opened. The seat was a wide wooden board, the size of the 'pit', with a round hole (square would have been uncomfortable); there could be two, three,

THE DASH FOR THE NETTY

THE ASH CART

or even four-holers, for family use – but the Rows had only one-holers (see *The Specialist*). The hole was covered, when not in use, by a loose board. The main cover was hinged at the back and lifted at the front for tipping-in the ashes, and was scrubbed weekly, as was the floor, which was finished with 'whitening' or 'sandy stone'. The screws holding the hinges had rusted and the wood rotted when one day, Mrs ... (who shall be nameless) dashed to do her stuff before the 'men' came, and the unfortunate lady, bare-bottomed on the hole, dropped, complete with seat, into the void below. No amount of frantic shouting brought rescue before the hatch was raised ... We can only hope that the 'men' were gentlemen.

Another time an agitated woman collared the colliery joiner on a Saturday morning and pleaded with him to fix the netty door, blown off in the wind. "Whey hinny," said he, "aarm sorry, but it's lowse (finishing time) and aal not be back afore Monday". Pause for thought, then, "But aal tell y'wat – just bring the 'Daily Harrald' (Herald) wi' yi' and spread it ower yor nees, then neebody'l knaa." The simple solution is always best!

Incidentally, these places did not smell offensively like the privies of old, or army latrines – loads of coal ash saw to that; nor were associated flies really a problem as everything was sealed when the lid and hatch were in place. Rats were definitely excluded.

Before making toilet rolls superseded mining as an occupation for working folk in the Mickley-Prudhoe area, newspaper was the normal netty 'furniture', pre-cut into squares and hung on string in the posher places, but whole, with bits torn off, for those who liked to choose their own size, or liked a bit read to pass the time – but very annoying when someone else had torn the end off the story you were reading. Don't ask me what they used before the days of newspapers. Life today is full of little luxuries.

That then, is where and how the miners of Mickley, their wives and families, lived – more or less.

Pits and Pitmen

With as many sons as he could muster, the miner worked in the bowels of the earth. Today, this is not easy to visualise, it is all at a distance and unreal. So allow me, if I may, to take you into a make-believe underground – with a bit of artistic license …

On a dark night, close-draw your heavy curtains so that not a chink of light enters. Put out the lights. Dark, isn't it? We are not used to total darkness; you should be unable to see a thing – stygian black. That is 'underground'. Now, the roof is only, at best, three or four feet high, perhaps only eighteen inches. So crawl under the dining table and mind your head, this roof is all rough and painful and you don't have a pit helmet: neither did early Mickley miners. The floor is all rough and painful too, on your knees, and wet in places, but we can't spoil the carpet with rocks and water, for realism. You can light a candle, for you can't work in the total dark. Candles – and matches were allowed at Mickley; it was never a 'fiery' pit, thank goodness, roof falls and tubs were the killers. Bryant and May were advertising in the *Hexham Courant*, in 1869, 'Patent Safety Matches' – light only on the box'. The public were cautioned against dangerous imitations. You have light to work with but although others alongside you and down the tunnel also have candles, they just look like yellow stars in a black sky, except for the slight glow close to the flame. All else is dark – 'coal black', so to gain a true impression, your walls, ceiling, floor and table would have to be painted black – sorry. Add a lot more table legs around the room, holding up the ceiling; then the air will have to be filled with choking dust. Alfred Nobel's invention of dynamite in 1866 made coal much dustier stuff. That is roughly, but not as rough as real, the 'working environment'.

Now for the work, but first of all turn up the central heating; it gets hot down there.

Don't forget your tools; you will need a pick, but not as big as the kind used for digging up roads, and a shovel, no longer wooden but heavy steel. The Company supplies these and the colliery smith keeps them in good nick. Picks in particular, needed frequent attention, blunt points made for hard and slow work. Now try lying on your side or kneeling under the table, or sit on a 'cracket' if there is room, and hack at the solid wall of coal with the

HEWERS AT WORK

point of your imaginary pick. There is a method and a skill in this but we will not go into that – just get a pile of coal loosened, then shovel it back to your 'marra' (mate), behind you, who will shovel it into the line of empty 'tubs' waiting on the little railway that the night shift have built through your kitchen.

These tubs would be pulled to the surface by tough little pit ponies, superseded for the long haul from increasingly distant workings by long wire ropes, hauling six, up to twenty, tubs at a time, worked by steam-powered pulleys. Ponies continued in use for a very long time, getting tubs to the main 'ways', and for general underground haulage. The last of these excellent little creatures were eventually 'pensioned off' when the last of Northumberland's deep mines closed in 1994: they were well cared-for and, at Mickley, 'walked out' (another of the advantages of the 'drift' mine) at weekends for sunshine, fresh air, a leg stretch and, yes, a BATH! Village boys vied with each other for the bareback ride at a seemly trot – they weren't made for galloping – up the hill to the long water-filled trough that they walked through – complete with boys, for a good sloshing around. Not quite the tin bath in front of the fire standard, but very welcome for them on a warm summer day for all that, and who wants a bath in the winter anyway?

You can come out now from your imaginary pit and put the light on. You will not need a bath, but I'll wager that your arms and legs are aching even without picking and shovelling – and you've only been there a few minutes. Imagine being stuck there for eight hours, six shifts a week, with only a pint-sized tin bottle of water and sandwiches, usually jam, also in a tin box – against the rats – for sustenance and a break. You didn't have rats for company under your table; they were standard company for miners, and ate everything they could get their razor-sharp teeth into. They ate the candles and would even carry them off alight (for a hot meal?).

Smokers at Mickley could indulge in a 'Woodbine', probably the cheapest cigarettes ever, at only a penny for a paper packet of five. Or they could have a clay pipe of 'twist baccy' (tobacco), thick or thin, like a rope of tightly rolled and twisted tobacco leaves, bought by the inch, foot – or yard, I suppose, if you had the money and a death wish. Simple, powerful stuff, it kept the flies at bay and most other things, and was probably less of a cancer risk than the sophisticated chemical-laden smokes of today. It certainly gave comfort underground in the absence of the continuous threat of deadly, explosive 'firedamp' that hung black-winged over the lives of less fortunate miners who had to forgo smoking and work by 'Davy' lamp. You think candlelight poor? You should try working by Davy lamp.

These little extras made life marginally easier for the men of Mickley – and for the boys. By about 1860 there were more than 130 men and 50 boys – boys being thirteen and over – working in the drift.

Another of the little bonuses in this harsh life was the short walk home, albeit with weary legs, through the delights of country days, or star-spangled, moonlit nights. This old Mickley was a glorious place – still today, like the Curate's egg, not bad in places, with lingering aspects of Bewick's tranquil paradise. Many of the trees have gone, and the heather retreated before the Enclosures and the plough, yet still, for the pitman, there was gorse and broom to blaze the 'fell' with springtime sunshine; bluebells and blushing anemones by the acre. Celandines, buttercups and daisies for childhood pleasure games; stately foxgloves in every corner, blackthorn, may-blossom and elder mimicking the winter snow, white ransomes underfoot fuming the air with garlic and the simple delight of that most English of flowers – the dog-rose, in gay profusion (before that lovely word was so sorely prostituted). All these were accompanied in springtime by an orchestra and chorus of avian artists, tiny throats no doubt giving ecstatic thanks for living in such a place and not having to work, like their canary cousins, in gassy pits. In autumn and winter, differently graced and clothed with smells and colours of the wearying year, and the prospect of a hot bath before a roaring fire, a good, hefty meal and well-earned sleep in a feather bed, and no mortgage or bank manager to worry him awake.

Personal Finance

Banks had no place here in Mickley – a man could carry all his worldly wealth in his trouser pocket, his biggest worry the undiscovered hole. No longer was a sword needed to ensure cash security, although there were still footpads and highwaymen about, looking for pickings. There was not much in the way of pickings in Mickley; the 3s. 9d. or so a day a hewer would earn, or a 'putter' – he moved the coals that the hewer dug – about 2s. to 2s. 6d., presented little problem in the carrying home, amounting to perhaps £1 for a full week, and no dodging if you didn't feel up to it. The pay slip detailed each worker's earnings, depending on how much coal he worked or moved, less his 'off-taaks' (deductions), which were small payments for benefits provided by the company. These increased in number through the years, from only rent and 'free' coals, to all kinds of 'luxuries' such as lighting, medical, welfare and recreation provision. The cash, less deductions, was collected on presentation of the slip, at the pay office which initially was in what is now some of Cherryburn Cottages. Here resided the Clerk, and no arguing – he wore a suit. The pound was worth a bit – a Victorian penny went a long way when you had one. Although the pitman made great play on being master in his home and usually gave his wife only housekeeping money, some wives got the pay intact – apart from a little spending money (beer and baccy) – and they all ran the economy, of necessity with a very tight rein. She might not be much of a hand at reading, the miner's housewife, but she certainly knew how many beans made five.

With no village 'Bobby' in the early years to mantain the law, and no close-by pub or shop for easy and legitimate cash-disposal, 'Pitch and Toss' was a popular, illegal, game for getting rid of pocket money, or, if a 'school', which was the name for a gathering of gamblers, waylaid you on the way home on pay-day, your whole pay. It did happen, quite a lot, in spite of attempts at rigid enforcement of the strict laws on gambling and drinking. Workers at Vickers Armstrong's factory had to pass through a veritable barrier of pubs on Scotswood Road, twixt work and home, but they were all firmly closed at going-home time. Pitch and Toss was never brought under control, over more than a hundred years; as late as 1950 there were 'schools' at 'secret' places – which we all knew about – in High Close and Low Close

MICKLEY COLLIERY.

No. 443 — Pay No. 11 1937

Name Albert Hubbuck — Shifts 1

	No.	@		Gross £ s. d.	Offtakes	s. d.
Tons			6 Shifts @ 1/9½		Elect. Lighting	1 9
,,			Amount		,, Lamps, &c.	
,,			Per Cent.		Coals	
xx. T.			Putting		Laid Out	
			Clay		Explosives	
Double			Hewing		Water	5
Wet			Subsistence Allow		Insur. Health	9
Ramble			Rent		,, U.E.	10
Help-up			Minimum		Picks	
Band					Reading Room	
Yds.					P. R. Fund	
,,					Weigh	
,,					Infirmary	3
Consideration			Compensation		Nurse	
					Band	
					Aged Miners	
					Ambulance	1
					Dr. Barnardo's H's.	
					Welfare Fund	
					Football Club	
					Lost Tokens	
				2 1 9		3 7

Nett Cash. 1 17 2

Any error on this pay note should be notified to the foreman before the pay commences.

X 456

MINERS' PAY NOTE

woods, where this simple, foolish game of chance was played – doors could not be closed on woods! By this late date the game had no social significance; miners were at last being paid a decent wage and no village child was likely to go hungry as the result of a game of Pitch and Toss. Mind you, right up until the last minute the village bobby, by then part of the fitments, sallied forth on an occasional 'raid' just to keep things right in the eyes of the law and he hadn't much else to do anyway. P.C. Rutherford of my time and, I expect, all those who went before, knew exactly where the 'schools' were – but the miners usually knew where he was! Lookouts were posted as in days of yore, and the ancient technique of 'melting' practised – to a fine art. They needed to be nimble, these gamblers; fines were heavy if caught – ten shillings could buy a fair bit of food – or pennies for tossing.

Coal and the Coal Trade

High quality Mickley coal was best converted into coke, so this stuff the hewers and putters were sending forth in tubs went down the slope to where the 'action' was – by the railway. No point in keeping coal lying about here except a bit to warm the workers; it went to where the need was greater – by rail. Both locomotives and lines were continually being improved and by 1860, just when the 'drift' was getting into its stride, steel rails were in use, reducing the excessive maintenance costs and delays caused by the frequent breaking of cast-iron rails – making the large scale movement of coal economical.

Large numbers of men were employed on the railways, and, as with the miners, housing provision had to be made where it was needed, so at about the time that the railway sidings were laid to serve the pit, which gave rise to this bit of Mickley becoming known as 'The Junction', twelve railway worker's cottages were built; one for the 'boss man'. Hardly a Stationmaster, he nevertheless had to handle a lot of freight, and quite a few passengers, although there was never a 'proper' station, in spite of being in the timetables for about seventy years. I have read, (although you can't always believe what you read!) that output from Mickley reached 100,000 tons a year but I find this hard to accept, as Wylam, a deep mine, only produced 50,000. However, if the figure was for the whole of the Mickley Coal Co., including Prudhoe and West Wylam, and Mickley output alone was, say, similar to that of Wylam, it meant a thousand tons of coal, raw or converted into coke, were being shunted out of these sidings every week – 150 tons a day. Perhaps not in the Premier League of coal mines, but Mickley was certainly not insignificant. It was a bustle of a place, especially down by the railway.

Here were the 'screens' where the coal, fresh from the face, was graded for size and thoroughly picked over for stones and rubbish as it passed along on moving belts or shaking boards. This work was done by women, before they were excluded from pit work; by boys being introduced to the ways of mining, and by men unfit for underground work, whose working lives could be extended by what was not entirely bosses' philanthropy – these workers came cheap.

Stones are a good make-weight in domestic coal, but make no coke, so the cleaning had to be thorough. The cleaned coking coal dropped into tubs which were pushed along to the ovens by the fussy little locomotive known as the 'Dilly' – probably from 'Billy', the original 'Puffing Billy'. There is a suggestion that the tubs may have been rope-hauled to the ovens, as they were from the pit: this is more than likely, but there is no evidence, one way or the other.

As for the coke ovens; one source assured me that there were six hundred, but it is probable that there were nearer two hundred. They were 'beehive' ovens, built of firebrick, ten to twelve feet in diameter and seven feet high and were filled through a hole in the top, from the tubs running on a raised track, with about seven to nine tons of coal, then sealed in except for a smoke vent on the top. The coal burned slowly for about 70 to 100 hours, releasing the 'coal gas' through the vent into the atmosphere, leaving a residue of 'cinders', by which this partly burned coal was known until the smelting of iron with 'coke' and the sole use of coal for locomotives.

Early locomotive builders believed that coal would quickly ruin fireboxes, and landowners didn't like the idea of these monsters belching thick, black smoke all over their trees and fields, so 'cinders' were stipulated as loco fuel until the early fears proved unfounded and people soon learned to accept smoke as an essential fact of life.

Consett Iron Works, the biggest in Europe at the time, came into being when Henry Bessemer developed his 'converter' process for making steel in 1856, and Gilchrist lined converters with dolomite. This enabled low grade iron ore from Cleveland to be used for the mass-production of high quality steel without having to transport haematite from Cumberland. The demand for coke for steel making increased dramatically and the little coke works at Mickley duly benefited.

When the coke had been cleaned of its gasses, which were wastefully cast to the winds (and a smelly, sooty business it must have been, down there by the river), it was spread out, hot from the ovens, with long-handed 'coke rakes', then cooled by spraying with water. This was done initially with

WORKERS AT THE SCREENS. THE OLD, WORNOUT, INJURED AND BOYS

hand-held hose pipes, then, as technology improved, through a system of overhead spray-lines.

The gas that was a by-product of coke making where the coal had a higher gas content, and in more urban areas, was 'cleaned up' by having the tar and chemical factors removed. Tar was produced in huge quantities and was the principal ingredient, along with stone chippings, of 'Tar-Macadam', the basis of modern road surfacing. I have vivid childhood memories, heavily laden with the pungent smell of tar, of gangs of men surfacing roads by pretty simple methods. The tar came in big wooden barrels, forty gallons, I think, and was decanted through a bunghole into a coal-fired tar boiler for heating to a consistency for pouring through ordinary gardeners' watering-cans with the spout flattened, with which the tar was spread across the road surface, aided by men with big brooms. I recollect the fun of watching the messy business of getting the bung back in the barrel with the tar flowing! Not much fun for the men, but they were adept at it. Still more men, armed with shovels, then threw whinstone chippings from carts, later lorries, as evenly as possible on to the hot wet tar. Then, finally, along came the clanging, huffing and puffing fiery monster steamroller to press the chippings, some of them anyway, into the tar. What a performance! That, with modifications, was how roads were surfaced into the middle of the 20th century.

The steamroller, and almost identical traction engine which had wheels at the front instead of a huge iron roller for flattening roads, (and little boys if they ventured too close, threatened the driver), were the roads' reply to the railways – steam on wheels. Built to last and still in use into the 1950s, they can often be seen today, preserved by enthusiasts, at steam rallies and agricultural shows, and are still a bit frightening, in spite of their superb appearance and gentle ways.

When the roads wore smooth, or where the chippings had missed, in certain summer conditions little blisters formed in the tar and it was a grand sport of children homeward bound from school, to 'plop' them with their feet. Sometimes water spurted out, which was even more exciting! – but if the tar stuck to your shoe you risked a beating when you got home – it needed butter to get it off.

Coal-gas was first used as 'novelty' lighting when it escaped to the surface from burning coal seams and was captured in animal bladders and skin bags then allowed to escape through a pinhole and ignited. The massive quantities produced from coke making found more useful outlets by way of gasometers (strange, 'rising and falling' Victorian architecture) and extensive systems of pipes into hissing, wavering jet lights in streets and homes and into the first alternative to coal for cooking, the gas oven. These caused almost as many explosions as the Royal Artillery, initially anyway.

None of this distant gas reached Mickley, candles and paraffin lit the homes, moon and stars the streets, and local coke oven gas went to the heavens. Only the coke was useful and it went off by rail, mostly to Carlisle and from there probably to the Workington area blast furnaces. Some of Mickley coal and possibly coke, went to Ireland. It was all good quality – there was no better coke. The very special 'cannel' coal went east – to Germany, until war in 1914 put an end to what was a good trade. This coal was rich in chemicals and the German chemical industry made good use of these, particularly in the making of aniline dyes. Rumour had it that we were short of dye for uniforms because the Germans had it all! Cannel was used for making 'jet' jewellery, although I understand

ROAD ROLLER

that real 'jet' was mined near Whitby, and the cannel of Mickley but a poor relation. Black was fashionable in Victorian times and cannel coal could be carved and polished and did not make dirt. Any pit lad could make his girl a ring or a necklace at no more cost than the price of devotion. I wonder how many potential artists were denied their development by calloused, gnarled hands? Bewick with miner's hands would have been no Bewick at all.

I understand, although some surviving miners dispute this, that weight for weight, cannel coal produced more heat than any other coal and that Mickley cannel fired the boilers of the *Mauritania* on her Blue Riband crossing of the Atlantic. It's a nice story – believe it if you like; I doubt if anyone can disprove it.

Coke was so much in demand that even the Bewicks, who continued the mining tradition long after Thomas had left the artistic scene, set up two ovens at Mickley Bank pit – it was a good way of using 'smalls' or 'duff', which was usually unsaleable to the domestic market. There is little in the way of evidence but they were in production at the end of the nineteenth century, possibly a little later. The coke, like their coal, would be sold locally, as although with low overheads in this small family business their prices would be competitive, the output would be so small, and with the railway at a distance, there would be no chance of breaking into a wider market. The only local use I can think of for coke was in firing boilers for water heating and there were not many of those until the few larger houses in the area installed the newfangled cental-heating and, perhaps more important, built glasshouses for growing tender plants. The most important advance in this area was when the family Richardson, whose business was in the ancient world of tanning, bought Wheelbirks estate, at the southern tip of the old Baliol lands. They set up a horticultural unit, with, for those times, extensive glasshouses which the noteworthy seed firm 'Finneys' leased, with a field, for their trials ground. These glasshouses used a fair bit of coke and would be a likely outlet for Mickley Bank.

As a point of interest, to gardeners at least, this land at Wheelbirks was subjected to continuous applications of just about the longest lasting fertiliser ever dreamed of – waste leather from the tanning works. It was brought by rail to Stocksfield station, thence by horse and cart the two miles or so to the farm, where I believe bits of hide could still be dug up until recently. Slow release indeed! Leather was the basis of the economy of this area for hundreds of years – nice to think that a bit of it lingers on.

The cost of this early coke was about 7s. 10p. per ton, of which 3s. was for the coal (hewing 8d., putting 4d., screening etc. 1s., materials (?) 3d., and rent 6d.). A ton of coal, 'led' (delivered) sold for 6s., a ton of coke from 7s. 6d. to 9s. Was the 'added value' worth the bother? It must have been, if enough was sold, and it was an additional outlet for coal. It also employed more men, in a pretty rotten job, even if it was free from the miner's eternal fear of the roof falling on him.

The heat and 'sulphurous fumes' from coke-making, when all of the work was done by hand, must have been horrendous. We hear no word of lung cancer (maybe these workers didn't live long enough to give it a chance), but there must have been a lot of respiratory disease and medical help was not much advanced on that available to poor old Robert of Micelee. One good breath of coke fumes from a brazier or raked-out boiler could make me wheeze for a week – how these men coped I just cannot imagine, even though most of the activity was out of doors and a good breeze would ease the wheeze.

More men were needed for all this activity around the pit than could live in the Square and labour had to be 'imported' from neighbouring places. Men from Ovington had to cross the river and although again it is difficult to find two people to agree on the number of boats plying, the ferry at its peak might have boasted as many as six – some say nine. This number may have included the salmon-fishing boats; this was an active fishing place. The procedure for getting across the river could be frustrating, hair-raising or hilarious, depending mostly on where you were standing. Although the landlord of the Hare and Hounds held the ancient rights and duties of ferry-keeper, the problem, if you happened to be on the other side, lay in getting his ear. With no one about and the gale in your teeth, getting an increasingly desperate and hoarse plea of "BOAT" through the distant inn door could be well-nigh impossible. With luck (or maybe not, if your rowing left something to be desired!), someone crossed from the other side and left the boat for you. With even more luck, and an element of kindness, if he liked rowing and had time to spare, he might take pity and row you across; this would absolve you from the fear and possible embarrassment of having to be rescued, at Prudhoe – or Tynemouth. You would not get me to row one of those boats – not even for a penny. At the end only one boat plied, occasionally, rowed, usually, by Nora, the slip of a girl daughter of the innkeeper.

The Hare and Hounds closed, and was demolished, in 1960 and then there was no one to row the boat and take the pennies.

Farming in Industrial Mickley

The magnetism of industry, or rather the money that went with it, drew workers not only across the river, but from farms everywhere, where virtual serfdom still existed. Industry began to superimpose itself on the rural scene, replacing the departed workers.

In Mickley, industry imposed itself but never overpowered the country aspect, as in less favoured places; horsepower on legs rather than wheels remained the motive source. Manpower, however, became an increasing problem as the attractions of urban life began the process of rural depopulation. Now, with man's inventive genius being harnessed to his new-found engineering skills, ways of applying industry to farming soon emerged and devices like mowing machines, reapers, binders and threshing machines, even steam-driven ploughs, took over some of the work of workers.

Harvesting the corn formerly required every able-bodied, and some not so able, person, young and old, in the village to pitch in for cutting, with sickles, tying into sheaves, and 'stooking' in sixes or eights for drying, to await carting to the stack yard ('leading'). In this new 'machine' age, it could be done in quick time by one, at most two men and a 'binder', pulled, because it was hard work, by two and sometimes three horses, and followed by a few women and children picking up and stooking the ready-tied sheaves. Men still took pride in building the stacks and a yard occupied by a good harvest, well stacked and beautifully thatched against the weather, was a sight to behold – and a good indicator of the standard of the farm. The stacked grain matured whilst awaiting the arrival of the itinerant threshing machine, which might be soon, or it might be well into the winter, depending on the number of farms to visit and the position on the route. These machines could not be whisked about at speed all over the countryside; orderly progression was the thing.

When the time came, a fuss and a commotion preceded the thresher procession. Farm gateways were made to fit carts, not multiple monster machines, and a mighty struggling and swearing was often needed to coax them into place, especially in a wet year. It was all too easy for machines to bog down, axle deep, and need hours of hard work to dig them out – perhaps even an extra traction engine having to be sent for to lend a hand. Farmers always seemed to put their gateways in the muddiest corners!

The thresher was a big, nay huge, wooden box on iron wheels, all pulleys, hatches and gadgets, pulled by the snorting traction engine and followed by a smaller wooden box on wheels which was the mobile home of the 'carer' – operator. Although it saved a lot of time and effort compared to beating the grain out of ears of corn with hand-held flails – the time honoured method prior to the advent of steam – machine threshing caused an awful stir around the farm during its annual one to four day duration, depending on size of farm and weight of crop. All non-essential work was put aside and all hands mustered; if there weren't enough people on the place, neighbours and villagers came in. The small children stood by, watching with the dogs for any rats that thought they had found cosy, well provisioned winter quarters – that is where the stack was not raised on rat-proof stone 'mushrooms' – the rats were shortly to become displaced, 'homeless persons' – lifeless too, if the dogs were any good.

The thresher would have been positioned by the first stack, with the stationary traction engine at rest and docile, slumbering boiler aroused before dawn and steam well up, awaiting the long hard day. The two working units were connected by a long flat, flapping belt, between the huge steam-driven flywheel-pulley on the engine and a small pulley on the thresher. Factory Inspectors, Health and Safety fellows, hide your eyes!

Gently coaxed into purring life by the pull of a lever, the traction engine sat there all the long day, doing its quiet job – there was not much effort for a traction engine in driving a pulley; it was almost a holiday, in fact. It had a few shovelfuls of coal to sustain it – only the best was good enough, and the farmer had to see that there was enough on hand – and an occasional drink from the yard pump or well; thirsty work, threshing. There was an occasional drop or two of oil from the oil-can, on shining bearings, from the hand of a caring master. He would rather go hungry than leave a bearing unoiled.

The 'action' was at the thresher end of the belt ... Men on the stack threw sheaves to women on the flat 'roof' in a non-stop flow – every minute of hire of this set-up had to be well used. One woman caught the sheaf and threw it to the next, who deftly cut the 'binder twine' and put it safe from risk of fouling the machine, and for future use for tying sacks and trousers; there was no end to the uses for binder twine. Then she dropped the loose sheaf down a hole into the spinning drum below. For myself, I'd rather have Robert's tree on me than fall down this hole. It was a gruesome way to die, and people did – mostly women and children. There was little to prevent anyone falling down until, in later years, short conveyors and guards were fitted.

Two or three women worked at feeding the thresher, in voluminous clothes and a rare 'glow', while the men sweated and the rats squealed. The straw, which in those days was long and strong (if wheat, suitable for thatching), now beaten grainless, passed on its way through the machine and came out into a pile for forking back into stacks for use as bedding, or tying into bundles, known as 'bottles', for easy carrying. Chaff, the thin outer casing of the grain, fell out of another hole and was not much use, although it was occasionally used as mattress stuffing and was sometimes mixed with animal feeds; it had little food value and could be a bother if it got into animals' eyes. Mostly it was burned. It had a nasty habit of blowing about all over the place, and up your nose, where it stuck. Threshing was no job for asthmatics – nor sleeping on chaff mattresses.

The precious grain, that all this work and worry was about, emerged in a golden trickle, or stream in a good year, from a third orifice with a chute that could be stopped or swivelled for sack changing, into sacks hung on hooks. These sacks were big, holding ten or twelve stones of grain and were responsible for men down on the farm (where men were men, I can tell you) being bent double before they could grow old. A stone was fourteen pounds in my day – you will have to work out for yourself what twelve stones would be in what at that time were recently invented kilo-whatsits – by the French.

The bags were tied, leaving 'lugs' (ears) at the corners for holding and hoisting on to the backs of the unlucky ones who had to carry them to the granary, as like as not up a steep flight of stairs, or with luck to a hoist that made ease of the job. Storing on the wooden floor under the roof of the granary completed any drying required. This was where, I believe, in the case of Eltringham Farm, some barley malting was carried out for Ovington Brewery. The attractive boiler-house chimney and granary building, sad and silent now, still bear witness to this activity. The barley for the brewery, malted or not, was taken west, upriver from the farm, across the ford directly below Ovington, and up the hill that would tax two good horses, to the brewery.

Sweaty, dusty, bone-aching toil though threshing was, an air of exhilaration and excitement pervaded the farm; even the chickens and 'gobblers', those frightening, fiery-red-turning-angry-purple headed turkey strutters that dominated even the hissing geese of the farmyard, got themselves all worked up at the prospect of feasts of extra pickings of fallen corn. This was the culmination, the high peak, of the farming year. Hay and harvest home were great reliefs, but only after threshing was the yield established and financial prospects for the year ahead gauged. It merited a thumping good meal – and farmers knew about food – for everyone involved, with perhaps a song or two, and a few drinks; thirsty stuff, thresher dust. We will not dwell on the bad years.

The traction engine rumbled its iron-wheeled way to the next farm, dragging its wooden boxes behind, and rural quiet returned. This industrialised farming was all very well, but was it not nice to get back to peace and quiet, and moving at the pace of clip-clopping horses? Even the winter jobs of hedge-cutting and laying, and ditching, which nobody liked, were done at leisurely speed – just enough to keep out the cold without making a sweat. The work got done. Hedging, especially laying, was another of those rural skills that evoked great feelings of pride and satisfaction in farm workers. Every field was hedged with hawthorn, which, with regular attention, gave total stock-proofing for hundreds of years, at no cost other than a bit of time at the time of year when there was not much else to be done on the farm anyway. There were competitions, along with ploughing contests, to test the skills, and stables became festooned with '1st', '2nd' or '3rd' award cards. Hedges were windbreaks, and superb nesting places for birds; they were the first to show green in the spring, and were beautiful. Alas for the demise of the hand-laid hedge.

Swede harvest was a rotten job too, but swedes, with mangels, made possible the keeping of livestock over winter on a large scale, even the maintenance of reasonable milk yields, and were an essential part of the crop rotation system which helped maintain fertility in pre-chemical farming days. They weren't bad for humans either (many a POW survived on turnip soup, but you would be unwise to remind him!), in spite of the 'scientific' farm adviser's claim that they were 'only water'. "Oh aye," said the old farmer, criticised for feeding them to his sheep, "but WAT WATTER!"

Swedes came home in carts from frosty fields and, if you were lucky enough, or hung around long enough to meet the homeward load, the kindly 'hind' (farm hand) whose son went to school with you, would reach behind, select a nice one and throw it down to eager hands. This prize, or the one fallen on the roadside from an overladen cart, was legitimate; it could be identified as such by farmer, policeman or parent, because it had been pulled by its leaves and expertly trimmed of first its roots then its top by slashing strokes of the 'turnip knife' before being 'hoyed' (tossed) into the cart. Inexpert turnip-bashers were easily recognised by their shortage of fingers! The stolen swede, top and root broken or hacked off with blunt schoolboy pocket knife, and gnawed by a half-starved child, was worth a five shilling fine and a jolly good larruping from the father who had to pay it from an income not enough to feed his children anyway.

The 'honest' swede, cubed into broth or mashed with potatoes, was a winter mainstay vegetable and yielded, in the preparation, chunks for pleasant enough chewing by children with sound appetites and teeth to match. It also yielded an occasional treat, in the absence of 'boiled' sweets from a distant shop, or home-made toffee. Your father had to be in a good mood and not busy with anything important like reading or smoking his pipe. He cut the skin off the swede then sliced it thinly and placed it on a dinner plate which it should fit comfortably, layer upon layer, liberally interlaced with sugar (brown moist if you had it). That's it! – Sweet Swede!. You had to be patient while the sugar soaked in, and I wonder now if it was worth the wait. Children looking for fun and something sweet were easily pleased – would even eat sticks of rhubarb dipped in sugar. Now teeth leap around at the very thought!

Gathering swedes was the sort of job where the horse showed its superiority over the machine – it would keep pace with gatherers, stop or start at a word, without the need for the driver to climb aboard or even be nearer than a word away. And it knew the way home, even from the pub. You needed to speak the language – 'Geedup', 'How-way', or an indescribable tongue-click from the side of the mouth – 'Tchk' – for 'walk on'; 'Whoah' for stop.

The influx of people to the village brought about by mining affected the farm economy in two ways, apart from drawing labour off the land. It provided a plentiful supply of child-labour for potato picking, when children could no longer work in the pits. This could be a rotten job in bad weather, badly paid, but it supplemented the household budget with a few coppers – and a bucketful of potatoes every day of the harvest. Some of the buckets taken for 'carrying home' were bigger than the children! The increase in population also brought a huge increase in the sale of milk.

Milk was still produced by simple, indeed primitive methods. Hygiene was at a premium, or non-existent; but the milk was produced in small quantities and sold and used quickly; no hanging about, no time for mischievous bacteria to do their stuff, and no one had heard of them anyway. Two or three cows would be normal stock for a small farm, pre-mining days, except for those near towns. Mickley cows did not supply milk for townsfolk, but when the pitmen came they were as good as a town to the cow-keepers. Ten or more cows radically affected farming practices. A cow would yield perhaps ten pints a day (a good goat will give that nowadays, and a milk-machine cow five or more gallons) on summer meadows of rich, healthy (organic!), virtually wild plants which were reflected in the flavour and quality of the milk. In winter they were housed and fed on swedes which were also reflected in the flavour and quality of the milk!

Milking was done by hand into open buckets, by dairymaids on bigger herds, or by farmer's wife, daughter, 'the lad', or even the farmer himself or the hind; who would, like as not, lubricate the teats on starting by applying the first squirt of milk to his palms – or by spitting on them! There's a thought for food inspectors. If the cow failed to kick the bucket (putting her foot in it didn't count) the milk was poured into churns through muslin to strain out the hairs and summer flies, which, especially the biting horseflies or 'clegs' were the main cause of kicking cows and spilt milk. Cooling could only be slow, at best by standing the churn in a trough of water, cold from the pump or well – and the dairy was usually the coolest room on the farm. Buckets, and where butter was made, scoops, churns, wooden 'hands' and tables were all thoroughly scrubbed with caustic soda – very cleansing. It cleaned the hands of the scrubbers too, I can tell you. Dairies had their own, pleasant, smell, of milk and butter and scrubbed wood and caustic soda and Mrs Rutherford's starched pinnies.

Cows on a good farm were a pretty healthy lot in general; they lived on good wholesome, natural food, lay on clean straw in winter, were never pressed to produce more milk than was comfortable and were milked gently by hand, not by high-speed machines. Mastitis was uncommon, not endemic as now, and the cow transmitted little in the way of disease to her customers – in spite of the spit; although she was blamed for the massive epidemics of tuberculosis which ravaged the country as a result of crowded, appalling living conditions and malnutrition. Nevertheless, in the mid-1800s there arose in the country a frightful scourge of cattle, 'Rinderpest', or 'Steppe Murrain', or just cattle plague. It claimed ten thousand victims a week at its peak, and reached Mickley in 1866, when the first farm in the north fell victim. One Charles Brannan, who lived in Prudhoe and farmed at Mickley, was fined £20 for infringing the cattle regulations, which amounted to a policy, eventually, of notification, slaughter, and control of movement. In the absence of Government aid only 'self help' by groups of unaffected farmers, who chipped in with cash support for the stricken, saved the farming community from devastation. The price of beef went sky-high – to 5s. 2d. a stone wholesale!

Here is, verbatim, (you think I'm verbose?) a gem of a report I found while poring over musty files of *Hexham Courants,* in 1995:

Rinderpest and its remedy

'It requires no great stretch of the imagination to fancy a political economist or student of veterinary science of 1966' (this was 1866) 'poring over a file of musty, time-stained newspapers of the present day in mute astonishment at the manifest inability of our veterinary faculty to grapple with the fatal malady that is now bidding defiance to all modes of treatment, ancient and modern, to stay its ravages or effect its cure'.

Eventually the plague abated under the policy of slaughter and strict movement control – shades of 'Foot and Mouth' – and farming in Mickley got back to normal. But the consequences at that time must have been far worse even than that of today's 'mad cows'.

Milk was trundled around the streets in churns, usually in open-backed little carts or 'traps', sometimes in hand-pulled carts or barrows that a boy could handle. You could collect your milk from the farm in a little can with a lid to keep out the flies and the rain, and small boys made a few coppers doing a private-enterprise delivery service of these. Otherwise you went out to the 'trap' with your jug or bowl and had your milk scooped into it, hairs and all. Hairy milk was still available by this method as late as the 1940s,

MILK DELIVERY

when Ned Brown of Hallyards Farm plied his horse-drawn trade around the streets. I never did determine whether the hairs were there because the milk had not been properly filtered, if at all, or whether they were 'value added' by way of Ned's coat, which he wore for handling cows and horses as well as milk. The arm that ladled milk from churn to jug dipped increasingly deeply as the round progressed and the milk level lowered. We were well on in the round. We got an awful lot of hairs. Inspectors of food were thin on the ground – but nobody seemed to die of hairy milk.

Butter, hand made and expensive, was a rare luxury for the poor; meat fat was still the commonplace spread for bread, and very good too. Dairy standards were higher for butter – the well-off didn't much care for hairy food and unclean butter quickly went rancid. These standards were mostly a matter for the people concerned; if you didn't like Ned's milk you went somewhere else, not that it would do much good. There was not much point in complaining – nobody to complain to. All this, however, was about to change and the kind of simple 'freedom' of the individual as known in the old order began the erosion which leaves us today beset by a form of tyranny made worse by the dominance of science and our inability to stay its headlong march.

The social link between farm and pit is nicely illustrated by another tale assembled from reports in old *Hexham Courants*, which began its life, incidentally, as *The Hexham Courant and South Northumberland Advertiser*, on Tuesday, 20th August 1864, price 1½d. This is the unhappy tale, in two parts:

> 'Mickley Coal Company, being short of miners' housing, rented a cottage from Thomas Humble, of Eltringham Farm, who then wanted it for his own use. There was acrimony, and when the wife of the miner-tenant went away to bring home her dying husband, her twelve-year-old daughter and eight-year-old son were evicted, with the furniture, into the torrential rain of a stormy night. An uncle forced entry and got the children back under cover'. The entire mining community was outraged by this callous act of inhumanity.

Shortly afterwards, on 4th. July 1866, the *Hexham Courant* carried this report:

Highway robbery with violence

'Two pitmen, Matthew Rowell and George Wilkinson, of Mickley Square, were apprehended by PCs Robson and Kennedy on 1st inst. on a charge of assaulting and robbing Mr Thomas Humble of Eltringham on 29th June, of the sum of £1.4s., one purse, one knife, one pair of stockings, and two pockets. The robbery was committed on the highway between the prosecutor's house and Mr Cook's public house at Eltringham boat house, and Mr Humble was very violently assaulted and much injured, being cut and bruised about the face. The accused were remanded for trial'.

This looked on the surface like rough justice, a bit delayed; miners had their own form, and long memories. At the Northumberland Midsummer Assizes the two accused were found guilty of assault and highway robbery and Mr Justice Lush sentenced them both to twelve months in prison, with hard labour. All three had been drinking and Mr Humble was very much the worse for alcohol.

Politics and Education

Kings and Governments of yore were concerned mostly with the defence of the realm and raising armies and taxes for that purpose; keeping the populace in order and reasonably content was part of this. On the whole the system worked, but dynastic wars had sickened England and weakened its kings. George the Third was the last monarch to lead his army into battle, and it was his long and messy reign and his going mad in the process that finally brought elected government into supreme power in this country. Monarchs in future might influence, but never again control.

Methods of election to Parliament left a lot to be desired – 'democracy' was for the well-to-do and influential; but 'well-to-do' was increasingly possible to the able and hardworking, and even within the grasp of ordinary folk. Not only that, but thinking men were as much a part of the 19th-century English scene as were engineers and craftsmen. Men like Wilberforce and Fox thought up the end of slavery and brought some humanitarian standards to human relations. Even the lowly began to be accepted as human, with feelings and lives to live. Men of vision realised that bosses got a better deal from workers if workers got a better deal from bosses. But it was a slow process.

The uncontrolled consequences of industrialisation, and the accompanying population explosion (a doubling, in the eighteenth century, and that was only a beginning), heavily concentrated in proliferating towns, brought urgent need for control, order, and even a degree of planning, into the nation's affairs. Social and political reform had to come; politicians assumed a more significant role and increasing power in running the affairs not only of the nation, but of the individual.

A pressing need was for a wider, better balanced system of electing Members to Parliament and the Reform Bill of 1832 developed the process of the emancipation of the working classes. Although the privileged could still have two votes and women none, the 'lower classes' at last began to have, and exert, influence in the nation's affairs. This in spite of the fact that the education system was still in the hands of the Church and the well-off, who guarded it jealously. Educated workers? Saints preserve us!

Oh yes, there were schools of course, and the 'mass-production' of relatively cheap books, pamphlets, song sheets and newspapers widened the dissemination of knowledge enormously. Above all there was a great thirst for knowledge, a yearning for betterment. However, the percolation of education down the social scale was still pretty slow, lacking a large scale, uniform system of teaching. What there was had to be paid for, and the needs of the body came first – the mind could wait, especially when the mind was that of a child who could earn a useful family supplement. Every penny counted.

Two things changed all this. The new 'humanitarian' thinking brought not only a regard for the plight of black slaves, but an awareness of the horror of the exploitation of child labour – what might be termed white slavery, in this country. Strangely, parents resisted the laws ending child labour as, in Mickley, they resisted 'netties' – out of ignorance. They failed to see that if employers were denied cheap child labour they would be forced to employ more adults and shortage of labour always enhances wages. But no one had a choice – Governments were encroaching into private lives. When not allowed to work in pits and like as not being infernal nuisances at home, children were better out of the way and school, where there was one, was as good a place as any, so parents quickly recognised their merit and were happy to see their children go.

The other important thing that changed thinking on education was the recognition of the undeniable truth that a rapidly evolving industrial society cannot be run on shovel-wielders only. There arose an obvious and pressing need for workers who could read, write and do their sums. The excellent Grammar Schools and Universities, sprung from the seeds sown by enlightened Kings and nobility such as the Baliols, were beyond the reach of the poor. The Church contributed greatly to education but this was based essentially, as you would expect, on religion, although dispensing a good general education as well. Thomas Bewick was a beneficiary of this. But again, vicars augmented meagre stipends by running their little schools – and charging; so it was only the better-off who benefited. In fairness it must be said that it was not unknown for caring vicars to waive the fee in the case of the poor child who showed promise and the will to work with diligence. The Bewicks could afford to pay – and the Vicar was a relative anyway.

For the rest, if they wanted it and could afford the coppers charged, there was the village school like that on the hilltop at Old Mickley, so hated by the young Bewick. The fact of his being a typically, possibly more than typically, rebellious boy, perhaps showed the school in a worse light than was fair. Teachers had a rotten job, teaching the unteachable – but then, as now, there were good and bad among teachers. Bewick himself acknowledged that the young James Burns, who followed the horrible 'Shabby' Rowns after Thomas had been removed to the care of the Vicar of Ovingham, was good and kindly. Burns, seemingly, was an example of the good dying young, we know not of what.

So, it was possible to receive a reasonable education at the village school of the eighteenth/early-nineteenth century. The great garden designer, 'Capability' Brown, feted and respected – and very well paid – by the nation's upper crust, had a good education at Kirkharle village school – in spite of the reason for his nickname!

But Mickley school held only a handful of pupils, and certainly had no room for the great influx of children that came with the 'Square', although at first it didn't much matter, as they were mostly too concerned with earning a crust or two.

With not a war in sight after Waterloo and no mad king to bother it, Parliament was able to concentrate on improving the state of the nation – and interfering increasingly in peoples' lives. Children no longer being allowed to work made for stony fields, pot-holed roads – and full schools. The production of the wage-earners of the future was still being applied to, assiduously, and there was a phenomenal growth in population, although this could not be attributed entirely to long nights and no television – Mickley must have been full of incomers. A measure of this growth can be gauged from these figures, for Eltringham and Mickley combined: In 1800 the population was about 200; in 1830 – 260; in 1850 – 700; in 1880 – 2,000; and in 1900 – 2,300. There were now a lot of people to be governed.

Governments have no money of their own, they trawl it from whence they can and they cheat – Gladstone promised, in 1866 that Income Tax, at 6d. in the pound, was only a temporary measure – so, when the Education Act of 1872 was passed and Universal Education made compulsory, no provision was made for schools – that was left, in the case of Mickley, to the good old Coal Company.

Parents were expected to make a direct financial contribution, and even a penny a child could be burdensome to the bigger families, so the bulk of the cost of providing and sustaining the schools seems to have been met with good grace, even magnanimity, by the coal-owners. Although they were known to quibble a bit when times were bad in the coal trade, as in the late 1870s, or when the miners, flexing their negotiating muscles, went on strike in 1877–78. Why should they help the children of miners who refused to work?

The Local Government Act of 1888 – what did I say about interfering? – removed a lot of the responsibility for local affairs from parish, Church and bigwigs, and placed them in the hands of elected – by ballot – 'Councils' with the right to raise taxes and employ staff to carry out their edicts. The thin end of a mighty big wedge, this. Mickley had had its own parish council. Now it came under Hexham Rural Council, within Norhumberland County Council. Mickley School forthwith became Mickley Council School and still bore that title on its exercise books when I arrived to grace its portals in 1936, from a school stubbornly remaining 'Clara Vale Colliery School'.

Whatever the name, after 1888, this school, like all others, was very strictly controlled by the Education Department of the County Council, acting to implement the Education Acts. Standards of teaching and discipline were set, and adhered to – or else! No more caning of bare bottoms, mounted pig-a-back on bigger boys, as in Bewick's time. Boards of Managers were appointed to oversee the workings of every school, and although the coal-owners continued to be well represented, as principle providers of the facilities and interested parties in the improvement of the pupils, they, and the Church, no longer held the strings of education.

The system has remained virtually unchanged to this day, apart from increasing interference from above, and was the basis of perhaps the finest education system in the world; probably, and sadly, no longer so. But Mickley still does quite well, I believe.

Mickley School

It was laid down in 1872 that all children of school age, that is between the ages five and thirteen, must attend school on five days a week, for specified hours, except for particular reasons, and that an Attendance Officer – School Board Man, of fearsome note – be appointed to enforce this law. That a Log Book be kept to record the school affairs. These Log Books cover well over a hundred years of school life and it would be tedious to dwell too much on them, but they make fascinating reading at times, so I reproduce a few extracts, courtesy of Northumberland C.C. Education Department. These extracts may give you a flavour of school in the early days of compulsory, controlled education …

Extract from the New Code of Regulations for 1872

'The Principal Teacher must make, at least once a week in the Log Book, an entry which will specify ordinary progress and other facts concerning the School or its Teachers – such as the dates of withdrawals, commencement of duty, cautions, illnesses, etc., which may be required to be referred to at a future time, or may otherwise deserve to be recorded.

No reflections or opinions of a general character are to be entered in the Log Book.

No entry in the Log Book may be removed or altered otherwise than by a subsequent entry.

The summary of the Inspector's Report and any remarks made upon it by the Education Department, when communicated to the Managers must be copied VERBATIM into the Log Book with the names and standing (Certified Teacher of the Class, or Pupil Teacher of the Year, or Assistant Teacher) of all Teachers to be continued on, or added to, or withdrawn from, the School Staff, according to the decision of the Education Department upon the Inspector's Report. The Correspondent of the Managers must sign this entry, which settles the School Staff for the year.

The Inspector will call for the Log Book at every visit and will report whether it appears to have been properly kept. He will specially refer to the entry pursuant to Article 39 and he will require to see entries accounting for any subsequent changes in the School Staff. He will also note in the Log Book any visit of surprise (Article 12), making an entry of such particulars as require the attention of the Managers.'

Big Brother certainly kept an eye on things, even in 1872!

Here are some entries for a typical school year, giving some insight not only into the running of the school, but into life outside:

'Headmaster John Graham' (until 1900)

'**2nd May** 1887. Miss Metcalf handed in her resignation of the post of Assistant Mistress in the School, the said resignation to take effect three months from this date. Isabella Dixon and John Newton, Pupil Teachers, attended drawing examinations in Newcastle.

5th May. Cautioned Isabella Dixon about allowing her class to read in a careless way.

10th May. Register called and found correct. J. A. Collingwood.

13th May. Usual weekly examination. Weak points: Std. 2, Spelling; Std. 1, Arithmetic. Std. 1 could not write numbers of two figures correctly. John Newton now takes Std. 1., Isabella Dixon Std. 5., Miss Bates Std. 4., J. Philipson Stds. 2–3., Miss Metcalfe, Infants, and I take Std. 6.

16th. May. Received HM Inspectors.

14th. July. Holiday given on account of Royal Agricultural Show at Newcastle. Many of the children are going with their parents.

26th. Sept. Several absent – gathering blackberries.

14th. Oct. Attendance low owing to blackberry gathering.

24th. Oct. Sixteen geographical readers (Std. 1) were found to be wilfully damaged by a page being torn out of each book. These books are in future to be kept under lock and key.

5th. Dec. Joseph Slack, who left school on Nov. 11th. to go to work, has returned to school this morning and been re-entered. They would not employ him at the colliery as he is not yet thirteen years of age. He has passed the 5th. Standard.

13th. Dec. The house of one of our P. T. s (Isabella Dixon) having been destroyed by fire last Thursday night and most of her clothing and books being burnt – she was absent from school last Friday and Monday, but is present today.

19th. Dec. Mrs — called to tell me that her daughter Jane is in such a delicate state of health that the doctor has forbidden her to attend school for some time to come. She has given me a doctor's certificate.

22nd. Dec. School closed for Christmas holidays until Jan. 3rd.

20th. Jan. 1888. Until further notice Std. 1 will work in the East Room every morning and the Class Room in the afternoon. There is not sufficient desk room for this Standard owing to the crowded state of our school.

24th. Jan. Received the 'Preliminary Papers'. Approximate numbers in Standards

returned to Inspector, amount to 251.
21st. Feb. Severe weather is affecting our attendance, particularly in the Infant's Class. Three boys are disabled by sliding accidents.
28th. Feb. Isabella Steel, one of our Infants, died suddenly this morning while at breakfast. She had been suffering from bronchitis.
9th. March. Std. 5 examined in Arithmetic. Found many careless errors in Bills of Parcels. Teacher will see to this next week.
16th. March. School closed this afternoon owing to very small attendance. The roads are blocked with snow.
6th. April, Friday, I propose taking the following pieces of poetry for repetition during the year 1888:
Std 1. 'Which loved best' Royal Reader p112.
2. The Beggar Mow.
3. Bruce and the Spider.
4. Wreck of the Hesperus.
5. Edinburgh after Flodden (Historical Reading)
6&7. The Battle of Killiecrankie and The Charge of the Light Brigade.
In place of Julius Caesar as a reading book for Stds. 6–7, I propose taking the 'Citizen Reader'.
10th. April. The following is the list of 'Object Lessons' for the year 1888–89 (Infant Class):
1. A Bird, 2. A Fish, 3. The Swan, 4. The Shark, 5. Cow, 6. Lion, 7. Elephant, 8. Camel, 9. Horse, 10. Sheep, 11. Sugar, 12. Tea, 13. Coffee, 14. Cotton, 15. A Candle, 16. A Bell, 17. The Hand, 18. Soap, 19. A Pea, 20. The Clock, 21. Money, 22. A Book, 23. A Letter, 24. Wood, 25. A Tree, 26. An Orange, 27. Paper, 28. The Whale, 29. A Pin, 30. A Pocket Knife.
19th. April. 'Exception' Schedule ('illness', 'delicate', 'weak intellect'). There were present in the school for examination 162 boys and 145 girls, in all 307 children.
30th. April. About half the older Scholars and many younger ones absent this afternoon because of a farm sale in the neighbourhood.
An Abstract from the Annual Report 1887–88:
'The construction of the offices does not tend to encourage habits of decency; separate privies with a door to each are desirable.'
7th. May. Owing to the depressed state of the coal trade and that Mickley Coal Co. are about to discharge a number of their men, the Managers do not intend enlarging the School.

Classroom temperatures are interesting – was there a shortage of coal?. At 10am. on 3rd. March the recorded temperature was 50 degrees Fahrenheit, on the 4th. – 50, 5th. – 52, 6th. – 52, 7th. – 54, 18th. – 56, 25th. – 48. I doubt if anyone went to sleep in lessons on 25th. March 1888 in Mickley School.

Isabella (what a popular name that was) Mary Bates started teaching at

Mickley School in 1884 and left in 1895, in which time her salary rose from £30 to £45. Here is something to puzzle over – was this yearly or monthly, or were they paid quarterly?. The log fails to say, but if this is monthly, teachers were very well off indeed at £11 a week in 1895. It must have been quarterly – if yearly they were worse off than farm labourers. If the increase reflected increments, they weren't bad, if they reflected the cost of living (whoever had heard of that?) inflation was around 4 per cent.

Mrs Craig was bracketed with Mr J. Craig on starting work in 1900, presumably headmaster and wife (jobs for the girls?). Her salary rose from £70 in 1902, when she became Headmistress of the newly built Infant School, to £90 in 1904. If her husband, as Head, got a fair bit more than his wife, they could almost have afforded one of those newfangled motorcars.

Whether monthly, quarterly or yearly, this income was not enough to keep J. Craig and his wife at Mickley; they only stayed four years and left suddenly. We know this because the Log tells us that John Smith took over as temporary head until Alex, or Alack? Cleghorn was appointed in 1905. He stayed until 1932 and was still talked of in my time, with great respect, and a certain amount of fear. A healthy combination in a Headmaster, it would seem.

New Pit, New Century

Sixty Glorious Years of Victoria and a peaceful, thriving country brought the nineteenth century to a prosperous close. Invention and industry created wealth; Great Britain was riding the crest of the wave of World Power. She 'ruled the waves', dominated trade and commerce, and, apart from an odd blip like the Indian Mutiny, the Crimean War, and the Boer War, remained at peace for a hundred years, until as great a threat as the French had ever posed reared its ugly head and messed everything up for half a century, in fact for ever. The Teutonic hordes marched West.

All this wealth sprang from, depended on, coal. Even killing Boers and various assorted natives around the world demanded coal to fuel the most powerful ever fleet, of steel and steam, bristling with Armstrong's mighty guns (made at Scotswood, while he installed his first electric lights at Cragside) that symbolised 'Britain'. Although the international oil trade plied its first tanker in 1886 and the internal-combustion engine turned the century as a working reality, there was no foreseeable threat to coal. The coal trade had got its problems sorted out by the century's end – it thought; Mickley Coal Co. prospered – they had not only Mickley Colliery and its coke works, they had Prudhoe Colliery (up and coming, Prudhoe) and West Wylam, with its coke works and an abundance of clay. Clay was, in a way, a by-product of coal, they lay together underground, and the marriage of coal and clay brought forth bricks, in abundance – 'Mickley' bricks, never made at Mickley, but at West Wylam by Mickley Coal Co. – 'common' bricks that grace no house exteriors, but form many sound and serviceable bodies. There was also Edgewell Colliery which fed coal and clay to Eltringham Brick and Fire clay Works, where Harrimans of Blaydon made firebricks and glazed sanitary ware, which was in great demand in the development of the sewerage systems. Workers for the new activities at Eltringham were housed in New Eltringham streets, some of wood, and their children were taught in the new Eltringham School, built in 1885 for 160 pupils. So Mickley Coal Co. seemingly had a secure and prosperous future – and might even consider building a new school for Mickley, to further the Government's education programme.

There was yet another source of coal in Mickley towards the end of the century – West Mickley Coal Company. They developed two drifts (a third proved too wet to work) just a couple of fields to the west of Mickley drift, beyond the Bullion Hills. Now there's a name to conjure with – Bullion, as gold? Or just a corruption of 'bulling', where the bull did his stuff? Little remains to mark the existence of this pit. Not of much note, it had a short life as pits go, of under forty years and not a great output; but it had its own pit heap, alongside that of M. C. Co.'s, where pit waste was tipped in long ridges rather than in the tall, pointed heaps that scarred the North-east landscape for so long, like brooding black volcanoes.

Incidentally, there is a little story in these heaps. They contained a fair bit of coal amongst the waste and, long after mining operations ended and nature, as is her way, had cloaked man's eyesores in a mantle of green trees and pretty wild things, some bright sparks came along and thought they could exploit this black bullion. They made an awful mess and went away almost empty handed – there was not enough coal to make it worthwhile. However, they stirred up not only the old sleeping heaps, they activated the New Thinkers – Environmentalists, I think they are called – who raised no end of a rumpus against the despoiling of their beautiful 'wildlife habitat'. I at times amuse myself wondering what they might have said, had they been about when these unsightly, barren heaps were being built beside the lovely Bullion hills?

Houses for West Mickley pitmen overlooked the heaps from a comfortable distance. Their village was unusual in not being built by coal-owners for coal-workers. Housing investment, this – speculative building as it was – and there was competition for the tenancies between Mickley and West Mickley Companies, but I think Mickley lost out. It came into being in its most unlikely location, because the Company fell out with Squire Humble over wayleaves. He was the loser, as, instead of bringing coal out of the drifts on his land, they sank a shaft in a corner of High Close Wood, where now children play on the 'Green', a short step and down the pit to work instead of the long but pleasant trail to the earlier drifts from wherever these workers lived before 'The Barracks' were built in 1910. 'The Barracks'? Geordie humour, most likely. Being built on a virtual cliff, West Mickley cottages, in streets, required a lot of 'dead-walling' to level them up and with not much in the way of windows on the downhill, north, side, they did look pretty much like army barracks. Still do, some of them, in spite of modernisation and attractive window boxes. They were built of yellow 'fire' bricks, produced for, and probably surplus to, the building of round 'beehive' coke and brick kilns and therefore slightly curved in shape. Impossible to build into a perfectly even surface, they nevertheless produce a rather attractive ripple effect, and walls of great durability. The roadside row of these houses, although tiny and without land for extension, possess a certain charm and a view beyond price across Bewick country. Perhaps they were 'Barracks' just because a lot of returned soldiers lived there – 'Gunner' Jackson did, in my time.

The wayleave story I cannot vouch for – it may have been that it was just an easier way to move the coal, by way of the shaft and a wagonway (wagonways – narrow gauge railways, were meat and drink to miners), eastwards through High Close Wood, through a tunnel under Eastgate Bank and the main road (tunnel no problem either) and across the fields to Eltringham Fireclay Works, rather than from the awkwardly sited drifts lower down, with no outlet except the main railway line.

West Mickley did little more than produce rivalry between the Barracks and the Square, and some more children for the school. The pit closed in 1922.

The original Mickley drift in the hollow west of Cherryburn continued to spew forth its coaly profits, enough to enable the Company to finance a new school, twenty years after the pressing need arose, to replace the one about which we know nothing except that it was too small, very cold and had nasty privies. Although the 'Kodak' camera made its debut in 1884 and photography had cast its dark shadow over engraving in book illustration, no one thought of, or was able to take a photograph of the original Coal Co. school, so we are, sadly, in the dark about its appearance.

Not so the new one – we know all about it and can take a look whenever we like; it is still there, almost unchanged – a monument to good building. A good building maybe, but I would like a word in the ear of whoever decided to put it where it is. I can only assume that it was either the cheapest bit of land available or of no use for anything else – the most dreadful place for a school, its only merit that I can see being that the boundary wall which protects it from the 20th (and 21st?) century is just a nice height for old men to lean on, to enjoy watching the children at play, and to reminisce. Only they are not allowed, nowadays, to look at little children – only reminisce. Time was, when the wall was lined with watchers.

You should try doing handstands in that yard. Space could have been found for a playing area, albeit sloping, but play must have been the last thing on the minds of educationalists of 1900, so they jammed the school within a few yards of the highway. The road was already there, so it's no use claiming that they didn't notice it, although it was only traversed by plodding horses, not by roaring container lorries. Just about enough room was left for the 250 pupils to stand shoulder to shoulder for the mandatory daily half-hour PT. (Physical Training, mark you, or 'jerks' – no soft options) designed to keep the mind in good order; done 'on the spot' – just as well, given the slope and conjestion.

The building looks so good I wonder that someone hasn't turned it into something else. Perhaps it is safe because it is tucked out of sight behind its defensive wall.

It was a Combined Operation, this new school of 1902, the year of mourning for the Glorious Old Queen and of relief from fighting Boers. William

THE SCHOOL AND SCHOOLHOUSE AS THEY APPEAR TODAY

Henry Wrightson was still lord of the place and owned the land, common and all. There was no munificence here; endowing schools for pitmen buys no place in Heaven. So he leased his plot of useless land to Mickley Coal Co. in Dec. 1898 and they proceeded to build and equip a school for 250 pupils, an Infant School for 140, and a Master's house – another good-looking job – all of which they leased to Northumberland County Council for 42 years, from 1903, at an annual rent of £132. Odd that the school should be freed from coal-ownership only a few weeks after Europe was freed in 1945.

The dimensions of the new school, given by the Coal Co. clerk on 17.7.03 were:

1. Schoolroom 50ft. x 20ft. x 19¼ ft. (as high as wide!)
2. Schoolroom 50ft. x 20ft. x 19¼ ft.
Classroom 23ft. x 18ft. x12½ ft.

The Log Book of 1904 showed the continued 'Big Brother' nature of the school development, but it is more detailed in the nature of the school work.

'Mickley Colliery Offices
Dec. 14th 1904
Dear Sir,

It was decided at the last Manager's meeting to ask the Head Teacher to enter in the Log Book the name of the teacher taking charge of any class when another teacher is away from school. Will you kindly make this entry, when necessary?

Memory. No simultaneous reading. Co-operation with Infant School (reading and sounds)
Arith. 1. Smaller numbers.
2. Problem. No problem is a real problem until it has two steps.
Composition. Std. 4. shall have much more composition, their own work; and this throughout the school.
Oral. Children must be trained to talk. No simultaneous work. (Think, talk, and keep moving).
More recitation. More Object Lessons, current events.
Std. 1. Conversation lessons. Inattentive and must work more quietly.
Std. 2. Short of desks. Two writing. Six more altogether.
Std. 3. More paperwork. Indistinct speech.

Although the emphasis was very much on basic, no frills education, it was remarkably thorough and opened up wide horizons for children of the poor. Being able to read and understand the great mass and range of books now available, brought pleasure and knowledge on a scale undreamed of little more than a generation before.

Churches

The Old Order, that revolved around Church and Lord of the Manor, although eroded, still played a part in local affairs; but the Battie-Wrightsons lived in Yorkshire, and the parish church for Mickley was still across the fickle Tyne at Ovingham which was all very well when Micelee was a widespread but sparsely populated township; now it had become a place of note, full of pits and people. But although coal-owners took some responsibility for the physical and even educational, needs of their workers, spiritual needs were not their concern.

In the Old Order landowners bought their way to Heaven (they hoped) with often very generous gifts to the Church, and the tradition of endowments died only slowly. In Mickley there had long been a need, perhaps not a pressing one, for a place of worship, and burial, nearer than Ovingham or Bywell., and in 1825, in probably one of the last of this kind of religious endowments, W. B. Wrightson gave land and finance for the erection of a 'chapel-of-ease' to the church of Ovingham. The Wrightson patronage continued and in 1873 R. H. Wrightson enlarged and extended the church by the addition of two transepts, a chancel and a porch, at the not inconsiderable cost of £1,400. The 170 seats were needed to fit the requirements of its becoming an independent Parish Church, St George's, in 1866 under pressure from the hordes of incomers. The location, midway between old and new Mickley (Mickelee and the Square) seems fair but I would say favoured the farmers on the hill – the work-weary pitmen had a pretty gruelling climb for their forgiveness and blessing. Perhaps some of them failed to make it – the churchyard had to be extended. This was in 1885, at a cost of £200. It appears that either the Wrightsons were a bit pressed or had had enough of subsidising miners (descendants of Bewick's 'heathen Apaches'?), because a third of the cost of the extension had to be met by the populace of the Parish of Mickley – at a rate of 2d. in the pound.

The living was raised in 1884 from £176 to £210 – not bad, you might think, for a country vicar, but it was a fair-sized parish and included for a time, Prudhoe as well as Eltringham.

Prudhoe (renowned only, I like to taunt, as the place where Wesley caught his fatal cold!) felt the blast of industry later than did Mickley. 1860 saw its

ST GEORGE'S CHURCH

colliery start, 1869 West Wylam, both beside the railway – a great advantage. Only the Castle had previously marked its presence; no use Mickelee folk walking there to do their shopping. Anyone inclined to worship had to cross the river by ferry as of yore, or, after Mickley came of religious age, walk the two miles to the pretty little new church on the hill. Doubtless some did, if only to 'have a look' – after all, it was their Parish Church now.

Mickley was really 'big sister' to Prudhoe, but not for long. When little sister grew, my how she grew – from a population of about 400 in 1850 to about 4,000 in 1900, by which time it had piped water (2d. per week) and gas (4s. 6d. per 1,000 cu. ft.). Prudhoe never looked back, kept on growing and became an independent Parish in 1881, with its own church to seat 300 and a living worth £240 – just in time not to have to fork out 2d. in the pound for St George. Little sister soon grew into Big Sister and eventually into Big Bully Sister. Ironically, Prudhoe (or Ovingham, depending on where you are standing) got its long longed for bridge just three years after the Church was built. Worshippers now could have walked to church dry-shod, but it would have cost them an extra penny toll to cross the bridge, in addition to the collection. Better that they had their own church.

Big, maybe, was this church at Prudhoe, but not in the same league, visually, as Mickley's St George's, and the stipend was only ten bob a week better; but the vicarage was quite grand compared to Mickley's square box with windows – it had enhanced status: Prudhoe was up and coming.

If penance was a part of religion, Church of England goers at Mickley paid

PRIMITIVE
METHODIST CHAPEL

their lot just in climbing the hill, especially in winter. Methodists, on the other hand, were a canny lot, had no need of such rigours, and built their chapels close by their homes; some people could join in the service just by opening their windows! Coal Companies were concerned with coals not souls, and Landowners were not so beneficent towards Nonconformists, who had to build their own chapels – and lease the land.

The religious fervour which developed from independent thinking, and the hard-won freedom to worship in the church of your choice, or not at all; the craving, in the masses of downtrodden workers, for some hope of a better future, if only in the hereafter, produced Chapels. They afforded, if not hope, at least a jolly good rousing hymn or two. Hundreds, indeed thousands, of chapels sprang up all across the land, in all shapes and sizes, without much pomp and grandeur – that would have cost money, which did not come easy and did not match the Wesleyan mood of 'good' living and simple ways, which debarred alcohol and gambling but not the odd bit of wife-beating. And in assorted names, but all with the Methodist or 'free' theme. Mickley built two chapels, by subscription – Methodists put their money where their hearts lay – and perhaps with just a teeny, weeny bit of an eye to the hereafter? R. H. Wrightson leased the land for twenty-one years and gave a subscription of £5 towards the first chapel.

Built in 1862, the Free Church was known in my time and possibly from the beginning, as Hubbucks' chapel, probably because this well known family of long standing contributed generously to its building. You don't have to be a Lord to chip-in for a church. Generations of the Hubbuck family worshipped in their chapel for a hundred years or so, until it went out of use in the 1980s when the fervour had declined and the Hubbucks too. It was converted into a house, as is the vogue, but it still looks like a Chapel, albeit better looking than many, being of stone and an attractive shape.

The second, hotfoot behind it just two years later, and almost next door, in keen competition – Primitive Methodist. Mickley Coal Co. gave a ten pound subscription. Whether these congregations spoke in passing, or threw verbal abuse I know not, but if deep divisions in forms of cant and hypocrisy existed in these new styles of religion, they were united in one thing – their freedom to worship in their own way.

My, how they celebrated this freedom – the rafters rang, the very air of the Square reverberated to 'Onward Christian So-o-eld- jeress'; the children went in droves to Sunday School, scrubbed clean and pious – what else could they be, scrubbed clean – just incidentally out of the house while the Sunday dinner was being prepared.

You could still be C. of E., if you could face the hill, so there was a good choice of churches, as good as that of cinemas in a later age – three. Seats in all for four hundred or more worshippers, and mostly filled, although St George's lost out a bit from the competition. It kept the traditional worshippers – farmers mostly, they paid their tithes anyway so might as well have their money's worth; and their workers, who usually followed the boss. Methodists lived mostly in miners' cottages and didn't follow the boss, not the workaday one anyway. John Wesley certainly filled the churches.

LAST WEDDING AT UNITED METHODIST CHURCH

Whatever their differences, there must have been at least an attempt at a coming together of Methodists, for in 1909 there was built a UNITED Methodist Church. Modern, in brick and quite posh for Methodists, with a boiler-house for central heating, a basement flat for a caretaker, not a lot different from, and adjacent to, the boiler house; and foundation stones carved with the names of notables who wished to be remembered as being

UNITED METHODIST CHURCH IN ITS DYING THROES

good, and contributing to the cost. The size of the stone denoted the size of the contribution, and, presumably, the standing of the contributor at the Pearly Gates. It seated 250 and replaced the Primitive Methodist Church, which was demolished in 1939 after becoming Nonconformist in a rather different way. That is a little story on is own.

Old Mickley on the hilltop followed the religious fashion and built itself a little Wesleyan Chapel in 1876, now Wesley Cottages. Many chapels were no bigger than cottages, indeed some no bigger, nor grander, than hen-houses.

Mount Pleasant, a little 'satellite' hamlet of a few mostly very old cottages occupied mainly in the past by pitmen, and an old pub, the Blue Bell, or Bluebell, built a red brick chapel seating about as many as the entire population of the place. Perched precariously on a precipitous hillside, near where the Bewicks mined their coal, it is almost a kindness to describe it as unsightly, yet it has a good and stout heart – and it survives, the only practising 'free' church in Mickley township.

St George's soldiers on, with a fair-sized congregation, but the just-retired vicar has not been replaced.

Gas and Water

With the advent of iron-built, steam-powered ships and dredgers the lower reaches of the Tyne became a deep, safe waterway, one of the busiest in the world. Making the fullest use of its coal resources, Newcastle drew to it industry, invention and innovation on a colossal scale and could afford to rebuild itself into a fine, modern city, with a good water supply, gas lighting and well developed sanitary system.

Mickley, for some reason, failed to expand even at the pace of its rapidly growing neighbour Prudhoe, where the march of science and disease-driven concern for water and sanitation had a much greater and quicker effect than on Mickley.

Prudhoe had piped water and gas by 1885. A lot happened between then and the turn of the century, but Mickley stood still – it didn't justify the cost, presumably. Gas, originally a waste by-product of the coke industry, became useful and highly profitable when the problems of storage and distribution were solved and, most important, the gas 'mantle' was invented. This clever device came in a little cardboard-cube box and was a woven, silk-like pouch with the open end fixed to a ring of fire-clay designed to hang on the open end of the gas-jet. When the new 'mantle' was 'fired', before the gas was turned on, the silk burned for a second and was left as a mere shell of ash that the very suggestion of a touch with match or taper caused to disintegrate; spare mantles were an essential of the gas-lit home. But this fragile thing contained and diffused the burning gas and transformed the smelly, flickering, hissing, dangerous jet into a well-behaved, quiet (apart from a scarcely audible murmuring hiss), brilliant blue-white light that put candles and paraffin lamps to shame and dazzled the reading eye. "We'll all be blind," said the die-hard candle users.

The gas stopped at Prudhoe, while the sulphurous fumes from coke-making darkened, rather than lightened Mickley.

As for water ... It still came in buckets, until after the turn of the century.

Newcastle and Gateshead Water Co. was charged with the task of supplying wholesome water to Tyneside, and to that end set up reservoirs at Whittle Dene, on the hill above Ovingham, within sight of Mickley Square and at about the same height above sea level. But the main concern was to supply the principle centres of population and the cost of an innovative system of leak-proof (hopefully) cast-iron pipes feeding initially to street standpipes, then to every house (lead pipes to the houses!), was enormous. Built to last, like everything Victorian, it has stood the test of time, and is only now being replaced, after a hundred years.

Mickley was well down the 'pipeline' and got its reservoir in 1914, nearly thirty years later than Prudhoe, and it was 1921 before this reservoir served East gate Bank, where a worker died whilst digging a trench at Tinkler Row, when it collapsed and buried him; it must have been exceptionally deep – two feet was normal for water pipes: perhaps it was a sewer. Water from Whittle Dene has since been pumped to this 'header' reservoir at Old Mickley, near one of the springs that served Micelee, by a pump placed on Eastgate Bank at the level of the Dene reservoir. Anywhere below this level could have had low-pressure water directly from the Dene before 1914, and it is possible that the Rows could have had their supply from Prudhoe at about the same time as they got their drain, in about 1900. It didn't amount to much – just a bit of lead pipe sticking out of the floor, with a brass tap at bucket height, under the bottom shelf in the dark, congested larder: no sink, no drain, just a bucket for the drips and what a mess when the tap washer failed. In tandem with the water came drainage – liberal water could have had Mickley vying with Venice for watery streets had the waste been cast out of the door as of yore. The Water Co. supplied the delicious water – and it was delicious; none of your polluted, chemicalised stuff – but they could not be expected to get rid of it, second hand, so this is where the blossoming Council showed its mettle. Prudhoe and Mickley came under the control of Hexham Council (it is true that if you keep a thing long enough it comes back into fashion – Hexham is again in control) and it laid a drain, or, more likely, forced Mickley Coal Co. to lay one. Nothing fancy, just to take the used water down to a simple sewage works just west (upwind!) of the new houses being built at North and South View. Why a sewage works, for only water? Forward thinking, that's why – it came in useful later on. For the moment, water was tipped from bowl or bucket into a gully, just outside the door, which could be reached easily on a rainy day without stepping outside to get either feet or head wet.

No Water Closets though. The Rows had only got their dry, ash, netties in the 1890s – no one was about to finance a fancy, elaborate system of waste disposal to replace what was perfectly adequate. It was also judged to be adequate for new houses . . .

Not only school space and desks were in short supply at the turn of the century, so were houses to accommodate the growing population. So M.C. Co. built some more, but of a higher standard this time. Water was built-in, and an earthenware sink with a waste pipe into the outside gully – they didn't even have to open the door on a wet day, and there was no excuse for a dirty neck at school.

New Housing

Having grown up with the 'Raas', pit folk took unkindly to fancy 'Streets' and 'Views', so 'East Street' became forever 'The Poliss's Raa' and North and South 'Views' the 'Neuw Buildins'. Still 'new', a hundred years on, to any natives still about.

Nine houses of East Street, running up and down the hillside, completed what had been an open-ended 'square'. They were unattractive looking white brick things, but providing much better living conditions, under pressure from authorities working to reduce the blight of infectious diseases. Not 'back to back', for a start; they had doors and windows on both sides and good healthy 'through draughts' to keep those germs on the move. There was a living room and separate kitchen, small but with a cooking range, and a sink complete with tap and waste pipe. Proper stairs led to two bedrooms above with windows to open, and all with ceilings at the statutory height of nine feet. Air was in vogue; but still no bathroom – and no WC. The ash-nettie was across the street in conjunction with the 'wash house'; a new one this, for – yes, you've guessed it – washing clothes, not people; they still enjoyed the tub by the fire. These wash-houses housed a 'set pot' for boiling water and clothes, a poss-stick and tub, mangle and a table. The new dwelling houses were too small to harbour all of this gear that was used only once a week. East Street and West Mickley houses were similar and the washing facilities shared between two households, the weekly routine being altered so that one washed on Monday, the other Tuesday.

By agreement with yet another new institution – the Police Authority – No. 1 East Street housed the village 'Bobby' – not so very long previously invented by Robert Peel and answering to 'Peeler' if you wished. Hence the 'Polisses Raa'. This formidable representative of the forces of law and order came to rank with headmaster and vicar in the village hierarchy. Nobody messed with the Trinity. No one ever knew where this P. C. was, night or day. He didn't patrol, silently he prowled; he knew everyone, where they were, what they were up to. Children, guilty or innocent (all children were assumed guilty!), quaked in their shoes at his passing; a word enough to bring the wayward to heel, or at most a flick of the cape or cuff of the hand. A fearsome last resort was the Magistrate's Court at Hexham where his word of evidence would invoke a fine of five shillings for stealing a turnip worth perhaps a ha'penny, or of seven-and-six for playing pitch and toss. Seeking warmth and shelter by the kilns at Eltringham Pipe Works, condemned the poor vagrant, and there were plenty of those, to 'hard labour', which believe me, really was hard. A few vagrants still sought refuge there until the place closed in about 1970 when vagrancy of the old kind was a dying vocation and their other refuge, the 'Workhouse', a day's walk away at Hexham, closed and was converted into a nurses' residence – some say, appropriately!

One particular Bobby gained a fine reputation at the local village shows, with his flower and vegetable exhibits. The garden that went with his house was well hedged-round from prying eyes, but grew no flowers or vegetables, prize or otherwise! Such was the power of the Law in Mickley. There was a local saying:: 'Better a smaall poke (sack) than a big garden'. Crime in the village was never a serious matter though. Sensible people, 'marras' mostly, living and working close together, could sort out their own problems – 'doon the gardens' if necessary, with fists.

The New Buildings comprised twenty-six houses in two parallel streets, similar to East Street and as unattractive, in brick, slightly bigger and on reasonably level land. They were innovative in a way; the move towards privacy, a 'place of one's own', brought about long, narrow,walled gardens – the width of the house front - to the fronts of South View, miniatures of those fine old Victorian kitchen gardens associated with mansions. Not quite mansions, these houses, but the gardens, facing south, grew some fine stuff and were but a step out of the door, for pleasure and convenience – but no hiding place for the gardener, like the distant, hedged allotment. The back doors opened into 'yards' with high walls like industrial Victorian city streets; high walls make for good neighbours, it was said. The coal house and the netty, still no WC., were across the yard and there was room for a bicycle shed or extra storage space. The Raas had no provision for coal storage, it lay outside or the miner cobbled up a shelter. The netty, as in the Raas, was emptied through an iron hatch from the street; but there was one to each house and the neighbours couldn't see when you went and it didn't matter anyway, there was no queue. Coals were cast into the coalhouse through a two-foot-square 'porthole' about five feet up the wall, having been tipped in the street. You needed a good eye and a powerful 'hoy' (throw) to avoid bouncing the coal off the wall and back all over yourself.

Lean times hit M.C. Co. once again and North View was never completed, possessing neither gardens nor yards. Netties and coal houses, yes, but it was 'across the street' for them, as in the Raas. Were N. View folk any less good neighbours, I wonder, for the lack of high walls between them?

The Co-op

Dependence for shopping on itinerant traders and journeys to Newcastle or Hexham by train, horse-drawn coach or carter's wagon, continued almost to the end of the century. The quiet revolution that brought shops to Mickley, or rather, to begin with a shop, began as early as 1844 in faraway Rochdale, when the Square was little more than a twinkle in the eye of Messrs. Cookson and Co. Like water and netties, shops were a while in reaching Mickley.

A small group of men, sick and tired of being exploited by monopolistic bosses-cum-traders, bought a bag of flour and a bag of sugar and sold it, retail, to their friends, at a small profit, just enough to buy more goods and expand into a small shop supplying the needs of their worker neighbours. The idea was born of dividing surplus profit between customers - 'members' – who had to 'join' to be eligible for a share. 'Shares' and 'Dividends' (the beloved 'divi'), previously the prerogative of the wealthy, could henceforth be enjoyed by working folk with barely the means to buy the weekly groceries. This was how the Co-op was born: Co-operative Wholesale Societies.

This novel idea, which put an end to the milching of already exploited workers by unscrupulous traders, all too often their bosses, spread like wildfire through the working North of England. It reached Newcastle in 1861 and by 1875 there were thirty-one societies in Northumberland. The whole county was fairly well covered, with at least one branch to every town, and many villages under promise.

A strange thing about the Co-op, hereabouts anyway, is that they developed intense rivalry and competition between Societies. Perhaps there was need, and room, for two of a kind (competition is good for the customer?) in a place the size of booming Prudhoe. Blaydon Industrial and Provident Society – what a name, it must have cost a fortune for sign-writers and no wonder they needed long shop fronts – set up shop along a prime roadside site in the centre of Prudhoe. Then, probably thinking, "Who do these Blaydon people think they are, muscling in on our patch?" West Wylam and Prudhoe Co-operative Wholesale Society set up shop opposite – and would need another sign writer: they liked a good title, did the Victorians – it added prestige. They built a 'shopping complex', and there they sat, glowering at each other for well nigh a hundred years.

The two societies built satellites all around – no one should have to walk miles to the shops. There was one of each, WW& P and Blaydon, at Prudhoe Station but separated by the line and facing the same way, so they didn't have to stare at each other. And they built another of each at Mickley Square, but separated by both time and a little distance – on different roads …

'West Wylam and Prudhoe' came to Mickley first, with a purposeful air – big, versatile, complete, serving every need, the ultimate in shops for the people; the culmination of forty-odd years of Co-op experience, and purpose-built. Unfortunately the builders, proud though they should have been of their fine, stone-built shop, failed to indulge in that little old-time whimsy of putting the date of construction on the front, in the manner of the Wesleyan Chapel, 1862; Bearl View, (West Mickley) 1910; and Blaydon Co-op, 1909. So we know not precisely when the WW & P Co-op arrived. My best guess is, in the 1880s, having been established in Prudhoe in 1872, in adapted premises which were replaced in 1900.

When the Co-op did arrive, how the good folk of the Square must have rejoiced – and let us not forget that Old Mickley up the hill still thrived and needed shopping, – this beat the newly built netties for 'best things'.

Of course Co-ops had been available at Prudhoe for a few years, just two miles away – a short haul compared to the Towns, east or west, at about ten miles distant, and probably with a delivery service; but – this was on the very doorstep, 'convenience shopping' that knocks the present-day Metro Centre at ten miles away, into a cocked hat. "If only we had a bit more

THE DRAPERY

money!" This institution, the 'Store', quickly became the focal point of the village, certainly where the women were concerned …

About one third of the 70 ft. frontage was taken up with the two small windows of the drapery department, separated by a recessed doorway, this being closed off, out of hours, by a padlocked iron-grille gate. Usually one window displayed men's clothes, the other women's, but the nature of the display, sartorial and artistic, was rather limited; the lass doing it hadn't been to Design School and the choice was hardly up to M&S's. But there would be at least a 'Best' suit for men, and a dress, cotton for summer, good wool for winter, or even a fine lady's suit, for dressing -up. It cost nothing to look, and even the poorest could dream – and they had their very own shop window to look in.

Everything in the shop had its chance of a place in the limelight of the window – except that there was no light, so there was no use looking on a winter's night.

Choice was a straight one – work clothes or Sunday clothes, which included weddings and funerals. Variety, or something special, could be had at Prudhoe, possibly, or failing that, from the 'Wholesale' in Newcastle, with a few days delay.

Inside, it was quiet – no bustling about in a drapers; there was a 'bentwood' chair to sit on. The first thing that struck you was the smell, oh, the special smell – of cotton and twill and leather shoes, and hanks of wool. My wife, (who knows about these things) tells me that the characteristic smell of cotton came mostly from the dressing used to make thin material look and feel thicker. It was the same smell that rushed out of the suitcase of Mr Landlass, the 'Traveller' of my childhood days, when he displayed on our kitchen table his 'pinnies', the wrap-round overalls with a tie-belt that disappeared in places around the waist, and colourful cotton dresses. It was the smell of leaning on your mother for childish comfort; she was seldom not in cotton. England was the cotton-shop of the world, and Mickley Co-op Drapers sold its share, and left nostalgia's nostrils full of the perfume.

At street level, a mahogany-topped counter stood at each side of the shop, with drawers of small items, socks, handkerchiefs, etc., ladies' on one side, gents on the other; you, and the assistant, had to switch counters if you wanted both. Mention of socks brings to mind that the Gents counter was likely to display, at opposite ends, two pairs of identical socks, one marked 'Pit Socks' 1s., the other 'Deputy's Hose' 1s. 3d. In the hope no doubt, that it would be considered worth 3d. in a pit village drapers to be recognised, if only in your own mind, as a Deputy's wife! Small drawers contained buttons galore (pretty things, old buttons, they deserve a chapter to themselves), pins on pink paper sheets, needles of assorted sizes in packets; knitting needles, pointed both ends for socks, big with a knob on one end for comforting scarves and school jumpers; hooks and eyes and newly invented press-studs – and Knicker Elastic, by the yard, for holding-up little boys' socks. All manner of useful things.

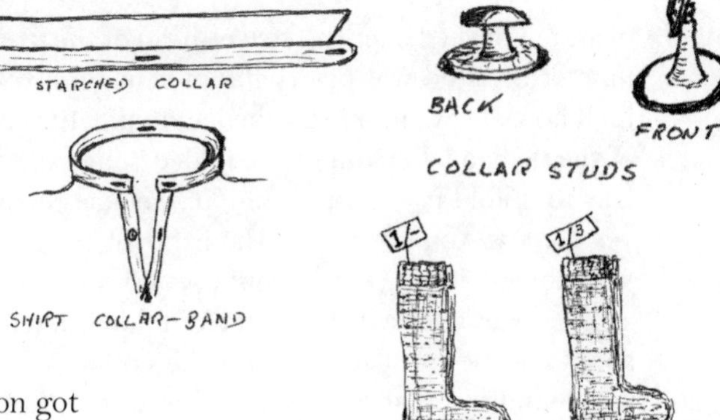

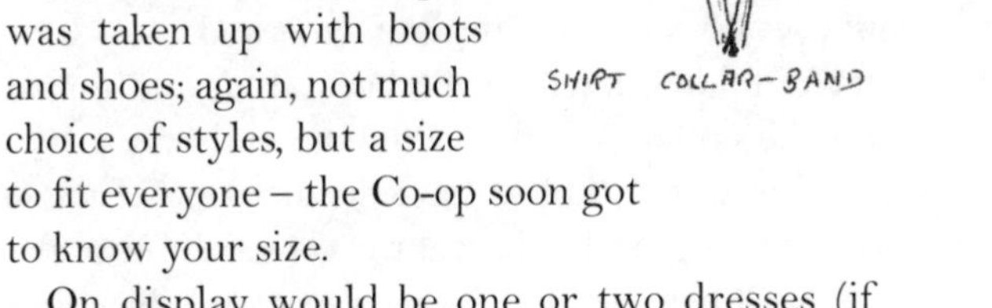

Much of the wall- space was taken up with boots and shoes; again, not much choice of styles, but a size to fit everyone – the Co-op soon got to know your size.

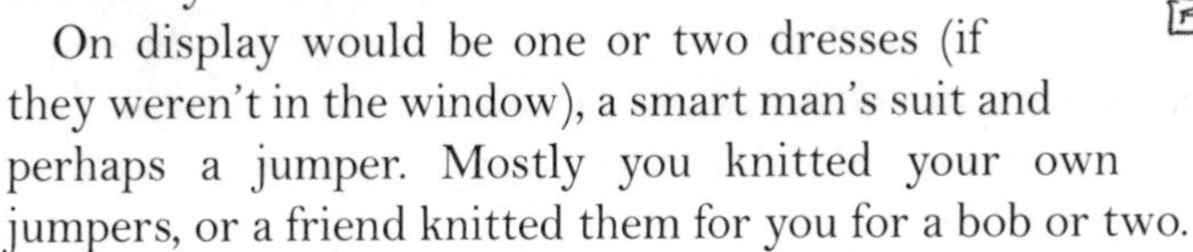

HABERDASHERY ITEMS

On display would be one or two dresses (if they weren't in the window), a smart man's suit and perhaps a jumper. Mostly you knitted your own jumpers, or a friend knitted them for you for a bob or two. The wool came in 'hanks' and you wound it yourself into balls with the aid of a press-ganged child's outstretched hands or over the back of a chair. Very mischief-inhibiting for small boys, was wool-winding. Some knitters had fancy wool-winders.

There were blouses for the ladies, for the prettying-up days, and plenty of shirts for men, mostly 'drill' for work, flannel for winter, but good white cotton, with separate starched collars for Sundays and 'going out'. Starched collars were essential 'dress', no well-dressed man would be seen out and about without one. They were the cause of much anguish in our household, when my father felt obliged to wear one on his Saturday afternoon jaunts to Town. They were fixed to the neck band of his shirt with two 'collar studs'. There's the rub – the fixing bit. The front stud was often quite a work of art, of gold for the flashy dresser, brass for workers, with an inlay of 'mother of pearl' on the round base that came into contact with the neck. From the base arose a short column topped by a smaller round head, which swivelled. The 'back' stud was a shorter one with a fixed head which was passed from the neck side, through the hole in the back of the shirt collar-band. Not too difficult – but don't get complacent. Then you opened-out the starched collar, which was doubled-over, and pressed the hole at the back over the head of the back stud. This could sometimes fray the temper a little if the collar was especially stiff and the hole new. So now you had two stiff white wings sticking out, either side of your neck, fixed at the back. Then came the tricky part. You took the front stud, swivelled the top so that it was on edge and passed it, from the inside, neck side, through the hole in one side of the collar-band, then the other. Things were tightening up! Now there were two options: you could place your tie around the open collar and fold it down so that the tie was held in place, hopefully, while each end was bent in turn, and I mean bent – it was as stiff as a board – around the neck and the hole in the front tab pushed over the swivel-head of the front stud. By which time the column of the stud was pretty full of shirt and collar – four layers in all, and the final hole always more starched and difficult than the others. Usually the ends of the tie had fallen out of the folded collar and the only way to get them back was to unfold it – if you could; it was like turning a bicycle tyre inside-out – yes I know, you are not in the habit of turning bicycle tyres inside-out; use your imagination. Or you could proceed in the alternative method ...

This was to leave the collar unfolded, fixed to the back stud, and forget about the tie until later. Bend the collar round and fix the ends on to the front studs so that you felt – come to think of it, looked – like one of those beautiful African maidens with the long necks. Swivel the top of the stud flat so that it doesn't all come undone. Then take the tie, pass it round the collar and tie the knot, being sure to get it exactly right before folding down the collar as adjustment is best avoided – this stiff collar, when fixed, had a rare grip on the tie.

The great explosion of anger which often accompanied this complicated operation, and my father was not alone in this, made the trip to town seem hardly worthwhile and sometimes abandoned in a huff, with a chastened wife (was it not all her fault?); and the children playing at a far, safe distance. But oh my – how grand the collar looked!

At the 'Drapery' could be bought the shirt, collar, (next door for the starch), studs, tie and pin to fix it to the shirtfront; a tidy suit with waistcoat; socks and suspenders for holding them up; and shoes – and a hat. The well turned out man would certainly need a hat – or at least a cap, but for real 'class', a bowler, in later days a 'dud' or a trilby. This was the 'complete outfitter' for the well-dressed working man. Women too, but I'm not so well versed in their clothes or how they got into them.

Up a short flight of stairs from the front shop were kept rolls of material, in good variety, mostly cotton. Although Mr Singer was making his clever machine for sewing in Boston in 1851, and it caught on fast, like most innovations, it was slow to reach Mickley. In later days nearly every house boasted a sewing machine and someone to use it. In the meantime, early rolls of material were hand-sewn by miners' wives and daughters; spinsters no longer spun – they sewed. Needlework was a universal, vital skill, passed on from generation to generation and now taught at school, to the practical advantage of poor families with lots of children to clothe. Not only useful, but decorative and artistic too; many a beautifully embroidered tablecloth graced Sunday tea, and blouses and children's dresses were an excuse to display often quite remarkable talent – and good eyesight. The pleasure of choosing the material for this activity, the often delightful prints, cotton threads and silks – even 'Dolly Varden' wool which intrigued me, was not the least of the pleasures brought to this little pit village by the 'Drapers'. They were not lost even on me – a boy.

The Grocery

Next door to the Drapers, to where you went for the starch, the grocery department also had two windows but much longer, with a similar doorway between: windows of little more than a shelf-depth with a back for display which was severely cramped artistically, compared to the Drapers, until the arrival of tins and pre-packed, 'untouched by human hand' products. These enabled shop staff on quiet days to vie with each other in skill and ingenious artistry in their stacking ability. Balance was the secret. These stackers would doubtless today qualify for grants from the Arts Council. In those days small boys sometimes amused themselves by thumping on the windows in the hope of setting-up vibrations that would tumble the works of art. They themselves got the thumping, if caught. Sweets of the day found a corner of the window, to tempt children with hard-earned pennies. They were mostly 'boiled sweets' in glass jars, the likes of which can still be found today if considered worth the search; they were pretty horrid but children were easy to please – would even eat 'sweet swede' – and they could always get liquorice in various forms.

Into the shop, and a very different set of smells – the smells of 'loose' food – basic, honest-to-goodness, no nonsense food. None of your 'convenience' foods here, well, hardly any; the smells you could almost cut, flavours taunted the appetite – you could always try a taste, as in 'high-class' shops. Walking in here, you scarcely needed to eat, the atmosphere was laden with nourishment – and you got your divi! The mahogany-topped counter (Victorian counters, as well as their furniture, decimated forests) here stretched the full length of the shop, with a good space behind for the to-ing and fro-ing staff. There was a lot of movement twixt goods and customers.

The counter top had clear spaces, where customers stood to be served and staff did the weighing and packing; it held scales and some of the foodstuffs for weighing, such as butter. It came in wooden barrels holding 28 lbs., which were lifted complete on to the counter, where the barrel hoops were knocked off, the 'staves' sprang open and together with the top lid, could be

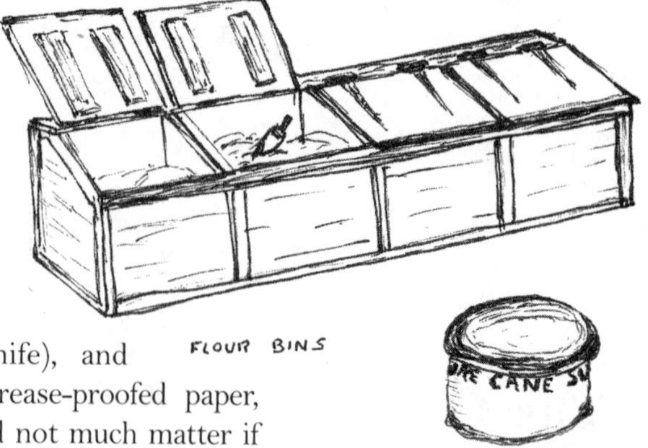

FLOUR BINS

lifted clear, leaving the butter sitting on the base ready for cutting. Incidentally, the staves, being saturated with butter, made wonderful firewood but, being tough, curved and springy, were brutes to split. Butter was cut with a 'gully' (big knife), and weighed on to sheets of grease-proofed paper, marked 'butter'. The shape did not much matter if the grocer hadn't time to 'pat' it with wooden 'hands'. You could buy as much or as little as need or purse dictated – a single ounce, if you wished.

GROCERY ITEMS

Cheese also came big. The biggest were rolled along the ground from cart to counter; fortunately with a muslin wrap and a thick skin to protect it from the grit and the spit. It stood, muslin removed, on the counter alongside the butter and was cut, with consummate skill and a 'cheese wire' with wooden handles, to any weight required. Grocers took great pride in their work, as did most people of the past it seems, and the ultimate skill was to cut a piece of cheese to the exact weight, any weight, at one go. 'Practice makes perfect' the school book said. They got plenty of practice, in the Co-op.

Then there was the bacon, at the far end, on the bacon board, which was beech or sycamore and could be scrubbed; sometimes there was a piece of marble. Bacon came in flat 'sides' (later rolled), and legs, including hams, and hung from ceiling hooks when not in use. Staff who lifted these became strong as well as skilled! Before bacon machines it was sliced by hand, with another 'gully' and more skill. The machine, as with all machines, saved a lot of time and bother, but it was a fearsome device. It had a huge flywheel on the right-hand side, which must have been awkward for left-handed operators, with a handle attached for turning. It in turn turned a big, circular, razor-sharp knife, like a circular saw without teeth, which sliced the bacon to the customer's preferred thickness as it was fed along on a sliding rack, worked by the left hand. It was a bit like the trick exercises that clever PE teachers get their pupils to do – making arms and legs go in different directions. Bacon machine operators often seemed to have bandaged fingers, with black leather 'finger stalls' to keep them – or the bacon, clean.

This – fatty – bacon was delicious beyond the understanding of the modern palate and consumed in huge quantities. It was cheap meat and 'convenient'; quickly fried in a big, thick pan on the open fire, with fat spattering all around, to a crispness impossible with our watery, tasteless, 'cultivated' bacon. The eggs, to go with the bacon, were fresh from the hens in the garden perhaps, or were quite good from the 'Store'. Even 'bought eggs', and known as such, were from hens that ran around farmyards and scratched in fields and boosted the farmwife's housekeeping money – or spending money, if she could get away with it. Dropped into the plentiful, boiling bacon fat and made companion to the plated rashers when the yolk was still soft but covered with a thin white film and the white crisp round the edges but still tender, they would be no use for heeling shoes, as are our modern day 'plastic' eggs. Finally, to complete this quick, greasy meal – bread, sliced thick and fried, again with all haste, (the bacon was waiting), again in plentiful fat; crisp outside, soft in the middle. Ah, the torment of recollection of good things gone forever.

If this 'good thing' – fat bacon – has gone, where did coronary thrombosis come from? Certainly not from this animal fat. The miners of Mickley would have been wiped out in their prime. Pigs were killed at weights of perhaps forty stone (14 lbs to the stone), mostly fat.

It has been said, by people who remember, that the first job of the summer morning for the boy in the shop was to scrape the blow-fly maggots off the bacon. If so, and it might well be true, no one seemed to be the worse for them; everything got a jolly good fry. The newfangled netties of Mickley could never have handled food-poisoning.

Sugar came in white, close-woven sacks of eight or ten stone and stood on the floor behind the counter, whence it was scooped into strong blue paper bags, weighed and bumped on the counter to settle the contents into a nice close pack. Then the bag top was folded over in a precise and particular way and tied around with 'sugar' string, with a dexterity to shame the best of mariners. Yet another little skill of the grocery trade. This sugar string was fine, white and strong – ideal for kites if you could get hold of a ball, and had the skill to make a kite out of bits of thin wood and brown paper stuck together with a paste made with flour and water. Mothers were very tolerant. The fun was in the making and trying – occasionally they did fly, if the wind was strong enough.

There was a choice of sugars, brown or white, and if you could get your grubby little boy's fingers on the lumps that came in 'Scots moist' they were as good as any sweets – and free; but a wary eye had to be kept for mouse droppings – the mouse was never far away, in spite of the best efforts of the resident cats, who worked at night, as did the mice, and slept on the counter or shelves during the day.

Peas, beans and lentils, rice and such things also came in sacks and were weighed out with scoops into paper bags. Flour was a bit different – being light, it was disposed to float about in the air, so was kept in big wooden 'bins' through a door behind the counter in a mysterious, dark 'back room' where also were kept the reserve stocks of goods in bags and boxes. Up a narrow flight of stairs from here were more bins, of hen-food, pigeon corn, boxes of soap, and the stock of hardware – scrubbing brushes, buckets, poss-sticks and tubs and the like. Tin baths. The mangle, at around £8 and cumbersome, had to be specially ordered. Up another flight of stairs, narrower still (have you noticed this assumption that the higher you climb the slimmer you are expected to be – or become?), to the loft, for paper bags, string etc. Up here was very dry and at one time there was an office where the dividend was paid, with access from the rear by a ramp/bridge above the yard area. The wooden stairs wore almost wafer thin with time. Grocers were fit if they worked in the Co-op.

Downstairs again. Tea came in wooden chests, foil lined to keep out the damp, later made of plywood when that became available and cheap. Empty tea chests were useful for storage, for recycling into doll's houses or smaller boxes, or, for anyone fortunate enough to own a 'fret saw', for cutting out into fancy patterns, not necessarily for a purpose, just for fun. The imaginative and skilled could glue a picture from a magazine on to a piece of plywood and cut intricately shaped, original, 'jigsaw puzzles'. I remember my father making these individual, durable puzzles for us, using the superbly illustrated covers of the 'Passing Show', a first class weekly magazine of the time. He cut the pieces to a size and pattern to suit our ages, and even made one without a pattern for my brother who I suppose was old enough for that sort of challenge, I thought it dull and wouldn't have swapped ten of them for mine with a pretty picture. I wonder what happened to that jig-saw-puzzle? Tea became much cheaper and more readily available to working folk in Victorian times, eventually was tax-free and not worth smuggling. The British Empire encompassed the major tea-growing areas of the world; if the British couldn't have cheap tea, who could? In 1669 imports amounted to 150 lbs.; by 1864 they were 125,289,016 lbs., and the price, advertised in the 'Hexham Courant', was 3s. to 4s. per lb. – 1s. of that being duty. By the following year, duty was reduced to 6d. and the price to 2s. to 4s. per lb. This put paid to home-brewed ale – and knocked the pubs a bit, as did the practice of coffee drinking – in coffee houses, not at home. Coffee was a long time in reaching Mickley Co-op. Although cheaper, tea was still one of the more expensive items in the household budget, not to be wasted; it called for care in the handling, but no longer for locking up. It was all very well to have the aroma of tea enriching the air, but smell went hand in hand with flavour, and once the chest was opened, much of both were lost to the atmosphere. So, one of the secrets of good tea was to keep the lid on the chest except when weighing out the 'quarter pounds', and at home keep it in a tea 'caddy' – the upmarket word for a tin box. Proper caddies could be bought but any pretty tin with a good lid would do. Decorated, often beautifully painted tins were plentiful, well made and cheap, in fact free – lots of things came in them. So anyone could have a caddy; it was kept handy on the mantleshelf. Mr Lipton made matters a little easier when he started putting tea in sealed, foil packets to keep the flavour in – 'Untouched by Human Hand', he boasted. He certainly started a trend. Ringtons were notable, locally, in not only following the trend and competing strongly with the Co-op. on tea sales, they also delivered it, their own blend and nothing else, door to door. They used striking, beautifully turned-out little pony-vans which became renowned and admired throughout the NE. They also had made for them, by the Maling factory in Newcastle, as a selling ploy, attractive, square, blue and white earthenware teapots with matching caddies. They came in exchange for the requisite number of packet ends and are now collectors' items, to prove which, the pair that we owned, battered and chipped, were recently deemed by rogues to be worth the stealing.

Ringtons had a depot in Mickley, until about 1940, in a tiny outbuilding at Eltringham Cottage, which had been part of the small farm that the Square was built on. The farmhouse became the Miners' Arms pub and the outbuildings housed the cart and the pony as well as the tea. (They still have a delivery service, by motor van, and retain their distinctive livery). It had been but a modest farm. In my time and probably long before, they also housed there the huge Clydesdale or Shire Stallion which was 'walked' at a slow, steady pace, to farms for miles around, when replacement transport was produced on the farm by mares, with the assistance of Mr Knox and his Stallion.

There were two bentwood chairs in the Co-op 'grocery' for the weary, the elderly or sick, or for those just not in a hurry and ready for a gossip. As Bewick's colliery had been the early-days gathering-ground of news in the village, and the Smithy its distribution centre, so the Co-op, being a place mainly for women, became the point of dissemination of news and gossip. A long wait to be served, and it could be long on pay-day, was as good as a picnic for relaxation; unless you got into a fight, in which case it was even better – for the onlookers! Not everyone could read as yet and, although Blaydon Co-op provided, at Prudhoe, a 'Reading Room' for its members (and for others at a small charge), where books, magazines and newspapers were available, no such facility was yet available at Mickley. Many a humble miner, or miner's son, read his way to Parliament, or at least to a better, fuller life by way of the Reading Room, but for the time being, Mickley had the Co-op and a good gossip.

On busy days the shop was full of pinnied, basket-festooned, standing-talking, customers and perhaps ten assistants busying about, serving, weighing, measuring, packing – making out 'checks'. These were little receipts contained in long books, in duplicate, interleaved with carbon paper, in which every transaction was recorded, for proof and accounting. The Membership number was needed to get these receipts and heaven help the childish messenger who forgot it and forfeited the 'divi', even on a tuppenny purchase. "Look after the pennies and the pounds will take care of themselves." The forgetful child was often saved from a fate worse than death by the assistant remembering the elusive number; they knew the regular customer's number by heart. The customers themselves, after a lifetime of shopping at the Co-op, had them engraved on their souls. Like servicemen's numbers in time of war, they were never forgotten.

The little slip, with value of purchase and number written in 'indelible pencil', so that there could be no cheating, was taken safely home and stuck (often with 'condensed milk' which, if you haven't tried it, makes a cheap glue for paper) to the big sheet of paper supplied by the 'store' especially for the purpose. This was hung on the wall in the corner by the fireplace, safe and accessible, until 'Divi' day.

Come the great day, which came 'quarterly' in an air of some excitement, the sheet, or sheets in the case of a big family, was taken to the shop, or until the quieter years, to the Office, high up in the attic by the string and bags, by way of the covered ramp at the rear. Here the operation could be conducted without interfering with the normal running of the shop. The Clerk or the Manager added up the total purchases, checked them against the shop copy, and worked out the dividend, which was variable, according to the Society profits. In the early years, and for many years, the 'divi' was around 3s. 8d. in the pound. This is hard to believe. Wouldn't you just like to have nearly 20 per cent off all your purchases credited to your savings account? Not only that, but if you chose not to take the cash on dividend day (it was used mostly for clothes and shoes and major household purchases), it could be left, recorded in your 'Pass' book, not only to accumulate, but to earn INTEREST. That way this remarkable institution, true socialism at work, set simple worker's thrift on the way to capitalism, banking and dominance by, not Barons or Bosses, but remote financial institutions. Serfs have come a long way in the course of this book.

The measure of freedom and independence – of having 'something behind you for a rainy day', and there were plenty of those, embodied in dividend and passbook, transformed the lives of millions of working folk, some of them in Mickley. But there were some drawbacks to this system. The Co-op sold only goods that it could buy in bulk, or, when it was firmly established, could make in its own factories and workshops. The emphasis had to be on 'value for money' – cheapness. Nothing wrong with that, to begin with anyway, when it was the only shop in the village, after centuries without one and forty years after the Square was built. Nobody was going to complain about the lack of choice, and if cheapness sometimes took precedence over quality, who knew about quality? At least most ordinary needs were catered for.

It was not even necessary to stand in the shop to be served and then carry the shopping home. Once a week, but not on washing day, a man from the Store, I think it was the clerk, but it could have been a spare assistant, walked from house to house around the village, soliciting orders. He carried a very long, very narrow book, on each page of which were detailed, in a column, all of the standard items sold in the shop; flour, tea, sugar, butter, etc., with lines at the top for name, address and Co-op number and spare lines at the bottom for any items not listed. Each item required was ticked and the quantity noted alongside and the torn-out sheet, duly priced and totalled, returned with the goods. Payment was required at the end of the week, after the goods were delivered; there was no credit at the Co-op.

Sometimes the 'order man' had time for a chat, teased the toddler, and passed on; sometimes, if the timing was right, especially on baking day, perhaps even a cup of tea. Two days later, the shop staff having occupied the intervening day (a quiet one, these things were well thought-out to fit the vagaries of the trading week) weighing, packing and gathering together, the 'flat' cart of the delivery man rumbled from door to door, delivering the goods – "Woa! —giddup; woa – tch-tch, giddup ..."

Other Ways to Shop

Hawking – selling around the streets – had been the standard method of trading before the arrival of shops. It continued, in its various forms afterwards, and as part of the Co-op, but the 'Store' hit the independents hard, although some of them survived, mostly specialists. I recall an 'independent', Charlton by name, (given up the reiving, he had) from along the road at Branch End still plying his 'loose' vinegar trade, midway through the twentieth century, from a little wooden keg on a tiny cart, pulled by an equally tiny pony, well cared for and cuddly. "Vinegaar," he would call from time to time – "Vineegaaar." and the faithful customer went out with a jug or bottle for a few pennorth and a 'hullo'. Pleasant buying, if tough on the hawker in bad weather.

Muffins came round in a big basket, covered in a snow-white cloth, carried on the head or switched from arm to weary arm, thick and fresh for toasting on forks at winter fires – they could never fit a toasting machine. No bell, that I ever heard in Mickley, like the London 'Muffin Man' of nursery rhyme, but a rousing call – not always welcome by sleeping pitmen. Americans don't know about muffins.

They all had their distinctive calls, the hawkers – how else would their presence and identity be known? The kipper man also had his distinctive smell, and sometimes came on foot with his supply in a wooden box, which must have been even more difficult to carry over a distance than the muffin basket. How many kippers did he need to carry and sell to eke a living at two for three-ha-pence? The cheap-est of all protein foods – except that no-one knew of

FISHWIFE AT LONGSTAFFES

protein; food was for pleasure, not analysis. Quicker than bacon and eggs for a meal-in-a-hurry, the kipper was always welcome, and tasty. The Co-op didn't sell fish – the smell, you know.

River fish could be had if you knew the right people, and you couldn't get fresher than that. Not only Bywell and Ovingham had salmon fisheries dating from medieval times – Mickley caught its share, until sewage spoiled it all. Otherwise fresh sea fish could be had from a weekly fish-hawker – Bessie Storey in my day – who toted her full 'creel' by train from Shields and then "Calla-harrin'ed her way on foot two miles from Stocksfield station, happily getting lighter as she came. Even with the creel in the goods van, Bessie must have been lively company in the close confines of a train compartment.

"Fresh fruit" or more likely: "Ripe Bananas" after they became all the rage and posters had to warn of the risks of broken limbs from slipping on discarded banana skins, was called from flat-carts. The independent fruiterer called on a different day from the Co-op, so fruit and vegetables were fresh all week; most of them came in wooden boxes of one kind or another, all of them having a supplementary use. Apple boxes made just the right size nest boxes for hens – double compartments, like some privies. Orange boxes had open spaces in the sides so were useful for transporting poultry. Both were handy for storage and were disposable so plentiful. Banana 'crates', on the other hand were robust and returnable and shuttled back and forth for ages on carts and trains, between warehouse and shop. The bananas, being fragile and prone to frost damage, had to be well protected, packed in straw in winter; so the containers were of heavy board, 3ft. 6 ins. long, 20 ins. wide, and 12 ins. deep. Just imagine what could be done with these when they finally became damaged and discarded ... rabbit hutches, hen 'crees', pigeon 'duckets' – you name it and the banana box could either make or mend it. Best of all though, for little boys, it made the 'bogey' – personal transport for riding on or moving anything from coals to little sister – the year-round equivalent of the sledge. A board from a banana box formed the chassis and sitting area; a short crosspiece, held to the front end by, and free to turn on, a heavy bolt, which were easy enough to come by in a pit village, carried the axle, fixed underneath with big fencing staples, and small wheels from a discarded pram. This provided the steering, by a short length of rope, or foot-power. Two more pram wheels for the rear completed the basic set-up. Big wheels looked classy. An open-fronted box to sit in, cut from a banana box and padded with an old cushion, provided 'Rolls Royce' standards of finishing touches. The grandest might even warrant decoration with a bit of leftover paint!

Meat, to the call of "Bootcher" or "Butchorr," had a special cart. Enclosed except at the back, it was nicely painted (with what was left over from bogies?) and scrupulously clean. All around the inside were 'S' shaped hooks for hanging the meat, with bigger cuts laid out on the scrubbed 'floor' which

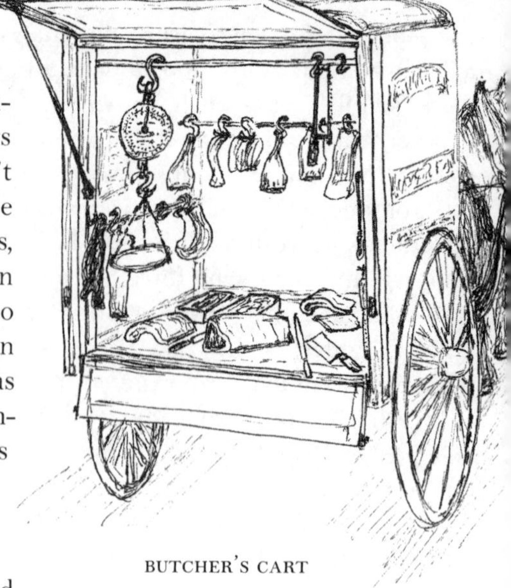

BUTCHER'S CART

had a full-width, thick but well-worn chopping board, with knives and choppers at the ready. A hack-saw hung on a hook. Most things hung on hooks, so that they couldn't fall about when the cart moved. The brass-faced, spring-balance scales, with a round tray hung below on chains, for weighing the meat, also hung on a hook, but it was taken down when the cart moved, as it was free to swing about and cause damage or be damaged. It always seemed to be 'down at the back', this butcher's cart, and swung up and down as the meat was cut, and I worried in case the horse moved just as the butcher was bringing down the chopper. The customer stood out in the weather for this service at the door, as did the butcher and his horse. The projecting canopy was only a token gesture – the wind always blew the wrong way. For indoor service or a better choice, although the cart carried a good range, unless the previous customer had bought the cut you wanted, there was the walk up the hill to the shop – one way or another the weather had to be faced.

More Shops

Yes, Mickley had a butcher's shop – Co-op of course. There had been a previous one, Potts, the name, in the Miners Arms part of the village. Potts had fingers in a few pies – Hare and Hounds pub, farm, shop.

The butchery development of the Co-op was up the hill on Eastgate Bank, past the side of the main building with its big-doored loading bay into which the delivery carts were backed. You can reverse lorries if you like – carts were 'backed'. Behind this bay was a messy, smelly cubby-hole, which could be reached from the back of the shop, and at a goodly distance from the food, where paraffin was kept in forty-gallon drums. Not the best of things for a food shop to sell, but it had to be done, paraffin by then was a necessity, and who else to sell it? Credit to the shopkeepers, not a lot of paraffin-flavoured food was sold.

Paraffin lamps filled the lighting gap between candles and electricity, and 'hurricane' lamps were the main source of light outdoors in stables, cow-houses or netties, and in the dark back areas of the Co-op where the paraffin was kept. Paraffin lamps lighted trains, some carts, although candles were the norm for these, and the front and rear of 'velocipedes', one of which was made in Newcastle by Geo. Angus in 1866 and demonstrated in Pilgrim Street 'before large crowds'. Everyone loved a crowd. Domestic paraffin lamps, having first been made in New York (USA) as long ago as 1854, were by now the normal lighting in all but the poorest of homes. The standard type lamp varied enormously in design, quality and appearance, but it was basically a glass, brass or copper bowl to contain the paraffin, mounted on a stalk on a heavy base. Atop the bowl and screwed securely to it but removable for filling except where there was a separate filler-cap, a brass fitting held cotton 'wicks' one or so inches wide and twelve long. These hung down into the paraffin and absorbed it, and were adjustable, up and down, in close-fitting guides which controlled the amount of saturated wick exposed for burning. The wick had to be trimmed and cleaned daily and adjusted to the height required for the optimum light; too much wick and it produced a poor light and smoke, which sooted-up the 'chimney', which was the clever bit. It was made of very thin, fragile glass, screened the flame from draughts and created a column of hot air rising through the funnel which caused the flame to burn steady and bright; its shape also magnified and intensified the light, which was good, and warm, easy on the eyes for reading white paper; and the smell was not unpleasant. But the lamp was never placed under paper Christmas decorations, for the column of hot air made for conflagration! The chimney also had to be cleaned daily, with great care, as it was easily broken. The proper stuff for cleaning was newspaper – nothing else would do, could do, the job properly – it imparted a sparkle. Newspapers had many uses. And a lot of paraffin was sold by the Co-op …

The Co-op Cobbler

There was a little way to go up the hill before the butcher's shop was reached. First there was 'the cobblers'. This was an odd, interesting wooden hut of a place with steps up from the road, that were more or less under cover, with the door positioned a bit precariously at the top. The remainder of the rather meagre frontage was taken up with window, facing west and on to the road, with behind it a workbench with two cobblers at their lasts, getting the best of the light.

Just within the door was a tiny counter, rough and cheap – nothing grand about the cobblers – where you plonked the footwear for examination, and, if not too far gone, acceptance for repair. One of the men bent at the bench in the window would finish what he was doing, which usually involved using up the tacks gripped between his lips, straighten his back, which no doubt was a welcome relief, and come to the counter. There he would determine the nature of the repair, enter it on a label with the name, and the day for collection, and place the footwear, in rotation, on the shelf along the far wall,

THE COBBLER'S SHOP

behind the only piece of machinery in the shop. This was a huge, floor-standing heavy duty treadle-operated sewing machine, not a lot used but quicker and easier than the hand-stitching of not so long ago, for the odd bit of work on uppers (soles were nailed – boots had welts), and for making belts in quiet moments. There weren't many quiet moments, boots were always needed in a hurry. "Ready next Monday", he might say, and if they were shoes and your only pair, which they surely would be, you were stuck at home without them. Pleading for them for the weekend, if he was in a good mood and kindly Mr Elliot – Norman – of my ken, usually was, would elicit, "Alright then, I'll try to have them ready for Friday." He always did; his pleasure was in the pleasing.

In the words of the song ... 'Prince and commoner, poor and rich, stand in need of the cobbler's stitch'. Few in Mickley were rich (possibly the Manager!) but everyone depended pretty heavily on the cobbler. Not much for the stitch either; this was a place for repairing, not making; more for tacks – but what would rhyme with 'tacks'? The cobblers didn't go in much for slippers and shoes either ('shoon'? – what some folk will do for a rhyme!), but were more for boots and pit boots. Substantial stuff, made for hard work and durability and from real leather; this area was noted for it.

Leather was the principal export from the Tyne, long before coal reared its ugly, profitable head. Fine leather and superb craftsmanship made 'Hexham Tans' supreme in the world of gloves, when they were an essential part of good dress. I knew of a man, you could say an eccentric I suppose, who always bought two pairs of gloves, so that he had one for each hand for warmth, and one to carry! Richardsons, up the road at Wheelbirks, tanned leather in Newcastle, possibly using bark stripped from the oaks of High Close Wood, where I now sit writing. This bark was as valuable a by-product of the woods as were hazel rods in the days of the corfes, and this industry went on for much longer; indeed there is still a limited demand, for high-class leather tanning, but no one here gathers bark any more. Maybe I could be more profitably occupied ...

The smell of leather, properly tanned, was another of those pungent symbols of simple times; it permeated not only the air, but the very walls of the cobbler's shop; a good, comfortable smell. It came from the pile of stiff slabs lying alongside the bench, from which the cobbler selected a sheet to suit the repair in hand. Thin for ladies and childrens' shoes, thicker for boys' boots, and pretty hefty stuff for pit boots, which probably took the worst punishment of any footwear ever made.

Pit boots were mostly what the cobbler mended. Nothing shoddy about these, they could be repaired over and over again, because they were properly 'welted', with substantial, durable stitching of the undersole to the 'uppers' with thick waxed linen thread. The main sole was nailed to the undersole around the edges and could be pulled off when worn through with a pair of fearsome-looking pincers. The cobbler in the window spent a fair part of his life doing this sort of thing, then drawing to rough size around the boot and cutting out the sole from his leather slab, with a sharp knife. Men who made a living cutting things kept their tools sharp.

The sole-less boot was then placed upside-down on a last of appropriate size. Lasts were cast-iron foot-shaped supports that fitted into footwear to give support for nailing. Portable ones were like 'Manx legs' with three feet of different sizes and a heel. My father used one of these for repairing our shoes at home. The cobbler had a range of different sizes, fixed to his bench The roughly shaped piece of leather was put in place and fixed with two tacks, then nailed firmly all round, close to the edge but not too close, with brass tacks. They had to be brass, to wear at about the same rate as the leather, otherwise the points worked their way through into the foot in the boot, and jolly painful it was too!

Heels were built up with odd bits of scrap leather, nailed securely layer upon layer; they took a lot of punishment. All, sole and layers of heel, were trimmed off with another sharp, curved knife and finished off neatly with a rasp; then painted, if 'good' shoes, with black or brown stuff and thoroughly buffed. If work boots, or hard-on-boots-little-boys boots, the soles would be 'hobnailed'. Hob-nails had tapered dome heads like miniature steel haystacks and were nailed in profusion in patterns suited to the mood and artistic bent of the cobbler. Hob-nails, with curved steel heel and toe-plates, took the brunt of the wear – saved the soles, as it were. They could be dangerously slippery on a hard surface and hobnailed schoolboys took due advantage of this feature, especially on ice. They made a rare noise, and were responsible for another of the memorable noises of my arrival in Mickley – the sound of an entire shift of pitmen trudging home down East gate Bank, not in step like marching troops, but like the approach of a charging storm of grapeshot over slate roofs. Now there's a noise to conjure with – not many people have heard that! Hob-nails were not good on wood and the bare boards of Mickley School had to be one and three-quarter inches thick to resist them.

Dubbing completed the treatment for work-boots, pit and farm. Let us not forget the farm workers, slaving away in all weathers. They also needed their boots mending and proofing and welcomed the Co-op cobbler as much as did the miner. Dubbing provided the proofing; it was just grease and was absorbed into the leather for waterproofing and preservation – but not for appearance!

That then, was the 'cobblers', smells and all. Oh – I nearly forgot. For winter warmth, for cobbling was not a warming job and handling small tacks with frozen fingers not easy, in the corner sat a round, coke-eating, cast-iron stove, cosy-ing the little shop and its workers and welcoming the customers. The tacks themselves would be warmed from being held in cobblers' mouths; this the time-honoured way of keeping them handy for use.

Understandably, conversation was not a strong feature between cobblers, and a coughing, sneezing one a positive danger to all within range.

The Cart Yard

Alongside the cobbler's shop through a wide gate was the stable and cartyard, again with its own peculiar smells, of manure and horses, hay and horse-leather (different from cobbling leather). More akin to farm than shop.

The carts, flat for general use and the van for meat, rested from work outside on the cobbles with their long shafts pointing to the sky. Stables built of yellow bricks similar to West Mickley houses provided winter quarters for the normal complement of two horses, who still had to be fed at weekends. There was space for the harness to hang on long wooden pegs, and it had to be dressed from time to time with 'leather soap', and polished, especially for Carnival days. A loft above held hay, with a hatch for dropping it through into the 'hay-heck' (rack) below, just as on a farm. There was a trough below the hay for a feed of oats after a hard day's work, and a big earthenware water trough outside, made at Eltringham Fireclay Works no doubt. All very compact and close to the main shop, which could be reached directly at ground level for loading, or at a higher level by way of the overhead covered passageway which was reached from the cart yard and was used by the dividend seekers. For loading the meat the butchers shop was also close at hand, next up from the yard.

Come the summer, getting the horses 'yoked' into their respective carts was more of a bother. They had to be walked from what we youngsters called the 'Store' field, beside the school, where they spent balmy evenings and short nights with their feet on the sward, feasting on fresh sweet grasses. First they had to be caught; would you fancy trundling a heavy cart around the streets all day, when you could be lying on the grass in the sun? Neither did they, and it sometimes took the lure of a sugar lump (Co-op of course) to entice them to work. It was even known for the cart to be late in leaving on its rounds if the mood was particularly intransigent. The walk to work was along the main road past my home and my memory is of this twice daily routine, to and fro, accompanied by the horse-man, Isaac, except on Sundays, when they were excused work and didn't even have to go to church like some horses. Isaac had a club foot and walked slowly, but horses were very accommodating that way. I long believed, and no one ever said otherwise, that this deformity was due to the foot, when young, being stood upon by a horse! I always held horses' hooves in highest regard and gave them a wide berth; they were so big, and hard, with iron shoes, and you never could be sure where they would put them down!

Next up the hill was a track, just wide enough for a horse and cart, leading from the road between two rows of miners' gardens, along which loads of manure were delivered.

The Butchers

Then, at last, the last of the shops – the Butchers. This was a red brick building, and built later than the main shop. Bigger than the cobblers but still quite small, the window also faced the road and west, perhaps not a good idea for a meat shop.

Inside was all white tiled walls (glazed brick, actually, like public toilets of the time) and cleanliness; not sterility, like today, but scrubbed wood and some easily washed marble, with liberal fresh sawdust on the floor every day. The chopping blocks were huge, trunk-of-a-tree sized, and the tools to match: full-sized meat demanded full-sized knives, choppers and saws. Poor they were, no doubt, but vegetarian not, these Mickley folk. They ate their share and more, of meat, especially on Sundays, when the 'roast 'was a ritual.

The meat hung 'whole' on hooks on rails and was cut to size as needed. Butchers were strong (they ate a lot of meat!) for lugging whole animals about. These animals walked to 'work' in the slaughterhouse behind the shop – there was no other way; even if they weren't local they had to walk from the station, and perhaps from Scotland before the railways arrived. They mostly lived a good life in the fields nearby and when the time came they walked the quiet early morning lanes to an end in better surroundings than a modern 'humane' abattoir. Travel between markets could now be by train and drovers became almost obsolete, but in the country meat was still on the hoof.

Being a butcher in those days meant killing and dressing the animals on or near the premises, they could not escape the reality of what they were doing; but people then had not gone sentimental over animals. They did not imbue them with human feelings, thoughts and emotions, but they treated them, mostly, with respect, so killing was all in the day's work, as was eating meat; it was known and accepted that it didn't come from factories.

Regard for any vegetarians who are still with me, denies my going into any gory details, but the Butchers was a very important part of the village life and must take its place.

The Co-op Manager and his Home

The last building in the Co-op complex, with its high yard wall bounding the butcher's yard, was the Manager's house – if anyone was to be bothered by the butchering it would be the boss!

This house was built much later than the main shop, at about the turn of the century, and was of a higher standard than ordinary workers' houses of the time, though not up to the rather grand affair in stone that the Prudhoe manager justified, but it was not bad at that – Mickley had some status, after all.

In red brick to match the butchers, like a slice off the terraces that clothed Victorian towns with solid rows, it stands well, with excellent views to the west towards Hexham. It boasted a sitting-room as well as a kitchen or living room, and a larder. There was a high-walled yard at the back with coal house and ash-closet – no 'netty' for the Manager! This would be one of the first houses in the village to have a WC, although not when it was built.

A quite attractive flight of stairs, with a handrail, newel and bannisters led to two bedrooms and a 'box' room; the 'box' borrowed for show from the better-off who had need of a storeroom for trunks, hat boxes and the like. Here it was really a third, tiny, bedroom, without a fireplace, but because of that, requiring a little open box of a ventilator through the wall above the door on to the landing; this to ensure the air circulation now required by law in bedrooms not ventilated by a chimney, to combat disease – although enough air entered through the draughty 'box' windows of the day to blow your hat off! The other bedrooms had attractive little fireplaces, which are now 'collectable', of ornate cast-iron and decorative tiles. Collectable for what, I cannot imagine – not for fires, they were seldom used even in their day except in times of sickness. Carrying coals up and ashes down, in the absence of servants – although a manager could probably afford a 'day girl' at a few shillings a week – was not indulged in unnecessarily by managers' wives. Even Managers and their families were inured to arctic-cold bedrooms.

Apart from status of a kind and a reasonable income, although Co-op employees at any level were never excessively well paid, the Manager had a job for life, unless he did something silly like 'cooking the books', which was not unheard of. Against this possibility, and presumably that of incompetence, he was required, on appointment, to give a security or bond, of quite a goodly sum – £100, at Mickley. He carried a fair bit of responsibility and needed to know his job – and usually did. He ran the Co-op and its staff of up to twenty with almost military precision and with the pride that goes with a well-run unit. Not quite on a par with the headmaster and the vicar, and way below – who wasn't? – that other manager in the village hierarchy, the Pit Manager, he nevertheless gained the respect of the people he served.

This, then, was the Co-op – the 'Store' – sole resident supplier of goods to the people.

Into the Twentieth Century

No part of the nineteenth century could not be described as a time of change; it galloped at breakneck speed and carried Mickley with it. Barely a slackening of pace accompanied the ride into the next century; development and innovation went on, but railway and pit continued to dominate.

Common cause, common interest and above all, common danger and hardship shared, draw people into close relationships, not easily understood by those without such experiences, and seldom experienced in our contemporary, comfortable, selfish world. War creates these bonds most obviously – for instance, in submarine crews, air crew, Desert Rats and Burma campaigners. Mining, however, was the most striking example of this human characteristic, of longer development and longer duration than any war. It spanned, in Mickley, one hundred and twenty years.

Building high walls to keep miners apart at home, giving them a modicum of privacy, was irrelevant in the context of life as it was lived. Hacking and shovelling coal by hand in the bowels of Mickley pits, in shallow, often wet seams, by candlelight, was indescribably horrible – and dangerous. Death lurked in every shadow. On 15th. November, 1866, Robert Robson, aged 14 yrs., was run over by laden tubs; he took a day to die, which was mercifully quicker than poor old Robert of Micelee all those years ago but no less awful. On 18th. March 1869 an inquest was held at Eltringham Boathouse into the death of Joseph Charlton, aged 51, who had been killed instantly by a fall of stone. A common way to go, for a miner. So it went on, year after cruel year. Miners, like soldiers under fire, got used to it, and also like soldiers under fire, they drew strength, support and comfort from their 'marras' around them, probably without knowing it, or making a show. They were all in the same boat – they needed their mates. That is not to say that they lived in perfect harmony, far from it: there were plenty of 'dustups', usually over little things. If there was a serious score to settle it could always be sorted, man to man, 'doon the gardens'.

Womenfolk mirrored their husbands, but screamed their differences from door to door, or across the street; but when illness or accident struck, the youngsters would be seen to, the garden tended, the need supplied. Crush a miner and the whole village bled.

A new baby's arrival, and they came aplenty, was a communal affair – such things could not be kept private in a place of shared experience. Even in the worst of times mothers never went short of their baby's needs. "Aal just gan and git one from wor Lizzie, she'll be done wi' hors."

Health Care

The District Nurse, who took over the role of Midwife early in the twentieth century from the 'Mrs Gamps' of the Dickens age, became revered in the Rows. The Doctor was respected but aloof and a bit mystical and feared. He was a recent phenomenon in the lives of the poor – he had to be paid for. Coppers a week, supplemented by a coal company that saw the need for a healthy work force, and increasing Council interference in health matters, covered the costs of simple health-care, and it was simple. Not a lot had changed in the world of medicine for ordinary folk since the days of Robert; either you got better or you died. Come to think of it, the wealthy fared little better except that they paid to be tortured in the name of medicine. Doctors continued to do the most gruesome things to their patients, in spite of the great advances like anaesthetics and antiseptics, but at least they were able to control pain to some extent. The pitman did what the doctor said – he never did know when the pain might be worse.

The 'Norse' (Nurse), on the other hand, lived in 'digs' (South View, I remember), in the miners' midst; was poorly paid – £1.3s a week – and worked whenever the need arose, night or day, weekdays or Sundays; sunshine or snow. They did as she said too, and loved her; she was a welcome guest in every home and she, above all others, could walk the streets and lonely roads at night in absolute safety. Anyone accosting, let alone molesting, the Norse would have had the whole village to answer to.

The last of the old-style pit village District Nurses still lives along the road at Branch End, well into her nineties; still known as The Nurse (posh place, Branch End), she is not above giving a private, free, consultation. This doughty couple, doctor and nurse, covered most of the medical needs of the village, now attempted by a veritable army of motorised, computerised assorted medical people, backed up by the most fantastic panoply of technological-miracle hospitals. She, Nurse Ingle (Stokoe now) cost £1.3s. a week; the NHS currently costs, I believe, upwards of one BILLION pounds a week – we lose count. But now there are more of us to be ill, and illness is different …

Turn of the century Mickley boasted the lesser, but still nasty infectious childhood diseases – mumps, measles, chickenpox, – but also had its outbreaks of the worse ones – scarlet fever, diphtheria, meningitis, and a steady toll of 'consumption' – tuberculosis. This ran through families, and the miracle was that there was not a lot more of it, given the living conditions. No doubt the good clean air, free for the stepping outdoors, was a valuable buffer against some respiratory and infectious diseases. Fresh air was certainly the preferred treatment for TB; fresh air and a bit of decent food. Perhaps it should be noted today.

We, some time later, had only mumps and measles in our house, but I well remember my father's firm rule against swapping comics, for fear of something worse, and our scheming, probably foolish but enjoyable evasion of it. If you bought a *Rover* with your precious pocket money, how could you not swap it for a *Wizard*, it for a *Hotspur*, and it for a *Skipper*? You could have ten-pen'orth of read for tuppence! And scarlet fever, we thought, was what someone else got.

The consequences of scarlet fever were dire; the victim was whisked off into a dread state called 'isolation' and the house, and everything in it, was fumigated. I never witnessed this but believe it was pretty dreadful; it had to be thorough, perhaps it worked or at least helped. Isolation certainly helped to control the spread and in addition, family contacts skipped school for three weeks, which was a bonus, but had work sent home, although, as it could not be returned for checking, it could easily be dodged. The unfortunate victim spent six weeks in isolation. Cholera and 'the fever' (typhus/typhoid, and scarlet) had pushed M.C. Co. into making available two cottages in the village for isolation, but by the turn of the century local authorities were making provision for isolation in proper hospitals. A huge,

SQUADRON 1248, AUTHOR 2ND RIGHT, FRONT ROW
THE FEVER HOSPITAL

hutted place was built at Woolley near Hexham, where air abounded and not much else, solely for the nursing of TB victims. On the breezy hilltop between Old Mickley and Prudhoe, which it also served, was built the 'Fever Hospital'. It was a strange little place, of wood and corrugated-iron made with two wards, girls' and boys,' holding about ten beds each, and another of those round coke-burning stoves that kept the cobblers warm, in each ward. A third room at the back and one or two cubby-holes housed staff, kitchen, stores and so-on. That was all. Fever in the poor did not command much luxury and most youngsters with Scarlet Fever were too ill to be bothered anyway. Those who were not too ill or were recovering, often suffered terrible homesickness; being away from home and family were dreadful afflictions, as bad as the fever. Thorough spoiling by kindly staff helped, but having an infectious disease was no joke and often left lifelong scars on those who survived.

I later had misgivings about lurking germs when, during Hitler's war, and the fever hospital no longer had a medical role, I got to know it pretty well. It was pressed into service as the headquarters of 1248 Squadron of the Air Training Corps and we young aspiring heroes spent a lot of happy, and hardworking time there, learning to win the war. We spent winter evenings after parade, sitting around the coke stoves that had warmed the sick, chatting and yarning before dispersing to our homes through the blackout. This was where I learned not to smoke ... Some of the lads were experimenting with cigarettes – not considered wrong or harmful then, except that we were a bit young. Being a 'Clever Alec' I decided to show off and go one better. So I raided the little 'smoking cabinet' where my father kept his pipes and borrowed a lovely black job with a long, curved stem and a small bowl. With it secreted under my uniform, I had an uncomfortable and worrying parade, but a glorious unveiling and lighting-up afterwards, leaning back on tilted chair, feet on hearth, wreathed in great clouds of blue smoke. I felt that even the C.O. was impressed, even a little envious, when he poked his head through from the back room which now housed officers rather than nurses, to see what the smoke was coming from. The lads were certainly impressed.

I was violently sick all the way home and have never since had the slightest desire to smoke!

I had occasional misgivings about the possible emergence of nasty germs that had taken up residence in our old Fever Hospital, especially when we held our 'social evenings', parties and dances. We crowded sixty or so youngsters into a room built to hold ten childrens' beds – what matter fire regulations in a war – then stirred things up by bouncing up and down (dancing!) with a fervour that oscillated walls and floor into a state of imminent collapse. Dense, fever-hospital dust filled the hot, sweaty air. But we seemed to suffer no ill-effects and who cared anyway, there was a war on – live dangerously! We took chances, 'swapped spit', with gay abandon, in the many and varied kissing games. Ah, sweet innocence, and the 'hazards' of war.

The Welfare

Coppers a week brought not only medical care. The 'Miners Welfare Fund' was set up by the coal company, towards the end of the nineteenth century, in co-operation with the workers, in an enlightened effort to bring recreation other than drinking into their lives. It was realised that contented, sober workers made better workers – although the Temperance League were forever active in the fight against the demon drink. As long ago as 1865 the 'Teetotallers of Mickley' had a picnic attended by 800 people, of whom at least 400 were served tea. 800 teetotallers in Mickley? – and what did the other 400 drink – water? The 'Welfare' needed a lot of weekly pennies to build recreation, but the Coal Co., as in school provision, was generous in providing the facilities. It built the 'Reading Room', a badly needed facility, in 1894. An uninspiring building, like a slice of North View, in white brick; it had, upstairs, one large room with a fire, chairs, tables, newspapers and books. A place for quiet recreation, peace, and

MINERS WELFARE HALL TODAY

refuge from children and washdays.

Downstairs there were two good billiards tables. Now the young blades of the village could 'miss-spend their youth' legitimately without having to go afar. This room gave leisure pleasure to hundreds, nay thousands of youngsters, through fifty years – but only if they, or their fathers, worked in the pit. I never set foot in it. Neither did the village girls; such a place was considered 'not quite suitable'. I ought to have done alright, with most of the lads inside and all the girls outside!

Football

More active amusement was to be had down at the football field – as though miners didn't get enough activity. This also was 'Welfare' and had a good wooden pavilion, with changing rooms and baths for home and away teams, and a veranda from which officials and the like could view the game in the dry. Wood or not, it also lasted fifty years, until the 'Age of Vandals'. Now, Council owned, the 'pavilion' boasts an appearance like a nuclear-bunker.

The field itself was ever open and free for any village lads who could find a ball to play with; you didn't have to be a miner's son, and there was seldom a time out of school when it did not sport a few boys 'kicking around'. A

MICKLEY FOOTBALL TEAM

fellow would walk straight from school, dodging, if he could, the ambushing mother with her irksome, delaying task or errand – better tolerated if rewarded with a slice of new bread and jam, or even condensed-milk, or even a ha'penny, in good times. If you could catch her off-guard, with a quick in, "Off to the football field", and away before she could collect her wits, you might manage a slice of fadge as you collected your pal, if he was having one to devour while walking the length of the Laa Raa to the field. Otherwise you hardly noticed the pangs of hunger if the playing was good.

The time-honoured way of collecting a pal was to stand at or near his door and call his name quietly, To-om, Joe-o, or Le-en. If he failed to emerge he'd already gone, or been caught and you tried somebody else. You never knocked – Dad might be abed. If there was nobody at the field with a ball you went home disconsolate and did chores – brought in the coals or ran errands – in the hope that they would stand you in good stead for the morrow.

Many good footballers developed their skills on this grass; miners were physically fit, very tough, and spent their spare time practising. Some would have been worth millions on today's transfer market. You will have heard of Milburns and Charltons from another mining village (and reiving ancestors?); Mickley produced its Bests, Youngs and Stokoes, Hepples and Middletons. The village team became quite well known, and Hughie Gallagher, of Newcastle United fame, made a guest appearance. His shorts were too long. Bobbie Stokoe, of recent times, played for Newcastle in their cup-winning team, and managed Sunderland to a cup win. Malcolm Young, a son of East Street and related to the carter who hanged himself, won his way to Cambridge University and there gained his Blues in soccer and rugby, and played rugby for England. In earlier times George Brown played for England, Huddersfield, Aston Villa, Burnley and Leeds and won three consecutive 1st Division Championship medals. That football field certainly made an excellent starting-ground for sportsmen.

The pitch had a pronounced slope at one corner, which gave the home side a pronounced advantage!

Demarcation between spectators and players was by thick, rusty, steel haulage-wire from the pit, stapled to railway sleepers on end and very robust, to withstand the pressures of the crowds – well ... Although there could be a hundred or two for an important game, and tempers not beyond fraying. Budding Tarzans had a high old time on the boundary wire.

Being 'selected' to play football for the school team was one of my first and unforgettable experiences on coming to Mickley. No one had seen me play, but I could run like the wind, especially in my once-a-year new sandshoes. I had kicked a small ball around, in the road and on grassy field; balls came in sponge-rubber, or were hollow, and all bonny colours until they wore off, and were used in any number of reflex-developing group or individual games – the most used and beloved of all boys' toys. With a bit of luck you got one, with your hard-boiled, onion-peeling-dyed egg, and an orange, from Auntie Cissie for Easter. They were easily lost, but I was the world's expert at finding them, so was never without one, either my own or somebody else's long lost. They did not amount, however, to real footballs. A spoilt neighbour where I hailed from had a real football, a 'casor', that was made of segments of stitched leather containing an inflatable rubber 'inner' like a spherical bike tube. It was inflated with a bicycle-pump, if the adaptor could be found, and the hole in the outer case through which the 'inner' was inserted, was laced-up tightly with a leather boot-lace. This laced part was the bit that got you on the forehead or worse still, on the nose, on an ice-cold day when the ball was water-logged ... yes I know, you are not supposed to head the ball with your nose, but we're not all experts! Balls, being leather and subject to wetting, were dubbined, which made them slippery as well as heavy. It took a real man to kick a wet ball from corner to goal mouth, let alone the length of the pitch, or even halfway. I doubt our modern miracle-players would have an unnerving time if the plastic ran out!

That is by-the-by; my neighbour, bless him, always ran home with his 'casor' under his arm if he wasn't allowed to score the goals, so I'm afraid I had had little practice with a real ball when I took the field for Mickley. Neither had I set boot on a proper field, with white lines and goal posts other than piled-up coats which were softer than stones or lumps of wood for markers. Nor did I know the team positions other than goalkeeper, which was self-evident, nor even the number of players in the team. Alright, I was an ignorant boy – but I knew of Drake and Hapgood, but only because I saw their pictures on cigarette cards. Otherwise football was just a boy's street game.

I had never seen boots with leather studs on their soles, although I knew that hobnailed, steel toe-capped boots were a considerable advantage over sandshoes except in matters of speed. I quickly became a firm advocate of 'shin-guards' when I discovered them. These were like miniature cricket pads made of cane rods stitched into a casing of leather or canvas so that they could be folded round the ankles inside stockings to protect the shins from painful kicks and grazes. Not only footballs were for men – football boots were pretty fearsome too.

So, I was selected to play for Mickley Council School, at Left Back, so I was told, against Ovington, across the river. I knew not where 'left-back' was, and I kicked only with my right foot. No matter, think of the glory! When the euphoria faded and I learned why I had been selected; it faded further. Ovington being such a small place, it was unable to field eleven players of an age to make fair combat with places like Prudhoe and Mickley, so these bigger schools were allowed to field only players of eleven years and under. We had eleven such 'players' (the dregs), Ovington only five – and six robust twelve and thirteen-year-old-worldly-wise-footballers. They even knew the team positions.

Furthermore, the fellow who so generously let me borrow his boots, just because he wasn't playing, he said, was a traitor. I think his dad came from Ovington.

We, The Team, foregathered at our school and proceeded down the hill past Bewick's place – how he would have laughed – to the river, boots slung on laces around our necks, 'strips' rolled under our arms, so that the whole village could be sure that we were the Footballers – no mistake. There must have been something else on because not many supporters supported us. A teacher came but I think that he was only there to row the boat; two loads, six in a boat. Then the long trudge up the hill, the weaker ones already exhausted and enthusiasm fading, to the school, sadly now long gone, where we changed into our glorious black and yellow striped shirts, like wasps on edge. The sight of ourselves in all this glory renewed our zest for the task ahead. Not for long; first there was the walk from school to field, a few hundred yards – or was it miles – up the hill. I knew the moment I set foot to road that borrowed boots are a mistake. You have heard of the traditional Chinese torture of 'a thousand cuts'? Believe me, it has nothing on borrowed football boots ...

Remember the little gem of information I gave you about using brass tacks for soling boots so that they wore at about the same rate as the leather? Well, the fellow who fixed the studs to these boots used sword-steel – LONG steel, RAPIER SHARP steel. By the time I reached the field there were at least a thousand half-inch long spikes penetrating my feet and I fully expected to see blood spurting through the lace-holes at any minute. We lost 13 to 1. Don't ask who scored the 1 – not I, for sure. I think they blamed me.

That ignominious walk of agony home, trying to pretend we weren't footballers, was assuredly the longest of my life. But the following pay-day my mother came home from shopping with a pair of boys' football boots.

In fairness, it should be recorded that I later earned my place on the team and had my mother take my photograph, in our backyard, with her 'box' camera, all lashed-up in my stripy strip, arms folded, just like a right-enough footballer. Played at 'right-half-back', I did (no such thing now) and scored my only ever goal in my last game at school, to give us a half-share in THE CUP. I think I must have been standing in the goal-mouth when the ball bounced off me. Don't ask me to explain how we shared a cup!

'Thought my playing days were over with my school days, ('hung up my boots'?) but came the war and my legs were voted the best in the A.T.C. team by the town (Prudhoe) girls! What fame, what glory – what opportunity – but I didn't learn about opportunity until later; too late, too late. It all began at Ovington football field, where I 'cut my feet', as it were.

I was supposed to be writing about Mickley Welfare football field. There is not much more to it, except that it has been played on for a hundred years, has had its sagging corner levelled to please the visitors and is still played on regularly, but not so much by children. The school would need more help than did Ovington to field a team; they only go up to nine years now at Mickley School.

The Church Hall

In 1885 £500 was raised by subscription, for the building of a Church Hall, or Parish Hall as it became known, and it was duly built, cheek-by-jowl with the Miners' Welfare Reading Room. I puzzle yet why the buildings that came first to the village in the way of welfare, recreation and enlightenment were built on the worst possible sites, even allowing that the whole place sits on a hillside. This was a daft place to put what was the social nub of the village; the land must have been dirt-cheap, or useless for anything else.

But it was a jolly good village hall by any standards, and did a right royal job for seventy-odd years, until struck by a plague of our age in the form of one of those chaps with 'Qualifications' who pronounced it 'unsafe' and it was sold to someone prepared to take the risk. It is still going strong in another role. The role of Church Hall was transferred next-door to the by then

PARISH HALL TODAY

redundant Reading Room, which was even more awkward, and dismal and inadequate by comparison. Perhaps it's no concern of mine, I'm not a church man; but the village could have done itself better.

The old hall was big enough to contain any social activity the church or village cared to organise, in the days when entertainment was still largely home-made. It was the place for wedding receptions, if miners had them, whist drives, and various celebrations – 'the relief of Mafeking'. There were good kitchens, and anterooms divided by folding partitions, like schoolrooms, where met the Sunday School and any committee that felt disposed to meet. It was a time of committees and committees weren't much use without meetings, so the anterooms did a thriving trade.

The small stage was just about big enough to hold the 'Prudhoe Gleemen' if one or two of them were indisposed and they all breathed in at the same time. Concerts were ever popular, either of local talent or itinerant performers; the tradition of the minstrels and mummers died slowly. 'Martin Bredis, Strong Man' once performed here, for a penny on Saturday. He amazed the village boys with his remarkable feats, like knocking six–inch nails through a plank of wood with his hand. The hall was packed, he was applauded and shouted to the rafters; there was nothing, is nothing, like live performers, and all the village boys who could find a six–inch nail had sore hands for a week. A few kitchen tables got a bit knocked about, too.

This Strong Man in the leopard-skin drape, from Europe, perhaps a refugee – he had few words of English, went on his sad way, putting on his act, gleaning his pennies from village hall to village hall. Memories lingered on, there are one or two who remember him yet, and others in the same tradition.

Mickley Band

Mickley Prize Silver Band rehearsed in the Parish Hall. It wasn't silver, just looked it. It was all shiny and impressive and made sometimes – mostly in fact, pleasant sounds. This was another of the institutions that miners wrapped themselves in as insulation from the harsh world (underworld?) of mining.

The instinct in man to make pleasant noises, evinced in the days of early Micelee in simple pipes and rattling sticks, developed by travelling minstrels playing tunes of their own creation, or passed by ear through generations, came forth in mining Mickley in the form of The Band. The printing revolution instigated by Caxton all those years ago made possible for the Common Man not only books but sheet music, which enabled him to share with the Masters the joys of beautiful sounds, by learning to transpose dots on paper into notes in the ear. The process could be excruciating.

Learning to play a musical instrument requires a high degree of tolerance in those around the learner. In the tight, congested conditions of the Raas this tolerance must have been tested to the limit; but, as in most good things, the end result justified the effort. Apart from the satisfaction of personal achievement the cumulative, combined effect embodied in The Band gave immense pleasure to village people who otherwise had little access to music other than of the simplest kind. That was in addition to pride in 'our' band – especially when it came home from a competition clutching the right to the title 'Prize' Band.

MICKLEY COLLIERY BAND

The cult of the brass band, and they were all brass, under the silver skin, sprang, like the Co-op, from the grassroots of need, but cultural rather than practical. It swept the industrial north of England; every worthwhile factory and pit village had one, they vied with each other for perfection and prestige, and went off to competitions in great excitement, instruments shining, and bedecked in uniforms copied from Ruritania. Bands cost a lot more than a Welsh choir or Prudhoe Gleemen to set up, voices coming free, instruments and uniforms expensive, but they got generous help from factory and pit owners and subscriptions from appreciative villagers. Mickley had its voices and contributed its share to Prudhoe Gleemen who gave their occasional, excellent concerts in the Parish Hall, but it was The Band that gave the village its musical heart.

The Band marched, or rather walked, not being of a military nature, about the place on special occasions such as the end of wars, 'relief of Mafeking' and Royal Jubilees, followed by hordes of children and admired by the village at its door. On May Day they led the procession of decorated 'floats' and carts of various kinds carrying arrays of gorgeous girls dressed in their best, often specially made. This is what the girls must have been doing when the lads were playing billiards! They vied for the title of 'Queen of the May' and the horses for 'best turned out', and 'floats' (flat carts), for 'best decorated'. The horses were worth seeing with manes and tails plaited and beribboned, leather shining and brasses gleaming, carts bedecked with balloons, ribbons and coloured drapes of red, white and blue usually, because it would double for any occasion; bells jangling and jingling. A lot of time was spent

MAYDAY 'FLOAT' ARRIVING AT FOOTBALL FIELD,
LOW ROW ON RIGHT, EAST STREET ABOVE

MAY DAY CELEBRATION

preparing, but it was fun time. The procession usually assembled at Branch End, with a great fussing and commotion – horse and cart processions are not easy to order, horses get excited too – and proceeded by the best route to give the most viewers a look, to the Football Field. Here everything that could be judged was judged, prizes awarded, horses rested, then the fun began. Maypole dancing as of yore – sports, side-shows, feats of strength for the men, competitions of quoits and darts, perhaps wrestling – but no jousting! There were teas and buns, perhaps served by the 'Temperance League:' a proper 'Fair', as of old. While the Band played on.

The May Days I remember were wet.

Bandsmen, like us all, needed Christmas at home, so we had our carols played around the streets on New Year's Morning and lovely they were too, especially on a snowy morn, except maybe for those with a hangover, of which there were surely enough. Hangovers must have been a trial for bandsmen – I doubt if many, if any, were temperate in Mickley, in spite of the 'League'. Keeping close company with a noisy great bass drum and a hangover must have been particularly irksome to the drummer. 'Christians Awake' would perhaps have suited him better on Christmas Morn.

The band played its last carols in 1958 and now the only band in the area is called Ovington but isn't; it draws its players from all over the area, and plays at Agricultural Shows and such occasions. Anyway, who needs a brass band, with transistor radios and 'Pop' music?

The ancient Fair, where goods and wares were bought sold and exchanged, had also been a place of fun – clowns, fire-eaters, sword-swallowers, strongmen like Mr Bredis, dancers and minstrels, tricksters of every kind, all out to make a penny from those able to afford to pay for a bit of pleasure, or from the gullible. Victorian England developed this fun side of life to a high degree, after fixed shops had replaced fairs and mobile traders. There were race-meetings like the immortalised 'Blaydon Races', agricultural shows and institutions like the 'Hoppins' on the Town Moor in Newcastle. On Ryton 'Willows', a flat area by the river, there were roundabouts and 'shuggy-boats' (big swings) and a kiosk where could be bought a pot of tea to go with the picnic.

Picnics were cheap pleasure for Mickley folk – everyone could afford a picnic. All that was needed was a fine day, a grassy bank 'over the Bullions Hills' or by the river; banana sandwiches, and ice-cold, delicious sparkling spring water that came forth from the hillside though a rusty, moss-covered old iron pipe into a stone trough shared with the animals of the field. Does your imagination run to water that was a treat to drink? To lying face-up on the harebell-nodding springy sward watching the soaring skylark heaven-bent on rapturous song? or face-down, making daisy-chains. Or sitting up to test friends and siblings, with buttercups under the chin, to see if they liked butter. They always did, unless the day had turned gloomy.

The Seaside

A train could be taken to the seaside, where the picnic was on the beach, giving rise, in our house anyway, to the name 'SAND-wiches'(!). There could be bought for a ha'penny that miracle confection, 'candy floss', or its making could be watched without charge, the watching being better value than the eating I reckoned. A stick of rock to take home would be a ha'penny, penny or tuppence – the entire spending money – but would have through the middle, that other miracle of confectionary-making, proclaiming in red letters where you had been; Tynemouth, or Whitley Bay.

If you could not afford rock there was always seaweed to take home, for forecasting the weather; or shells for listening to the distant waves or mermaids singing. There was the temptation, if you dared, to take a little crab from a pool for your sister. All day could be spent building a sand castle, even with help and the pretty tin pail and wooden spade that you couldn't afford to buy but which your spoiled sister had got last year and you had remembered to bring to show off on the train that you were seaside-bound. Only a few sad minutes to watch the demolition of your fragile fortress by the relentless tide – in spite of frantic efforts at defence. Boys of a romantic, seafaring disposition could sit on a rock and do a 'Boyhood of Raleigh', watching the numerous ships leave the Tyne for distant shores – or more likely with coals for London. Many a budding sailor felt his first yearning to explore the oceans on a day trip to the seaside. Today he would be hard-pressed to see a ship – with luck, maybe a ferry to Norway.

Formerly there was great confidence in the therapeutic properties of 'the waters' (spa), and sea air. Thomas Bewick took his dying sister to stay at the seaside in the hope that it would better her. Our nearest spa is at Haydon Bridge; the water tastes and smells like rotten eggs, if you know what that is like, and perhaps is why Haydon Bridge is not as prosperous as Bath or Harrogate ... or is their water just as horrible, but their promotion better. Tynemouth air is farther than Haydon Spa but doesn't smell so bad.

The 'Coast' certainly has plenty of sea air; usually cold, wild and wet, sea air; and I cannot for the life of me understand why anyone would believe that it could possibly do anyone or anything any good. I would not trade my grassy bank for a thousand seasides – although the train journey was fun. At least Blackpool had attractions other than seaweed and candy-floss, so the posters on the train said; but who could go to Blackpool from Mickley?. Not yet awhile.

The 'Royal'

Mickley folk and their children could also train-it to Newcastle, and they did. We know, because the School Log tells us that, on July 14th, 1887, the school was closed because 'many of the children were going to the Royal Agricultural Show with their parents'. The Royal Show, best in the land, travelled from place to place in those days and came to rest on the Town Moor that year. It was too good to miss.

Were pitmen interested in agricultural shows? If all of the fathers took a day off the pit would close; if only farm children went, that would hardly close the school. Perhaps the Headmaster wanted to go – it was something of an occasion. The school did close. If this happened at every school within rail-reach of the Town Moor there must have been a mighty throng of carbolic-scrubbed, Sunday-best-dressed youngsters and their parents, looking at carbolic-scrubbed, Sunday-best-dressed cows, sheep and horses. Mickley Junction must have been chaotic. Not being a 'proper' station, although in the timetables – it had five passenger trains a day, the first, 6.15 a.m. to Newcastle – 9–20 Carlisle; the last, 7 p.m. to Newcastle, 8 p.m. Hexham, with two trains only on Sundays – it boasted no waiting room or proper ticket-office – just a room in an adjoining cottage with a hole in a small window for serving tickets through. There were only short wooden platforms that were 'temporary' for seventy-five years, and no fancy iron stairs like those at Prudhoe and posh Stocksfield for crossing the line and looking down on the trains. A good level-crossing with gates large and small was controlled, night and day, from a proper signalbox, by relays of signal men. It handled a lot of traffic, did Mickley Junction, in its heyday.

There was a bit of a crush then, on Show Day, but crowds were comforting to nervous, imaginative children (and some adults!), embarking on journeys to far-distant places like Newcastle. Not everyone could get on the first train that came because it was already full of excited day-trippers from Stocksfield, Riding Mill and stations west. But there would be as many trains as it took – excursions were meat and drink to railways.

Early railway coaches were not the most comfortable, especially those dug out of sidings on special days. So I reckon that by the time the village contingent had completed the return journey, with a hard day of pleasure at the show in between, and climbed the weary Station Bank to home, collective parental tempers would be pretty frayed around the edges. Work next day would seem a welcome relief. The 'Royal', though, would fill childish memories for ever, and be the subject of 'composition' at school – you didn't get a day off for nothing.

This 'day out', special though it was, indicated a degree of 'prosperity' amongst workers, and a means to indulge, courtesy of the railway, in pleasures to be found only away from the village, including, for the better-off with the inclination, Music Hall and the Theatre. Steam was opening up the world for workers.

The Village Show

Ambitious ideas brought home from the 'Royal' and gleaned from books and magazines – gardening magazines for garden-crazy Victorians – set going Village Flower Shows, as distinct from Agricultural Shows and traditional fairs. The main feature of the Village Show, which, in Mickley, was held in the Football Field, was a large Marquee. It housed long rows of trestle tables on which were 'staged' hundreds of entries in the various classes of flowers, vegetables, and, under 'crafts' and 'domestic', anything that ingenuity could think up to test local skills and artistry, like jam, cakes and bread, embroidery, knitwear, corn dollies and jet jewellery. Entries were set out the night before where feasible, and guarded overnight, or arranged early in the morning. Judging started early and was done by impartial experts brought from afar if possible, against the risk of angry losers!. There were very few of these; it was all taken in good part. Prizes amounted to only a shilling or two; it was the WINNING that counted – taking home the treasured First Prize red card. The best gardeners festooned their sheds and greenhouses with them, and boasted like mad.

HALL YARDS FARM FLOWER SHOW

Sweet peas, roses and hosts of other flowers; bread; sun-warmed canvas, perfumed the Marquee air, and foot-crushed damp turf – more smells for memory's stockpile.

Lesser tents housed refreshments, top-notch stuff by the village ladies, and possibly beer, if 'Mickley Total Abstinence Society' had failed to get their way; and all manner of side-shows and stalls – balloons, noisy cardboard trumpets, celluloid windmills on sticks, flags, and gold-fish in bowls, condemned to death. All lots of fun, and no train needed.

Whippet racing and showing was

ever popular, and at times an 'Eighty-yard Foot Handicap' with a prize big enough to attract runners from afar, and bookmakers, just like the horse races, all of which, argued some, would bring the Show into disrepute. "There's always trouble where there's big money," they said. The 'Big Money' was all of £100.

The 'Hoppins'

When the 'Hoppins' people dispersed from their Race Week gathering on the Town Moor, reputedly the biggest of its kind in the world, if that's worth boasting about, they split into small groups and went about their various ways, spreading their noisy, raucous fun across the country. A few days here, a few there; people soon tired and anyway the money ran out. One such group attached itself to Mickley Show, although others came at other times to other sites. They chugged and rumbled their iron-wheeled fiery traction-engines along the rough-roaded length of Laa Raa North to the football field, past, within a few feet, forty-two cottages with windows cleaned and doorsteps whitened, brasses gleaming through open doors. Everyone and everything going to the show passed these houses, or their twins in Laa Raa Sooth, so they had to look their best – it was a matter of pride.

Dragged behind, like giant threshing machines, came various assorted fairground entertainments, in bits; and caravans for living in – two, perhaps three trailers, to an engine. Negotiating corners was tricky, but the trailers could always be unhitched and handled separately; there was no hurry anyway, not with traction engines.

They laagered for the night on the waste land alongside the football pitch – didn't dare set foot on it! – and spent a whole day putting things together, like Meccano sets; watched over by hordes of youngsters scheming how to raise enough money for a few rides, or wangle a free one. Little hope of that; these folk perhaps couldn't read, but were wise to all the tricks!

Come Show Day evening, and all the flowers and vegetables carried home for vase or cooking pot, and prize cards, 1st, 2nd, 3rd or just 'Commended' displayed for the time being on the mantelpiece, and it was back to the field for the 'Hoppins'. Noisy, exciting stuff this, and there was the chance of getting to know a girl!

Vying for centrepiece with the big roundabout and its up-and-down horses, was a noisy work of art: the steam-organ. It played steam-powered tunes that more than matched the whole day long Prize Silver Band, and not a musician to be seen, nor even a pause for refreshment, unless the steam ran low. The versatile, ever willing traction engine quietly did its stuff in the background of the fairground, providing the steam that moved the rod that turned the wheel that lifted the flap that dropped the arm that pressed the knob, that worked the thingamajig. In the words of the song ... 'The music goes round and round, Yo-o and it comes out here'. Anyone with no money to spend could stand all evening, and many did, watching this great machine clash its cymbals and blow its pipes to 'Blaze Away' and 'Colonel Bogey' – non-stop.

For quieter amusement, the beautifully made and decorated roundabout horses provided a sit-down ride. Again steam-driven, they went up-and-down on poles that the rider hung on to, except for the daring 'bronco buster' who raised his hands in the air for a show-off as they did their monotonous gyrations. A penny for a ride, was collected as you rode – on the hoof, as it were – by an intrepid dodger of flailing hooves who never missed a fare or dropped a penny in the works from the long column of coins in his hand. Real skill, that was!

Side-stalls abounded, where money could be lost with skill and forever the hope of a win. Such a choice ... throwing darts at playing cards on a board; coconut shies, where I'm sure the nuts were fixed with glue, so you had to buy one to take home to show how good you were; shooting galleries, with bent-barrelled guns where there were prizes; straight barrels where a chap only wanted to impress the girls with his Wild West prowess. Come to think of it, perhaps they were bent as well! There was the ancient skill of throwing wooden balls into sloping buckets, and 'Bool-a-penny' (roll). This, in my time, was my very favourite – money could be won, and skill exercised, so it appeared. I once won 3s. 7d.! Knew when to stop!

I'm a bit out of touch, but they tell me that it is possible occasionally to engage in these harmless little games, or variations of them, at Blackpool, the Town Moor, or even at one of the increasingly rare descendants of the Hoppins.

The noisy fun went on late – until ten-o'clock! But children were allowed to stay to the end because parents knew where they were. The atmosphere begat romance and many a first, tentative touch of the fingers, hold of the hand, or behind-the-shooting-gallery-in-the-dark clumsy kiss that set young couples on their way to married life, happened at the Hoppins after Mickley Show.

If the pickings were good these nomads might stay three nights, by which time the village would have had enough, then they trundled off, and life returned to humdrum normality.

Turn of the Century

Far away in the outside world, and not so far away – Newcastle was no laggard – inventive science and industry continued headlong through change so fast that even little Mickley scarcely dared to blink for fear of missing something. Momentous things were happening: in America, where gimmickry flourished, someone thought of toothpaste in tubes! That was in 1891, but tubes weren't seen by Mickley folk for another thirty years or so ... what was toothpaste for? They gnawed raw turnips and bones, and brushes were for floors, not teeth. Gibbs came first, with 'Dentifrice' in solid blocks in highly coloured little tins, so that each family member could identify their own. Gibbs didn't reckon with the Bateys; with so many children their house would have been psychedelic with dentifrice tins, and there wasn't enough room anyway, and probably not enough colours in the spectrum. So Mickley made do with its turnips and if teeth did eventually rot, put up with the pain and the stumps. Dentistry was a gruesome business, and you had to pay for the suffering; few from the village would put their fate in the hands of the dentist who visited Hexham once a week, on Market days, a fellow name of Tinn, with the initials G.E. – G.E. Tinn – Get In? I like to think he specialised in fillings. He held his surgery in a shoe shop.

Toothpaste in tubes didn't reach the lowly, in my recollection, until the 1920s, when the instructions in large letters on the tube had to be observed – SQUEEZE FROM THE BOTTOM UP. Otherwise the peppermint-flavoured contents might well end up on your foot, scientists not yet having mastered the technique of a foolproof seal to the bottom of the tube, by which it was filled – clever stuff.

What did have an instant impact on Mickley, and what the civilised world was waiting for, the men folk anyway, was Gillette's invention – the 'safety' razor, again from America where change was even faster than it was here. This was the classic example of the principle that the world will beat a path to your door for a better mousetrap – or razor. This clever little device transformed the lives of shavers everywhere and saved not a few lives – apart from making a fast fortune for Mr Gillette and putting a lot of barbers out of business. What with advances in medicine, they were having a rotten time. Previously the well-named 'cut-throat' or 'open' razor was the only way of iii.

18TH YEAR OF ATTENDANCE IN HEXHAM.

PAINLESS DENTISTRY.

MR. GEORGE TINN,

SURGEON DENTIST,

16, Saville Row, Newcastle-upon-Tyne.

ARTIFICIAL TEETH.

Since the introduction of Artificial Teeth, which has enabled many to continue the mastication of solid food to a period of life at which they otherwise must have swallowed it without being properly masticated, longevity is on the increase. Whether the Dentist is really to claim this fact as a triumph of his art, or whether it be due to a generally improved system of Hygiene, we will not discuss, but as mastication is so absolutely necessary, even to the strong and healthy stomach, we may fairly suppose that many years are added to the lives of those who are thus enabled to save distress to the digestive organs by the use of Artificial Teeth.

Mr. G. T. solicits the attention of the public to his new style of fitting Artificial Teeth on a Vulcanite Base, which for beauty, durability, and comfort far surpasses the Gold Plates usually made. The Teeth are manufactured of the purest and strongest materials, most suitable to resist the acids of the mouth, and fit so accurately as to defy detection. So perfect are they in every respect that they are an excellent substitute for the natural Teeth. They are inserted without the removal of stumps, or causing the slightest pain.

A PERFECT FIT GUARANTEED IN EVERY CASE.

CONSULTATIONS FREE.

Artificial Teeth from 5s. per Tooth. Complete Sets (Upper or Lower) from £2 10s. per set.

SPECIAL NOTICE.

Mr TINN attends Hexham every Tuesday at 27, Fore Street (opposite the Sun Inn). Attendance from 11 till 5-30 p.m.

DENTIST'S ADVERT

shaving, since the flint or your dagger. And a risky job it was too, even in the hands of an expert barber. No doubt a fair bit of blood was shed in the cause of becoming 'expert' – and quite a lot in the cause of murder – although Mickley had no 'Demon Barber of Fleet Street' – he supplied a pie shop in London. Cut-throats were diabolical weapons and, along with coal-gas, a favourite way of taking your own life. 'Melancholy Suicide' proclaimed the Hexham Courant all too often, and like as not with a 'cut-throat'.

That is not to say that the new devices were not capable of inflicting a nasty wound – there was still a skill involved. Some men stuck to their old-fashioned cut-throats – they cost nothing to run, Gillettes needed blades, which, at a penny a time, weren't cheap, and the shaver was lucky if he got more than two shaves for his money, but this was still cheaper than a trip to the barber, for he who couldn't trust himself with a cut-throat. 'Convenience' shaving, 'Gillettes' caught on fast, and lasted; they are still around in spite of competition and new ideas on shaving. An even bigger fortune awaits the fellow who can persuade hair to grow on the pate rather than the face.

In 1884 'Evaporated Milk' in tins ('from contented cows' – slogans were all the rage) and COCA COLA in America, did nothing yet awhile for Mickley, but the Kodak Box Camera had implications for the future; it made possible for posterity a photograph of the whippet or even the children at the seaside.

In 1898, with progress running amock, came Mr Kellogg's Corn Flakes, the first 'health food': he thought he was doing the world a good-turn. Then, in 1903, to set the century firmly on its way to scientific tinkering with food, 'Kraft Processed Cheese' ('Velveta Spreads Like Butter') was invented to use up a lot of cheese that was going to waste because it wouldn't sell. 'Processed', which made it sound special, into being soft, and in a clever pack, it sold well at an enhanced price, but was the same cheese; pointing the way to 'value added', or rather 'profit added'.

Another impact on Mickley at the turn of the century was the creation, 'doon the toon', at Newcastle, by Joseph Swan, of the carbon-filament electric light bulb. In 1878, it put a bright, reliable glow on the wires from Faraday's dynamo, fifty years after its invention. The bulb enabled Armstrong, who made a fortune from hydraulic cranes and with his guns a better way of killing than his namesake reivers, to light his mansion at Cragside, near Rothbury, entirely by water-generated electricity, the first house in the country to be so lit.

Not far behind, Mickley, by 1908, was on terms with Cragside and in the very forefront of the electrification of street lighting and workers' homes. It made a change for a pit village to be showing (lighting?) the way. Paraffin lamps had not long superseded candles as house lighting in the Raas, where in fact candles were still widely used, and in pits like Mickley deemed to be 'safe'. In some such pits 'carbide' lamps (calcium carbonate) superseded candles. They were highly portable, could be fixed to miners' hats and to bicycles and carts and gave a brilliant but ghostly bluish-white light. They were really portable gas lamps, the gas being produced 'in situ' in a simple but ingenious way. The process began when water from an upper chamber, controlled by a tap, dripped on to lumps of 'carbide' in a lower, screw-on container. The carbide, that had a peculiar smell, was bought from the Co-op, out of a metal drum with a tight-fitting lid to keep out the damp. The water made the carbide 'fizz' and produce acetylene gas which passed through a pipe to the 'jet', which had to be kept clean with a fine wire 'progger' (pricker), where it lit with a satisfying 'plop' and a quiet hiss. Miners leaving work knocked the residue of expended carbide out of their lamps on to the tops of fencing posts and if little boys were lucky, and quick enough, they might find bits unused – sometimes quite a lot. With a fine hole in a treacle tin, they could have their very own lamp for a short time. Getting it wrong, or arranging it deliberately, produced a bomb good enough for any Marxist plotter, but not spherical as in the 'comics'. On a good day cans and lids flew in all directions, with some force. A wonder we weren't all maimed.

Waste gas from Mickley coke-making darkened daytime skies, lit no night-time mantles; the roads were as dark as Turpin's except where lit by travellers' lanterns, and the Raas illuminated only by the dim glow of candles and paraffin lamps through curtained windows, or chinks in shutters.

Electricity in the Village

Electricity was soon found to be a very useful and versatile asset in mining. It could be very dangerous but with proper precautions, it provided, for the first time in the history of mining, effective lighting for men to work by. It enabled ventilation fans to go where no steam-driven one could go, and water pumps, although not at Mickley, where water was a discomfort and inconvenience rather than future-threatening, as at Clara Vale which produced more water than coal. Water and electricity were also, and early, found to make uncomfortable, indeed deadly, companions and were best kept apart.

Electricity was strange stuff, not easily understood, travelling silently and unseen along, initially, cotton and varnish-covered copper wires, which gave the careless or unwary an awful thump if the bare bits were touched – not to be messed with. However, it made life in the pits a mite easier and speeded the work – and the rats couldn't eat it as they did the candles, even the lighted ones; mind you, they were not above gnawing through the insulation and causing short-circuits and fires, and themselves a nasty headache.

In Mickley the magic light was generated in a special 'house' by steam-powered, belt-driven dynamos, and carried to where it was needed above ground by thick wires held at a 'safe' height on 15 ft high poles – which any self-respecting lad could shin up. There was a night-time surplus of power, so why not put it to good use?. So the little poles marched up the hill from the generator-house beside the pit, carrying their two wires on glazed earthenware insulators, by way of the New Buildings, to the Square, thence through the loft of every house. Tappings were made to provide two lights, one upstairs, one down, wearing 'coolie hat' style shades, white below to reflect the light, green or blue above. They were 'on' and 'offed' by heavy, brass-covered porcelain switches, just inside the door, and at the foot of the stairs. That was it!. No sockets, no 'power', no earth, only lights. Lighting was the function; bright, unflickering light, at the flick of a switch. But it only came on when the day shift ended, and went off when the 'fore' started. The pit needed all the electricity it could get when it went to work.

This marvellous electricity pole-vaulted from the Laa Raa to East Street then crawled through the lofts of the High Raa and ended there, being only a small marvel. Not so small that it couldn't manage to light the streets on the way, with 100 watt bulbs in 'butterfly' reflectors, twelve feet up the wooden poles spaced 50 yards apart; but lights only on alternate poles – no point in being extravagant.

Yes, Street Lighting, in 1910. Can you imagine the excitement? No, I doubt if you can; nowadays we seldom see the star-speckled sky, the Plough, Pegasus, Vega and Altair. Artificial light makes night into permanent, bird-confusing day. The first lights merely diffused the edges; you could still see the stars, walk by moonlight, find a shady corner for a cuddle, yet not fall over anything (like drunken Mattie) on a dark night. Under street lights were great new playing places in the evening for children no longer confined to indoor mat-making or homework, or even reading, about which there was some concern: bright light on white paper might cause blindness; the bright light being a 100 watt bulb in a sixteen feet square room!. Perhaps they were right – eyesight is not what it was.

Youngsters could play marbles by streetlight, chucks, tops, they could skip and play most street games, but they were disadvantaged compared to gas-lit children, who could speel up the lamppost and light a rolled-up piece of paper at the mantle, being careful because mantles were tender and too many broken caused questions to be asked. Nor could 'electric' bairns enjoy the twilight sight of the lamplighter on his bike, with a long pole over his handlebars, pointing fore and aft; it had a hook on the end, and a tiny acetylene jet, fed by a long tube from the carbide container at the other end. Carbide lamps were versatile. The lamplighter stopped his bike at every lamppost, upended the pole, pushed it through the flap that we pushed our rolled-up paper though, turned the gas-tap with the hook on the end, and lit the fizzing mantles, two or three of them, with the carbide jet. That was a street light, gas style. There was a poem about it, which I forget – I do wish I'd tried harder.

Gas street lights eventually got automatic timing devices and lamp-lighters vanished into memory and poetry. I do wish I could remember that poem about the lamplighter. Electric street lights came on without any fuss, on their own, like magic. A house at the end of each section of Row had in its electrical system, as well as a fuse that served the section, a third switch, separate from the others and up the stairs a stretch. It could not be put on by mistake. It was the duty of someone in the house to put this switch down at dusk and up before going to bed. It controlled the street light on the pole outside; automatic timing system, Mickley style!

This wonderful service did not come free; it was deducted from the miner's pay. So many 'off-tiaks', I wonder he had anything left. But at 1s. a week it was good value I would say, even if the bulbs were only 100 watt; mind you, they didn't half show up the dirt, and he who worked the street lights got no rebate.

Wonderful it was, maybe, possibly almost miraculous; but problems lay ahead, when clever things other than light bulbs came along to be worked by electricity and there was only a little generator.

Blaydon Co-op

Considering that, in 1888, Mickley Coal Co. was laying off men and could not, 'because of the deplorable state of the industry', afford to enlarge the school, there was a remarkable turnaround in fortunes for the village – the brand-new school in 1904; electricity in 1908 – and another Co-op in 1910.

Building another Co-op might seem like a risky speculation, in competition with a well-established bigger one, even if Co-ops did enjoy glaring at each other. Blaydon Industrial and Provident Society perhaps had wind of developments to come; or merely hoped for them; perhaps there was a recognised need for more shopping facilities, a wider choice. The British Empire was at peace and awash with good things, cheap good things for a prosperous nation to buy and enjoy.

Built in brick and not ashamed to proclaim its date – 1910 – Mickley branch of the Blaydon Co-op served the 'bottom end' of the village: the New Buildings, Laa Raa area; those who could not be bothered to climb the hill (my, how having a shop in the village made people lazy!), or wanted a change, or had got mouse droppings in the sugar, or were just tired of having to wait for ages to be served by over-stretched staff. It sold much the same things as 'Prudhoe'; had an adjoining draper's; paraffin and tin baths at the back, but no cobblers or butchers. The red bricks were added to an existing stone-built building which was used as a warehouse with a loading bay, and the Manager's house. This part predated the new shop by some considerable time I believe, and was probably, like the Miners Arms opposite, a part of Old Eltringham. Potts the butcher probably had his shop here, and Mrs Bolam her shop and Post office.

This Post Office is a puzzle. With the Penny Post being established the year that Mickley's pit first opened, and a postal service through Stocksfield station before Stocksfield amounted to anything, it seemed a bit daft to have to bring the mail for Mickley two miles back, by pony or on foot, when it could have been dropped off at the Junction. There could not have been much mail to tax Ellen Bolam, Postmistress at the turn of the century, but it arrived at her office at 8.40 am and 7.40 pm and despatches were at 9.30am,

STATION ROAD, MICKLEY, LOOKING SOUTH WITH THE CROSSROAD ABOVE THE SECOND CART AND BLAYDON CO-OP ON THE RIGHT

2.45 and 8.30 p.m. It was a long day for Mrs Bolam, but think on that for service – for a penny.

With a postal service and another Co-op, Mickley was flourishing. Pitmen now had some spending power, crumbs from the rich man's table maybe, but nice crumbs. They certainly weren't paying their rent in a pound of pepper. So, as could be expected, the Private Sector moved in; there was room for private enterprise and a bit of speculation in those days, it was what made Britain Great. Anyone could build their house, or chapel, or club, or shop, anywhere they wished, subject only to the recently imposed Building Regulations, and buy and sell anything they wished, although 'The Council' – Hexham Rural and Prudhoe Urban from 1910 – was beginning to keep a closer eye on things like sewers, ceilings and meat.

Worker Power was beginning to flex its muscles, test its fledgling wings. Socialism emerged as a political force – weren't you warned what would happen if you taught workers to read? The first rays of sunnier times struggled through the murk of Victorian industrial oppression; thunder storms aplenty lay ahead but the Hope and the Vision emerged, for workers. Not only for men – far away, a small voice was heard. Mrs Pankhurst raised the voice of women.

Back at home, there was a little money in Mickley pockets.

Entrepreneurs, just little ones, but important in the village context, saw the possibilities. The New Mickley began to materialise.

The New Mickley

The first Private Enterprise of which there is clear record (Ellen Bolam and Potts the butcher are shadowy figures) is Edward Stobart, General Dealer, who traded from a 'prime site' corner shop: corners having two sides meant extra window space and windows sold goods.

The Main Road frontage west from Station Bank top, was the first part of the private development of the village. On the corner Mickley Social Club reflected the recreational mood and needs of the times. Social Clubs sprang up across the Northern lands, as had Co-ops and Brass Bands, to satisfy a demand. In this case a need for a place for men – not women yet – to gather socially; to drink, have concerts – when guests were allowed, including women – and to stage leek shows. Run on strict Club lines, with very firm rules, these institutions drew strength from numbers of Members, in much the same way as did the Co-op movement. 'Affiliation' and 'Federation' meant

COMMERCIAL INN, HIGH MICKLEY

that membership of any Club assured entry to any other affiliated club and they sold their 'own brand' beer at privileged low prices. And of course, they were non profit making. Big by Mickley standards, 'The Club' was built in 1900, in red brick – the colour of the times, and the future. It was, I believe, the first Club to be 'Affiliated'. It was razed by fire in 1924 and immediately rebuilt, in its present form.

The old pubs and inns; the Hare and Hounds, or Boat House, of Bewick's time; the Miners Arms in the heart of the village on Station Bank, the Blue Bell at Mount Pleasant and the one for country folk, the Commercial Inn at Old Mickley, were only drinking places and too small to provide for the needs of the times, although they did well enough until the pits closed.

Alongside the Club was a small piece of land, probably left vacant for potential extension but in fact only providing for a 'quoits' pitch: being a modest kind of activity, quoits didn't ask for much. Played originally, in the distant past, with horseshoes on a clay bed, by country folk, it involved pitching heavy iron rings or quoits, as close as possible to an iron peg, and to knock your opponent's quoit off if it rested on it. Something like that. It sounds simple, perhaps it was, but it filled many a happy, harmless hour, caused a bit of excited shouting and made a loud, distinctive, metallic ringing sound that told the village that a game was in progress. I believe there has been something of a revival, but not here.

Stobarts

Next along the road, west from the Club, was a block of two houses, seemingly sliced off a typical street of the time, like the Co-op Manager's house. Side by side front doors opened directly on to the pavement and back doors on to stone steps leading down to enclosed yards with 'the usual offices' – coal house and ash-closet and a cellar or basement to accommodate the sloping site. The first private housing in Mickley, built for Edward Stobart.

The second of the two houses had its sitting-room intended from the beginning to be a shop, with big windows taking up the whole of the front and half of the side walls. It is quite astonishing that at last when houses for ordinary folk were being designed and built with two rooms for living in, they should choose, in many cases, to live in only one. The other, the 'front room', or 'Parlour', was largely unused except for special occasions such as the three day 'lying in state' of the family dead, with all the house curtains tight-closed. Stobarts wouldn't have been able to do this – they needed the parlour for a shop, and why not. A shop could be set up anywhere; West Mickley had one in a wooden hut, and many a successful enterprise started off in the 'front room'.

Edward Stobart, when he got going, sold everything from paraffin, kept down the yard, to snuff, candles, knicker elastic, zinc ointment for mending sores and 'camphorated oil' for rubbing on children's chests, to Fry's chocolate, bacon and eggs, to pinnies and clay pipes for a penny and the 'twist' tobacco to go with them, hacked off what looked like lengths of tarry rope and probably tasted like it. 'Fine tooth combs' for the ritual of 'nit' removal when long hair had been in too close association with the wrong heads. He had enamelled kettles and pans and 'pot menders' for when the fire, which was still where pans and kettles were boiled, burned a hole because enamel wasn't meant for coal. Enamelled kitchenware was cheap, and light to handle and needed no black-leading, but, intended for gas, it didn't last long on coal fires, so 'pot menders' did a steady trade. They were two tin discs with a rubber washer between; one disc, with the washer, on the inside of the pan and the other on the outside and a little bolt passed through all three and the

STOBARTS SHOP

hole, tightened with a nut, and 'Presto' – a good as new pan. Some pans became more mender than pot.

Best of all, in Stobarts' (Nichols' later), there were sweeties; far superior to the Co-op's and designed to waylay children on their way to school. Only the glass separated the footpath from the shopwindow; pedestrians could not help but brush shoulders with it. The display area was a two feet deep shelf at low window-bottom level, a little below small boy's eye level, backed by opaque glass sliding doors for access from the shop. This shelf held flat boxes of such delectables as 'liquorice novelties', egg and milk caramels – worth a ha'penny of any bairn's pocket money, toasted coconut balls, packets of white candy 'cigarettes' with red ends like real 'Woodbines' that big brother smoked when he thought no one was looking. He bought five in an open-ended paper packet for five pence when he was old enough to pretend to prefer them to those cocoa-nutty sticks, brown one half, pink the other, that were my favourite; or long flat bars of 'nugget' (nougat), with real nuts and cherries and bits of green stuff that someone clever said was 'angelica'. Even dates rolled in cocoa-nut or coated in chocolate were jolly good, and all of these were temptingly displayed right there in the very front of the window.

A window-long shelf atop the glass sliding doors held a row of glass jars of every kind of 'boiled' sweeties imaginable, and others besides, from aniseed balls to gob stoppers that did, and changed colour as you sucked them. These jars were continued on rows of shelves behind the counter inside the shop and it was not too much trouble for the shopkeeper to remove the screw lid from every jar in the shop so that you could have a sweetie from each at 2d. for a 'quarter' (4 oz.), or just a few for your ha'penny. Which reminds me of the story of the little old man in his sweetie shop, designed, like Stobart's, to ambush children on their way to school; these shopkeepers had to accept the consequences …

"A pen'orth of those, please," said the first boy, pointing to the farthest away jar on the topmost shelf. The old man carried the steps the length of the shelves, climbed up, brought down the jar, carried it to the scales, opened it, weighed out the pen'orth, poured them into a 'poke', exchanged them for a penny, closed the jar and returned it to its place up the steps. "And what would you like," to the next boy. "A pen'orth of those please." The same jar. The same procedure. "What would you like?" The same jar … and so on. To save time and effort after the fifth pennyworth (he wasn't daft, this old man), he turned to the last boy before putting the jar away and asked, "I suppose you want a pen'orth of the same?" The little boy shook his head, so back went the jar to its place on the top shelf at the far end. "So what would you like?" "A ha'porth of them, please."

Perhaps I should explain a 'poke': before cheap ready-made paper bags became available, or for economy's sake, shopkeepers made their own packets out of squares of newspaper. Here's how it's done if ever you have need of a 'poke' … The paper square – made in advance, another job for winter evenings – is held in the palm by a corner between finger and thumb, then twisted with the other hand, around the fingers in an upward spiral, ending with a tight twist to make a seal and hold the thing together. The finished packet looks like an ice-cream cone with printing. It would hold anything from sugar for rhubarb dips (mothers could twirl paper to some effect too) to chips, although the grease released the print and the chips were a bit inclined to turn black; I can't remember if it enhanced the flavour, perhaps printer's ink then was of a better quality.

Twentieth century sweets certainly came to Mickley with Edward Stobart, and little boys had to learn to make important decisions – the choice was bewildering; no longer only highly coloured fishes, mixed fruits – the same as fishes but without tails and round and knobbly to mimic raspberries, round and smooth for gooseberries – barley sugar and acid drops. Up-to-date sweets came in up-to-date containers that were not only nicely decorated, but were useful for keeping things in. There were 'Dainty Dinah' toffees and Horner's 'Vanity Fair', in round tins with pictures of stage coaches and crinolined ladies in pretty colours, all grace and good living so it seemed. These were favourite toffees because they were mixed sorts, and wrapped in transparent coloured 'cellophane' that you could look through and see things in red, blue or yellow; and coloured tinfoil, 'silver paper' that could close-wrap hanging ears of oats to give to grateful mothers for attractive winter decorations, just as welcome in a jam jar as in a vase – you thought!

MAIN ROAD MICKLEY, LOOKING EAST

'Black Bullets' remained for ever popular; they came in tall square tins with round lids and you waited, if you could, until the lid had been left ajar long enough for the bullets to assume a thick coating of soft sugary candy around the hard, minty centre. They might also stick together, and the tin need a bang on the counter to separate them. They are extinct now, these sugary treats, killed off by hygienic wrappers. Black Bullets never go sugary in wrappers.

Pounds take care of themselves, if enough pennyworths of sweets are sold, and so the industrious Edward Stobart soon retired to 'Rosedale', the house that he had built a few yards to the west. That was a posh innovation for Mickley – a house with a name!. The shop became J. Nichols and Son.

Rosedale was yet another slice off a terrace – 'detached' like the Co-op Manager's house – quite aloof, in fact. Because of the sloping site it boasted an extra storey, and, because Edward Stobart was worth a bob or two by the time he retired, one or two superior touches. The front garden, enclosed by iron railings and entered from the roadway through an iron gate, was tiny, as with all such houses, but had room for the roses that climbed around the fine pitch-pine, panelled door, which opened into a lobby with panelled wainscot. An inner door, even grander: panelled and half-glazed with beautifully engraved glass, to greet the visitor with a good impression, led to a short corridor with a 'dado' and good panelled doors off to sitting room and kitchen. A marble fireplace decorated with roses, pink roses, which also ornamented the rich green tiles of the hearth and jambs, dominated and graced the sitting room. The fire would only be lit on Sundays and special

ROSEDALE. EDWARD AND CATHERINE STOBART WITH DAUGHTER MAGGIE

occasions, which the Stobarts could afford more than most. It looked high-class, this fireplace. The ceiling had a plaster cornice and an ornate central rose with a pendant gaslight.

The stairs too were attractive, with a half-landing, newel-posts with knobs on, and well-made bannisters. Two bedrooms and a 'box' upstairs, with a tiny iron fireplace in the rear one and a superior but slate, rather than marble, one in the 'master' room.

Downstairs, the second door off the corridor, at the foot of the stairs, opened into the kitchen which, as ever, was where life was lived. It was dominated by the fine cast-iron range – a 'Glendinning'. Lots have been written about these cookers; they may seem today to have been primitive, but in their time they transformed cooking, and life for the housewife, just as the round oven had done a hundred years earlier. But coal was still the heat source, so there was dirt and dust, black-leading, carrying coal and ashes – everything up and down stairs at Rosedale, and across the yard. There was stoking the fire to heat the oven, and carrying water for the side-boiler and kettle – but only from the brass tap in the scullery, not from the stream. The result was worth the effort, though – it looked fine, did this Glendinning, all glowing black-lead and burnished steel parts, and the dancing fire emitting warmth and goodwill all around, to say nothing of its slaving away at the cooking. Oh yes, the cooking, it was good at the cooking. Real bread, Yorkshire Puddings good enough for Yorkshiremen, and roasts fit for Royalty, quite apart from the cakes and pastries.

The scullery – a posh house term, so why shouldn't the Stobarts have one – was really just a walk-in larder with a white-glazed earthenware sink and a brass tap at the end of a lead pipe. The water emptied into a drain – *à la* New Buildings – but neither did this one serve a WC. There was an ash-closet, not a netty; they were for the Raas; this was upmarket, West End stuff – but the same ash-cart emptied it. To reach it, and the coal house – they went together, for convenience, as it were – was as far across the yard as across the street to a netty. The same rules still applied in keeping privies at a distance from the food. The difference at Rosedale, from the Rows, was that there were flights of stairs to reach the yard from the living area; eight stone steps from the back door, out of the kitchen. There were three doors out of this room – it was like Heath Row, and as windy. Dark wooden stairs led into the 'cellar' and thence by a ground-level second back door to the yard. Great fun for children. This internal route shortened the exposure in bad weather; the outside steps were a place to pause for the summer view, perhaps to sit awhile to enjoy the bird song, and maybe in later years to enjoy the 'Pastoral' symphony from the open door – or the hymns from the Chapel over the wall.

The 'cellar', really a basement and the internal way to the yard, was a second kitchen, with a simple brick fireplace like those in the Rows, with bars, round oven and setpot, with a lead pipe fixed to the wall above it, with a brass tap on the end – no sink, no drain. A low hatch of a door opened into a dark and dank 'real' cellar with no window, where a ghost would feel at home. Rosedale basement was a place for washing clothes and for wet day drying on lines strung across the low, wooden-boarded ceiling, and for children's wet weather playing. Every house should have a cellar.

The concrete yard was alright for playing in too, skipping and tops and hopscotch, but, down another flight of stone steps (if you build your house on a hillside — !) was the garden: big, steep and difficult, though some, especially children, might say that it was the grandest part of Rosedale, because at the bottom of the slope that was full of fruit trees, bushes, flowers and vegetables, ran the stream – the river 'Mick' quoth my dad, and he knew all things important. It came out of a secret tunnel, a 'cundy', from under the road; in summer a 'mere pencil thin trickle' as of pre-water-tap, bucket-filling days, rising to a raging torrent in thunderstorms and winter rains. This was Riding Dene, running through Rosedale garden; great for making dams and sailing little home-made boats.

A gate from the yard opened into a cul-de-sac which also served the 'Chapel' caretaker's house and boiler-house.

Rosedale was the first detached private house in the village, but was still only a slice off a terrace.

The United Methodist Church – the 'Chapel' – built in 1909 to replace the old stone chapel at the other end of the village, was almost as grand as the competition – the Club – and was in the same red brick, with an imposing arched entrance and rows of foundation stones. It could, and did, seat two hundred and fifty worshippers, and the pavement outside was wide enough to accommodate them nearly all, dressed in Sunday Best, when they gathered in after-service groups to hold earnest, no doubt pious, conversation – prolonged to give opportunity for display of the newest hat or suit.

Although Wesleyan fervour had mellowed somewhat by this time, these Methodists took their religion very seriously. In today's freer, more enlightened times many of them might have been classed as bigots or hypocrites, but, beneath the show, they believed in what was preached, sang a good hymn and in the main, applied a high moral standard to their lives. Besides, they forked out a fair bit of hard-earned cash on the road to heaven – a building like this did not come cheap; it had central heating, a WC, one of the first in the village, and like Rosedale alongside, gas lighting. Gas had at last reached Mickley, via Prudhoe.

Water and WCs

The juxtapositioning of this early twentieth century development is interesting, catering, in a very small group, for most human needs – housing, Social Club, shop, school and church. All haphazard and unplanned, but what more could anyone wish for? Adequate piped water and drains to get rid of it were the keys to development, and Prudhoe got them in the natural progression from the main urban seats of disease, long before Mickley, which as a consequence stagnated and remained a village while Prudhoe became a town.

However, the village eventually, at the turn of the century, got the services needed, unlike the old village on the hilltop, which had to wait another twenty-five years.

Pressing, health-driven need got the new school Mickley so much needed with long awaited, up-to-date 'offices': separate WCs in separate yards for girls and boys, and a smelly urinal for the boys, but all flushing away into the newly laid sewer to the newly made sewage works, upwind from the New Buildings. Separate white-tiled cloakrooms had rows of white-glazed washbasins with brass taps. Washbasins? – what's wrong with sinks?. And the rows didn't even have those … With roller-towels and soap, there was no longer any excuse for dirty hands, neck or ears – they were inspected daily. But there were a lot of dirty roller-towels about. A cast-iron drinking cup – like a bell without a clapper – was chained securely near one of the taps.

The United (Central) Methodist Church, practising, no doubt, the principle that Cleanliness is next to Godliness, went to the expense of installing a WC in the new vestry, and a tap and sink. At least now the Minister could be clean as well as Godly. This was only reasonable, as, unlike the Vicar on the hill, he had no close-by manse and had to travel from Prudhoe or farther, on foot or by horse-transport. There was a second WC downstairs, just outside the caretaker's back door; luxury indeed. WCs did not need to be so far from the food.

The Social Club also afforded WCs, on its rebuilding.

These few WCs hardly justified an extensive drainage system and sewage works yet it was a long time before much other than washing water was treated. Although the water was there, and the sewage works, it was nearly fifty years before Mickley privies went 'wet'.

All of the private houses built prior to about 1930 were of standard terrace design, with iron-railed pocket-handkerchief-sized gardens at the front and high-walled yards at the rear, with a cobbled, cart width road between two terraces. They had gas – electricity was still only for the 'privileged' Raas, – water and sink but no bath other than the tin one before the fire, which was a Glendinning or similar. The drain removed only water, the ash-closet was still the preferred sanitary option, 'across the yard', although not so far away as the earlier ones. The yards were smaller, and perhaps 20th century flies had a shorter range. Anyway, why change a system that worked reasonably well, was cheap and you had got used to? Ashes and the increasing amount of household waste such as tins and bottles that could not be burned and didn't command a penny on the return still had to be disposed of in any case. Besides, although few mentioned it at the time, did it make sense to flush sewage into water then try to remove it before drinking the water? There had been a move in Hexham, fifty years earlier, to return from WCs to ash closets, because of the state of the river, which was like a cess-pit until sewage works were thought of. Fortunately, by that time Mickley's water came from the newly built Catcleugh reservoir, away in the border Reiver country, by way of Whittle Dene and Prudhoe; and good it was too – you could even drink it. Unless an encounter with a freshwater shrimp in your glass bothered you!

Gas and Gadgets

Every room, except the boxroom, in every house in the new Mickley had a gas lamp, the principle ones on long stalks from the centre 'rose' of the nine-foot high ceilings, with long chains to control the 'on-off' valve and a big coloured glass bowl to soften the harsh white light. Bedrooms and lesser places like passages and sculleries had curvy and rather ornate wall-brackets with a tap to turn the gas on. Gas lights caught on; they produced some additional heat in winter and used a lot of oxygen, but who cared, there was plenty more where that came from, through the doors and windows.

The controlled convenience of the gas-cooker, on the other hand, was slow to supercede the faithful Glendinning range. An element of fear was associated with them as tales of terrible explosions persisted from the early days, and desperate people were using gas-cookers, instead of cut-throat razors, to take their own lives. Few in the new Mickley were prepared to take a chance, they were accustomed to their faithful ranges which didn't go off bang, and the fire was on anyway. Some adventurous housewives saved their pennies and bought a gas iron, which was a fearsome, hissing, fiery device that frightened the cat and worried the children – and the user initially – but speeded-up the ironing no end and ensured sootless laundry. Controlling the heat took a bit of practice, so there was still some dancing spit around, scorched cheeks and singed clothes. The long, flexible, armour-plated tube was a nuisance too, connecting to the gas-nozzle with a tap. A careless move could send the monster crashing to the floor like a fiery dragon.

A similar tube connected the gas supply to another innovation, a 'copper' – a further attempt to ease the work of washday. It was a galvanised steel stand holding a lift-out-for-emptying, copper water bowl holding six or eight gallons which, heated by a gas ring below, produced hot water even in the summer when the coal fire was not needed. They were for private homes where coal had to be bought. Mainly they boiled the whites and things that needed to be germ-free – germs were having a rotten time just then, everyone was getting at them. Not as now, when they are twirled around a bit in a machine to make them dizzy, with tepid water and some weird chemical that probably does more harm than the germs.

Shortage of servants and their increasing cost, as women found some freedom to choose their way of life, encouraged inventions that eventually made workers of the wealthy, and slaves to the machine. They learned to do their own housework, with mechanical and technological help. On the other hand the humble housewife, who had to do her own work in any case, reaped enormous benefit as the Age of Invention and Innovation in the Home brought not only gas irons and boilers, and cookers for those who dared – apart from fire and explosion, would the food taste funny? There came the 'dolly tub' and stick, a great advance on the poss-tub and heavy tree-trunk of a stick. The dolly-tub was galvanised steel, light to carry, and small enough to tuck under a table when not in use, where it could hold dirty clothes. The tub had a lip to prevent splashing in use, and the cleaning power was provided by a 'dolly-stick' which was just that, a broomstick, with a copper dome with holes in on one end. Pushed down into the hot from the 'copper', clothes-filled lather in the tub, the combination of the dome and the holes created a very efficient 'suck and squirt' effect. There were midget versions for doing a few clothes in a bowl or sink. Science rather than brute force was applied and took a lot of the ache out of washday, and soap-powder in packets was at last available in Mickley to make, with the dome, the foam.

So also did the little 'Acme' wringer take a lot of effort out of washing; few believed it would work, but it did, indeed it did. It fixed to the edge of a table with clamps like table-tennis net clamps so that it could be removed for storage, but it had to be a sturdy table or the edge broke off, or it wobbled around the room under the stress of squeezing water from sodden clothes. One thing about the old iron mangle – it didn't wobble! The water from the Acme ran back into the dolly-tub and the clothes slid through on to the table. Like the Dolly stick, the little Acme wringer made use of science, although it still called for a fair bit of physical effort. The rollers, being rubber, had to be dried and kept apart when not in use, otherwise they went 'claggy' and stuck together. A common shop sign of the times was: 'Wringer Rollers Re-Rubbered'.

Washday Blues became a little less 'blue'.

Floors in the new houses made life a little easier and more comfortable, too, being of wood and warmer, and dry, and flat. 'Linoleum', though, was what transformed floors. Cut by the yard from six foot wide rolls in all manner of colourful designs, it could easily be cut to fit any size and shape of room. On the other hand 'Congoleum Squares' were ready-made squares patterned in the style of, and the nearest most working class people ever hoped to get to, a carpet. They covered the centre ground and the 'surrounds' were made to look, more or less, like polished wood flooring, with oak-patterned 'parquet' lino; all shiny and smooth and easy to brush, mop or scrub.

Hooky mats still had to be lifted and shaken in the yard, or banged on the wall, but 'cocoa-matting' rugs could be bought for lighter shaking where the warmth and comfort of the clippy or hooky was not so important.

Lino found its way into the Raas and was excellent upstairs although cold on winter feet if they strayed off the mat, but it had a short life on damp, uneven downstairs flagstones and was often protected by thick under-layers of newspapers. Most housewives found its labour-saving cleanliness well worth the cost and the Co-ops sold a lot of lino.

All of these modern comforts and devices could be had at the Co-ops, but there was now a much wider choice in a whole lot of shops in Prudhoe – a street full of them in fact – or, better still, in the big 'Department' stores in Newcastle and Hexham, where Robinson's and Robb's led the way. What could not be carried on the train could be brought out by horse-drawn carrier for sixpence or a shilling.

Little flat boxes on wheels, with wheel-driven brushes inside and long handles arrived on the scene – 'Ewbank Carpet Sweepers' – more likely 'floor sweepers' in Mickley, where carpet from Robinson's at 3s a yard was an expensive luxury; no newfangled sweeper would keep it from getting mucky and who would shake it? These simple devices were handy, although they didn't work in corners; but neither did they just stir the dirt around as did the brush, and the even newer-fangled 'Hoover' needed electricity, which the Raas didn't have enough of, and the new houses none at all. Anyway, Hoovers were far too expensive for ordinary folk.

The Bicycle

Bicycles now, were different; they had moved on somewhat since George Angus tried his 'Velocipede' in 1866; they were no help in the home, but my goodness they were fun out of it. The most economical and efficient form of transport ever thought of, to this day, it almost made the horse redundant as personal transport, and brought wheeled mobility to the masses – and immense pleasure. And it could be kept under the stairs in the Raas.

The 'Penny-farthing', so-called because of the huge disparity in the size of the wheels, had been an adventure to ride – not for the chicken hearted, or ladies. The 'Safety Bike' brought cycling within reach of everyone, even ladies – though it put them into 'knickerbockers' which shocked the prudish but launched women on the road to sartorial freedom. The cycle brought problems of course, such as learning the new skill of balance. Back-pedal brakes broke a leg or two, to say nothing of skirts in spokes and trouser bottoms in chains before skirt guards and trouser-clips were thought of. If the venturesome ventured into Newcastle he needed to keep clear of

EDDIE LONGSTAFFE ON PENNY FARTHING, BESSIE ON SCOOTER

tramways because if his wheels got into the sunken tramlines, he was sunk! There were none of those in Mickley fortunately; only rough roads. Bicycles quickly became very popular and pretty safe – the internal-combustion engine had not yet made its nasty presence felt, although Henry Ford set it moving in 1908 with his 'Model T'. Bicycles, unlike the first trains and motorcars, didn't much frighten the horses but, as you might expect, there were madcap speedsters hurtling along at breakneck speed and faster – downhill!

Once the bicycle was bought, which was not easy, costing as it did eight to fifteen pounds in 1900, running costs were minimal. A good bowl of porridge for breakfast and Aunty Ada's special scones for lunch could propel a bike fifty or sixty miles in a day on reasonable roads, with a following wind. It needed no stable, just a little shed in the yard or a space under the stairs if you lived in the Rows; but it was cared for as the Huntsman did his horse. Wiped dry after every wet ride and cleaned thoroughly once a week, which was worth a penny extra on a boy's pocket money! The only other expense

MICKLEY CYCLING CLUB

in running this masterpiece of engineering design was a drop or two of oil on the chain and bearings and, very occasionally, a new tyre. Mr Dunlop had made the bike comfortable.

Every young, and not so young, man, aspired to own a bike and ride it to far distant, hitherto inaccessible places. As the maxim of 'safety in numbers' applied to distant travel, cyclists went in groups; Cycle Clubs became the order of the day: Mickley had one. They gathered, perhaps ten or even twenty or more of these intrepid travellers, on Sunday mornings, all dressed up in special gear if they could afford it, plus-fours and the like, or at least with trouser-bottoms tucked into stocking-tops. Bike chains and trouser-bottoms in combination could cause nasty spills, or at the least oily trousers and gave rise to tucked-in trousers and 'trouser clips' for holding flapping trousers tight around ankles. I seem to have mislaid mine. Country roads were choc-a-block with happy cyclists on Sundays and the Chapels took a beating. Routes were carefully planned, sometimes calling for meetings during the week, which extended the pleasure. They sometimes booked in advance by letter – phones were still thin on the ground in cycling country – at watering-holes for lunch, which otherwise might be picnicked on a grassy bank or woody glade.

One such stopping place, favourite for cycling townsfolk, was the 'Temperance Hotel', by Stocksfield railway station – hotels and stations were a happy association in the days of steam. The Lord of Bywell still had a bit of clout, although not on the same scale as the Baliols, and he didn't much like the idea of drunken peasants on his patch, nor even cyclists, so the hotel was 'tea and lemonade only'. Nothing wrong with that, lemonade was still made with lemons, believe it or not, and was as refreshing a drink as any on a hot summer's day. Or there was that old stalwart ginger beer, that needed thick stoneware jars to curb its vigour and was a bit frothy for cycling. Even the lemonade was powerful enough to need a stopper with a clever spring wire clip to restrain it in its glass bottle. These bottles superseded those with a marble in the pinched-in neck, held in place by gas-pressure, that were equally clever but expensive to make and cumbersome, and preceded those uninteresting ones with screw-in stoppers, and those VERY interesting ones that had metal caps pressed on with a machine. They almost needed a machine to get them off too, or at least a special tool, which in time came to be incorporated in the multipurpose pocket knife beloved of boys and the antecedent of the 'Swiss Army' knife. These bottle caps had all manner of designs and pictures on them in bright colours and made classy, collectable badges. You were somebody if your pullover breasts were covered with these emblems of boyly power – like Generalissimo Presidents of Latin-American countries. To make a bottle cap into a badge the cork lining, or washer, which sealed the bottle, had first to be carefully prised out, using your 'Lamppost' knife; then the tin cap held, right way up if there was one, against the pullover and the cork washer pushed back into place from the inside. The pullover got somewhat puckered but who cared so long as the badge held firm. As good as proper Sheriffs' badges they were – well, almost.

Temperance was best for cyclists. A disadvantage of the bicycle compared to the horse, apart from the fact that no-one could look dignified on a bicycle, was that it couldn't take you home drunk, it would pitch you into the ditch. Mind you, you could be fined for being drunk in charge of a horse (was not the horse in charge?) – still can. Venturing out at night on a bike without lights could bring a fine too. Bicycle lamps were dinky little things, mostly paraffin, some carbide, jobs with small red and green lenses in the sides for port and starboard! I never actually met an amphibious bike. The front lens was clear for showing the way and on a clear night just about illuminated the front wheel; the rear lamp was red in case someone came up fast from behind. They hardly showed the way but gave others the chance of seeing you coming – or going.

Cyclists could also be fined for riding two-on-a-bike – why does somebody always have to spoil the fun? – but it didn't stop them. I've seen six – but that was a built-like-a-tank RAF machine and the riders irresponsible – some said mad.

My first taste of speed-induced thrill, and fear, was on the crossbar of a brakeless 'bone-shaker', downhill at speed, at the hands of my brother. What was a bone-shaker? It was an impoverished boy's first bike, made up of discarded bits and pieces of others; usually just a frame and handlebars on

AUTHOR HOLDING A BICYCLE FOR HIS BIG BROTHER

wheels – buckled. Tyres were a bonus, the seat an old sack tied on with string, and brakes extravagant luxuries. They were an introduction into the science of engineering, and a testament to the will of little boys to survive!

At the other end of the scale, my mother, voluminous skirts and all, rode eighty-odd miles from Yorkshire on the rear 'carrier' of my father's bike during a rail strike in the 1920s. Two on a bike ...?

Great things, bicycles.

The Cinema

This 20th century was blossoming in Mickley, with the first real advances in living standards since Norman, even Roman times for the poor – their first personal transport. But it did little for a wet winter's night. Then, wonder of wonders, came cheap, accessible entertainment of unbelievable variety and novelty – the CINEMA!

Moving films developed fast after the Lumiere brothers scared the wits out of their first French audience with moving pictures of a steam train hurtling at them from a flickering screen, in 1895. By 1911 there was a thriving film industry, electricity in the Raas – and the old Primitive Methodist Church, built for £240 in 1864, standing empty in favour of the brand new United Chapel at the other end of the village. Even Primitive cinema needed electricity to function and a dark place to blossom in: the ex-chapel was already pretty dark by its nature, and it straddled the gap between East Street and High Row, where the electricity wires passed. Could Mickley Coal Company, still the dominant force in the village, and Controller of Electricity Supply, be persuaded to supply a private venture? – in the evening, when demand was low? Of course they could; it would make for happier workers without causing headaches as did pubs. Besides, the Manager and his wife fancied a look.

'The Manager' and his family already had available to them a new form of entertainment not within financial reach of the workers – the Phonograph – novel in-house music without the need to learn about notes and practise them. Thomas Edison invented the Phonograph in 1876, at the time that Alexander Graham Bell (Telephone Bell?) produced that other great pain, bane and blessing of life, the telephone. Neither could have realised what they were starting!

Music out of a machine started off as a pretty innocuous kind of private pleasure needing no electricity, gas or coal – or blessing from the church, so long as it wasn't played on Sundays. But playing too loud posed no problem – phonographs couldn't, and had no volume control in any case. They, and what followed, supplanted singing round the piano as family entertainment, but Mickley was short on pianos anyway; they cost 40 guineas and took up a lot of room. The Band saw no problem – it had the volume.

The Phonograph was, in the manner of the times, mechanical, and acoustic – another new word. The mechanism was similar to a clock – Clockwork. A large spring, tensioned – 'wound-up' – with a handle, provided the power and the recording was made by the performer singing, loudly, into a huge 'sound horn' like a jumbo-size ear-trumpet that the hard of hearing of those days required you to bellow into. The 'vibrations' were concentrated by the horn and transposed by way of a diaphragm and steel needle on to the surface of a slowly-revolving wax-coated cylinder. To reproduce the sound the procedure was reversed; the groove vibrated the needle, which more or less re-created the original sound by way of the diaphragm, amplified by the horn. 'The music went round and round, Yo-o and it came out here'! Some music.

This was a great time for applying often newly discovered scientific principles to engineering and mechanical skills and putting them to practical and sometimes pleasurable use. The Bicycle, Phonograph, Cinema, and, dare I say it, the internal combustion engine, all arrived on the scene at about the same time, as did the 'entrepreneur', looking for ways of exploiting them.

The Branch End Connection

Along the road a little way towards Bywell, at Branch End, which was long a part of Micelee Township in the Barony of Baliol, and where had stood a turnpike tollgate, there came to live a man called Longstaffe ...

Branch End was inclined to distance itself from its workaday, grimy neighbour Mickley and associate with the upstart Stocksfield with its fancy station for the reception of Royalty visiting the Lord at Bywell. Like Ryton, Wylam, and pleasant country 'places west' with railway stations, Stocksfield was a Mecca for well-off Newcastle business men seeking escape from the pressures of work and unpleasant town living. They came at first for weekends and pottered and picnicked on plots of farm land at Painshawfield where the remains of the area's last water-mill were, at Ridley Mill. An 'intellectual' recently tried to hi-jack the Lampton Worm here from Penshaw (Painshaw?) Hill, on the Wear ...

These plots continued to be known in Mickley as the 'Allotments' long after they were filled with high-class houses at not less than £1000 a time – the rabble-excluding rules stipulated – surrounded by high-class gardens. Even more disparaging, this area became known by the miners, after the 'nobs' moved in, as 'Debtors Retreat', occupied by people who were 'Aal forr cotes' (fur coats) 'and nee knickors' (no knickers)! Pitmen still did not care for the ways of the wealthy – but they had no qualms about making use of them when they could.

Painshawfield Estate became a place of good – mostly – if poorly paid, employment for Mickley girls in 'day service', where in addition to being 'skivvies' they might learn to lay a proper table and, sometimes, the skills of housekeeping and the etiquette of 'society' – they needed no lessons in scrubbing floors. Many an ambitious lass from the Raas pulled herself up the social ladder on the apron strings of 'The Allotments'. Lads too, looking for an alternative to grim pit life, almost as grim farm labouring, or the 'buildings' (building trade), and not wishing to be a 'cissie' in a shop, might find work of a more congenial nature as gardeners on the Estate. Later generations enjoyed the results of their efforts on Sunday walks, when sharing other peoples' gardens by peering over hedges was popular.

Mickley children of a later time also shared another pleasure with the Estate. For tuppence they could fill the biggest shopping basket available with apples from the orchard of the kindly Mr Kidd. He kept bees, that discouraged scrumping, and bred apples, among them reputedly, although I cannot vouch for it, Kidd's Orange which can still be bought occasionally, imported from New Zealand. These apples, those that survived the walk home to Mickley, went well with blackberries from Hyons wood, and were almost as cheap. The good Mr Kidd could not have been out to make a profit, even if he did live in 'Debtors Retreat'!

Longstaffes

Branch End, centred on the old tollhouse, was like the new, modern Mickley of terraced houses, piped water and gas, Shops and Enterprise. Edwin Longstaffe – now there's a name from Robin Hood times – was a philosopher, some say a dreamer. He thought a lot, read incessantly as was the wont of those out to better themselves, tinkered and dabbled. He played with things scientific such as 'perpetual motion', and later built an observatory in the garden which was no Joddrell Bank but impressed the neighbours and filled the night hours. All this while his tough, practical wife got on with raising their children Eddie, Greta, and Bessie, and the practicalities of making ends meet. She had the ubiquitous Glendinning type range in her little end house in Meadowfield Terrace and was good at baking, so she sold a loaf or two to neighbours who weren't or couldn't. This was in the not-so-long-ago, when the people of this country could still do much as they pleased. It went as far as being able to sell, without permission, a loaf of bread from your kitchen. So, before you could blink, she was baking full-time and needing more than a Glendinning for doing it.

MAIN ROAD, BRANCH END. LONGSTAFFE'S ON RIGHT

INSIDE LONGSTAFFE'S SHOP

Like so many others at the time, her little business just grew and grew and went on growing for over half a century. It moved down the street and occupied as a shop the ground floors of two houses at the end of Alexander Terrace (the name dates it), with the proud boast LONGSTAFFES in big letters above, and the bakery filling the yards at the rear. Then it spilled across the lane behind, and down the street.

Eddie, as soon as he was old enough, and strong enough, carried baskets of bread on his back to outlying places, in all weathers, thus beginning the renowned delivery service which carried on with horse-drawn vans, early petrol vans, and travelling shops. Lonstaffes were in the forefront of mechanisation and innovation, owned the first 'Stanley Steam Car' in the area, if not the country, and got bread to Hedley in 1947, the worst of all winters, long before helicopters or powerful snowploughs. The founder of this institution, for that is what it became, is reputed to have carried ten-stone bags of flour on her back up the ladder into the loft above the bakery! Now men demand a machine to lift four stone. Greta and Bessie worked in the shop and the bakery, and I mean worked – this was a real family business. Bessie

EDWIN LONGSTAFFE, PHOTOGRAPHER

inherited some of her mother's daunting characteristics, and some of her father's artistry. She married Andy Liddle and between them, starting in a shed behind the shop, established Branch End Garage. That is another story but further illustrates the opportunities of the early twentieth century, there for the taking by anyone prepared to have a go.

Edwin the Elder, in between his reading and philosophy, repaired bicycles in a hut. Although a steady trade, it was not much to his liking once the novelty of the bike had worn off. Cyclists came from Mickley and all around, but not as many as flocked to his studio when he set up as the first professional photographer in the area; he saw a niche, and filled it. This is significant, as it is his work that provides us with most of the photographic record of life in the area, early this century.

People came, dressed in their Best, for posed portraits; individual or in family groups, to display their prosperity and to see for themselves just how handsome they really were – permanently recorded by Edwin Longstaffe, the Poor Man's Gainsborough. How they puffed themselves out, while their wives looked meek and the children glowered and no one dared blink. Edwin cloaked himself and the wooden-box-on-a-tripod camera, that had a huge eye of a lens sticking out at the front, and a door at the back for loading the glass photographic 'plates', in a black sheet, to keep out the light. Light, except when controlled through the lens, was fatal to photographs.

The lens shutter was operated by a hand held press-bulb on a tube, or a plunger on a wire and if the light was inadequate or the children fidgety, a tray of magnesium held high and ignited at the precise moment of shutter release, gave the required split-second flash of light – and blinded a lot of photographers – and possibly some of their subjects. This early system of photography called for a certain dexterity, and nimble feet if the place went up in flames and was not for the chicken-hearted. Outdoor photos, in natural light, were much easier and safer and, although the methods and equipment were positively crude, the results, on glass plate negatives, could be quite masterly and compare with the very best of today.

Quite a few of Edwin's photos are still about, with his name proudly displayed in ornate style – ornate was what impressed!. His portraits are good and interesting, but it is in his out-and-about record of life of the times that the value lies, incomplete and dispersed though it unfortunately is. I make no apology for claiming him, and Longstaffes, as part of the history of Mickley.

The 'in village' equivalent was John Nichols, who bought Edward Stobart's shop and continued it in the same vein; but his story, and Longstaffe's for that matter, if I am to attempt to follow some sort of chronological order, was interrupted by something nasty.

Most faraway happenings impacted slowly on Mickley: the Wright brother's flying machine and the 'Model T' didn't mean much except new

GRANDMA RUTHERFORD HOLDING THE BABY

wonders to read about in the newspapers. War was different – it hit hard and it hit fast. Mickley had had its share through the centuries but ordinary folk still didn't understand what it was all about, except that they were required to go off and be killed. Now they could read all about it in the newspapers, along with aeroplanes and cars, but where was this Sarajevo anyway (still there, you will notice, in 1996), and who was the Kaiser? A cousin, or nephew, or something, of Queen Victoria, or Albert – he couldn't be all that bad, could he?

The Great War

Press Gangs and the 'King's Shilling' were long outmoded but 'Your King and Country' still needed you when the chips were down, and there hadn't been a decent war for ages, so why not go and teach these horrible Huns a quick lesson or two and be home for Christmas. 'Time we had a bit of fun, a free holiday in France, all that wine, and those beautiful girls. That was the mood in August, 1914 – alas, alas.

Coal was just as important as guns in making war, and miners as useful down the pits as in the trenches, where they made some of the toughest, bravest soldiers in the world and they could even turn their hands to a bit of tunnelling – underground came natural. But getting coal was no fun; so they volunteered, for the fun and the sun. No one told them about the Hun and his Gun, his howitzer and his rattling machine-gun; nor about Flanders mud. Many did not come home, not for next Christmas, nor any other.

In this war young men, and some not so young, and some just boys, volunteered together (safety in numbers?), served together, and died together – and not only the miners; the farmers, joiners and shop-boys too. There is no record of how many left the village, but what passes as a war memorial, in the Church on the hill, names seventy-three as having paid the 'price of freedom'. There could have been few who were fit and did not go. Every single loss scarred the whole village, which still amounted to only a handful of streets but although the common cause helped to spread the load, some names bore disproportionate suffering. Four Scotts, for instance; three Stokers, and two each of eight other names. Such sadness – in a bronze plaque on a wall.

The survivors, some with minds and bodies torn and twisted, were welcomed with the Band, some flags and everyone in their Sunday Best, but no honoured place on a plaque. The limbless got a niggardly pension.

Mickley built no grand marble Cenotaph for those lads who did not come home, but had the noble thought of building a Nurse's Home as a fitting and more practical memorial, and a fund was set up. Prudhoe built its Nurse's Home, and a Lych-gate Memorial at the Church; Stocksfield built a Nurse's Home and a marble column where poppy wreaths are still laid on Armistice Day. Mickley bought a plot of land on Eastgate Bank. Ironically, opposite

BOER WAR VICTORY PARADE

this plot was built a row of quite pleasant cottages, in a fine position, for elderly miners to retire to; built, complete with plaque, to commemorate Sydney Bates, coal boss. The Nurse's Home got no farther.

What happened to the deeds for the plot and any money raised is anybody's guess – there could not have been much money, miners still did not have a lot. I do know that, after another war had come and gone, a surviving trustee and Councillor, applied unsuccessfully for planning permission to build himself a house on this commemorative plot of land and it has long reverted to a part of a field. Should we doff our hats as we pass? Few if any, of their generation are now left to mourn the lads of the village who went to Flanders fields, and who else will spare a tear? War is a bore.

This, the wealthiest nation in the world, bled itself dry in the fight against tyranny, came out empty-handed, exhausted and depleted of a generation of its sons. Those who returned found no place for them in the 'Land fit for Heroes'; no houses, no jobs, and for many, no food, while farmers ploughed crops into the ground, poured milk down the drains and well-nigh starved themselves. This country was, for many, a sad, bitter place, without even the crutch of religion to lean on – Wesley would have preached to deaf ears. Boys had gone to war teetotal, non-smoking, 'signed the pledge' Rechabites and Methodists – came back swearing, drinking, smoking men, prematurely old men, with nightmares. Atheists. They had been through Hell, saw no Heaven, returned to a life without hope. Nobody seemed to care. There might have been revolution in the land, there were those who would have tried, but there was no real will for it – 'enough of strife, just let us have food in our bellies, shoes on our children's feet'. Without war there was little need, not only for guns and ships, but for coal and miners; Mickley felt the pinch.

Although we, my family, did not then live in Mickley, my father's story is typical of many, and we came here on the tide of inter-war events ...

A Land Fit for Heroes

He carried stretchers, this boy, my father – at Passchendale and the Somme; got his legs peppered with shrapnel, and a dose of gas. Like many, he met his wife in a parcel …

Women and girls at home knitted like fury – 'comforts for the troops' – scarves, gloves, balaclavas, socks; all gratefully received. Letter home to Blighty in thanks for socks – 'Dear Lady, I received your knit – some fit; one I used as a helmet, the other as a mitt. Some day I hope to meet you, when I have done my bit, but where in the Dickens did you learn to knit?' The comforts went off in parcels, with Auntie Ada's scones (if they could sustain cyclists, why not soldiers?), and books and photographs and little reminders of home. Some were sent to friends and family members, others at random; many were 'lost in transit'.

My father got several books – diaries, Ella Wheeler Wilcox poems (never heard of her? – just say her name, never mind the poetry!); a beautiful, precious little fine-leather bound edition of *The Rubaiyat of Omar Khayam*, which he rested on the stretcher and learned by heart on the long, long, carries out with the wounded. I know not which book contained my mother's name, but I like to think the Khayam – 'Dreaming ere dawn's first light was in the sky …'

There was a photograph – she was a beauty, my mother, enough to will any young man to survive the war! She lived in Clara Vale, where the wet pit was, and had for a father a mining village 'entrepreneur' like Edward Stobart in Mickley. He had been a colliery 'winding man' – who worked the mechanism for lifting the cages up the mine shaft – lost an arm in an accident, and set up a typical little shop in a room in his house to become General Dealer and Sub-Postmaster.

The Postmaster got himself a horse and flat cart and left the shop in the care of his wife and daughters while he hawked fruit and vegetables around the wealthy houses of Wylam. He had a stable and warehouse which I later passed on the way to school and where I could gain an apple by presenting my outstretched hand, tugging at his empty sleeve, and grinning; he was stone deaf, as if having only one arm wasn't enough. He would respond with a scowl, then a reluctant smile, and slap an apple into my hand with : "Y'll

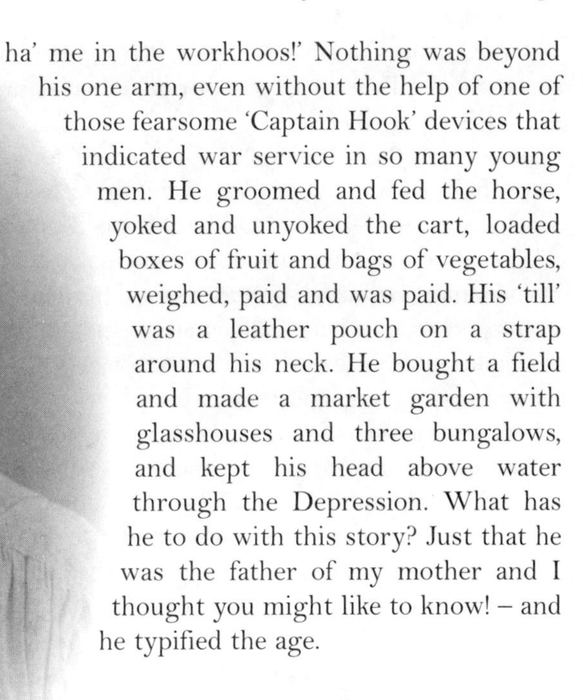

ha' me in the workhoos!' Nothing was beyond his one arm, even without the help of one of those fearsome 'Captain Hook' devices that indicated war service in so many young men. He groomed and fed the horse, yoked and unyoked the cart, loaded boxes of fruit and bags of vegetables, weighed, paid and was paid. His 'till' was a leather pouch on a strap around his neck. He bought a field and made a market garden with glasshouses and three bungalows, and kept his head above water through the Depression. What has he to do with this story? Just that he was the father of my mother and I thought you might like to know! – and he typified the age.

AUTHOR'S PARENTS

He was Thomas Smiles; my mother, Bertha.

My father, who was from Sunderland, came home with his nightmares and lost no time in marrying my mother, then, like so many survivors from the war, took her off in search of their idyll to a delightful village in Yorkshire where he plied his woodworking skills while she sank the ducks on the village pond with her early attempts at rice pudding. He might have succeeded in better times, but after being reduced to making deck-chairs for a shilling a time, made his way back to Clara Vale, where he rented a piece of land, built a cottage and greenhouses, and market-gardened; he reckoned that if people didn't need deck-chairs, they had to eat. But they didn't – couldn't afford to. So we were like the farmers of the time, only instead of ploughing the crops in, we had to eat them – Brussel sprouts, I remember, all winter long. Do I like Brussel sprouts?

Those who tried and failed got no 'dole' for six weeks. Six weeks is a long nightmare with no money and a family to feed. No 'Family Allowances', no 'Social Security' – nothing, The 'Means Test', which doesn't bear mention. This craftsman father, this one of the many heroes, left his house at seven in the morning as though going to work, perhaps on better days with tuppence in his pocket for a bar of chocolate to sustain him through the long day, and he walked the wide world in search of work, asking at every workshop, at every building site, and there were precious few of those – 'What chance of a job?' Five and a half days a week, home never before five, sometimes seven. When his soles wore through he cut cardboard insoles to save his feet and carried a pocketful of spares. This was a man who could mend his own shoes for the price of a piece of leather and a few tacks. He got a job, eventually, shovelling sand in a quarry just along the road, at £2.10s. a week and when the Newcastle firm of builders who owned the quarry discovered he was a joiner, they gave him a job and he got £3.7s. 6d. and his self-respect. Not for long – no job lasted in the Depression, but this time having been in employment, he got the 'Dole': £1.10s. a week for himself, wife and four children. We got by, and there was always someone worse off ...

One summer evening a haggard, weary man passed our way and asked for directions to Newcastle; we were off the main road somewhat, so he came in for a cup of tea and a bite of what we had to eat before going on his way. He was a shipyard worker and had walked from Glasgow, alone, in search of work. Shipyard workers to Jarrow? – coals to Newcastle.

Pride, and lack of business acumen being my father's weaknesses (is pride a weakness?) drove him to abandon the ignominy and despair of the dole and try his hand at independent woodworking again, and fail again. He worked too well and charged too little and the depression was not quite at an end – not quite.

I clearly recall, as we were about to leave our home, hearing a man on the road calling to the farm hind, passing on his cart: "The Ities have gone into Abyssinia."

Children sang, to the popular 'hillbilly' tune 'Roll along covered wagon, roll along': "Will you come to Abyssinia, will you come, Bring your own ammunition and a gun. Mussolini will be there, shooting peanuts in the air, Will you come to ..." The depression was at an end – it had taken another war.

To Mickley

The country had just celebrated the Silver Jubilee of King George V and got an aluminium beaker proclaiming it; I had let the relay team down, and we all sang 'Land of Ho-up and Glory' with gusto, 'conducted' with great aplomb by Mr Pinkney after weeks of assiduous rehearsal – he had waited years for this. Then I moved away – some said because I daren't face the relay team, but it was really because my parents went.

School at Mickley

The yard of Clara Vale school was surfaced with ashes from the pit boilers, which were also standard surfacing for side-road footpaths, and were horribly rough when newly laid and fearsome on bare knees (I have the scars yet), but the ash broke down into quite a good surface for playing on – marbles, football, even cricket of sorts. Mickley had a tarmacadam slope good for little except 'tag' and skipping; it was too crowded for anything else and anyway the windows were too low to allow for ball games. 'Chucks' was alright, in the water channel by the wall under the windows – when it wasn't raining – and 'Munty Kitty Finger Thumb' on the only level part at the rear; both new games to me. I liked chucks; it was gentle and we could make our own out of clay from the 'Padduck (frog) Pond' in the wood, where pitmen on their way to work would gather a wet handful for use as underground candleholders. This was quite good clay – good enough for potting – and it could readily be formed into small cubes and baked in the oven after the bread or roast was done, to make passable imitations of chucks which from the shop cost precious pocket-money and played no better. Pocket-money was better spent on marbles, if you couldn't win them or swap cigarette cards for them. Clara Vale solved the problem of bouncing balls and wandering attention at school by putting the windows

CHUCKS

high up and opening them with long cords: Mickley walls were low and therefore the windows; children sat with their backs to them – only the teacher could see the outside world (and the arriving Inspector), and woe betide the child who twisted in his seat! Bouncing balls were fatal to low-level windows, so were proscribed.

Clara Vale school warmed itself with coal – in big, square, black, cast-iron stoves, close to the teacher and surrounded by high wire-mesh fireguards that wet clothes could be dried on. The teacher fed the fire occasionally from a coal-scuttle – so she should – she got most of the benefit. Children at the back of the room got cold and were allowed occasionally to flap their arms to boost the circulation. Mickley had its own coke and therefore a boiler for the school, in a boiler house at the rear, with an almost-flat roof that was just made for climbing on but you weren't allowed to – not if anyone was looking. The radiators served by this boiler were chunky and 'cuddly' in the manner of the early days of central heating, stood beneath the windows and were never cold – coke boilers worked all night. A far cry from 1887 and 48 degrees Fahrenheit: Mickley school was now warm.

One long blast on Headmaster Mr Bryson's whistle stopped everyone dead in their tracks, girls and boys in their separate yards; they could fraternise in class, in an academic way, and on the way home, but not in the yard – no nonsense there! Who was interested in girls anyway? I was taken with the gorgeous long, auburn hair of a not very bright girl who kept on asking me for help with her arithmetic! A short 'toot' – it was one of those sonorous whistles that distinguished Headmasters from lesser teachers who had only little tinny whistles with a pea inside – set everyone marching briskly, in complete silence, with arms swinging, into orderly 'lines', by classes, facing the school. Another 'toot'; right turn. "Forward", and follow-my-leader into the school and distribution into the appropriate class-rooms, where everyone stood at their desks, seats tipped up, until the teacher entered with a, "Good Morning, children". "Good Morning Miss" (or Sir). "Sit down" – with a good clatter as the seats were lowered. Then a short silence apart from rustling, while things were arranged and the Register brought out. The day was awake and ready to begin.

"Allen?" – "Present Miss." "Bell?" – "Present Miss." "Coulson?" – silence. "Coulson, where is Coulson?" "He's not well, Miss" – and so on, through the class. Names of absentees were recorded and the 'School Board Man' called later to examine the register and go off to

MUNTY KITTY

check on the missing. If he was seen approaching, out of school, children would cross to the other side of the street for passing, such was his fearsome aura.

On wet days, but not in the cold or snow, children were allowed indoors during 'break', or 'playtime' as it was more attractively known. In the cold they ran about to keep warm, and in the snow, threw snowballs; on wet days they sat on or near the radiators and took the rare opportunity of looking out through the windows at the dreary rain. They all went home for the mid-day meal, except those from High Mickley who couldn't make it in time, what with birds nests and interesting things on the way.

I, a frightened mouse of a boy, was pitch-forked on my arrival, into Charlie Hall's class. I had never been taught by a man – and what a man! He was a Martinet and became a legend. Not very tall, he towered above the world, with a back like a ramrod and the eye of an eagle and one at the back. He must have been a sergeant-major in a previous life. "Lost a sixpence, Boy," he would bawl, if you lowered your head, even when you thought you were out of sight. How he tied his shoelaces or washed his feet was a mystery – he only ever looked straight ahead; although he could see backwards!. No hand ever entered schoolboy pocket except for handkerchief or pocket knife when Charlie was about.

He dressed immaculately, almost 'dude'-like – if you hadn't known him better; he was no dude, in his well-made brownish suit with trouser creases that could cut bread, and a waistcoat bedecked with a silver, medallion-hung watch-chain (was he 'Masonic'). No idle ornament, this chain: it held a gold 'hunter' watch – or was it a 'half-hunter? – which he pulled delicately, 'pinkie' finger extended, like ladies at afternoon tea, from its nest in a waistcoat pocket, to check from time to time that the big-faced school clock on the wall above the door wasn't cheating. He couldn't stand cheating. Only he could see the clock; pupils couldn't clock-watch; he could clock and watch-watch. I suspect that he also checked from time to time to be sure that he really did possess a gold 'hunter' watch.

Another waistcoat pocket – there were four – housed gold *pince-nez*, for occasional use and more often peering over, balefully usually, quizzically sometimes.

Not only cheating – he could not stand wrongdoing or dishonesty of any kind. He gave one boy an open note for his next teacher, on moving up, saying : 'This boy is a cheat!' Nevertheless he was, I believe, a thoroughly good teacher of the time. What you learnt from Charlie Hall you never forgot – or else!

He viewed me, this skinny, shy, frightened boy, with a suspicious eye. At eleven I was of an age when I must have taken the 'Grading Exam' which determined my future: Grammar School and a career as a teacher or bank clerk, or staying on until fourteen then becoming a worker. So I must have failed and was therefore a potential cheat, 'dunderhead', 'nincompoop' or 'blithering idiot'. He was not to know that the exam at Clara Vale came in two parts and I had passed the first part but had been off school with some trivial affliction for the second. Headmaster Mr Pinkney had come especially to ask my father if I could attend school just for the day to take the exam; my father left it to me! But he knew full well that had I, or my clever brother, passed a thousand exams, he could not have afforded to send us to Grammar school. For my part, I declined because I didn't want to leave my pals and the school that I knew – besides, who wants to be a bank clerk? Mind you, I thought teaching wasn't so bad – teachers got lots of holidays.

Within a few weeks I had left not only my pals and school at 'Clara', but my home and the very place that I loved; where I passed to and fro to school by hedges and weedy banks with dunnock nests and yellowhammers for the finding and quiet, gentle enjoyment. Some boys claimed that taking 'only one' egg from a nest did no harm; they pierced a hole in each end and blew out the contents, then displayed them in a box with lots of others, everything from 'kitty-two-fingers' (long-tailed-tits) to partridges and peewits, all barren things that hatched no next year's 'Dawn Chorus': so sad and pointless, collecting eggs, and pinning butterflies to boards. There I had watched frog spawn in the boggy places hatch into wriggling tadpoles, grow legs and metamorphose into shiny, hopping baby frogs that disappeared into the wide world; I had drunk from cupped hands the ice-cold spring water at Potpie well, shared with the frogs and my wild friends, and, in high summer, rode perched precariously behind sweet-vernal scented pikes of hay on horse-drawn 'bogies;' while the sweating, struggling hind berated whoever had built the pikes too big. In out of summer farmyard, searched the idle seed-drill chutes for hibernating hordes of earwigs – did they really get into your brain? – and speiled up iron rods and stanchions to lie doggo atop the barned hay while friends searched carts and crannies down below; called 'guissee guissee' over the pigsty wall, thrown a crust to the eager occupant and perhaps shared the pleasure of her numerous family for a few minutes, and the smell of the never offensive pig-warmed, straw-bedded accommodation.

I kept a discreet distance when the massive bull was walked to 'work', on the end of a long wooden pole hooked to the ring in his nose, his nose, and wondered how many farmers he'd gored to death, and which tree I could climb if he broke loose. I was wary of the geese and gave a wide birth to the 'gobbler' turkey whose head always seemed to turn purple with rage whenever he saw me if I went just along the road a few yards to the Colliery Farm for a pint of milk if we ran short.

I would stand in the doorway of scrubbed-clean, sweet and sour smelling dairy (yet another of those eternal smells no museum can recapture) while Mrs Rutherford scooped milk from a big churn into a bottle and closed the top with a cardboard disk firmly pressed into place. These bottles were a great advance on jugs and cans for carrying milk. The cardboard tops at this time developed a clever little modification; a 'press' bit for inserting a straw to drink through, when all schoolchildren were given a third of a pint of milk a day, in an effort to combat rickets, and it was considered bad to drink it too quickly. Children weighed and found wanting got a full pint and probably glandular TB from untreated milk! Everyone got showered with milk because, when the 'press' bit was pressed, it didn't, but the whole lid did – down into the milk, where it acted as a plunger, to some effect. It was easier, and safer, to prise out the lid and sup from the bottle.

Mrs Rutherford at the farm also made butter in a big wooden churn that looked like hard work – I never saw it in use although I lived in hope.

All these happy childhood pleasures I left behind, without even the compensation of Grammar School and the prospect of a 'good' job and a life of leisure as a teacher. I traded it for a hundred yard walk to Charlie Hall ... Clara Vale had nothing to compare with Charlie.

He sat me in the front row, in the desk nearest his, in company with the class dunce, and 'kept an eye' on me. Next day he moved me to the back row and we never thereafter had reason other than to respect each other – not that I enjoyed being in his class: an element of fear pervaded the atmosphere. But he liked triers and anyone with a nose to the grindstone had little cause to worry.

He stalked the aisles, thumbs in waistcoat pockets, from which he occasionally produced a bone or ivory toothpick to pick a tooth or two. He quietly whistled, or rather hissed, through closed teeth, the popular tune of the day: 'Twas on the Isle of Capri that I found her ...' He had been to Capri on holiday; it was the beginning of 'holidays abroad' for the likes of schoolteachers. When the music stopped the class kept its head down, as when a time-bomb stops ticking; trouble then assailed some hapless child – a thump, a slapped head, a twisted ear, by which he would be propelled to the front for special treatment. Shame on him! He wouldn't get away with it now, but even the recipients of these 'assaults' now smile, albeit somewhat wryly, at the memory of Charlie.

He lived half a mile or so away, in Beaumont Terrace (it was the turn of the Beaumonts of Bywell to have things named after them), on the main road western fringe of Prudhoe, from where he to and fro-ed on foot to work; he disdained buses for those with legs but at times when things got a bit hot for him, he is reputed to have walked to 'Truman's' at the far end of the village and bussed from there to the Co-op – about 200yds, rather than run the gauntlet of the angry mothers of High Row South where the footpath was within broom-length or slop bucket reach of the doors – all thirty-odd of them.

There was also the tale of when he was old but still irascible, teachers having been allowed to work on beyond retiring age during Hitler's war, and he fell foul once too often, of a bigger than him, and fitter, older boy – and a Best to boot. The Bests of Mickley would not stand trifling with. The outcome, I believe, although these tales are inclined to be embellished in the telling, was a pretty vigorous chase amongst the desks, about the school, of Charlie, hotly pursued by the Best, hotly pursued by Mr Bryson (I question the 'hotly pursued' by Mr Bryson bit – he wasn't made for hot pursuit), cheered on by the more excitable and daring children. The discreet ones, with an eye to later, would no doubt maintain an overawed silence. I have not checked to see if this event was recorded in the School Log – as an example of 'Class Warfare!

My final, quite fond, memory of Charlie is of walking home from my last woodwork lesson at Eltringham School, where two ex-barrack room huts were used for woodworking lessons and cookery lessons ('domestic science') for girls. Mickley had no space for these recent facilities for instruction in rice pudding and dovetail joints, so we walked the half mile once a week for a half day lesson, and graduated, in the case of boys, from wooden 'soap holders', by way of bathroom cabinet (in genuine 'Satin Walnut'!) to a small piece of furniture – workbox, table or such.

I made a 'bedside table' in my last term, in oak, the best of all woods, and it was this that I was a bearing home when I met Charlie, marching to lunch. "Put it down, then, and let me see," he said. Being secretly pleased with my effort I welcomed the opportunity to show it off. "Very nice," quoth he: "Well done," and as I moved on, "Good Luck" – with a rare and kindly smile; knowing that I was about to set forth from school into the wide cruel world. The Demon had a gentle heart.

I sometimes wonder if he ever remembered his pupils and hoped that he had helped them on their way with a bit of discipline. Maybe a few teachers in his mould might not go amiss today.

School After Charlie

Mr Robinson was the antithesis of Charlie – quiet gentleness personified. He did wonders for confidence, and encouraged me in 'Art', as did Miss Murray, who took the class below Charlie's as well as the whole school for 'music' (which was 'singing'), much to Charlie's disgust – he had no choice but to hear it through the partition. She got nowhere with singing with me, for I had been put off for life by the horrible Miss Melrose at Clara Vale. I always had a cold for singing lessons and wiped my nose vigorously whenever Miss Murray passed by, bending her ear for the off-key; and 'made my mouth go' when she was out of hearing, as I thought. She must have known, bless her, and kept mum. How nasty memories stick, and bring a cringe. I still enjoyed listening to the songs when other classes sang – 'Drink to me only', 'Strawberry Fair', 'The Keel Row', 'Waters of Tyne', and hosts of others, all good stuff and worthy of a listen.

Miss Murray must have seen my stumbling efforts at painting because one day during 'break' she invited me to her classroom to see one of her oil-paintings that she had brought especially to show me, of Ovington House, across the river. This was the first 'real' painting I had seen, oil or otherwise, and it left a lasting impression, not least because she had taken this trouble in a kindly attempt to encourage some small talent in a boy who couldn't sing. "Try oils," she said. "They're easier than water colours." Twenty years later I did. They are expensive, and very messy.

These teachers of yore were gems beyond compare, dedicated to the betterment of 'their' children. Let this effort of mine, be it of any merit, this painting in words of Education in Mickley, stand as my modest tribute to them.

The Other Teachers

The 'old King', George V, died the year after his Jubilee and although I have only vague recollection of it, the country went through the trauma of his sad son Edward's unacceptable romance and inevitable abdication. Then we enjoyed a distraction; a day off and a bit of bally-hoo for the Coronation of Edward's brother, Good King George the Sixth. The British are good at that sort of thing – never miss a chance of a party.

Mr Robinson was good at 'sayings'. He would look over a shoulder and compliment a drawing with: 'A Thing of Beauty is a Joy Forever'; "Patience is a Virtue', if you couldn't get it right; one for every occasion. He teased me to tell him which way the wood grain ran on a varnished panel and when I thought I had done a clever painted Coronation decoration, rampant lions and things with 'God Save The King' for a finishing touch, all he could muster was "Nice hymn". He knew when to praise, when to gently put down. He set me up for life.

We got a china beaker for this celebration, and a propelling pencil; both attractive and both useable. Either Mickley was better off than Clara Vale, or the depression really was coming to an end. I also won a tie in the sports. Who needs a tie?

After the pleasant experience of Mr Robinson's class, on to Miss Burns, plump and cuddly but you wouldn't dare – no nonsense. You will notice that only unmarried women teachers worked – home was still where wives belonged – there was little enough work for men as it was. All of that wasted dedication and ability though, just because girls got married – what a shame.

I wrote long 'compositions' for Miss Burns, in well-nigh illegible writing that was the bane of her life but tolerated, only just, in a good cause – you couldn't write long and fast and readable, at least I couldn't. She ticked me off soundly for spelling 'alarum' for a clock; I'd seen it in a dictionary and thought to be clever. Not a hope.

Memory Training was synonymous with Poetry and I detested both. 'The Wreck of the Hesperis' in 1888 was no better than 'The Wreck of the Hesperis' in 1937 ... 'The boy stood on the burning deck (the Captain blew his Whistle, and down the mast came Uncle ...). I remember more of the childish parody than the poem. But I remember even more the effort and the failure – the intense dislike, especially of Scripture learned by rote – but how I have since wished I had tried harder, or had the gift of memory, or had Miss Burns earlier to encourage me. I married my wife 'For Better or for Verse' and envy her her head packed with poetry. You are never alone if you can conjure up a poem!

Miss Burns did her best to overcome my obvious dislike of poetry by offering exciting stories in verse, or beautiful descriptive pieces. I can recall as a result of her efforts, not word-perfect and only in snatches, 'The Highwayman', 'Bess the landlord's daughter'; and him 'lying there like a dog in the highway, like a dog in his blood in the highway', 'The Lake Isle of Innisfree with its nine bean rows' and 'bee-loud glade', not so different from my High Close Wood; 'The Slave's Dream' that yet makes me weep; but who wants to know about the boring old 'Hesperis' or the 'Battle of Killiecrankie' anyway?

I remember, I remember – Miss Burns. She must now be about ninety, if she's still alive; I hope she married and had lots of lovely children to read poetry to – and teach net ball. She 'took' the girls' notable team, and good they were too, I believe – visiting teams couldn't cope with the sloping yard. 'Old Girls' I speak to do not seem to have cared much for her – she kept a short, thick stick in her desk, and used it. But she was alright, and taught good English – tried her best, at least!

Finally, at Mickley school, there was the 'Top Class', with the Headmaster, Mr Bryson, and the prospect of leaving school at the age of fourteen. He was obviously the headmaster because he sat at a prestigious flat-topped desk with a kneehole and drawers down each side. The other teachers had tall, narrow desks with sloping lids that lifted for hiding behind (eating chocolate?). He was mostly absorbed in things other than teaching – like walking about the school looking important, carrying some papers or a book. He was held in awe and signed the 'Reports' that gave parents a rough idea of how their children were doing.

I don't remember learning much in Mr Bryson's class, except some Algebra and a reluctant piece of 'Portia's Speech'. We read a lot, and Miss Burns, whose class shared the room, kept an eye when he went walkabout, and used her cane more generously on her neighbour's than on her own class.

The 'Boss', as he was known, invited me to stay on another year but there were no facilities for further education and I didn't fancy another verse of 'Portia', so I declined the kind offer; I could read at home, and my mother needed every penny.

I didn't go to school on my fourteenth birthday – I went to work.

There was still a lot to learn, I soon discovered, but this was the finish of formal education for a Mickley child in 1938. Looking back on it, I have few regrets: these little village schools certainly didn't fill heads with erudition, but they laid firm foundations on which the willing could build, and in many cases did, once dislike of the process had worn off. Some Latin would have been good to have and an extra language, and perhaps if I'd been taught to sing?

Education eventually withered on the vine at Clara Vale, where the school is now a 'Community Hall' (popular stuff, Community), but at Mickley, after a period in the doldrums, the old school flourishes and vibrates with vitality.

I returned to the school in short time, not, like some, to 'Night Classes', which never seemed to do much except give teachers a spot of extra income, but to the 'County Library', a recent and wonderful idea. I had so missed access to school books – although my father brought home second-hand books from every Saturday afternoon in Newcastle, at 3d., 6d., and at the very most, 1s. a time, they were not enough. Zane Grey, Jeffrey Farnol by the score, Hopalong Cassidy, Sherlock Holmes and P. G. Wodehouse in numbers, Mark Twain, Chesterton – there were never enough books. Even when he lashed out £1.10s., half a week's pay, on a huge set, almost too heavy to carry, of blue and gold bound, 'Illustrated Works of William Shakespeare', it was not enough. (Shakespeare not enough? – how dare I?).

I needed my books. This great yearning must have been a leftover from Victorian times, the heyday of reading, when books were the principle source of pleasure and enlightenment. Not being a miner and therefore excluded from the 'Reading Room' and its 500-odd books, I even contemplated trying the chemist's shop at Branch End with its sign saying – Stationery. Circulating Library, but was still not so big that I couldn't get my ears boxed for enquiring how a circulating library could be stationary. Anyway, it cost 2d. a week for a rubbish book. The County Library arrived, in Mickley School, just in the nick of time for me – like the Relief of Mafeking. There were books galore, free for the asking and a hundred yard walk – and a chat with Mr Bryson in his new and extra role as Librarian. The 'Library' was in square bookcases mounted on spare desks against the only bit of blank wall in the school, at the back of Std. 2 classroom. On two evenings a week Mr Bryson unlocked and took down the doors, stamped the books and filed the tokens, and was delighted if a particular book was requested. He also had first choice of books, in particular the new ones, when they were changed twice a year, and probably ordered ones he fancied. He was taken aback when I asked for Lawrence's *The Seven Pillars of Wisdom* – "You'll find it hard going," he said; but he got it, and I read it, every word. It was hard going.

Browsing through the books was enjoyable – so was going back to school! Not for the learning – for the nostalgia and the smells, again the smells – life's punctuation marks. School was chalk and books, ink and paper. Ink had its own character: It came in brown earthenware bottles and was dispensed by the ink 'monitor' into little china 'wells', two to a desk, for dipping into, and shaking off with a rattle, with wooden pens which had nibs that 'crossed' and were useless if misused. 'Misused' was being laid at right-angles across the end of a ruler projecting over the edge of the desk, the free end then being struck hard in an attempt to impale the pen by its nib in the wooden ceiling. Failed attempts carried a risk of impaling pens in children's heads. This game was strictly for when teacher was out of class. At other times, as when she was at the blackboard, pellets of blotting-paper dipped in ink could be fired from catapults of golf-ball rubber tied to finger and thumb (secreted in the palm). Otherwise ink could be used for writing, and making blots, and staining fingers if the pen was dipped too far into the well. A good supply of blotting paper was important. Do computers have a smell?

Riding Terrace

During the time that I took you off through my family's Depression, Mickley pressed quietly on with its own and not a lot happened, but there were a few developments. The land to the west of Station Bank being the 'development area' of the village and Wrightsons the owners, ever looking to raise a bob or two, had parcelled it off at the turn of the century to various speculators. They began building private houses in earnest, but got no further than eight each in Newton Terrace and Riding Terrace, and twin purpose-built shops. Purpose-built in that they were intended from the outset to have their front rooms used as shops, otherwise they were ordinary street houses, with built-in enterprise. The enterprise of the first occupant of one of these shops, a Mr Christer – the second private shopkeeper in the village, was sadly cut short when he failed to return from the Kaiser's war.

Ovington Brewery bought a chunk of land, either for another brewery, or more likely, for just a pub. They were reputed to have made 'Guinness' at Ovington but I doubt it would only be black beer; it's a nice thought though – 'Guinness' brewed in Mickley. It would have saved crossing the river with the barley, although the hill was no less steep. Either way, it didn't come off and Blaydon Industrial Provident Society bought the site and built their answer to 'West Wylam' in 1910, when shops were springing up like mushrooms.

Riding Terrace, being a prime site for shops, on Station Bank, made quick use of its front rooms. No. 2 was a barber's shop, complete with red and white candy-striped pole sticking out from the wall by the door, symbol of blood and bandages, from the time when barbers led a double life. You might well ask who cut the hair of Mickley previously: anyone with a pair of scissors and the courage, unless vanity could afford a trip to Hexham – they even had a dentist and a solicitor up there!

The 'dunce' who sat beside me on my first day in Charlie Hall's class lived at No. 2 Riding Terrace He wasn't such a dunce – he knew about money – more than most. He was the 'lather boy' in the barber's. Whenever a customer entered needing a shave, the barber tapped on the door to the kitchen and the boy emerged with a mug of water, boiling from the kettle on the range; a shaving brush and stick of soap, a towel for draping around the customer's shoulders and a smaller one for wiping lather (or blood) from where it oughtn't to be. He wet the stubble with brush and water then proceeded to work up a rare old lather with the aid of the lavender-perfumed soap-stick. It took ages – the more prolonged and thorough the lathering, the softer the stubble, the smoother the shave. Task completed, the boy (I forget his name) retired to his mother's kitchen to wash the gear ready for the next man in, who might be one of a continuous flow on a busy day, or not another all day; but the boy had to be there, and ready, just in case. The barber could do his own lathering at a pinch, so an evening at the pictures was always possible for the 'lather boy' – he had the money. Homework did not fit comfortably between shaves.

The razor was a great advance on a dagger or a piece of broken glass for shaving, and carbon steel at its best, no longer needed for Knightly swords, made superb 'cut-throat' razors. A fearsome weapon in unskilled hands, properly used it could give the best of all shaves. There seemed to be a selection process involved between the several razors laid out on the bench; perhaps the weight or 'set' of the blade had to be suited to the type of growth – perhaps just to the whim of the barber. Possibly he chose a blunt one for the disliked customer (didn't give a tip last time?). It would take a brave man to offend his barber! The chosen blade would be given a jolly good 'stropping' on the leather strap hanging from the bench – flip-flop, flip-flop, flip-flop. Most barbers began proceedings with a flourish, like Mr Pinkney about to embark on a 'copperplate' application of chalk to blackboard but infinitely more threatening. It was the nose and the ears that seemed to be most at risk and were firmly twisted, it seemed painfully, out of harm's way. Strangely, customers never seemed to bleed unduly – these barbers really were a dextrous lot. All the same, I was glad as I sat waiting my turn – and it could be a long wait in a barber's at a busy time and if the talk was good – that it was only a haircut I needed and no young shaver would ever practise his skills on me.

A 'proper' haircut was only called for when I was old enough to worry about what Winnie Barnes thought of my appearance; before that my mother did the job on my brother and me with a pair of hand-clippers that could no doubt have been used on sheep, they pulled the hair if she was in a hurry: once my father did it but because my brother winced he went off and left the shears dangling. He never did get near my hair. 'Short back and sides' was the norm at the barber's, or 'just a trim', if you were going out for the evening. Either way it was 'short back and sides'. That was as far as hair-dressing artistry went. A 'singe' was value added for an extra penny on the nine pence for boy, shilling for a man. "Seals the ends," he said; it made an awful smell – burning hair does, doesn't it? Then: "Anything on?" – it would be 'Sir' in town but only Mr Bryson and perhaps the Manager got 'Sir' in

Mickley – it would have been nice, though, at fourteen! I remember feeling ten feet tall the first time the 'Commissionaire' in his fine uniform opened the door and 'sir-ed' me at Bainbridges – until I began to worry in case he was watching to see if I bought anything. And who was I to be kowtowed to by a man old enough to be my grandfather and who had probably been at the Somme. The 'Anything on?' if it took your fancy, was a dollop of green stuff from a bottle without a label so that you couldn't blame anyone if your hair fell out. Smarmed down and combed and the spare hair brushed from your shoulders to join the mounting pile on the lino (you got a good brushing-down, and it was free), you sallied forth (self conscious if it was your first time) looking like Sir Malcolm Sargent at the Proms and smelling like a chemist's shop.

Those who preferred to do their own smarming down did it with 'Fields Lavender Brilliantine', bought in an oval tin with a difficult-to-get-off lid, from the barber (he scored either way), or 'any good shop' for that matter. It was universally popular, especially after the advent of films (Rudolph Valentino) and dance bands, whose leaders seemed to use it liberally. Coloured green (green was the colour for putting on hair), it had the consistency of axle-grease and a powerful smell of lavender. Mickley pit lads smelled awfully like wartime Polish airmen! It fairly stuck the hair down, did Brilliantine – no breeze would dare, to ruffle a hair.

The barber didn't sell much else, and the place was a bit seedy, but you could get razor blades and something in a packet out of a drawer that was asked for in a low voice; this was before cannabis.

The Post Office

Next door to the barbers, at No. 3 Riding Terrace, was the village Post Office, again occupying the front room. Customers entering the front door could have gone straight up the stairs to the bedrooms, but instead turned right, and could then have gone right through the P. O. into the Carrs' living room with its Glendinning range and clippie mats, just like next door's.

If you think the barber's seedy, the P.O. was downright dismal and depressing. It was all-over brown, on the theory, I suppose, that it was easier to keep clean, or didn't show the dirt. There was nothing in the room except a counter (brown) across the middle with drawers for cash and postal orders and forms (yes forms, even then). The counter was surmounted by a wire-mesh grill, presumably to keep stray fingers out of the drawers – it would have done little against Kalashnikovs. Not that there was much need – the contents of the till were measured more in pennies than in pounds and anyway people didn't go about robbing little shops and Post Offices. The mantle-shelf of the fireplace, which was never graced or lightened by the flames of a fire, even on the coldest of days, held the 'stock' – a packet or two of cheap note-paper and envelopes, some pencils and pens and packets of nibs, and a bottle of ink. A picture postcard of Mickley (oh yes, Mickley rated picture-postcards) would more likely be found at Branch End.

The counter held a telephone and telegraph pads. The telephone superseded the telegraph-key for the transmission of telegrams by the turn of the century and Mickley P.O., being a Telegraph Office since the days of Mrs Bolam, had its telephone when Dave Carr came home one-legged from the war and took on the P.O. as a job he could handle; at least it was a job.

Previously Telegraph Offices were run by people with a knowledge of the Morse Code and the training to send it along overhead wires (we could hear the messages buzzing their way, we thought), by way of an arm on a board that was pressed up and down to make electrical contact in the form of coded dots and dashes. 'A' was . -, 'B' was - . . ., 'C' -. -., and so on. At the other end of the wire the process was reversed and the electrical pulses translated by a buzzer into audible dots and dashes for the telegraphist to decode and write down on the yellow form which became the harbinger of doom for wives and mothers of soldiers of the war.

Dave Carr didn't need the skill of the telegraphist; he had a telephone. But it was a strange device – a stalk on a stand with a mouthpiece – a small microphone – on the top for speaking into, and a separate ear piece that hung when not in use on the rest, which was also a switch, on the side of the stalk. There was no dial, initially, and contact was made with the operator by jiggling the 'rest' up and down to jangle her ear and draw her attention if she was having a cup of tea or a chat. She made the necessary connection and could listen in (and join in!) if so inclined. The Telephone Exchange bid fair to oust the Co-op as the centre of traffic in news – the village Reuters.

After a while there was a dial; it was 'O' to raise the operator, and local numbers could be dialled direct, although 'trunk' calls still needed the help of the operator – female by day, male at night. The night-time facility was not much use when the only phone was in the P.O. and only accessible in opening hours – when it could be used for tuppence by anyone with the courage and someone at the other end with a phone. It was unnerving to hold a conversation with someone at a distance who couldn't even be seen! Eventually there came an 'open all hours' phone in a public kiosk by the club, but the telephone did not exactly take Mickley by storm – in 1950 there were no more than about a dozen, for a population of around 2,000.

So Dave Carr's telephone was used mainly for the transmission of telegrams, and a much used and valuable service it was, and cheap. But even at a penny a word, the cost was counted. The resulting almost cryptic messages were rushed, and I mean rushed, for they could be urgent, to their destinations. At bigger offices they were an excuse, like flashing blue lights on police cars, for high-speed dashes by 'telegraph boys' on bicycles, who would wait for a reply if one was called for. At Mickley, Dave closed the office and peg-legged his high-speed telegram to its destination, and if anyone wanted a stamp in the meantime, they just had to wait while he peg-legged his way back.

He was a sad, sad man, with good reason; working in this miserable office and trying to bring up his two sons on what the Post Office paid him, plus the miserly pension that the grateful nation paid him in return for his leg; mind you, he got a wooden peg in exchange, so he did as well as the veteran of Minden!

Sadder still, one day there was a fuss, with the village bobby busying about in High Close wood opposite the school and Dave Carr was taken away. He had tried to drown himself in the few inches of water that here made up the stream previously noted for filling buckets. The near tragedy was all because of some trifling discrepancy in the P.O. accounts. One of his sons, it seems, had been taking coppers from the till for sweets, and Dave couldn't face the consequences. The lather boy next door had plenty of money for sweets …

Taking your own life was in those days a criminal as well as a religious offence, but Dave wasn't unduly punished for trying, and he kept his job. Not long afterwards, his younger son Gerald was killed in a road accident while travelling as a passenger in a lorry. Ten years old, I think he was. The other son, John, became what every boy was supposed to dream of becoming – an engine driver – steam engines of course. He made complete the tragedy of the Carr family by dying young – before his parents.

The Dolly Sisters

Down the street was No. 8 and Scotts' – another shop in a front room; a mini general dealer, but this time unmodified to the tune of a shop window and with only the ordinary house window for a very limited display of a few bottles of sweets on a high shelf and one or two trays below and a few odds and ends – the usual array but less of it and more difficult to see. Inside, when the opening door had tinkled the delightful brass bell on a coiled spring to summon one or both of the 'Dolly Sisters' to enquire your needs, there was barely room to stand before the tiny counter – one was a crowd, and no doubt a busy day. This room was chock-a-block with stock – almost as much as the Co-op, it seemed, but don't ask me what. My recollection is that these Dolly Sisters were expert at leaving loose the round lid of the square tin of Black Bullets, so that there was always a supply with a sugary coating, for weighing on shining brass scales. Sometimes a tiny, black-dressed, white-aproned old lady, wearing lace headgear which mother said was a 'mutch', flitted away into the kitchen, like a ghost out of Cranford. They sold yeast for bread making, and babies' dummies, and were open when the Co-op wasn't.

My family were forever giving names to nameless ones: the chap who wore one of those sleeveless army-surplus leather jerkins, winter and summer, was 'Leatherjacket', the fellow who was perpetually in the green long-sleeved pullover (his wife was a dab-hand at knitting) was 'Greensleeves'; he who shot rabbits (and an odd pheasant when the Squire's back was turned, and your dog when its days were ended), was 'Twelve Bore'. The Scott sisters got their sobriquet because one of them was 'Dolly' and is to this day, although which one is the survivor, at 93, I know not – she is the 'Dolly Sister'. She lives alone in No. 8 and has witnessed the rise and fall of shops in Mickley.

Fish and Chips and Wormalds

The shop that was Christer's, who did not come home from the war, adjoined a fish and chip shop. Fish and chips were not the first 'convenience' foods or 'take-aways'; there had been roast chestnuts and baked potatoes in city streets for donkey's years, and hot pies and cups of peas with vinegar in the Raas. But in the first half of the twentieth century 'fish and chips' took off in a huge way, as a moneymaking business and a tasty, nourishing (although nobody knew or cared about that) and easy meal – and cheap. Alright for working folk at threepence for the fish and a penny for chips and some 'scranchums' thrown in (the bits of batter that fell off in the fat and went crisp, that children begged).

Anyone could set up a fish and chip shop and many did, but it needed more than a bag of flour and a scoop; there had to be room for a pretty big two or three pan frying range, which, with the counter, just about filled a room, so that at busy times the queue went outside. Fish and chips contributed enormously to the nutritional well-being of the nation, in spite of what you hear about fry being 'bad for you' – and all that salt! and heavily dosed with vinegar, and eaten with grubby little fingers out of second-hand newspapers; oh yummy – they were 'scrummy'. Better than now, and that's not just an old man's fancy.

SCOTT'S SHOP, 8 RIDING TERRACE

When 17 Riding Terrace gave up fish-and-chipping it

joined in close company with No. 18 in the plethora of General Dealers arising in the village. The Wormalds took on the shop at No. 18 when the war-widow Mrs Christer couldn't keep it going. 17 and 18 were intended to be shops – they had big, double windows, but they still sacrificed the sitting room: Mrs Wormald also sacrificed the small bedroom upstairs to a ladies hairdressers, which was innovation if you like, in a village where 'short back and sides' was the only hairdressing known. If men could have their hair singed, women could now have theirs clamped in red-hot irons! So indeed they did – all crimped and curled, and some of them dyed, the hussies! Jolly high time too, that the ladies were able to spend a bob or two on themselves, even if it had to be skinned from the housekeeping. Before long they'd be using lipstick! It indicated somewhat better times.

Better times certainly showed in the number and variety of shops where money could be spent – Riding terrace became the Oxford Street of Mickley, with seven shops, including Blaydon Co-op 'supermarket', in a distance of little more than a hundred yards, a fair part of which was taken up with the great social experiment of 'Council houses'. These provided homes at low, subsidised rents for the poor, and released many from the tyranny of the 'tied cottage' system, which virtually bound a worker to his boss, whatever the circumstances – no job, no home. Prudhoe Urban District Council did its duty in this direction, spurred on by governments now becoming more involved in the social affairs of the nation and the welfare of the people. It bought up the land in 'private enterprise' Riding Terrace between Scott's and Wormald's, which had gone undeveloped because of the war, and filled it with Council houses, which put an end to Oxford Street, as there were rules about living in Council houses, such as not using them as shops! A private attempt to continue Riding Terrace down the hill beyond the 'Blaydon' got no further than two houses, one of which became yet another shop, couldn't you guess, but it was the final one in the street and an innovation – Christers' paper shop.

The Paper Shop

Selling newspapers was enough in itself to make a shop, and 'Christers' was never taken seriously as a challenge to the Co-op, or even Scotts. It sold a few sweets and broken toffee in trays, but had a monopoly of papers and as they were delivered to the doors, the shop was really just a distribution centre from which children plied their little trade, before school in the morning with the 'Dailies', after school with the 'Evenings' and magazines, and on crisis days, like Abdication and War, a dash around the streets shouting "SPECIALL-EXTRAA". Newspapers were how the news was spread, even after wirelesses came within the reach of ordinary folk They came by rail and pony-cart and to the door at no extra charge; every household got one, mostly the *Newcastle Journal* – sprung from the old weekly *Newcastle Courant* which ran from 1720 for approaching 200 years, starting at 2d. – or *Evening Chronicle.* They were needed for personal hygiene and cleaning paraffin-lamp glasses.

The emancipation of the working classes, their education and social awareness, gradually developed a political aspect to their lives. Trade Unions and Socialism became a force to be reckoned with in the affairs of the nation; workers felt that they at last had a voice, a voice to be heeded. They had come a long way since the Massacre of Hexham in 1761, when workers were suppressed, and shot, when trying to resist conscription. Although the workers of Mickley gained nothing from the General Strike of 1926, and did not become embroiled in riots such as those at Blaydon and Crawcrook, they talked, in pubs and clubs, of Politics. They learned the power of words, the skill of debate; they used their votes and elected fellow-workers to speak for them on Local Councils – and in Parliament, the garrulous ones who read a lot. They read the *Daily Herald.*

It was a matter of principle for working men to read the *Daily Herald,* the official voice of the Trade Unions, after it arrived in 1934. I was brought up on it, and although it missed out a bit on local matters, I believe it to have been a pretty good paper. It carried a horrible but compelling story (I was rather young), in instalments, about hordes of naked midget people trying to take over the country (or world), leaping on to shoulders and slitting throats with 'cut-throat' razors. I don't recollect how it ended, but they didn't succeed! No doubt they increased the circulation of the *Herald.* Perhaps it is significant that Mickley miners, now literate, having read their newspapers, used them as toilet paper! Whatever would they have done with the *Sun*?

The shortcomings of the *Herald* in local matters could be overcome with the *Hexham Courant.* It had started as a courageous venture in 1864 as *The Hexham Courant and South Tyne Advertiser* (took up half the front page for its title, on the Co-op principle that you can't beat a good name for attracting attention!) and at first was more Advertiser than Courant, at three-ha'pence a time, twice a week. It immediately grew from four to eight pages and within a year reached a circulation of 2,000. Most of the news in the early years, indeed for some time, came from London and was of a National and International nature, like the American Civil War, the Irish Problem, Parliamentary affairs, murder and suicides – always 'melancholy', 'most horrible', or at least 'strange'. My, how they used words, these Victorians – never two when ten would do, in close-packed print without illustrations, which were confined, in simple form, to advertisements.

The *Courant* made a name for itself in the early years in being in the forefront of the establishment of the freedom of the press. It fought for, and won at some cost, the right that Editors and Newspapers could not be held accountable in law for the views of correspondents – a principle enjoyed by the *Daily Herald* in its time, and the *Courant* (and the *Sun*!), today.

Advertisements filled the front page – of course, they were being paid for and had to be seen; news could be searched for. Local news took up only a few paragraphs on the back page, half a column in the first issue; there was either not much of it or not many gatherers. Mickley figured quite prominently in the early days, for a place of its size, but it must be said, more in notoriety than fame! Otherwise most local news was in the form of verbatim reports of meetings of various kinds where people aired their views, usually at length. The Hexham Board of Guardians carried some column-weight; they often discussed the 'deplorable state' of sanitation and water, and threatened to call Mickley Coal Company to book, as the responsible party hereabouts. The danger of 'fever' and cholera greatly exercised their minds and kept the typesetters busy. In 1866 the Board requested (when did a request become an order?) M.C. Co. to set aside one or two cottages for isolating cholera victims, should the need arise.

A major early event of importance to be featured was the very serious outbreak of 'Cattle Plague' (Rinderpest or Steppe Murrain) which swept the country in 1865–66 and killed 10,000 cattle a week at its peak. It was centred, in the North East, on Mickley, where a Mr Brannen was fined £20 for failing to report his first case and had his entire stock wiped out. The wholesale price of beef rose to 52s. per stone. It is interesting to note that farmers relied on self-help to see them through the crisis – there was no other way. Those fortunates whose stock were not afflicted, and who benefited enormously from the high price of beef, chipped in for the less fortunate (is there a lesson there?) The *Courant* covered it all – very fully.

Police Court and Assizes got good coverage too; separate but related cases paint a realistic but rough picture of life in the village. A poor village woman claimed £4.10s. from a local landowner for assault on her 13yr. old daughter. It seems he wanted possession of the cottage the family occupied, which he had leased to M.C. Co., and when he failed to get it waited until the woman went away to bring home her ailing husband. Then he burst into the house, 'in great anger' and threatened the girl to such an extent that she and her two little sisters had to 'depart the house into the rain, whereupon he proceeded to throw out their clothing and bedding and what possessions he could handle after them into the mud and the wet and locked the door'. They were eventually, with help, able to make re-entry through a window but one of the children became very ill as a result of her ordeal. The family retained possession but the father died after reaching home and the case so outraged the Judge that he awarded it to the widow, regretting that he was unable to award greater compensation, but charging all of the costs of the case against the landowner, Mr Humble – "As much as possible," he said.

Not only the judge was outraged – the pitmen of Mickley didn't like that sort of thing either, and rough justice bettered 'costs' in their eyes. The outcome was a report in the *Hexham Courant* of July 4th. 1866 headed – 'HIGHWAY ROBBERY AT MICKLEY', and the commitment for trial at the assizes of the two pit men concerned: Matthew Rowell and George Wilkinson. They each received twelve months hard labour.

Other early reports said that the 'cat' was used for the first time in Newcastle; that Mickley Coke Ovens Permanent Benefit Society had 87 members, an income of £57.6s. 9d. an expenditure of £44 (good housekeeping), and a tea in the School.

There were frequent reports of 'Penny Readings', especially at Bywell.

There was an account in the National news section, of an attempt to blow up a non-unionist saw handle maker in Sheffield (diabolical attempt!).

After the Hexham hirings, when farm workers offered themselves for hire, like slaves, in the market place, John Stokoe of Mickley Square had an eye destroyed by a woman who threw an earthenware pot at him after he had called her 'foul names'. She got 21 days hard labour.

John Scott of Mickley was accused of the attempted rape of a 48 year old widow. He had 13 children and was a friend. Found 'not guilty'!

Telegraph poles were to be erected from the stations at Corbridge and Prudhoe to the Post Offices (telegraphs followed the railways).

Hexham streets were to be lit by gas.

Lawn mowers (noiseless!) were advertised for £3.10s; Prize Medal sewing machines 35s., and meat was too dear at 2d.–3d. per pound; but you could send by post for Downies Italian rough balsam, Healing Ointment and Life Preserving Pills, although the prices weren't quoted.

The *Courant* office was closed on Sept. 29th 1869 for a staff trip to Kelso. By rail, from Hexham to Kelso?

Thus did the *Hexham Courant* lay the foundations; set the pattern, for the dissemination of local news on paper, kept the readers of Mickley informed, through dark days and fine; saw the *Daily Herald* come and go, and still keeps its place, although much bigger and more technological (makes more mistakes), but still finds space for an occasional mention of Mickley.

The East End

With the prime sites built on, development moved east and the next and last shop to take its place in the village was Trumans', which was another purpose-built general dealers on the lines of the house with a shop in the sitting room, but this time with an extra room or two. It was quite 'upmarket' in fact and it seemed doubtful if the Trumans needed a shop if they were that well off! They were 'detached', and alongside the cricket field, which was status, if you like. Next along, and in keeping with the 1930s trend away from terraces into 'semi-detached', or semi-attached, I suppose, were two houses joined together. Again they were somewhat above the standard of previous building - 'modern' and all that: separate kitchenette, (little kitchen!), WC, gas not only for lighting but for cooking, in addition to the easy to work and clean, tiled 'Triplex' range. Makes you wonder how the housewife filled in her time! There were only two of these 'privileged' housewives; just along the road a few yards were some who certainly were not. They lived in the Bungalows (euphemism for huts), which were rushed into service as temporary 'homes for heroes' after the war, and were still in use fifteen years after the next one. These ubiquitous Army huts adopted some useful roles, from fish and chip shops to school classrooms, but it was as homes, the Great War equivalent of 'Prefabs', that they fulfilled their greatest role. Simple – primitive – they were, maybe, but with modern fitments such as gas cookers and lights and water on tap, they became, with a bit of devotion to the skills of homemaking, cramped but cosy nests. Wood makes for warmth: it also makes for fires – one hut went up in flames, but no one was hurt – they were easy to escape from. Being only six in number, but semi-detached into twelve dwellings, and set apart from other houses, the huts were really quite select and in a very attractive location, green field site and all – with 'easy access to all amenities'. Today they might happily be 'holiday chalets'. They formed the most easterly development of Mickley – getting on for Prudhoe.

Cosy Joe

With the opening of Trumans ', the last of fifteen shops in this tiny village, which had none when the *Hexham Courant* was first published, there seemed little scope for any more adventurous entrepreneurs, but Joe Stokoe – Cosy Joe – found a gap. He came from Halfway, on the way to Prudhoe – halfway between Gateshead and Hexham, in fact – and, like Edwin Longstaffe and John Nichols, saw potential in innovation. He latched on to the craze for the cinema, or Picture House as it was first known, that swept the country, knocking live theatre and Music Hall for six and not doing much for Martin Bredis either; now he could have a rest from knocking nails in with his hands. The cinema was novel, it was cheap, and any dark building that would hold a small crowd and had electricity on hand was suitable; in towns, theatres lent themselves admirably to conversion or to a dual-purpose 'Jekyll and Hyde' existence. These conversions couldn't satisfy the huge demand, so specially built cinemas erupted across the land like colourful warts – huge, ornate, ghastly looking eyesores reflecting the taste, or lack of it, of the times. But they were exciting and enticing, with lots of bright electric lights, colourful ones, and on the biggest and best, like the Stoll, the Odeons and hosts with names as splendid, NEON lights to proclaim their gaudy presence to the heavens. At the doors, wide and handsome, with lights enough to welcome a Prince, stood a Commissionaire resplendent in uniform to shame his counterpart at Bainbridges, or even a Mickley Band member; he didn't do much except keep an eye on the proceedings, but it got him off the dole and he did feel grand – when he'd got over his initial embarrassment; the white gloves looked especially good.

Inside was usually even more ornate than the Commissionaire; like a cheap theatre, with Terrazzo floors in the foyer – they had to have a foyer – and wide, sweeping stairs to carry the crowds, and there were crowds, to the circle and balcony. The cheaper stalls were straight in from the entrance, under the balcony, and close to the screen. Everyone sat in plush tip-up seats, with ashtrays on the backs for the people behind, and while they waited, watched columns of different-coloured lights playing up and down the huge curtains that hid the screen when it wasn't doing its stuff; or admired the great decorated areas of 'stippled' walls and the luminous clock, and the lights that faded just before the curtains opened as if by magic. The novelty of such things, although at first almost worth the entrance money, soon wore off and then some of the bigger places relieved the boredom of waiting by having a noisy, some might say musical, 'Whurlitzer' organ emerge from the bowels of the earth, like some Satanic monster, complete with the organist himself seated at the mighty keys and arrayed in appropriate gear – black bow tie, and tails. The two together played non-stop until the show was about to start, when together they disappeared Satan-wards to await the next interval. It kept some organists off the dole, and left some pleasant memories.

If the lights went out before you found your seat, there were Usherettes to shine you there with long electric torches: if kitchenettes were little kitchens, were usherettes little ushers? Electric torches had been thought of as long ago as 1891, not in America, but in England – Bristol – but didn't come into their own until the age of the usherette and later, the Blackout. Torches were also good for Christmas presents for boys who already had a 'Lampost' knife, but they were different from Usherettes torches; they were flat for fitting into pockets, and had, as well as a clear lens for lighting up the clouds, little red and green ones for I don't know what, except Port and Starboard if you happened to be at sea – or on a bicycle. Ordinary ones were good enough for Usherettes I suppose; mind you, they had dashing uniforms – like little Commissionaires!

In the early days of cinema and in lesser places, there was none of this ostentation, just a dark room with seats and a simple screen with a flickering picture and no accompanying sound except that of a piano playing 'atmosphere' music – the atmosphere depending on the ability of the pianist. Words to match the action were shown on the screen but it didn't much matter if you couldn't read – the actions spoke louder than words!

Crawcrook, just up the road from where we lived prior to Mickley, had no spare building suitable for conversion but was big enough to warrant a real cinema, so the purpose-designed Globe was built, with a hint of theatre, in the name at least. Otherwise it was a shoestring affair without even a foyer or coloured lights; but it had a balcony of sorts, although no Usherettes, not for Saturday morning matinees. There was a big fellow, not a Commissionaire because he didn't have a uniform, who shouted at us to be quiet and if we weren't, more or less, the rotter opened the exit doors alongside the screen to let the light spoil the picture. That shut us up, which wasn't fair because making a noise was part of the fun, especially when Tom Mix – in the white hat – shot the villain – in the black hat – or when Tonto came dashing to the rescue just in the nick of time, but you had to wait till next week to be certain. What a cacophony!

It was a penny, downstairs; for tuppence you could enjoy the privilege and pleasure of throwing your peanut shells over the balcony on to the 'pennies' below. Our version of vandalism.

Altogether, the cinema was the most exciting and adventurous development of fun in the lives of working folk, especially children. Mickley didn't justify a purpose-built cinema – not at that time – but it did have electricity, and a redundant Methodist Chapel, dark inside. Would God, the Authorised Methodist version, approve? Of course He would – they needed the money, and Joe Stokoe had some – and would soon have more, there was profit in films. All the chapel needed was an extra door, both made to open outwards and fitted with 'panic bolts' to conform with new safety regulations for cinemas after the terrible disaster in Sunderland when more than 300 children died because the doors opened inwards and someone shouted "Fire".

Of course there couldn't be a cinema without a white screen, mounted high, so that it could be seen over the heads in front, above a tiny stage with hand-pulled curtains. A slope on the floor improved the view still further as there was a limit to how high the screen could go. At the rear of the hall were a few rows of second-hand tip-up seats with armrests and plush seats with fleas. These posh seats were separated by a passageway from the bulk of the seating, which was without armrests and knee-room. The front stalls, at the very, and I mean very, front, were two rows of wooden forms with neither backs, armrests, velvet – or fleas (too uncomforable!) The front row had plenty of knee room and they did tip-up – end-ways if everyone stood up except the one at the extreme end. The crick in the neck from looking up at the almost overhead screen was the worst problem with the front row, but then these seats were cheap, at 3d. in the evening. Come to think of it, the other, 'good', seats were not exactly bank-breaking at 6d. for most and 9d. at the back where sat the Manager and the Deputies and the better-off (the lather boy?) Just like Woolworth's, who made a fortune at 3d., 6d., and 9d.

The film projector and 'projectionist', or in posher places Bioscope Operator, stood at the back, raised a little but separated from the best seats only by cigarette smoke, which rises. If anyone in front of the projector stood up their silhouette filled the screen, to the detriment of the picture and howls of outrage from the audience – those in the cheap seats anyway – the Manager didn't howl. Frequent breaks in the film, which had to be mended, also caused uproar in the cheaper seats, where best behaviour was not so much called for.

On Saturday mornings entrance was 1d. and 2d., just like the Globe, and I was told, but didn't dare put it to the test, that you could get in for a jam-jar – you never could trust Geordie humour. I never saw one being proffered, nor were there piles of them at the entrance, but I could well believe it – they were normal currency if not legal tender. A 2lb. jar traded in at 1d. A soda-water syphon was worth 1/- but more difficult to come by. You might well ask what the people of Mickley did with soda-water syphons. I can tell you what one hard-up housewife did … In the absence of a pawnbroker she used a syphon to tide her over till pay day! Some shops gave credit ('tick'), so she bought a syphon on 'tick', went outside and squirted the contents into the gutter, then returned it empty to claim the 1/- deposit – cash! How's that for high finance? It certainly beat stock-broking for losing money – at 3d. interest – the cost of the soda water in the gutter – on a shilling for a week or less!

Also on Saturday mornings the entrance ticket, which was just a numbered cloakroom ticket, served as a free raffle ticket. The 'front of house' man, one of the three sons of the proprietor – Joe, Jim and Ralph, who ran the place – climbed on to the stage and drew a ticket from a shoe-box. The holder of the other half of the torn-in-two ticket – my, how you held on to them – won a bag with, I think – I never won it – an apple, an orange, a few peanuts and sweets. Apples and oranges were not scorned as gifts or prizes in those days: this largess was totally unnecessary but added enormously to the excitement and fun. Perhaps it compensated for not being able to throw peanut shells from the balcony. But nothing could have kept children with a penny away from Tom Mix, The Three Stooges, and Tarzan on a Saturday morning. The 'Cosy', what a lovely name for a little cinema, knocked marbles and tops into a cocked hat and ran football close. No-one could say it was bad for children – sedentary and nonparticipating – there was no shortage of activity and participation at Saturday morning matinees!

I remember the Stokoe brothers as being rather sad and unsmiling, which seemed strange, running as they did, a place that dispensed so much pleasure. Perhaps it was having to cope with all those noisy children; but not excessively unruly – the 'Polis' lived next door.

I well remember my first evening visit to the Cosy – to see King Kong – in the thre'pennies, front row. Could I ever forget? Can you imagine, on a wooden form, petrified with fear, pinned all round with hordes of other terrified boys (no little girls – Winnie Barnes sat on a radiator at the side, when she might have held my hand and comforted me; perhaps she didn't fancy the crush of other boys), with this huge monster trying to get at you from a screen only three or four feet in front and above you? I had read Edgar Alan Poe and John Buchan – and even 'Gaboreau' – but never in my wildest dreams did I imagine anything like this. Oh yes I know, you've seen it on telly and laughed your head off; but this, believe me, was completely different; never before experienced, scary – and close.

There were no end of good films – and a lot of very bad ones – to be seen, some of them still bearing comparison with today's, and the choice was really quite remarkable. In later times the serious cinema-goer of Mickley had a choice of three changes of programme a week at the Cosy. Mon-Tues-Wed, Thurs-Fri-Sat, and on Sunday usually a Western – in an ex-holy place, shame on you … Plus another three changes at the flash new purpose-built 'Electric' at Prudhoe, with its neon lights that could be seen for miles, after the makeshift 'Palace' had been destroyed by fire, and before the 'Rio' gave everyone within walking distance a choice of a different film six nights a week and three on Sundays.

Cinemas were even more profitable than shops and soon the Stokoes had made enough money to build themselves a fair-sized double fronted house, with WC and 'all mod. cons.', rubbing shoulders with the surviving competition – Hubbucks' Chapel. But religion was fighting a losing battle with films.

The Stokoes had land with their house, built one or two glass houses, and grew bedding plants, tomatoes and chrysanthemums. With not much doing in the cinema during the day, when the womenfolk did the cleaning, gardening enhanced the profits – and the tomatoes were good. There were always several places in the village where a pound of 'organic' tomatoes could be bought during the summer. There were no others, horse manure was plentiful and chemicals cost money – and ruined the flavour. Like boiled peas with vinegar in a cup on Fridays, or delivering newspapers, or lathering beards, gardening was a way of supplementing still meagre incomes.

The threat of the Electric at Prudhoe and the possibility of something even bigger to tempt patrons away from discomfort and makeshift, led inevitably to thoughts of a proper Cosy with more seats and comfort. Low investment costs and overheads, and with all staff, including usherettes, being family, continuing popularity and profit made it possible – the future looked bright.

The New Cosy

In 1939 the old chapel closed its doors for the last time and before you could blink it had disappeared. As the bell went for the next round of the war Germany versus the Rest, the Gamesmaster said to the Stokoes, "You have started, so you may finish"; so the new, purpose-built Cosy arose on the rubble of the old, in the calm before the storm of Hitler's war.

Ugly as any building could be, and cinemas were by their nature ugly, it was made worse by its cheapness; made worse by wartime restrictions, which denied even the consolation of vulgar ornamentation. Profits, good though they had been, and supplemented by tomatoes, ran only to cheap bricks and square box, function first, construction. It was a proper cinema though, with a foyer, and a shop selling sweets, chocolate, cigarettes and ice-cream: outside, there was a canopy for the queue to shelter under – oh yes, there were queues at the Cosy. What with the war and the blackout, the canopy never got its neon lights and eventually fell off. Because of its location on a hillside, Cosy patrons walked in off the street at the level of the balcony, and it was the poorer patrons – even pitmen were patrons – who had to use the stairs, down to the stalls. This was clever use of the site, but the architects didn't get it quite right, and on the opening night the local bigwigs who got complimentary tickets, and those not so big who had paid full price for the best seats – 1/6 – all this lavish extravagance would have to be paid for – couldn't see the screen for the heads in front. This was very disappointing because it was Deanna Durbin in 'Three Smart Girls' and everybody loved her. It takes a fair slope, upstairs in a cinema, to be able to see the screen. So, amidst a flurry of red faces, the place had to be closed for a few frantic days of tearing out of seats and up of floors, sawing and hammering and alterations. When the job was finished, and clever it was, there were fewer rows of seats, which was a pity for the profits, and patrons could no longer walk on to the balcony on the level – they had to climb three or four steps before descending to their seats. The seats were very comfortable, quite up to city standards and included a line of very special seats down the wall at each side, separated by gangways from the main block of ordinary seats in the middle. These were double seats, without an armrest between, like small settees, and were used by those who didn't really go to watch the film. For young lovers who were happy enough on summer's grassy banks, but with nowhere to go in pursuit of cupid's sports in dark wintertime, these little couches, warm, dry, dark and 'cosy' were the very stuff of Paradise. With Eldorado close at hand.

Many a lasting troth was pledged in the side-seats of the dear old Cosy.

Another great leap forward in the cinema was the usherette with a tray, suspended at her waist by a cord around her neck, containing goodies illuminated by her torch – chocolates, cigarettes, sweets; and one with 'Eldorado' ice cream. This arrived at the end of your aisle after a brilliant advertisement, the best ever, in my opinion. To the accompaniment of 'Perpetuum Mobile' through the loudspeakers, the whole progress of the ice cream, from manufacture, packing, transporting with wheels turning in rhythm, to its being carried into the cinema, was shown on the screen, and as the lights went up, there it was, in a tray at your elbow, complete with usherette. It was brilliant, and sold a lot of ice cream bars – Eldorado.

Solid bars of ice cream, sometimes coated in chocolate to make 'choc-bars', and wrapped in paper for easy handling, were a sensation when they came on to the streets in the mid-1930s, in white painted boxes proclaiming 'Stop Me and Buy One', on white-painted tricycles ridden by white-coated vendors calling 'Eldorado', with the 'o' high and extended. These blocks were ideally suited to trays in cinemas, where Tony Marchetti would have been in the way dispensing soft ice-cream with a scoop from a tub, even without his pony.

That was how we got our ice cream previously, when the weather was warm enough. It was made at Crawcrook, by Tony, Italian Master of Ice Cream Making, and scooped, unimaginably delicious, from tubs that wobbled around in containers of solid carbon-dioxide that gave off icy mist. It was carried around the streets in a tiny 'trap' pulled by a diminutive pony called 'Sausage' and it was easy to see why. He was a tubby version of those that spent dismal lives pulling tubs of coal in stygian tunnels; but he lived a life of bliss by comparison and ate too much ice cream. The most beloved by children of all horses.

The ice cream filled the cone be it a ha'penny, a penny, or – sheer luxury, spread in a 'sandwich', for 1d. or 2d. Different techniques evolved over the years for dealing with cones and sandwiches and you had to be quick; good ice cream melted fast on hot days. The cone was much like today's in eating technique, but light-years apart in pleasure: the sandwich called for a quite different approach. You licked progressively round the edges, quickly or the ice cream ran out, while pressing the wafers together, until the edges met and turned soft. Then you nibbled them off all round, soggy with a touch of crispness and a taste of ecstasy. The first lick and the last tiny morsel of soft-edged, crisp-centred ice cream-laden double wafer were the best! Mind you, the bit in the middle wasn't bad.

Tony and his pony didn't come to Mickley – five miles was too far for the cuddly little mite of a pony, so we as a family suffered from very serious ice cream deprivation when we moved. Cosy Eldorado, though nice enough in its way, and novel, was not the same; indeed ice cream has never been the same.

Deanna Durbin, that refreshing, delightful girl whose joyful film inaugurated the new Cosy and stole the hearts of those rugged mining folk (I wasn't rugged but was fourteen and loved her), introduced a new dimension to music in the village. Now you could see, as well as hear it sung and played and be right there at the performance, almost like a real concert. But you couldn't take it home.

At home Edison's 'Phonograph' was pretty primitive and few local folk bought them, except Edwin Longstaffe who liked novelties and the chance to make a bob or two. He sold his recording of 'Gladstone's Speech', in broad Geordie accent, at a penny a listen. The Phonograph was a questionable improvement on the tin whistle except in that it needed no musical ability to play. On the other hand the gramophone with grooves cut in flat revolving disks, was a huge improvement. The sound it made was loud and real for those who'd never heard real 'real'; you could listen to Dame Clara Butt, Peter Dawson, or Harry Lauder,or even the D'oyley Carte with Gilbert and Sullivan's vocal gems, singing just for you and your family right there in your own home. Everything stopped for the first playings of the first precious record. The neighbours were invited – no point in keeping something like this secret – and everyone gathered round in perfect silence and some awe of this device that conjured magic sounds out of a box with a big 'horn' on top and a handle on the side that had to be turned quite a few times for the winding-up process that preceded every tune. This winding tensioned a coiled spring in a drum, like a big watch spring (you've never seen a watch spring?), which turned cogs and things that were controlled by a wonderful twirling-round device called a governor, when the 'brake' on the edge of the turntable was released. So many new words to learn. The turntable then, as you would expect, turned – at a controlled speed of, for some strange reason, 78 revolutions a minute. The flat disc with grooves on only one side to begin with was removed from its protective paper sleeve and placed very carefully on the turntable; very carefully because early records were inordinately brittle and couldn't stand, for instance, being sat on if they were foolishly left on a chair. Or, as my father did (he gets blamed for everything, doesn't he?), put a pile – well three, which was a pile if you had just bought them, on the empty bus seat beside him on his return from his Saturday jaunt. Of course a fat lady sat on them – not that thin would have saved them. Three shilling's worth – shattered.

Apart from being sat on or carelessly scratched with the needle, the records were very durable in use and wonderful value at about a shilling each. They came under many strange names, in their distinctive covers … Odeon, Parlophone, Regal – and H.M.V. with the memorable label which perpetuates the image of the dog listening to 'His Master's Voice' coming forth from the trumpet or sound horn, which was the precursor of the electric loud speaker. Unfortunately there are not as many of these old records still around (a-round?) as there might have been because they were continually mauled by the steel 'marlin-spikes' that passed muster as needles, before styluses.

Needles came in little tin boxes, about one inch by one and a half with pictures on the lids (nothing was ever left plain) and were supposed to be changed after every playing but weren't – they cost money – to the detriment of the records, although it didn't show at first. Apart from making poor quality sound, which few would notice, blunt needles wore the grooves off the records and grooves were important – vital, in fact. I have seen records without a trace of a groove – perfectly smooth, that still managed to hiss out a tune of sorts. But they were much better with grooves.

The needle vibrated in the groove, in the manner of the Phonograph; it was fixed with a tiny screw into the edge of the sound-box (which had a 'diaphragm' which was nice to know) which was on the end of the curved, swivelling hollow-tube tone arm, which conveyed the sound vibrations to the horn, which provided the final amplification – 'Yo – o and it comes out here'! All this was 'acoustic' – nothing electrical; not a wire in sight; but at least the gramophone could be seen working, if not quite understood.

The choice of music became quite remarkable, in a range from the best of classical to the most popular of popular. This was the wonderful age of the 'tune', the 'song' that everyone could whistle or sing, hum or tap a foot to. The reproduction may have been primitive, but the words could be heard and understood and the notes made music, not noise. The Great Performers live on – Caruso, Nellie Melba, John McCormack – their voices enshrined in black discs with grooves (Nellie also in ice cream with peaches!)

The snag with the gramophone, other than the fragility of the records and having to go to a shop to buy them – although this was really a part of the pleasure and soon there were record shops even in Prudhoe – was the need to jump up and down all the time, to wind the handle, change the needle and turn or change the record. But this was surely a small price to pay and all part of the ritual, in a life where doing things came naturally and turning the handle helped to make the music. £2.10s. for a gramophone took a bit of finding – the miner had to shovel a few tons of coal, but the effort enhanced the appreciation.

The Wireless

The next 'in house' entertainment that swept the country and intrigued simple minds was more difficult to understand than the gramophone, but less effort to operate. Remember that it was only thirty years after literacy became compulsory for working folk that Marconi sent his signals though the air without wires and named it wireless-telegraphy. Another thirty, and wireless-telephony came to Mickley – the Wireless.

Marconi found a way of casting dots and dashes, in the style of Morse, into the air and catching them afar; then throwing and catching words and music, which was more difficult but came eventually. It is strange that the first method used a fixed wavelength quartz-crystal which was superseded by the radio-valve which in turn was made redundant by a return to the fixed wavelength equivalent of the crystal – the 'transistor'. The first receivers were simplicity itself in construction; any schoolboy could, and many did, make one – they could buy the parts. But it took a genius to grasp how it worked.

Children sat around in even greater awe than of the gramophone and were given a turn at listening through the earphones to the band playing in far-distant London, while father gently tickled the crystal, which was held in a fixed holder with a wire leading from it, with a very fine wire – the 'cat's whisker', gripped in a holder with a knob for holding, held on a spring-loaded arm on a pivot with a wire leading from it. The two wires led, by way of a coil, which was wire wrapped closely round a core, to the earphones. The secret lay in the crystal, but it had to be searched for with the 'whisker', and believe me, it could take some finding; only if it touched the precise spot did the sound emerge – and woe-betide anyone who caused bad vibrations that dislocated the whisker!

The signal, if it could be found, was 'crystal clear', if faint; you could not only hear the band as it played in London, but even the announcer reading the news – in immaculate 'square-gob' English. Something not much heard in Mickley.

Only one person could listen in with the earphones (guess who?) while the rest of the household sat in static silence, so wireless was little more than a novelty until valves were thought of and the wireless arrived, in a wooden

THE WIRELESS

box with not only valves, but condensers and coils that moved and batteries – crystal sets needed no electricity.

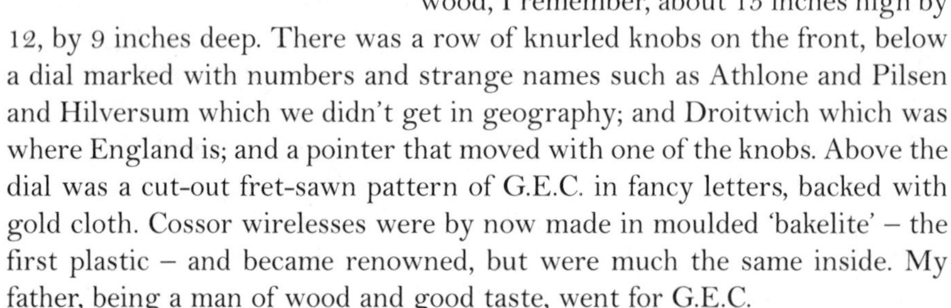

One day in 1935, before we came to Mickley, when my father was in a job, he came home laden with a parcel. This didn't often happen – parcels cost money – so it was cause for excitement and a gathering round. The string and brown paper duly removed and stored for future use revealed a tidy looking wooden box – oak-faced plywood, I remember, about 15 inches high by 12, by 9 inches deep. There was a row of knurled knobs on the front, below a dial marked with numbers and strange names such as Athlone and Pilsen and Hilversum which we didn't get in geography; and Droitwich which was where England is; and a pointer that moved with one of the knobs. Above the dial was a cut-out fret-sawn pattern of G.E.C. in fancy letters, backed with gold cloth. Cossor wirelesses were by now made in moulded 'bakelite' – the first plastic – and became renowned, but were much the same inside. My father, being a man of wood and good taste, went for G.E.C.

Not being technically minded and the thing needing some setting up, I'm not sure that help from next door, where lived an Engineer, wasn't called for. The back of the wireless had to be opened, to reveal a rare box of tricks. A shelf held the 'set' which was made of valves and coils and tubes and little boxes, all joined with lots of wires fixed with tiny nuts and bolts and soldered here and there. Wires issued forth with little round plugs on the ends in different colours; these were duly plugged into appropriate sockets in a 120 volt High Tension battery which was flat, about 9 inch x 6 inch x 3 inch and fitted under the shelf. Two separate plugs went into the 9 volt Grid Bias battery, about 9 inch x 4 inch x 1½ inch, on edge. The final two wires (if there were any more left you'd got it wrong) had terminals like flat, metal lobster's claws that fitted round threaded pillars on top of the 2 volt accumulator and were secured with big knurled nuts, red for positive, black for negative. Wireless owners had to know about these electrical matters and soon learned. The accumulator terminals had to be kept well coated with vaseline or they 'corroded'. Corrosion was like green metallic gangrene and had the same effect on batteries as on soldiers' wounds.

The accumulator was a nasty little beast containing something called acid which was held in fear and dread – it could eat you all up, like the Lambton Worm, if it wasn't treated with the utmost respect. The container was a heavy glass jar, 6 inch tall by 4 inch square, slightly larger if high capacity –

to last longer between charges – which would break if dropped – with dire consequences. It fitted into a metal frame with a wooden handle for carrying, and carried it had to be, all the way to the wireless shop in Prudhoe, (Mickley really was falling behind), once a week for recharging, or more often if you 'listened in' a lot or it was getting old and not holding its charge. Battery shops did a roaring trade at tu'pence a time, fully charged, you hoped, in exchange for the 'flat' one. Wet batteries, as accumulators were known, were not allowed on to buses, but there was an alternative to the risky long carry, if they could be cosseted through the full week. Andy Liddle at Branch End Garage ran an active charging and delivery service which cost 3d. and saved the risk – if you had the extra penny. John Nichols at Mickley missed out, which was a pity for us. The most frustrating thing about this kind of wireless was the accumulator that gave out in the middle of a favourite programme – Band Wagon, Monday Night at Eight, In Town Tonight, or The Brains Trust, which quickly established themselves as routine listening.

Having got all those wires in their proper places the next job was to fix a short length of wire to a scew-terminal marked 'Earth' on the edge of the shelf that held the works, take it out through the window, by way of a small hole in the frame if you had a brace and bit and knew how to use it, and fix it to a copper earth-rod driven into the ground, or a bit of old bed-iron or thick fencing wire at a pinch.

Another length of wire, as long as possible this time, was connected to the terminal marked 'Aerial', taken up the wall into the loft and strung across the rafters – several times if you were a long way from the transmitter. Or, if you had a long pole, the aerial could be stretched above the garden, ostensibly for better reception but in reality for ostentation – to let the whole world know that you had a wireless. But you would need a licence.

I am not now sure of the merit of this – a firm rule – but at the time saw the reasoning ... If thunder threatened, these two wires, earth and aerial, had to be disconnected from the set and joined together. The theory was that any lightning looking for mischief, that was attracted to the wire in the air would 'run to earth' by the wire in the ground, rather than blow the set – and anyone near it – to smithereens. After all, it could be reasoned, wirelesses by their very nature must be objectives of forces of nature like lightning!

If you as a boy were the only person about and felt obliged to shoulder the responsibility of directing the lightning on a safe path, and the thunder was brattling all around as you fumbled with the wires, the fear of this wayward lightning blasting your head off on its way along the wire to 'earth' was very real indeed; that it didn't happen wasn't for want of imagination. It was like some great film, where the hero had to save the train from impending doom and just made it. If the hero felt as good afterwards as I did, it was worth it – saving the wireless was vital.

Every wire connected, everything in its place, we all gathered together and at the proper time – and this is what it was all about, this fuss and my father spending £3.10s., a week's pay, on a G.E.C. wireless – a knob was turned, a light went on in the dial, another knob turned, the pointer moved and a very cultured BBC voice spoke from the fretwork hole. "We are now broadcasting the first instalment of The Count of Monte Christo by Alexander Dumas". We were transfixed; this was the stuff of Merlin, issuing forth from a little box with knobs on and loud enough for everyone in the room to hear without anyone being 'hushed' – not that they needed to be. The instalments went on for weeks and all work, all play, housework, activity of any kind, grown-up as well as childish, was suspended for the half-hour of its enactment. Never was there such stimulus to the imagination – for me never again; one of life's great experiences. I need say nothing of the look of smug, complacent self-satisfaction on my father's face or the quiet smile of my mother, who had to make ends meet on a short budget – £3.10s. would buy a lot of food. She did enjoy the wireless though; there was little fun in the lives of wives, and it was better than being made to lie abed on Sunday mornings to read a chapter each week of another of my father's 'best buys' – a huge, ton-heavy, beautifully bound and illustrated edition of *Lorna Doone*! Perhaps she enjoyed the long lie, but she was no great reader of books, there was always something to be done. Things could be done while listening in.

The little wooden box with knobs on came with us to Mickley and was a treasured source of pleasure for many years, as the wireless was in most homes. It propagated plays and stories and, like the gramophone, music – and it didn't need winding. I remember the dance-bands; especially, after Children's Hour and before the six-o'clock news (with Stocks and Shares in between), Henry Hall and his Band and 'Here's to the Next Time'. The dance tunes; foxtrots, quicksteps, waltzes, with Carrol Gibbons, Roy Fox and the rest. Then there were the songs – whatever happened to songs?

If I could sing, or when there is no one about, I could still manage the words, and in my mind the tunes, of Tiptoe Through the Tulips, Easter Bonnet, Miss Otis Regrets, Little Old Lady, Red Sails in the Sunset (parodied, as boys did, on a notorious murder case – Red Stains on the Carpet, Bloodstains on the Knife, Oh Doctor Buck Ruxton, You Murdered Your Wife!). Then there were the Hill-Billies that were in great vogue – Old Faithful, Roll Along Covered Wagon, The Old Pine Tree; the list is without end. They all had one thing in common – the words could be sung, the tunes whistled – when did you last hear a boy whistling a tune? Furthermore, not one of them gave you a headache. They are still there, some of these old tunes, stored on transpositions from the old 78s., but many, I'm afraid are lost and gone forever, like Darling Clementine. Perhaps one day there will be those with an ear for the gentler things who will again find pleasure in those that survive.

Wireless and gramophone worked well together, were a happy combination and didn't stand in the way of anyone going to the Cosy for a night out, nor reading a book or making a clippie mat. If there was nothing special to listen to, and there was money for an evening at the 'flicks', another little pleasure could be indulged in – fish and chips on the way home, or just chips. The fryers timed their operations to have everything ready for the 'pictures cummin oot.'

Fish and chip shops blossomed between the wars – they were everywhere. They were in a wooden ex-army barrack hut run by our entrepreneur John Nichols. His chip shop traded across the road, isolated from the shop and house in its ugly black hut. With its vats of fat heated one by coal, the others by gas, it was a fire hazard supreme – and a food hygiene inspector's nightmare, had there been one. But it never caught fire, no one ever seemed to be ill from the chips, and it was less than fifty yards from our house on the way home from the Cosy – and the fish and chips were out of this world. Not only that, the impecunious little boy who had the sense to wait for a lull in the serving before trying his luck could poke his head around the door with a cheeky "Gissabaga scranchums?" or perhaps with a better chance of success – "Please have you any scranchums?". You know what 'scranchums' are! They are really just waste, but boys enjoyed them, acting, as boys do, as waste-disposal units; and all the while kidding themselves that they were privileged to get them; but they tasted good, cooked in real dripping. Better than crisps, and better still for being free.

Fish and chips and General Dealing were not the only interests of John Nichols; like Andy Liddle at Branch End, he early saw the potential in one of the last of the great inventions of the nineteenth century – the internal combustion engine, that mixed blessing which came to dominate most of the next century, as had steam in its time. The early manifestations of the monster required a man with a red flag walking before, warning of its approach, which is a giggle, considering the noise they made. With the help of the Wright brothers it launched man on wings into the air and propelled him towards the mass-destruction of cities and women and children; but as compensation also powers lifesaving ambulances and helicopters and humanitarian aid. It acted out its modest part at Mickley Garage, by the chip shop.

The Motor Car

Once the principle of the internal combustion engine was established and oil tankers, albeit baby ones, plied the oceans, it was only a question of time before petrol engines superseded not only steam, but horses themselves as man's main source of transport and power. The skills of steam engineering were assiduously applied and the early cars, which were little more than carts with engines, rapidly developed into superbly designed and built vehicles. They entered the age of mass-production in 1908 with Henry Ford's 'any colour so long as it's black' Model 'T'.

By the outbreak of war in 1914 enough of London's buses were petrol-driven to justify requisitioning them for war purposes and it was not long before petrol engines were in use to power death-machines – tanks and aeroplanes. However, just as the Napoleonic Wars accelerated the development of the railways, so the Kaiser and his lot caused the rapid improvement of petrol-powered transport, to peacetime benefit. No sooner had the war ended than 'Omnibuses' were commonplace and although the established use of electricity for powering tramcars in cities retarded buses in Newcastle, the work of Telfer and MacAdam bore handsome fruit in making possible smooth roads for buses to Mickley. Not only buses – motorcars, especially after Dunlop invented the pneumatic tyre, which cushioned the way for cyclists too.

Longstaffes, in the forefront as usual, went for petrol-generated steam – the Stanley Steam Car, a clever idea that failed. The passengers had to provide a considerable and continuous supply of chewing-gum (another horrible American practice that swept the country – to the benefit of steam-car owners!) for repairing the steam-tubes that were forever failing. So I heard. There are still one or two Stanley Steam Cars in use, and no shortage of chewing-gum.

Doctors and Colliery managers went for straightforward petrol and the car became a great boon to doctors when it became reasonably reliable. Dr McCoull at Prudhoe, home from the war, was an early owner, but keeping them running wasn't easy; this brought another village innovation – the garage, which also obviated the need to buy petrol in cans from chemists' shops.

Just as blacksmiths had pioneered engineering, and there were still plenty of them around, worrying about a future without horses, it seemed natural that garages should evolve from blacksmiths' shops, but the men who had the early interest in petrol hereabouts were neither of them smiths – they were associated with shops, which I suppose gave them some financial support. Andy Liddle drove buses for Newcastle Corporation and had a mechanical bent – it was hardly possible to be a driver without it, and after he married Bessie, daughter of Longstaffe, he set up a little workshop in a shed behind the bakery. Hard work brought its reward and he moved to a prime site for a garage, opposite the shop on the main road, where the hut grew into a substantial establishment – Branch End Garage, employing mechanics, had four petrol pumps under a heather-thatched canopy, rockeries with a fountain and a big clock on a high stand, all designed, and the rockery built by, Bessie, who had an artistic as well as a practical bent. All very attractive and a credit to the place; a loss when the heather went up in flames, but fortunately not the pumps.

John Nichols lacked much mechanical aptitude but the 'and son' could drive and saw a future for buses – stage-coaches with engines, as competition for trains. Without the constraints of rails, able to go wherever a good-enough road would take them, the future of the bus looked good. Nichols went into partnership with a Mr Cowen of Apperly, possibly the same who had taken over the Derwent pack of foxhounds from Joseph Humble, and they ran the first commercial bus service in the area. Details are hard to come by, but it was rather limited, with only one, some say two, buses plying between Prudhoe and Hexham.

The uncontrolled and chaotic bus services, resulting from too many people seeing the potential, were brought into some semblance of order by Government legislation. This in effect reduced many small operators to running excursions and put many out of business, while the main, busy routes were plied by urban Corporations and large town-based companies. A lot of capital was needed to run the frequent, reliable services demanded by a public anxious to avail themselves of this fast, comfortable mode of transport. Well, it was more or less comfortable – compared to stage-coaches – and dry, there were no seats on the roof; not here anyway. Anyone sitting on the roof of a bus from Mickley to Newcastle would surely have banged his head on one of the low bridges that carried railways across the road at Scotswood and Stella (one of the collieries near Blaydon named after the daughters of the coal-owner) where the coal still came down to the staithes in trains. No double-deckers plied to Mickley – not till the coal ran out at Stella.

The 'Blue Buses, which were those run by Newcastle Corporation, crept out into the country as far as Ryton by 1920, and ran a fifteen-minute service; then to Crawcrook, then to Branch End. In 1925 they inaugurated

ANDY LIDDIE AND CORPORATION BUS

the first regular service between Newcastle and Hexham but it ran into trouble when the first trial run was delayed one and a half hours by private buses which gathered at Scotswood bridge on the city boundary in protest at Corporation buses being allowed to run outside the town. They drove ahead at their slowest speed, to a rare grinding and boiling, no doubt, all the way to Hexham.

By 1930 three services ran through Mickley; the Blue Buses terminated at Branch End, which seemed appropriate, running half-hourly. Bright red United Automobile Company buses ran all the way to Hexham, also, so we did well, with a fifteen minute service to Newcastle which took forty minutes at its best; and a half-hourly service to Hexham, taking 25 minutes – about the same distance but with fewer stops. Anyone wanting Corbridge had a usually wet and windy walk across the bridge. It cost, for a long time, for deflation was the economic order of the day, 1s 3d return to Newcastle; 1½d return to Prudhoe; half price up to fourteen; under fives free. Children had to stand if the bus was full and gentlemen stood for ladies anyway – some even doffed their hats.

The third service through Mickley – Norfolks, was different. Their buses were blue, but a prettier blue than Corporation, which were sombre townie things (so as not to show the dirt?). Norfolks superseded Cowen & Nichols as local bus operators and Johnny Nichols was not a partner but had an arrangement to drive a bus when he wasn't peeling potatoes for his chip shop, or selling petrol. At night he drove the bus home and stored it in the wooden garage that was built alongside the chip shop when hopes were high that the Cowen partnership would flourish. He owned a car and ran a kind of half-hearted taxi service, while his wife or daughter might, if the shop wasn't too busy, sell petrol. There were two pumps, stately things with glass heads, one oval, the other round, proclaiming, 'Cleveland Discol' and 'Esso Ethol' at 1/-per gallon for ordinary Discol, 3d. extra for Ethyl. A joggling-back-and-forth handle on the front, like a water pump, drew petrol from the bowels of the earth into the tank, fortunately not in large quantities – only a gallon or two at a time: a long journey called for an extra two gallons in a can strapped on the running board. The running board was a platform outside the car door for gangsters to stand on while making their getaway. Pumping petrol by hand was hard work and perhaps why Johnny preferred driving a Norfolk's bus, which was comfortable and could be booked for a trip to the seaside. They plied their bus-service between Newcastle and a remote cross-roads on the A68 south of Riding Mill – Scales Cross. It sounded like Highwayman country and I sometimes wondered, in idle moments, who would want to go there on a bus, although if you had an eye for such things it was a pleasant run on a fine day. The bus also ran on wet days and it must have been a useful, non-profit making service for the few folk who lived out that way.

Norfolk's were limited by silly regulations, so that passengers were not allowed to get both on and off between Newcastle and Branch End. They could get on anywhere between Newcastle and Branch End but only off after it had turned off the main road on to New Ridley Road, or on before it joined the main road Newcastle-wards; so it was a service only for the people of New Ridley and its road, which must have been limiting to its profits, but it was a well-used service in its day. It was very useful for the lasses of Mickley who found work as 'day-girls' ('skivvies' to some) for the wealthy folk of Park Estate. So long as they got off beyond Branch End going, and on, coming back, they could get on and off at Mickley!

Notices were an important part of buses; there was one on the back of the seat in front: – 'Lower Your Head When Leaving Your Seat' (or you banged it on the luggage rack). 'Pipe Smokers Please Occupy Rear Seats'. Smoking was as fashionable as riding on buses – it was often impossible to see across the width of the bus for smoke, so how putting pipe smokers at the back helped I couldn't imagine, when the bus was full of cigarette smokers. 'Ring Bell Once to Stop Bus'. Only the conductor was allowed to 'ring twice' to start it. Before bell-pushes worked buzzers in the driver's private compartment (which could only be reached through a door from the outside, safe from drunks and irate passengers), the bell was a bell, like a miniature of the Scotts' shop bell, and manually operated. It went 'Ding', or 'Ding Ding' when a cord stretching the length of the bus ceiling was jerked. Primitive but fun.

The classic notice was 'Refrain From Spitting. Fine 5/-'. Directed at pipe smokers I suspect, but pitmen with their lungs full of coal dust did a lot of spitting.

Why the person who collected the fares and punched the tickets was called a 'conductor' I never did discover; they had no music and no lightning. I once saw one help an old woman down the steps – I suppose he conducted her off. Bus conductors now seem to be extinct.

Bus tickets varied in style through the years and at first were like train tickets but paper instead of card. They were in various colours, with printed numbers indicating 'fare stages' along the route and conductors carried racks of them: they at first used a punch to indicate the duration of the journey with little holes in the ticket numbers; then a machine was used that went 'Ding' ('Dings' were important in the world of buses) as it bit a bite out of the edge of the ticket to prove to the Inspector that neither passenger nor conductor were cheating. Kindly conductors were known to let nice little children off paying their fares, but if the Inspector called everyone had to have a ticket, except policemen; they always seemed to ride free, but they stood in the doorway and appeared to be waiting to catch someone for not paying their fare. The Inspector was never a particularly popular figure, but his role was understandable. The inspector is one of Nature's great success stories, like Collared Doves, and lurks everywhere; the bus variety hopped on and off at all sorts of unexpected places; he wanted to know 'why' if the bus was late – he'd been waiting around in the rain – but his main role was catching cheats. He examined the tickets, "Tickets please", and checked passenger numbers against the conductor's count. Conductors had to be numerate. There is the story of the trainee, given a tip on counting the passengers on a full-ish bus, just to count the empty seats and subtract, who proceeded to count the empty seats when there were only three passengers!

Fares went into a leather pouch like those worn by the hawking butcher or greengrocer – security was of little concern.

Buses played a most important part in the social and economic life of mid-twentieth-century Mickley. The choice of shops was now enormous, in Prudhoe, Hexham and Newcastle; the problem had been in reaching them – and lugging the shopping home, especially after the railway station closed. Buses changed all that and transformed the lives of villagers. Even if there was no money for shopping, a day out looking cost only the fare. It was worth it, through boy's eyes anyway, just to see whining, grinding, sparking trams that went 'Clang Clang' to warn of their coming and carried thousands of passengers stuck around the outside like flies when workers at Armstrong's ended their shifts and Scotswood Road had a solid core of trams to take them home. Or when 'United' had a home game and 50,000 fans erupted from Gallowgate and were scooped up and away as if by a giant vacuum cleaner. Trams were the environmentally friendly movers of the masses par excellence – and great fun for lads on a trip by bus to Newcastle.

Not only the thrill of trams was brought within easy reach of Mickley folk by buses, but city lights – the streets became Fairyland as evening fell. Mickley's early electricity was a dim affair, but adequate in the country – it showed the way and didn't keep the birds awake at night. In town, though, when they caught up with Mickley and got themselves electric lights, but kept gas as well, they had lots and lots of them and everything was brilliant; the shop windows positively sparkled – and what shops: where did people get the money?. They fairly put poor old Mickley Co-op in the shade, although it still had much to offer, especially when times were hard, which was most of the time, and it continued to be easier to shop locally and have the goods delivered. Not only that, if in Newcastle you bought for a penny one of those newfangled 'carrier bags' to put your shopping in, like as not the paper would tear, or go soggy in the rain and you'd be left halfway down Clayton Street, on the way to the bus, with two pieces of string in your hand and a scattering of loose shopping on the ground, broken if it was gramophone records, squashed if cream-cakes (a rare treat indeed). Hey-ho for the village shop!

Buses also opened up the world for workers – the choice for lads leaving school was no longer the pit, farm or building trade. The fares reduced take-home pay, and travelling to and fro lengthened the working day, but a job in the 'Toon', or even Hexham, paid better and was often more interesting – and skilled. A weekly or monthly bus 'pass' not only cheapened work travel, it gave bonus, in effect free, rides to St James' Park on Saturday afternoons, or the Theatre, Music Hall or super Cinemas showing the latest films.

A STEAM LORRY

At the Theatre Royal, which overawed the young newcomer with its glories, could be enjoyed Shakespeare (by those who had recovered from Portia's Speech), or an Opera, for nine pence in the 'gods' where the seats were little better than the front row in the Cosy only you didn't notice. This after standing perhaps an hour or more in the rain or snow for something special, but all the while being entertained, often to some effect, by buskers playing tunes on flutes or fiddles, tearing clever patterns out of newspapers, juggling and conjuring. A whole new world of beauty, culture, and excitement opened up for villagers, by way of the bus. Even the Hancock Museum became readily accessible, and the Laing Art Gallery with its paintings by the Masters, that brought to mind Miss Murray and where was she now? …

Just as farm workers had left the land for pit villages, so village dwellers left to work in towns, but didn't need to leave their homes – unless they were pitmen, in which case they could apply for a Council house – or turn their backs on the rural scene. Commuters arrived – by bus; although without a fancy name at the time.

The petrol engine gave the cart-horse, as well as the coach-horse and the steam engine a serious, indeed fatal setback, but prior to the rise of the petrol engine, efficient steam-driven lorries were developed.

Coal, and manure from the stables, was delivered locally by horse and cart, and, as downhill was easier for horses, coal was brought to the surface by the ventilation shaft on Eastgate Bank, behind the Co-op, where three loading hoppers were in steady use for many years, and are the last standing evidence of mining activity in the village. Steam lorries broke no speed records, but they were quicker than horses and coped better with heavy loads and steep hills – and coal for fuel was free, for Coal Co. lorries. But the change to lorries was speeded by an unhappy event in 1931 when the horse used for round the village carting was gored by a bull while grazing.

People who spend their lives in close company and working partnership with animals develop affection for them. A man, called Young I believe, carted the coal, and his horse would mean a lot to him – probably his livelihood too, as carters didn't readily adapt to things mechanical such as steam lorries. Perhaps he blamed himself for the horse being in the field with the bull; whatever the reason, he disappeared and was found hanging from a clothes-post in his garden. The horse was not replaced: instead a steam lorry was bought.

Then another – did it take two to replace one horse? They chugged around the village and were housed in a building that still stands, adjoining the old electricity transformer house. They needed no feeding or grooming at weekends and no field to graze in so were not likely to be attacked by bulls, but they did need a lot of maintenance. Steam lorries, like steam cars, never stood a chance against petrol.

The End of the Drift

A hundred years, a little more, the coal under Mickley lasted, that had lain undisturbed all those millions of years, and precious little was left to show for it, except a bit of a mess and a few houses, some of them with shops in their sitting rooms. Oh yes – and the Co-op.

By the early 1930s the mine workings had moved so far south, right under the hill that housed old Micelee and its fatal tree, that it became cheaper and easier to work from the valley beyond – 'Hedley Bottoms' – and take the coal east, to West Wylam. The pit at West Wylam had been opened in 1869 and grew into a major operation, with coke-works, brick-works and coal-washing plant – even, eventually, a miner-washing plant – pit-head baths!

The whole of the area from West Mickley to Wylam, from the river Tyne to Hedley, was cleared of workable coal by Mickley Coal Company between 1840 and 1960, with a little help from West Mickley C. Co. on the western fringe, while the Bewicks toiled quietly away at Mickley Bank. They easily held the record for perseverance – something like 250 years, from the early 1700s to about 1950. After this only small pockets of coal were left in the area and these were worked privately by the Walker family of Stocksfield, on land east of New Ridley Road.

Although Mickley Colliery is officially recorded as closing in 1934, I clearly remember being shown the 'drift' entrance when we came to live here in 1936, and tubs of coal were coming forth on little rails and wire rope. I was struck by the quiet, almost gentle nature of the operation compared to the horrible cages, turning wheels and gushing water at Clara Vale. Not that the hole in the hillside wasn't dank and frightening enough, and the nearby blacksmiths' workshops still fiery and fumey even if they by then weren't making much more than sledge-irons and hoops-and-girds for children.

The coke-works had been in decline for more than twenty years, ousted by more efficient methods, and when the last ovens went cold in about 1930, then the coal stopped coming out, the extensive railway sidings by the river grew silent, the shunting stopped and the Junction slept in peace again – or perhaps couldn't sleep for the quiet ... The little Dilly fussed about for a while, helping with the clearing-up work, then departed, some say to the breaker's yard, some to a new home – hopefully not to a murky town, having spent many happy years – if Dillies can be happy – down by the Tyne in Bewick Land.

West Mickley Coal Co. drifts closed somewhat earlier than Mickley, in 1922; I was shown their silent, ghostly entrances and ventured in a short way: it quickly grew dark and the roof was not to my liking so I didn't linger, but wondered that such places should just be abandoned, like relics of a gold-rush. The Company ceased to exist and its workers dispersed to other pits, some of which could now be reached by bus. Pity the girl in her summer dress who occupied a bus seat after a going-home miner.

Working at Hedley Pit

Hedley pit, the 'out-by' extension of Mickley, was not on a bus route, so the miners of Mickley, and those formerly of West Mickley who had switched allegiance – intense rivalry marked relations between the Square and the Barracks – had to commute by boot when the 'works entrances' closed – only a few yards from their homes in the villages. Who said you could be too close to your work? Those commuting hobnailed boots provided me, on my arrival in Mickley, with my second great 'audio impression' – poss sticks on Monday morning being the first.

ROAD TO HEDLEY DRIFT

It was a puzzle, this new noise – distant at first, like the ominous sound of spears on Zulu shields, steadily growing louder until it reached a crescendo as the out-of-step army scraped and clattered its weary way down the steep tarmac of Eastgate Bank, picking up speed on the straight towards a hot bath, meal, and a hard-earned sleep. Hobnailed boots down a hill don't make a clear-cut noise, like marching men; it is – was, a lost sound – a clash and scrape combined. Multiplied by a whole shift of men, it was some noise! Certainly there was no excuse for the bath not being ready – wives had ample warning of the coming of the workers.

For those of you who do your commuting by car, and press buttons when you get there, picture this for a working day – fore shift, say ...

Rise in time to be at work by 2.30 am – alarm clocks by now had the march on knockers up; have a mug – like as not a pint pot – of tea and a substantial breakfast. If any lads were old enough to work and were on the same shift, chaos could arise in the cramped conditions but harassed mothers usually had a system for getting them away, while the none-workers slept on. It was important that each got his bait in its rat-proof tin; not that there was much variation; strangely enough bread and jam was generally preferred, the quantity varying only within the limits of the tin. Which reminds me of a little tale ...

His mother gave this fourteen-year-old on his first day at work, a sandwich for his 'bait' and enquired on his return if it was alright. "Fine," quoth he, "But not enough." Next day he got four slices – still not enough; next day six – not enough; working hard, and still growing. In exasperation she cut the loaf in two and thought she'd surely fixed him this time. "How was your bait, did you have enough?" "Aalreet, but aa see y're back t' two slices."

In the larger households each worker might be allocated a tread on the open, almost ladder-like stairs and his loaded bait tin placed on it, youngest at the bottom, father's at the top, always in the same order. Don't ask me what happened if boys outnumbered steps! Each grabbed his tin on the way out, along with a tin 'bottle' of either cold tea or water. These two small tins provided sustenance for the whole long day.

The initial climb from the village to work at Hedley Bottoms was of Alpine proportions, something like 1-in–5 or 6, I'm guessing – but steep, although not quite so steep towards the top, where had lived the cottars of 1292 and where now worked their modern day farming equivalent, machines and all. Then a short half-mile jog (difficult not to) down an even steeper rough track to the 'bottoms' and the noisome drift, and a further underground walk, or possibly a ride on the tubs, for the face workers, to the coal face.

Eight hours of hard work and I do mean hard – even, as time went on, with the help of some machinery, which kicked up an awful lot of noise and dust – was relieved by a half-hour break for bait, and an occasional Woodbine or clay pipe of baccy. Smoking was a great consolation for these miners, who were favoured with gas-free working conditions.

Then 'out-by' again, sweaty and black, with white, red-rimmed eyes and mouths like the then popular Kentucky Minstrels, into the clean air and whatever the weather had conjured up in the meantime. Up the weary, heavy-legged climb out of the hollow and down the long easy clatter home – not much short of two miles in all, and not, perhaps, too much of a trial for a fit young twenty-year-old, but for the sixty-or-so-year-old with backache, this must have been a sojourn in the Vale of Torment – six days a week. If it got too much there might have been an easier job at an 'easier' pay, on the surface, perhaps at the screens with the boys and the disabled.

It still had to be journeyed, this unpaid extension to the working day, come rain or snow no matter how deep. A cleared path could only be with shovels; building workers laid off by the weather cleared main roads and town footpaths, but in the country people dug their own way, or if the snow lingered long it got packed hard if walked enough by hobnailed boots. No matter how much underground lighting improved, with electricity and lamps that fixed to miners' hats, coaly underground was still pretty black and to emerge from this to a world cloaked in virgin white snow must have been a mighty shock to the system, especially to the gritty eyes – but what a glorious shock!

Perhaps the manner of his life, the harsh cruelty of it, made the miner particularly susceptible to the charms of nature. At leisure he loved his garden, his whippets and his pigeons, his caged birds – had he an affinity with these? and he must surely have been enchanted, on emerging from his subterranean world, by Hedley Bottoms in the snow, in spite of the added effort of getting home through it.

But life for the rural miner was not all black and white; his ugly scar of a pit lay in the remains of what our new-world 'ecologists' would term Ancient Woodland where the folk of Micelee had sought refuge from the pillagers of yore. Not much forest now, mostly birch and light-hearted stuff, the big trees long gone, helped along by Robert in his last gasp. Where the trees were cleared to make way for the muck and the mess of mining, and the muck and the mess did not quite reach, there sprang up another forest – of the most vigorous and luscious blackberries. So for the miner's wife too there was profit and pleasure to be had at Hedley Bottoms. Blackberries grew at Mickley Square, of course, and I thought myself clever in picking a shopping basket full in an hour in High Close Wood, but those from the Bottoms were beyond compare, in quantity and quality.

Wives – and children, for blackberries were still an excuse for staying off school, although less readily acceptable – went in groups and made a day of it, and a picnic; the love of a picnic lingered. It was so delightful and peaceful over there in the valley, in Hyon's Wood, cut off from the hubbub of village and domestic life. The pit hardly intruded, being a drift and having electricity, but it was reassuring to know there were husbands at hand – 'just in case'. This was usually in September – the so-called Blackberry Week holiday in October was more appropriate to tatie picking, for which children were paid, but not much fun – not much pay either, for that matter. All they got for blackberrying were thorny hands, as many blackberries as they could eat, and blackberry jam for ever – as well as the fun and extra time off from school.

They walked the miner's road home, without hob-nails, but just about as tired, laden as they were with the spoils of the day. Two women in partnership, with a clothes-basket or tin bath lined with a cloth (blackberries had an odd effect on zinc) between them, laden to the brim, and a two gallon bucket or a shopping basket, in the other hand. Enough berries to make jam to cover hungry, homecoming children's slices of new bread (hadn't they worked for it?) and worker's bait for a goodly part of the year – while sales of Co-op jam plummeted and the penny returns on empty jam-jars were held in abeyance; not for ever though, they lost nothing for a second using!

As well as jam there would be tarts and delicious blackberry and apple suet pudding – Nature's Bounty at its best. Blackberrying was the domestic equivalent of hay making or harvest on the farm; everything stopped for it, and it was a major factor in the economy, especially in large families where jam-eating was a principle pastime. A good harvest was cause for satisfaction and a small celebration – perhaps a slice of new bread, more thickly spread than usual (more jam than bread) with nobbly 'full fruit flavour' real fruit jam, another of life's lost delights. A bad season, when fruit hung mouldering on the branch or at best made jam reminiscent of 'claggy taffy', meant frugal spreading and bought jam for the year except maybe, some made with rhubarb from the garden.

Bought jam was mostly Co-op, often in seven-pound earthenware jars, and raspberry – reputedly coloured turnip pulp with added wooden pips. Wooden raspberry-jam pip-making became a major source of employment for girls with nimble fingers; so my father said. There was also strawberry – the same but without the pips (cause of unemployment in little girls with nimble fingers?), which claimed an association with fruit by having a genuine strawberry floating in the top of each jar. This caused an early form of child abuse, as they had to sit around at every new-jar opening, while father took this solitary fruit, before they were allowed to dig into the pulp below. At least the pulp was sweet; hungry children would eat almost anything – but thank goodness for a good blackberry season.

The End of the Forests

As the brambles flourished, the ancient woods of Mickley continued to decline, ending their part in providing timber for Baliol estates, and almost lost their role as hiding places.

Only two areas of the ancient forest that had surrounded the clearing on the hilltop known as Micelee, in the barony of Bywell, remained as forest in 1928 when the Battie-Wrightsons, lords of the Manor of Mickley, of Cusworth, Doncaster, decided to finally sever their links with the inherited, eroded possessions – including High Close Wood, south of the Gateshead – Hexham turnpike (the A695), and Low Close Wood, to the north.

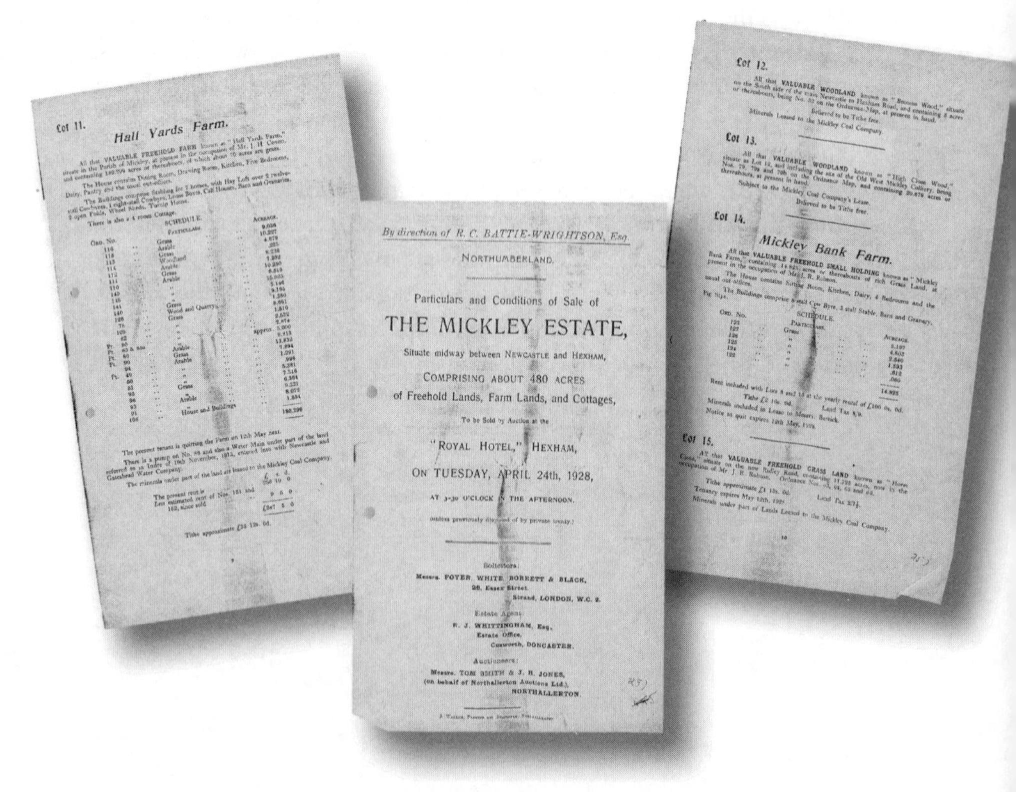

Lot 11.

Hall Yards Farm.

All that VALUABLE FREEHOLD FARM known as "Hall Yards Farm," situate in the Parish of Mickley, at present in the occupation of Mr. J. H. Coven, and containing 180.299 acres or thereabouts, of which about 70 acres are grass.

The House contains Dining Room, Drawing Room, Kitchen, Five Bedrooms, Dairy, Pantry and the usual out-offices.

The Buildings comprise Stabling for 7 horses, with Hay Loft over 2 twelve-stall Cowbyres, 1 eight-stall Cowbyre, Loose Boxes, Calf Houses, Barn and Granaries, 2 open Folds, Wheel Sheds, Turnip House.

There is also a 4 room Cottage.

SCHEDULE.

[illegible]

The present tenant is quitting the Farm on 12th May next.

There is a pump on No. 88 and also a Water Main under part of the land referred to in Indre of 10th November, 1913, entered into with Newcastle and Gateshead Water Company.

The minerals under part of the land are leased to the Mickley Coal Company.

	£	s.	d.
The present rent is	256	19	0
Less estimated rent of Nos. 151 and 152, since sold	9	6	0
	£247	5	0

Tithe approximate £33 12s. 0d.

By direction of R. C. BATTIE-WRIGHTSON, Esq.

NORTHUMBERLAND.

Particulars and Conditions of Sale of

THE MICKLEY ESTATE,

Situate midway between NEWCASTLE and HEXHAM,

COMPRISING ABOUT 480 ACRES

of Freehold Lands, Farm Lands, and Cottages,

To be Sold by Auction at the

"ROYAL HOTEL," HEXHAM,

ON TUESDAY, APRIL 24th, 1928,

AT 3-30 O'CLOCK IN THE AFTERNOON.

(unless previously disposed of by private treaty.)

Solicitors:

Messrs. FOYER, WHITE, BORRETT & BLACK,
26, Essex Street,
Strand, LONDON, W.C. 2.

Estate Agent:

R. J. WHITTINGHAM, Esq.,
Estate Office,
Cusworth, DONCASTER.

Auctioneers:

Messrs. TOM SMITH & J. R. JONES,
(on behalf of Northallerton Auctions Ltd.),
NORTHALLERTON.

Lot 12.

All that VALUABLE WOODLAND known as "Brooms Wood," situate on the South side of the main Newcastle to Hexham Road, and containing 8 acres or thereabouts, being No. 32 on the Ordnance Map, at present in hand.

Believed to be Tithe free.

Minerals Leased to the Mickley Coal Company.

Lot 13.

All that VALUABLE WOODLAND known as "High Close Wood," situate as Lot 12, and including the site of the Old West Mickley Colliery, being Nos. 79, 79a and 79b on the Ordnance Map, and containing 20.679 acres or thereabouts, at present in hand.

Subject to the Mickley Coal Company's Lease.

Believed to be Tithe free.

Lot 14.

Mickley Bank Farm.

All that VALUABLE FREEHOLD SMALL HOLDING known as "Mickley Bank Farm," containing 14.825 acres or thereabouts of rich Grass Land, at present in the occupation of Mr. J. R. Robson.

The House contains Sitting Room, Kitchen, Dairy, 4 Bedrooms and the usual out-offices.

The Buildings comprise 8-stall Cow Byre, 3 stall Stable, Barn and Granary, Pig Stye.

SCHEDULE.

Ord. No.	Particulars	Acreage
123	Grass	5.197
127	"	4.802
128	"	2.540
125	"	1.593
124	"	.612
122	"	.080
		14.825

Rent included with Lots 8 and 15 at the yearly rental of £100 0s. 0d.

Tithe £2 10s. 0d. Land Tax 8/9.

Minerals included in Lease to Messrs. Bewick.

Notice to quit expires 12th May, 1928.

Lot 15.

All that VALUABLE FREEHOLD GRASS LAND known as "Horse Close," situate on the new Ridley Road, containing 11.795 acres, now in the occupation of Mr. J. R. Robson. Ordnance Nos. [illegible]

Tithe approximate £1 18s. 0d. Land Tax 2/7½.

Tenancy expires May 12th, 1928.

Minerals under part of Lands Leased to the Mickley Coal Company.

FARM SALES

They were offered, at an auction in the Royal Hotel, Hexham, on Tuesday, April 28th, as Lot 13, about 21 acres of 'Valuable woodland' including the site of the old West Mickley Colliery and subject to M.C. Co. lease, and Lot 6, about 14 acres. Mickley Bank, where Bewicks still mined, was Lot 14; Hallyards Farm, lot 11; and Mickley Grange Farm, lot 18. Other farms and land had been sold previously and on the day only 480 acres, with farms and cottages, went under the hammer. Much of the land was bought by M.C. Co; it was easier to buy the land – when farming was in the doldrums – than to haggle over wayleaves and mineral rights, even if they had no immediate use for it – and most farmers were happy to continue as tenants, no matter who the landlord. Strangely though, the Coal Co. didn't buy the Close Woods.

It is said that a timber-merchant named Heugh bought the trees without realising that the land was included. A bit far-fetched, but he certainly wasn't interested in the land; I also question if his name was Heugh, although there was such a man. It would be a long stretch of the arm of coincidence if a man named Heugh bought land including Heugh Dene, a name of unknown and distant origin, as was Bellasize Burn that runs through it. I would dearly love to know who or what 'Bellasize' was; Heslop's *Northumbrian Words* mentions Bellases, or bellows, for livening up blacksmiths' forges; Godfrey Watson defines Bellasis, a Northumbrian place name, as the Fine, or Beautiful Seat of some Norman immigrant, so was there a Norman blacksmith hereabouts? The timber merchant would no doubt recoup his outlay, and show a handsome profit in quick time when, after the Great War, there was a great demand for English hardwoods – not for the first time in the annals of Bywell.

BARKING IN MICKLEY WOOD, 1868

This land, that had always been forest, was well managed, fenced, and drained with a network of ditches, kept in good order – and cropped. Timber was a precious asset to the Baliols, Nevilles and their like; they knew its value and always looked to the future and preserved the resource. Apart from the crop of heavy timber, oak bark for the important tanning industry and hazel coppice for a dozen uses ensured the proper care of the Close Woods for many centuries. So they were superb and beautiful, stocked with huge and stately trees as well as young ones coming on. The main road that runs between these woods was canopied with verdant green in summer, sparkling fairy trees in winter frost. There are those – now only a few – who remember them yet.

Mr Heugh, if that was his name, was perhaps an early Modern Man, who cared naught for the future, only for the money – money was the thing. He decimated this woodland, took his profit, went off. He left behind a pile of sawdust, that burned for weeks when I inadvertently set it alight thirty or so years later when taking on the role of owner of High Close Wood. A buried slab of concrete – which I inadvertently tried to cultivate – alongside the sawdust, indicated where the sawmill had stood. The biggest horseshoe you ever did see, presumably left behind by one of the team of heavy horses used to haul the timber, I found two feet deep when digging a base for a greenhouse. Interestingly, the trees were felled and moved by methods not much changed from those of Robert's time – axes, saws, animals and brute force. Only the cutting into planks had the benefit of mechanical circular saws. The biggest oaks that were felled might have dated from Robert's time, which puts our role in perspective. The land, clear felled like the Somme battlefield, was left, as the saying goes, to God and Good Neighbours. Mr Heugh was under no duty or obligation to replant. But God, or Nature if you are not of a religious disposition, reclothed the land with dense scrub, and seedling survivors of the 'holocaust' gradually re-established themselves, as reminders of the past and perhaps talismans and guardians of the future. Isn't Nature wonderful?

The 'good neighbours' of Mickley, particularly the children, were not slow to 'take care' of this new adventure playground, where wild flowers and blackberries grew and no farmer shouted 'Get off my land'. Here were streams to dam, still a few trees to climb, that weren't good enough for timber, and plenty of cover for caves or camps. Mr Robinson crossed the road from the school for nature walks with his class and pointed out Cranesbill, Lady's Smock and Ragged Robin, which children painted, or tried to, in the art lesson that followed. But it was in the autumn that this new freedom of the woods really came into its own. Every boy, and not a few girls, who could muster an old saw, a chopper (axe), meat-cleaver, or gully (big knife), or at the very least a pocket knife – with lamp-post on the blade – no matter how blunt or rusty, repaired to the woods, hacked down trees and dragged them home. Burnham Woods never did move like Mickley at bonfire time.

Hands raised in horror would today greet this wanton vandalism, which probably delayed regeneration of the woodland, but it was mostly scrub, and no-one would notice now. The children enjoyed themselves and Nature has a way of dealing with these matters – she even began to clothe the old pit-heaps.

Guy Fawkes was the chap responsible for all this mayhem in the woods, and his famed memory, on 5th of November was duly and properly celebrated with a bonfire in a garden in every street or section of street, which amounted to a lot of bonfire. The woods provided most of the combustibles and took a beating as boys vied with each other as to who could build the biggest bonfire. The amount of work involved was prodigious and the excitement intense, increasing as the day of assembly drew nigh and homes were ransacked for extra material like broken furniture and worn-out clothes that wouldn't make clippy mats but might make a Guy, stuffed with rags and newspapers.

It had to be on the 5th – none of this business of the nearest Saturday, for the convenience of grown-ups: this was a serious business and nothing to do with grown-ups, although they could have the wood-ash for the garden when it could no longer sustain a semblance of fire – after three days if it didn't rain.

Ha'pennies and pennies, carefully saved over weeks and months, and perhaps an extra threepence or sixpence from parents who kept a distant, wary, but enjoying eye on proceedings, could be spent at most shops on fireworks, either Brocks or Standard, but the best and biggest choice was at the newsagents, or, best of all, at Coulson's the bicycle shop in Prudhoe – the journey enhanced the excitement. Most were ½d or 1d; rockets cost more – 3d, 6d, or even 1/-. Often the cheap ones didn't work, nor the Catherine Wheels that needed a pin and a post and fell off or didn't twirl. Roman Candles and 'sparklers' were as good as any, and cheap. 'Bangers' and 'Jumping Jacks' were for horrid boys to frighten girls with and were dangerous.

When the fire died down enough to get near, baked taties were a good way of rounding off the proceedings but they were usually pretty badly charcoaled – and what was wrong with that – or even lost in the embers. I don't recall anyone being seriously burned – nothing that a bit of butter wouldn't mend! Nor do I remember the fire brigade being called.

The brigade had been called in 1924 when the Club went up in flames, and had to gallop from Prudhoe and I must say that they did not much look, on the photograph, like galloping-type horses – perhaps a gentle gallop. By which time the piano had fallen through the floor and the sound of exploding bottles was like the Somme again. People were evacuated from Riding Terrace as the high gable wall at the rear threatened to collapse. A night of high drama in the village – as good as any Guy Fawkes, 'bangers' and all.

With the passage of time and in spite of Guy Fawkes, the woods grew dense again, lonely places for little boys and not so much frequented except by pitch-and-toss players and wild-bird catchers. Then, in about 1935, along came a fellow named Barker, a builder, with advanced recycling ideas. He recycled the old redundant coke ovens into houses, some might say 'Jerry-built' houses – but now they are 'desirable' – in the Winlaton area. He got his eye on High Close Wood and thought it an attractive site for more – lots more – of the same houses, and not so far to haul the bricks. He actually employed a couple of village lads – one called Jerry! - to start clearing the scrub – by hand. This was still the age of the shovel and wheelbarrow, before bulldozers. Events overtook them, as they did Bernards, the brewers who owned the Miners Arms and aspired to something grander and more in keeping with the changing, more prosperous times. A pub, even an hotel, on the main road would not only serve the village, it might catch some of the increasing passing motorised traffic that kept us young Seymours sitting on Sundays in the windows of Rosedale thrilled with the sight of all the different makes and colours of cars on their jaunts to the country. Bernards bought from Mr Barker a corner of the wood next to John Nichol's garage; but that was as far as their hotel got.

Some passing traffic of a different kind greatly exercised the attention of boys at this time – aeroplanes. Twenty-five years or so had passed since the Wrights first got off the ground before aeroplanes first began to buzz, and buzz they did, around the skies where Bewick had watched his birds. I heard my first in 1930 at Clara Vale, when the whole school was agog, teachers too I suspect, but trapped in lessons, so condemned only to hear and not to see. It took ages in the passing and no work was done during it – they might as well have turned us out for the watching!

Later, during breaks or after school, whoever first heard the distant drone raised the cry 'Aeroplane – Aeroplaaa-in' and dashed to get the best vantage point, followed at speed by everyone in earshot, from where this wondrous thing could be watched into and out of sight – and oh! the thrill if it decided to do a turn or even go right round and back the way it came. Thus died the aspirations of boys to be train drivers – it was flying, from now on.

Mickley was not so good for watching aeroplanes; there were fewer, and it was more difficult to get a clear view from the school yard. But they became more common and the sight and sound of these gentle little flying machines, with double wings and purring engines fixed their role as part of peaceful, sunny summer days. Certain boys began trying to make models that would fly, or at least glide from Rosedale yard in an orderly manner into the garden. Alas we were big on enthusiasm but short on aeronautical knowledge; our revolutionary designs were leaden footed and crashed – ignominiously. Fortunately, as with the Wrights, there were few onlookers.

Some of the aeroplanes passing overhead began to have a more urgent sound – and snarled.

Mickley at War Again

The wooden box with knobs on was not much listened to during the day – batteries and accumulators had to be saved for important things like Band Wagon and anyway daytime was for doing things. So we missed the drama of Prime Minister Chamberlain's monotonous, tired voice making the pronouncement that has echoed down the years as a turning-point in the affairs of man. It was followed by the wailing of sirens and scurrying for shelter in London, where it was thought that a demoniacal version of our little buzzing moths would rain death and destruction from the skies immediately on the declaration of war. We knew that it had been tried out, this new way of waging war from the heavens, on the women and children of Guernica, in the Spanish civil war.

Here in Mickley we didn't really expect war, although we read our *Daily Herald*, and the first we knew was a boy running up Newton Terrace with a satchel of newspapers, waving one and shouting, 'Extra – Extraaa'. News by now was quicker – it came by telephone and tele-printer and petrol-driven vans and though not everyone was listening to the wireless, we got the news fast on Sunday, 3rd September, 1939 – on foot.

The news made little impact on me – at 14 there were other things to think about; but I remember the haunted look on my father's face and he went very quiet. Too old now to carry stretchers, but he had two sons, fourteen and eighteen.

Nothing warlike happened. I, still 14, finished building the Cosy, my father the Rio at Prudhoe. There is a piece of board above the ceiling of the Cosy with written on it the news item: 'French tanks advance' – what a laugh – in retrospect. There was talk of war work: building stopped, the Rio made do without neon lights and instead of an occasional grey lorry-load of gravel toiling slowly up the hill past Cherryburn, from Christer's gravel works by the river, suddenly there was a continuous flow, up and down every few minutes, of bright yellow lorries marked Wimpey. There was a lot of concrete mixed in the next few years.

We got identity cards and went back to school for another whiff of chalk and ink and paper and to be fitted with gas-masks – an ominous and serious business that brought everyone up short – this war was perhaps not only for soldiers. My father declined to go for a mask, which seemed strange for one who had encountered gas and its consequences at first hand, but he couldn't bear to wear a mask again. These things were awful, apparently designed to frighten the enemy to death, and they didn't do much for us either. Hysterical children posed a problem; they wouldn't even look at them, let alone get inside. Masks had the smell of a rubbery cellar – it was like being trapped in the inner tube of a bicycle (literary licence – a big tube). The window part misted up even if you used the whole supply of anti-mist stuff on it, so you couldn't see out; and they made a rude noise when you breathed out and the rubber vibrated on your cheek much to the delight of the worst boys (who were beginning to enjoy things) and the embarrassment of their mothers. The masks came in square cardboard boxes with string for putting over the head and went everywhere with you. I made a wooden box for mine, with a leather strap, and carried it for a while like everyone else. Then it was discovered that they were useless – 'I told you so,' said You-know-who, in support of his not having one – and they had to be taken back to school to have an extra box of charcoal, or whatever it was, taped to the end of the pig's snout that you were supposed to draw breath through. Enthusiasm for carrying these infernal nuisances soon waned and most of them were consigned to the backs of cupboards, where, no doubt, many of them languish yet. We knew where they were if needed and they were probably a wise precaution but it was a blessing they were never needed; going about our affairs encased in these would have been a nightmare.

AUTHOR'S ID CARD

This new war produced none of the wild: 'Let's go and teach the Hun a lesson and be home for Christmas' enthusiasm of the previous one – my father's expression said it all, only twenty years on. A dying German officer had predicted to him the next war – within 25 years. There was conscription from the beginning which got rid of the dole queues – there could no longer be reliance on masses of volunteer fools; but as producing food and weapons was as vital as fighting, certain jobs were designated 'essential' and exempt from military service. Coal mining, the principal occupation of Mickley men, came into this category, as did building army camps and aerodromes. This meant that few sons of the village went to Hitler's war, compared to the Kaiser's. The only way a miner could get into it, if he was daft enough to want to, was to volunteer to serve in RAF air crew. Strangely, most of those who did volunteer were not miners – one was a butcher, one a cinema projectionist, one a joiner.

Mickley just got on with producing coal and food and even when U-boats again made their deadly, sneaky mark, rationing never had the impact it made in towns. Miners got extra cheese and meat to supplement the standard rations. The sort of rations that townsfolk had to live on was, per person per week:

One shilling's worth (8oz.) of meat; 1oz. of cheese; 4oz. of bacon; 8oz. of fat, including not more than 2oz. of butter; 2oz. of jam. The amounts varied through the war but these are about the quantities that people lived on. Mercifully, bread was never rationed until after the war, in 1946, when the Americans stopped being kind to us. Special arrangements were made for mothers and babies – they and their well-being were important, the nation would need replenishment. The National Milk Scheme provided 'expectant and nursing mothers and children under five', with a pint of milk a day for 2d. – free to the poor. After 1942 they also got cod-liver oil and orange juice, rosehip syrup and blackcurrant puree. Schools were collecting centres for the rosehips, and the syrup was delicious. National Dried Milk was introduced so that mothers could go to work and leave the feeding to others – something the Germans never did. That certainly started something – working mothers, and granny feeding the baby.

Everyone with a garden dug for victory – and full bellies – like mad. We at Rosedale were fortunate in having a big, well-stocked garden, and my father kept bees, so all our relatives from town called to see us from time to time. We never really went short, or at least we came to no harm from hunger. And we had lots of visitors.

I became fifteen and got involved in 'war work' which was a bit unreal, as there didn't seem to be one. The Germans in their Siegfreid Line and the French in their Maginot seemed quite content to sit it out, while the poor old Poles got knocked about and England pottered as usual, playing bowls and 'Phoney wars'. I worked at making fit for soldiers an old house in Ovingham, next to Bewick's Church and a lovely little white cottage that looked as though it had been there since the beginning of time. The cottage housed a similarly lovely and ancient looking little lady – was she there when Bewick passed her door? – who gave me daffodils for my mother and bulbs for Rosedale garden, whose descendants I can see from my window in High Close Wood. The soldiers were to be next to the village bakery that produced the most heavenly smells and pasties – some billets!

I walked the two miles down the hill to work in the mornings, paid my penny toll and crossed Ovingham bridge, which I didn't like because I could see the river far below my feet, through the gaps in the planks, and they rattled when a car crossed and you had to step aside. This bridge was a 'utility' job, built for horses, but it is still there, carrying more cars than it can be comfortable with. The walk home at the end of the day's work was also two miles, and, like the miners', steep, uphill; but walking to work anything up to four miles was still not uncommon. On a good night I met Winnie Barnes, which lightened my steps, but I never did, alas, pluck up courage to ask her to the pictures – but I did wear my cap at a jaunty angle (faint heart ne'er won fair lady, Mr Robinson would have said!)

Making a Start on the Real War

7.30 a.m. on 10th May 1940 was glorious, I might have sung, as I walked to work, looking down on the mist-draped river valley with the ancient church tower of Ovingham probing the sparkling early sunshine while songbirds probed the still air with their vibrant love-songs. The skylarks sang, then, in Mickley Square. A knot of serious people stood by the bakery, neglecting the pasties. "The balloon's gone up," said one – it had indeed; some balloon. The Hun was on the move again, into Holland, Belgium and France.

There was not a lot I could do about it, so I got on with my work, listened to the news at night and looked at the rapidly changing maps in the *Daily Herald.* I worked in the garden. The news got worse, my father became even more serious. The new Prime Minister, Churchill, soon to become 'Winnie', spoke to us through our faithful wooden box with knobs. I thought he was drunk – it was a while before I realised that that was how he spoke – but his words were stirring and frightening. It was strange stuff, this war, for a fifteen-year-old.

We made sure the wireless batteries were in good shape, the accumulator charged, and stopped everything for the news, every hour – "and this is Alvar Liddell" – or Frank Phillips, or Stuart Hibberd – "reading it". We thought it odd that for some war reason we needed to know who was reading our news; but they were ever so nice, always calm and unruffled, and spoke beautifully. Some folk – traitors we thought, but really they were just looking for a laugh – listened to 'Lord Haw-Haw' at night, but you couldn't mistake whose side he was on – he had a funny voice!

The wireless played a lot of organ music, nothing else in fact. It kept Sandy MacPherson busy at the Theatre Organ and perhaps made his fingers sore. I cannot abide organ music.

The country wakened up, girded its loins – and braced itself. The Prime Minister's call to arms produced the Local Defence Volunteers – charged with the task of supporting the Army in the defence of the Realm – with broomsticks.

In Mickley the L.D.V. formed themselves at the school, without uniforms or weapons, but full of spirit and good intentions. Mr Bryson, who stood at the gate at going-home time and tooted his whistle and crooked his finger to bring back for talking to any miscreant youth, was ideally suited to the roll of prototype 'Cap'n Mainwaring'. I forget his rank but he looked and played the part to perfection.

They shortly got their uniforms, so that they began to look like real soldiers, then some old rifles and a few grenades and eventually they were quite well equipped and trained – and no joke, believe me, had they met the Bosch – on a dark night in the rain ... Some of these fellows had met a few Germans in their day, and had no liking for them. Many of these amateur, spare-time soldiers were boys, like me, but I didn't join them – had no interest in 'Brown Jobs' (the Army). Mind you, I knew all the secret hiding places that no Hun could ever find, and had plans to harass and destroy the whole German Army – single-handed, if they ventured here. At fifteen you can do that sort of thing.

My early enthusiasm for aeroplanes had a boost when I spent my only ever holiday away from home, within sight of Usworth RAF station, near Sunderland, and watched aircraft busy about their various activities. They looked like flying tadpoles, with big heads and long thin tails, and were also black – Handley Page Hampdens, I identified them as – clever stuff, I thought. They were affectionately known as 'Flying suitcases' (some said coffins). I blew all my spending money on a flying model aeoplane powered by a rubber band. It flew, but only into things and when the band broke it wrecked the fragile structure, so I was left to build my own again – without much success I must admit, although improved on the early attempts, and I did carve a rather natty propeller.

Lots of young men, like Douglas Bader and Peter Townsend furthered their early interest in flying by joining the RAF, or Auxiliary Air Force, and made a career of it, but only if they were from a good background, with a decent education. Flying was not for uncultured duffers. However, I thought I'd found a way into flying, before the war, when I saw a newspaper advertisement for Boy Entrants, and Apprentices, so I wrote off, secretly, for application forms. My poor mother was horrified when she discovered, but need not have worried – they only wanted tradesmen, the form said. It was many years before I discovered that lots of Halton Brats as they were known, went on to achieve fame and high rank in flying. I, with bitter disappointment, took the matter no further, to my mother's relief – and the RAF's loss? ...

When war came I watched the 'planes fly over Mickley and learned to recognise them; then there were books to be read; after all, if the war lasted long enough and I bettered myself the snobbish RAF might just have need of me. I dreamed not just of lobbing stolen hand-grenades into passing German lorries – from High Close Wood – but of becoming the New Age Biggles. In the meantime, there not being much war-work in the village, I was sent to grow food – at Wheelbirks, where the Richardsons had spread their leather waste. It really was a part of the ancient township of Micelee, in the Barony of Bywell, if I need justification for including it here.

A well-known firm of seed-merchants, Finneys, had their trials grounds there, but were duly diverted into war work, which was growing food – cabbages – in the field, and tomatoes in the glasshouses. I planted cabbages – millions, it seemed – with another lad from the village and a couple of Land Army girls. They were the feminine equivalent of the Home Guard, but their weapons were hoes and tractors and their efforts largely unsung but prodigious. These two must have been from 'good' backgrounds because they didn't fraternise with village lads. They ate in the house with Percy the Manager and his wife, while Jerry from the village – the same lad who had set about clearing High Close Wood by hand – and I ate our sandwiches in the greenhouse and didn't dare add a tomato because that would be stealing, and they were needed for the war.

This Percy deserves a mention, though he was not really a man of Mickley, except in nature. He came from afar – either Lancashire or Yorkshire, and had learned his gardening in the best of all schools – private service. There was little about gardening that he didn't know, nor about the country. He could shoot rabbits with a catapult, and would no doubt have despatched Germans with equally silent adroitness had the need arisen. He was a fine athlete and could have played for Sunderland but the money was poor and the prospects better in gardening! He had done his bit in the 'first lot' and joined the LDV, now renamed the Home Guard, with alacrity.

We heard the planes above the cabbage field and stopped to watch, when Percy wasn't looking, the Hurricanes and Spitfires limbering up for combat overhead as the Battle of Britain intensified in the faraway killing-skies. Fighter pilots needed urgent practice and politicians, belatedly, no longer skimped the petrol, so make-believe 'dogfights' between friendly adversaries thrilled and entertained the young cabbage planters. Pilots probably enjoyed them too – that's what they had joined for; the thrill and fun of flying. Not the dying.

I decided, there at Wheelbirks in that glorious summer of 1940, that as soon as I was old enough I would fly Hurricanes. They could out-turn Spitfires, if they couldn't catch them, and I heard that they were better gun-platforms. Biggles look out!

On 15th August a bank of cloud ran from the coast right up the Tyne valley and over Wheelbirks, with clear skies to the north and south.

The German warlords played their trump card. While – they thought – the entire RAF fighter force was being bludgeoned in the south, their Norwegian-based air Armada would devastate the North-east and bring England to heel. The lads who had been entertaining cabbage-planters with aerobatics gave these arrogant Huns a bloody nose and sent them packing; but before they went home – those who made it – a group of them ventured as far as Wheelbirks.

We in our field heard a remote thump or two and then an eerie drumming in the sky above the clouds, more sinister than poss-sticks or even poss-sticks and hob-nails combined. Percy dashed into the house and returned with one of his sons, who was also in the Home Guard, bearing a dining chair each, a tin hat, and a rifle – loaded presumably, I didn't ask. We non-combatants kept on planting – the nation must not go short of cabbages. Now that I think of it, we planters didn't even have tin hats …

They sat on their dining chairs in the field, back-to-back – Percy and Arthur; helmets on, rifles across knees, awaiting the imminent German invasion. "They Shall Not Pass". Their names alone should surely have given the intruders second thoughts – Heaven help any Hun who dared to set foot on Wheelbirks and disrupt the planting while Arthur (King) and Percy (Hotspur) stood, or rather sat, in defence of the realm.

Whether it was the presence of our two stalwarts, or the cloud concealing Wheelbirks and, incidentally, Mickley, the enemy gave up and turned for home without even dropping a bomb on our cabbages. It was almost an anticlimax – and we didn't even get a look at them. Only a part of the force came our way but there were enough to weigh the air with that peculiar sound that German bombers made – quite distinct from 'ours', which made friendly noises. At 190 or so m.p.h. it took a long time to fly from the coast – about twelve minutes, and twelve back again, but I was unable to show off my identifying prowess to warn if they were just bombers, or troop-transports bent on invasion, so it was an anxious few minutes. There was relief, disguised as disappointment in the 'troops' when they realised they were not to get a crack at the enemy after all, as the sound faded towards the east and we were able to pay proper attention to our rural pursuits.

The rifles were left leaning on the chairs – just in case they came back. But they didn't, not ever.

Thus the one and only large-scale daylight assault on our area came to an ignominious end. The RAF had their best day against the Luftwaffe, and rightly so – how dare they come swanning over our clearing in the forest, disturbing the quiet with their ghastly noise.

The Dark Days

Soldiers had come to Mickley after Dunkirk; and the road signs were taken away so that nobody knew whether they were coming or going. Air raid shelters were hastily built in the school yards, of Mickley bricks from West Wylam, with thick concrete tops of gravel from the river bed at the Junction. Inside slatted wooden benches lined the walls for children to sit uncomfortably on and a heavy roll-down gas-cum-blast curtain closed the entrance. Cramped crowded conditions and lack of light prevented much in the way of activity; kissing games would have been alright but they weren't allowed – games had to be educational – so only word games and singing were practical when air raid rehearsals were held. The real thing never arose, the nearest being 15th Aug. Just as well – direct hits on concentrations of children in blast shelters could cause the most ghastly casualties. The ancient ploy of dispersal, of melting into the woods, would have been better advised, saved on bricks and gravel, and lent itself to nature-study lessons. Anyway, this was provision for safety of the children by day, regardless of what the night might bring.

MICKLEY CLUB SIREN TOWER

Being just too far from a major target, Mickley did not qualify for air-raid shelters except at the school, nor for a siren; but it had Air Raid Wardens and a 'Post'. Now where would you locate the Post if you were Mickley miner-wardens? In the Club basement of course, next to the beer cellar – bearing in mind what had happened to all those bottles in the Great Fire of '24. No point in taking chances.

Prudhoe had the siren and on a quiet night with the wind from the east, and if you were down the yard – in the nettie – or walking home from the Cosy, it could just about be heard. This was really not good enough for Mickley, so they got their own Private Enterprise siren on the tower-like structure atop the Club that must have been built with sirens in mind – or Reivers. Only it was not a siren – it was a Klaxon Horn. Now what's a Klaxon Horn?. It was the first electrically-operated warning of approach of the motor car, after the man with a red flag and the rubber bulb on a bugle that went 'honk', or 'honk honk' when the bulb was given a sharp squeeze – or two. The new style audible warning worked by button so didn't need the hand to be stretched outside the car. It produced a most gruesome, indescribable noise in two tones – a warming-up, and a main blast, mercifully short-lived if the finger didn't linger on the button. On a car in the street it must have caused a havoc of heart-attacks and bolting horses; mounted on the Club and activated by a Warden's finger in the Post below, primed by a phone call from the control-centre at Prudhoe, it curdled the blood of the village, but made a passable siren. A finger was pressed in short bursts – like a braying donkey – for two minutes for the 'Warning' and continuously for the 'All Clear'. All it did was bring everyone out to watch the searchlights – which were ever so pretty but never seemed to do anything except light-up the clouds – and to see if there was anything happening 'doon the Toon' in Newcastle. What else could be done? There was no point in hiding under the stairs when they were little more than a ladder and it was quite a walk to the drift, which would certainly have afforded good if grimy protection if things became serious.

West Mickley, now, were an independent lot and though they had no siren they could have a free listen to the Square hooter and they made their own shelter in a remaining part of the old pit, which was close enough to the village. I believe it was pretty good as shelters go – miners knew a thing or two about holes in the ground. Some had lived in trenches. They had no Warden's Post, but what was the point with no Club to put it under?

Stocksfield had to build their own shelters if they wanted them (who would want to bomb Stocksfield, said Mickley), and they could stock them with tins of Spam and fruit and I hope they went rotten, said Mickley.

Watching searchlights soon palled as a pastime and people returned to ordinary evening pursuits, with a few wartime extras for some ...

The Army lads who had come to live in our midst were a long way from home; where that was we didn't know, in spite of the odd accents, because units were secret and insignia strange. My father being away from home building airfields and army camps, we at first did not have soldiers to Rosedale but they were made welcome in the village, in the manner of Northumberland and the times. Any who wished could always find a hearth to warm his feet at, and a cup of tea and perhaps a slice of home-made bread and blackberry jam; the lucky ones a pretty girl to take to the Cosy. The Cosy flourished – it had got built just in the nick of time – every night was a full house. Likewise at Prudhoe, which also housed an extra population of troops. The local lads lost out a bit on the girls – who would want a coaly pitman when she could have a brave, smart soldier? At least they weren't Americans, with dollars – a British soldier's shilling a day didn't go far, when a tuppenny pie cost fourpence. The secret of success for girls was to be pretty enough to date a sergeant, or even an officer. One family of three beautiful daughters made bets as to who could date the highest rank; one of them managed Captain, although it was said that she had the advantage of having had her appendix removed so had the scar to show off!

This was, whatever has been said and written to the contrary, still a time of some innocence and decency; these soldier-boys were alright, most of them, and respected the girls – who stuck to the rules, because the leather belt still hung by the fireplace – and they valued the village hospitality. They were issued with prophylactic treatment against V.D., which was a scourge of the Army, but, although there was no 'Pill', they left behind no bastards. That is not to say that one or two girls didn't make reputations for themselves; one, of simple mind, was reputed to have made herself available for a penny. Village talk I expect, but she certainly hung around the soldiers.

The Army at war meets its needs in the field largely by requisitioning: at Mickley some of them lived in Nissen huts in the field off East gate Bank behind the Mission Room. They cooked their food in a concrete-block built cookhouse adjoining, that would have sent any self-respecting Food Inspector into convulsions, and served it through a window-hatch into the main hall, which was the 'mess, other ranks'. Sergeants' Mess was the Miner's Reading Room next door – complete with billiards tables, which never recovered. The food was the same, and everyone drank the same horrible 'char', or 'brew'. The water for this tea was alright when it left the tap, was boiled – although not always – and was usually 'smoked' (you've never had smoked tea?) in mobile coal-fired field boilers, like set-pots on legs, with chimneys. Depending on the whim of the 'cook', who was probably a squaddy on 'jankers', copious quantities of tea leaves were cast into the water and left to stew for a while, or else the tea was put into big urns and the water tapped into them. Either way, it ended up like tar and either stewed or cold, and coloured yellow with great quantities of Carnation milk, still from contented cows, out of tins savaged open with old bayonets – and where might they have been – or gullies, to get them open fast. Sugar was not optional – there was a wartime belief that it was good for you – gave energy; so the result was that anyone falling into a vat of sugared tea would have floated, like eggs in brine. This tea could almost be cut into slices and was to be avoided whenever possible – except when refusal might give offence to a big cook with

NISSEN HUT

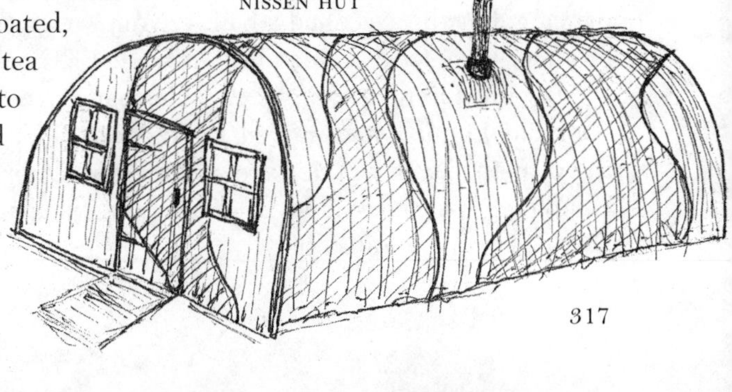

a gully, or a kindly one with a pound of butter or tea to spare. It was difficult to believe that there was a war on – food was wasted beyond belief by the Army. Later on, they would get a shock. Meanwhile, the pigs got the benefit – Dearly beloved brethren ...! Soldier's tea was made even worse by having bromide added; it was thought to reduce sexual appetite and the attendant risks.

Officers messed at Bywell – where else. I don't know if they got bromide in their tea.

Soldiers dug zig-zag trenches for air-raid shelters – and practice at digging trenches – in the field above the Nissen huts, where the nurse's home would have stood. They parked their little Bren-gun troop-carriers in the cricket field and slept in the pavilion, but had no use for the bowling-green (wrong service!), reputedly the best for miles around. So pitmen could continue to relax on the fine sward, and their children on the adjoining swings; or play tennis in the summer, at the Welfare.

This sporting complex was the last, laudable, example of co-operation in the field of welfare, between penny-paying pitmen and munificent bosses. They made a great team, recreation-wise.

The cricket field was respected by the Army and hardcore laid around the perimeter for the 'carrier' tracks to run on. Practice driving – for Hurricane pilots were not alone in needing to hone their skills – was done in the field by the Nissen huts, and in High Close Wood, which had recently been burnt from end to end, the fire almost reaching Nichols wooden garage. It also destroyed enough of the fencing to allow unrestricted access from the road, so with no one about to say 'nay' the Army made full use of this ideal training-ground. They would have done anyway, being the Army. They requisitioned Johnny's garage and Norfolks' bus lost its shelter so that trucks and tracks could be serviced under cover.

They mounted a Bren-gun on a tripod by the Nissen huts for anti-aircraft defence.

On Saturday nights they hired a band – the Services did a lot for Bands – and held dances in the Mission Room; this war was a mission, was it not?. Typical 'sweat box' stuff; any fire and safety regulations there were in those days went by the board, there was a war on, you know. The walls pulsated, cigarette smoke fogged the atmosphere, and the very air of Mickley reverberated to the sound of jolly revelry. I am not sure if many village lads went dancing, but the girls had a ball ... War was not entirely gloom.

There were football matches – Mickley F.C. v The Army.

All winter long, into 1941, the Germans wreaked their vengeful havoc on poor old London and spread their doom-laden shadow over nearly every town in the land. Sunderland was battered horribly and an Aunt of ours, completely paralysed and helpless, was evacuated from there to Rosedale. The Germans followed her ...

It was 4a.m. when the Klaxon went and nobody bothered to get out of bed, so we are not quite sure what happened. A German bomber – you could tell by the unfriendly sound! – passed noisily overhead and there was a close – a very close, rattle of machine-gun fire. We leapt out of bed – I can assure you. Some said we were under attack – well, it was something to tell your grandchildren; others that the defensive Bren-gun had loosed off on our behalf. What had actually happened was that an enemy aircraft had been caught in the beam of a searchlight that operated from a field across the river between Ovington and Ovingham. Whatever would Offa have said? The aircraft had fired down the beam to try to douse the light, that was all. But it had happened overhead and sounded mighty close. Our friendly Bren lost out on the glory, and helpless Auntie Florence in her bed at Rosedale did not enjoy the experience.

Night Raids

In order that fire-fighting appliances would not suffer excessive losses in the early stages of a raid, the A.F.S. – Auxiliary Fire Service – later changed to National – reserves were withdrawn to the country – Ministeracres Hall. It must have been better than having your ARP Post under the Club. Every evening when weather conditions made a raid possible and there was not enough of the usual filth hanging in the air over industrial Tyneside to hide it, a convoy of lorries from Ministeracres passed through Mickley townwards. They towed little trailers with chimneys and were for making smoke, heaven help us, as though we didn't have enough. As a result of their efforts, so it was said, the shipyards and factories of the Tyne, strung out as they were along the river, were very difficult to find and escaped major damage. Manors goods yard, in Newcastle, must have missed out on the smoke because it was hit and made its own – we could see it from Mickley and it burned for days – sugar, I believe, and flour as well, some said. A smoky combination. Alright in cakes.

Blaydon got more than its size justified, and a mention by Lord Haw Haw. Perhaps it was too small to waste smoke on. The Marshalling Yards were hit, according to Haw Haw, who kept us posted on what was happening, German version. His 'gen' was 'duff' and they missed the railway, but hit a small factory and houses and shops. There was a mess and people were killed and it brought the war close. It came even closer the night Branch End was bombed – well, sort of.

It was the night of the big Glasgow raid of March 1941 when a lot of bombers passed over here. We guessed it was Glasgow's turn, poor souls, as the monsters drummed their way overhead with their distinctive sound. They unsynchronized their engines (set them at slightly different revs.) to confuse our acoustic direction-finding equipment. It didn't confuse R.D.F. one little bit – Radio Direction Finding – Radar when the Americans got their hands on it – but it didn't much matter as we couldn't do much about them anyway.

I doubt if the bombing was deliberate – Longstaffes was not all that important a target. It could have been a jettison on the way to Glasgow, but it's doubtful; if anyone was in trouble or wanted to run for home, which was unlikely in the absence of opposition, the whole load would have been dropped and the bread would certainly have risen! No, it was most likely a 'hang-up', a bomb that failed to release, that the crew finally persuaded to 'go' on the way home – over Branch End. They are not good things to take home, hung bombs – they can go off 'bang' on landing, and crews made every effort to get rid of them and didn't care where. It could have been tough on Branch End.

Anyway, the wayward bomb was probably made by slaves and failed to explode. It made a hole in the field just a few yards east of Brettonby Avenue – the occupants would have had a headache, had it gone off. As it was they had to clear out while those intrepid Bomb Disposal lads from Close House at Wylam, next-door to where Stephenson was born, dug it up and defused it. For cool, calculated bravery those fellows took some beating. They had nothing in the way of sophisticated devices to ease their way and never knew the nature of the fuse until it was uncovered or heard ticking – whether it was dud and therefore harmless, a new design, or delayed and therefore potentially lethal at any moment. Hairy stuff indeed; the making of posthumous V.C.s.

The retrieved bomb, a five-hundred pounder or its metric equivalent, if I remember rightly, was put on its base, pointing skywards whence it had come, beside the Esso pump at Branch End Garage. People went warily to touch it – trusting that it really had been defused – during one of those weeks that punctuated the war, in which we were exhorted to put our money, because there was nothing to spend it on, into National Savings for the Government to spend on weapons – Governments are a devious lot when it comes to ways of relieving us of our money. There was Wings Week (£5,000 paid for a Spitfire they said, but it didn't), Warship Week, and I think this was Army Week or words to that effect. Branch End people, thankful that The Bomb had not gone off, saved generously and Stocksfield easily reached its target as indicated on the barometer by the garage. So did Prudhoe and everywhere else in Britain – it was a question of pride and patriotism. Mickley was included with Prudhoe, not big enough to have a pride of its own. Anyway we were hard-up.

There were parades and marches – and amateur concerts in the Rio and the Cosy – where the stage held no more than a duet – and children's 'concerts' in Rosedale backyard; and dances and whist-drives and apart from the money, everyone felt they were doing something to help and morale got no end of a boost. It was badly needed, things were pretty black for an endlessly long time – in more ways than one ...

It was so dark one moonless, cloudy night, that I became disorientated walking home from Prudhoe and lost my sense of direction until I recognised the hedge I fell into. The 25 minute walk became a one hour grope; like being down a pit without a candle. This was Blackout, and pretty complete; difficult to imagine. No street lights, not a chink from any house – 'Put that light out!' – and seldom a car abroad at night; any that were had only one headlight and that was hooded, so that it cast only a small pool of light two or three yards ahead, hopefully on the curb if there was one – on most country roads there wasn't. Driving off the road was a common mishap, but few motorists other than doctors ventured out at night unnecessarily. Anyway, petrol was very strictly rationed – questions could be asked of motorists.

Men came to the village with lorries and took away the iron railings from around the churchyard and the tiny gardens of Riding and Newton Terraces to be made into weapons (ploughshares into swords?) and they were still lying in rusty heaps when the war ended, perhaps to be made into rusty cars. They were neither paid for nor replaced. War was an excuse for all manner of foolish and naughty goings-on.

Housewives were also asked to sacrifice their aluminium pots and pans to be made into Spitfires. Aeroplanes were now made of aluminium instead of wood – except the brilliant little Mosquito, which might have changed the course of the war on its own if its potential had been recognised earlier. Wood was good.

It is a strange irony that if Mosquitoes had been built instead of Stirlings and Halifaxes, people would have kept their aluminium utensils and perhaps become ill as a result of aluminium poisoning ... It was forty years before the dangers of cooking food, especially making tea, in aluminium was recognised. If the bomber didn't get you the teapot could.

Talking of bombers – word went around, for rumour was an essential part of war, of a big new airfield being built at Harlow Hill, a knob on the skyline to the north of Mickley, within sight of Rosedale windows, for the defence of Tyneside, or better still we hoped, for the bombing of Germany. It must have been planned a while, it was no quick-build emergency job. The buildings were brick and permanent, apart from the added-on parts like dispersals, which were the ubiquitous Nissen huts, and wooden huts for the Women's Auxiliary Air Force quarters, at a distance from the main buildings – outside the airfield, in fact. A thoughtful attempt to keep the girls, bless them, from harm, at least while they slept.

I was directed to do my war work at Harlow Hill, or, as it was officially named, RAF Ouston, and travelled the eight or more miles on a special workers' bus that had a struggle getting up the hills. It was full of old men, and boys who sang all the way there and all the way back – 'Roll out the Barrel', 'I've Got Sixpence', 'The Quartermaster's Stores'. What a lot of songs to sing; songs to cheer. Someone had a mouth-organ; wherever you went during the war, someone had a mouth-organ; they could be carried in a pocket. You couldn't carry a guitar in a pocket.

The night before I started work at Ouston I watched from the stair-head window the red flashing identification beacon atop the wireless mast on Harlow Hill and practised my Morse Code. Not much to practice on, just BE, I think, but can't be sure now. The identification letters were supposed to be for the benefit of RAF flyers, not the Luftwaffe. I watched the lights of the flarepath behind the hill and landing lights gliding in on the approach. Then all the lights went out and there were bright flashes in the night sky followed by a series of 'crunches' as the bombs exploded. An audacious Junkers 88 intruder with a spot-on navigator had feigned an RAF approach, hit his target, opened up and got clean away. Caused a bit of mayhem and a few red faces – 'Might have waited until the damn place was finished, don't you think'. We civilians were not allowed to see the damage. We had to have special identity cards to get past the guardroom, but anyone could have driven a herd of elephants in across the fields and no one would have noticed. We all managed a sneaky look and found that they had hit the very nerve-centre of the Station – the NAAFI. Oh horror of horrors! But everyone buckled-to and before you could blink the place was rebuilt and ship-shape – if the metaphor is Air Force acceptable – and 'tea and wads' flowed freely again. The NAAFI, for those who don't know, was the Navy (in order of seniority!), Army, and Air Force Institute and served roughly the same purpose as the Miner's Welfare – the well-being of the workers, but food and drink orientated, perhaps more on the lines of the Co-op, with a piano. Servicemen could buy, at non-profit-making prices, supplies such as writing paper, boot polish, razor blades, toothpaste, and oh yes – for the RAF, 'Brylcreem'. Chocolate and cigarettes were restricted and servicemen could never get enough 'fags' and weren't always keen on chocolate, so non-smoking chocolate-eating civilians like me could benefit. Shops got an allocation of things that were not rationed and divided them amongst their 'registered' customers (you could only buy your rations at the shop where you were registered). Cigarettes and chocolate were among these items, so I was able to buy my allocation of cigarettes, and my father's too when he was away, from Nichols' shop and barter them for chocolate at RAF Ouston. Thus are made Captains of Commerce ... Mind you, there was no money in it, and hardly enough chocolate to rot my teeth.

After they had taken over the role from the distinguished WVS, the function for which the NAAFI became renowned and which it performed with courage and distinction, in spite of the jokes, and to the eternal gratitude of countless numbers of service men and women, was in providing 'char and wads' – tea and sandwiches, but don't forget the cakes. Not within an hour before a meal (in case it spoilt the appetite for service food!), the canteen opened for morning break, an hour after midday meal, and all evening from six till ten, when beer could be served and the piano came into its own. There was always someone who could bang out the Warsaw Concerto; sometimes one of taste and accomplishment who could hush the room with Chopin or bring a tear with a sentimental ballad, or else had a rousing song to sing. I hadn't thought till now, but piano-making must have been essential war work.

Although the tea and wads were essentially for the Services and civilians not allowed to buy in the canteens, when the NAAFI van came around dispersal the kindly girls would often beckon the young worker from his labours for a welcome break, when everyone had been served (why did he always look hungry?). I never understood what NAAFI cake jokes were about – I liked them. Mind you, they could never be a patch on Church Army, WI, or WVS – which were like mother made.

At Ouston I fixed shelves and blackout curtains in Nissen huts and saw how Servicemen lived; sat on the grass at bait time and watched Spitfires at work and rest, whittled models of them out of scraps of wood and decided that, after all, if the war lasted and there seemed no good reason to suppose it wouldn't, these were what I would fly. I was still fifteen and Mickley had seen the last of aerial warfare; sneak raids still kept the sirens wailing and the searchlights probing, although increasingly to point the way to crippled RAF bombers groping for home. ARP wardens played a lot of cards under the Club.

Time to Don Uniform

Our soldiers left and others came, and we got to know what these were – The Kings Own Scottish Border Regiment – reivers gone straight. They had a good band; it played in a field at Bywell, to entertain the ghosts of Baliol, and we walked to hear it on Sundays. Mickley Band had nowhere to practice, the Army had all the best places. What I remember most about the KOSBs was their Beating the Retreat in the roadway at Branch End, by the garage – perhaps as part of Army Week or something. They stirred my blood into a froth – these were stirring times. I had never seen kilts on the march, to drums, never heard bagpipes in bulk – my little dog had howled to the heavens on hearing only one issuing from the wooden box with knobs. The sight and sound of all this pageantry almost made me wish I were a Scot – but not quite. They really were magnificent – but they got soiled in Burma, poor souls, where the reiving came into its own, I believe.

The Air Training Corps was intended to prepare boys for service in the

RAF, unlike the Home Guard, which was an active defence force. But ATC cadets were trained to use weapons and would have joined the fray if needed. The uniform did not come up to kilts and sporrans for romantic appeal, for the tunic was designed to go over shirts of working lads who could not be expected to buy special shirts and ties. It also made for a quick and easy change for evening parades, after work; and it was RAF blue and I was for flying so, one evening, without telling my mother, I dressed in my best, as though taking a girl to the pictures and took myself off to Prudhoe, where I walked up and down several times before plucking up courage to enter the Parish Hall where the ATC were meeting, and placed myself at their disposal. This was a momentous step they were taking. They were a disorganised lot, compared to the Home Guard, with no fixed meeting place – the next meeting being in a school. My mother must have thought it serious – dressed up two nights running. The same nervousness tormented me but I felt more at ease in a school and stayed on for a maths lesson – back to school indeed. I discovered that the C.O. was the blue equivalent of Mr Bryson, Home Guard, and years later realised that he was a better prototype Cap'n Mainwaring than Mr Bryson in that he was a Bank Manager during the day. When Mainwaring eventually materialised on our television screens, he was the image of Flt. Lt. Wallace, Manager, Martin's Bank, Prudhoe. We at Mickley knew nothing of Banks, except that there was one in Prudhoe. We kept our resources in our pockets and paid cash. But had I had need of a Bank Manager then I would have liked him to have been Mr Wallace; a kindly man, few as kind, even if he was a bit pompous.

When my intentions were considered by 'the command' to be serious I got a uniform and swung my arms with some pride – up the High Row and back again; if I had disdained the bus to Prudhoe previously, I certainly wasn't going to use it now, even if my precious uniform got wet! I turned a head or two, or so I thought, and didn't mind being looked at any more. My mother did not seem to mind, in fact I think she was quite proud of her little boy.

Churchills in the Village

The Borderers left and another lot of soldiers came, with a great noise and creaking and bustle. They brought massive Churchill tanks and parked them in High Close Wood, amongst the trees and under camouflage nets, so that the Germans couldn't see them.

They made an awful noise and mess, practising and churning and getting repaired in Nichols' garage – only just: it was a bit tight for tanks and the vibrations shook the structure. They had lorries and motorbikes and all manner of gear and were very impressive. The Hun would get it in the neck when they met these – so we thought. The British Army was pulling itself together, and a fair slice of it seemed to be parked in Mickley. The Royal Armoured Corps drank the same kind of tea as the others, danced in the Mission Room on Saturday nights with the village maids and enjoyed the hospitality.

I continued to march back and forth to Prudhoe in my uniform. It does strange things to a chap, does a uniform. I played soccer for the Squadron (1248) on Saturday afternoons, and made it an excuse – no time to change, to go in uniform to the dance at the fine Queens Dance Hall in Hexham, with the rest of the team for support, of course. The uniform was to impress the girls – no hope that my dancing would, I'm sure; another of life's little failings. We travelled en masse by train to Hexham and had fun on the way, and on the way back in the dark with the light bulbs removed – wartime fun was great fun, at least we thought so – still do. The sound of 'In The Mood' still evokes fond memories of 'The Queens' on Saturday nights, with its floor of a thousand springs (not with rotten joists for the bounce, as in the old Fever Hospital at Edgewell that eventually became the ATC Headquarters), the Boston Two Step, Palais Glide, and Bradford Barn Dance, and crowded to the limits, mostly with uniforms. Then the late (ten o'clock finish) night walks home from Stocksfield or Prudhoe station, two miles, or three the long way, in the company of youngsters of no unruly intent, only of a mind to enjoy themselves before going off to win the war.

Buses were not much used for wartime travel to dances, petrol was too precious; it came from afar, across the U-boat infested seas, in tankers that were their prime targets. By 1941 the sneaky monsters were sinking more than twenty ships a week and took their toll through most of the war. Men's lives were not to be lost so that we could bus to dances. Miners risked their lives in the battle for coal and were uncomfortable, but not on the scale of the mariners, and miners lived at home, the coal was beneath our feet – and Mickley made its due contribution to the war effort.

So when we could, we travelled by train – good old coal-fired trains, or we walked; that was nothing new, what

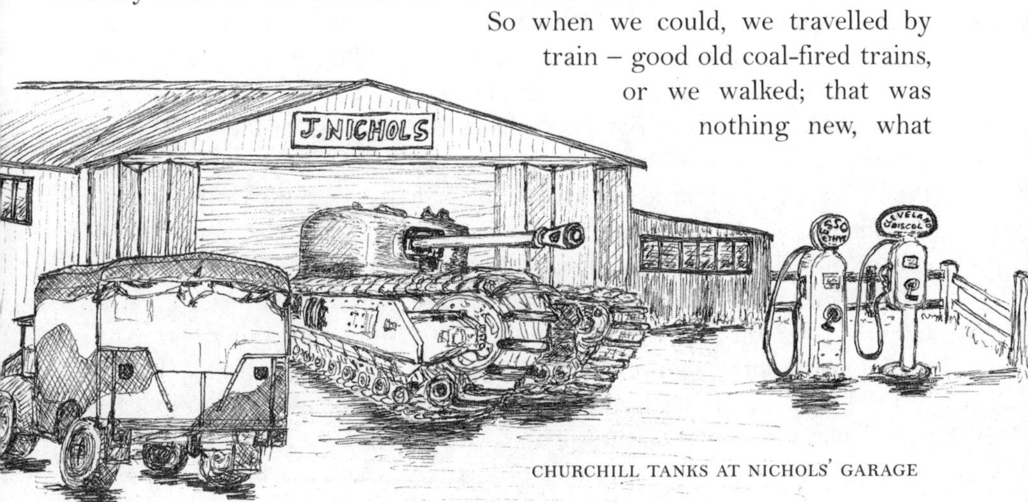

CHURCHILL TANKS AT NICHOLS' GARAGE

legs were for, quoth Charlie Hall. Those who did their war work in Newcastle, which was in the forefront of the industrial battle, travelled by bus and grim it was too. They queued for ages without shelter then packed into buses like sardines in smoke-filled Black Holes (Calcutta, not Space), with not enough room to move and not enough light to read. 'Utility' (everything in wartime was 'utility') buses, which replaced the old 'Leylands' that could no longer be coaxed to function, were stark. They had slatted wooden seats along the sides so that passengers faced each other across the wide aisles, or would have done but for the solid mass of standing passengers between; rather on the principle of cattle trucks, where the tighter the packing the less rolling-around there is. Conductors (-esses, most of them) had a tough time but in general they, and their passengers, remained good-natured. Good nature is another of the characteristics of the British in adversity, but it was somewhat strained in bus conductors and barkeepers (who also worked in crowded and difficult conditions) by Chinese Bank Notes. You don't have to believe this but it is true – in the middle of a very serious war …

A ship bound for China was sunk off Druridge Bay and its cargo washed ashore, just where my brother happened to be working on coastal defences. The cargo included pencils, blotting paper – and Chinese Bank Notes. Men died for them.

The blotting paper was not a lot of use by the time it came ashore, and Geordies didn't do all that much writing; they might have used the pencils for practising, and budding Bewicks might have drawn with them – but they fell apart when they dried. That left the Bank Notes, which had remained dry for some reason (apart from the watermarks?) and what use to make of those? The Geordie rogue perhaps didn't have a lot of use for wet blotting paper, but he wasn't daft and although he couldn't read Chinese he jolly soon cottoned on to the fact that a Chinese Bank Note in the dark was very much like an English Bank Note in the dark to a harassed conductor, or barmaid in the not quite so dark. We had our share of wartime 'spivs' and 'drones', 'wide boys' and black-marketeers and they passed off these notes in considerable numbers. It was an unpleasant business, especially when you consider that conductors had to make good any deficiencies out of their own pockets. I heard of no one ever being caught for passing Chinese notes but I hope they were. My brother kept a couple for many years, out of interest.

Conductors, as well as drivers and passengers, also had to suffer 'Charcoal-burners', a clever idea to save petrol, thought up by someone from Norfolk where it's flat. These strange buses might have been good for a laugh if you didn't have to ride on one for want of something better to get you home. At first glance they looked pretty innocuous, just like any other bus but with a little trailer lurking behind, like an 'Emmet' creation. It was rather like the smoke-makers of the AFS without the chimney but with a warm glow about it and a smell of charcoal, like a barbecue without the sausages. Great for roast-chestnuts and baked potatoes you might think – but for powering buses? Strange though it may seem, this invention worked quite well, so long as the journey was downhill. Not too bad on the level, with the wind in a favourable quarter; uphill was the bugbear, and there is a lot of that in these parts. They often refused even to make the effort uphill until all the passengers, and the conductor (the driver was excused), had dismounted and walked up the hill. Sometimes the young and fit had to give a push – and there was no refund on the fare!. No doubt there were a few charcoal-burners going cheap after the war. The gas that was produced in the trailer by smouldering charcoal was conveyed to the engine by a long pipe where, with luck there was enough to provide motive power, like the cars that carried bags of coal-gas on their roofs, in the manner of African porters.

One who never suffered from either charcoal-burners or queues was one of our village characters – Kitty by name. She was short, round and cuddly, packed a mind like a razor and came gift-wrapped in one of those pinnies that was standard wear for village wives; or else all in black for going to town, 'just in case' the worst happened. It was as well to be prepared – there was a war on.

Kitty appeared to have the greatest difficulty in walking, especially near busy bus stations; she leaned heavily on her stick, and could only just make it to the bus queue – the front end. There she would stand, breathing heavily, and gasp, "Oh dear," looking despairingly down the long length of the queue. "Howay Hinny, on y'gan," would say the work-weary head of the queue and help her up the steps into the front seat. Here she sat, poor old soul, regaling the passengers with her well-rehearsed story of how she knew she ought not to be on a bus at that time of day (shoppers were asked to leave town before 4 o'clock) but her poor dear husband was terribly ill in hospital, not expected to live and she wanted to spend as much time as possible with him and, oh dear, she hadn't noticed the time. She had them almost in tears, while all the while he was actually asleep at home after a hard shift with a pick at the pit.

She would be helped off the bus at the Co-op – "Noo are y'sure y'can manage?" – and set off painfully for her High Row home – until the bus was out of sight, when she would pick up her stick and stride briskly off before too many neighbours enquired what was wrong. Not that they didn't know. Alas, there is no one like Kitty in Mickley any more.

Moving Towards the Action

I came of the age for making war, seventeen and a quarter – and the war still raged, so I offered myself to the RAF and went off to far-distant Doncaster for three days to see if I was of any use to them. To a lad who had been no farther than Whitley Bay on a Sunday School trip and had yet to find his way around Newcastle, this was High Adventure, and all free. There were lots of other lads there with the same ideas about flying, and from widely varied backgrounds. I discovered bawdy songs that I couldn't understand.

I was asked by one of an imposing bevy of officers behind a desk, with scrambled egg on his hat and wings on his chest, why I wanted to be a pilot. I replied that that was what I would be best at! I thought they believed me, but I was really only acceptable because the losses of air crew over Germany were so great (the Air Force equivalent of the Somme) that lads from any kind of background were now welcome. They recruited so many that the training schools were chock-a-block, so instead of putting me in an aeroplane they sent me home on 'Deferred Service', to continue my war work around army camps. I was, however, 'sworn in' and given a number and small lapel badge – RAFVR (Volunteer Reserve) to wear with my little round ATC one when in civvies; and now I could wear in my forage-cap, when in uniform, the white 'flash' that proclaimed to the world that I was an Aircrew Cadet!

None of that foolish horror of the Great War, the white feather, was seen in the Greater War. People did their whack in many different ways, not always obvious. But it could be seen that you weren't shirking if you wore a badge; the VR badge was one to be worn with pride – had not many of the wearers of these fought and won the Battle of Britain? So I was shaken to the core, when working at a place where there were Welsh soldiers who had been mauled in France and saw no RAF at Dunkirk "Yellow bellied * ——*s". They saw my badge pronouncing RAF and a group surrounded me, bent on wreaking revenge on a lad who was not long out of short trousers at the time of Dunkirk. Only the timely passing of an officer saved me from a roughing. Their unhappy experience had left them still bitter after all this time – it was now 1943 – the Battle of Britain, and the grievous losses the Air Force were then suffering over Germany. I sometimes wonder how they got on when they returned to France and if they had reason to be grateful to the despised RAF ... C'est la Guerre! I have never much cared for 'Taffys' since.

The Last of the 'Brown Jobs'

The Churchills and their ringmasters suddenly disappeared and left the village quiet for a time, and the girls lonely; but not for long. The dashing 'Inns of Court' regiment arrived with their armoured scout cars that had big rubber wheels and little guns – made for rushing around looking for trouble, and finding it too, we later heard, in Normandy. They hid under bushes in

High Close Wood and were mended in Johnny Nichol's garage, where they were an easier fit than the Churchills. They were altogether less noisy and troublesome than tanks, but we did miss the big fellows and often wondered where they went and how they did. Many ships passed in our long night of war in Mickley. The 'anti-aircraft' Bren-gun in the field behind the fish and chip shop was long dispensed with, but guards were still mounted on important points, to village puzzlement; we could understand the need to protect the cookhouse, it was vital – but who in their right mind would want to steal a Churchill tank or even a bit off one? Maybe a Scout Car ... I did find a piece off a Churchill many years later and hoped it wasn't a vital part. They must have been careless – too late to worry now anyway.

My father now being home, all the camps and airfields completed, two of the new army lads were able to come to Rosedale for a cup of tea and a chat and a feeling of 'home'. They were there most nights when I came home from ATC parades and I suspect had a quiet smile at all my showing off, white flash, insignia and all – "poor fool". They were grand lads though and we had the highest regard for them. One of them showed great interest in my father's carvings, especially that of his RAMC cap-badge, so he offered to do one of theirs – the Inns of Court, and I got the job of doing the drawing. It went off to Normandy and we never knew whether it and the lads survived. We heard that they, and the Churchills, had a rough time – the German Tigers (formidable tanks) had them for breakfast. It would be nice to think that the oaken cap-badge carving, by my father, a veteran of the Kaiser's war, might now grace the mantleshelf of a veteran of Hitler's.

Only a detachment of Royal Engineers came to Mickley, most of them were in the Corbridge area, but they made their presence felt. Needing practice at their bridge-building in many different circumstances, they ranged the area for suitable places to bridge. Heugh Dene, at Mount Pleasant, was as nasty a little dry gorge as they were likely to meet, so it got its Bailey bridge, and a rare commotion it made, in such a small place. The locals really had no need of a bridge over Heugh Dene and it went nowhere anyway, so they didn't mind when it went away, but it was fun while it lasted. Not so the full-size Bailey on pontoons across the Tyne at Mickley Junction This was an ideal spot for a bridge – it led to Ovington and Ovingham and places North, East and West and had long been a busy ferry. A bridge had been argued for for years and an effort made to start a fund to launch a Company like that which built Ovingham bridge. I suspect that all efforts failed for the same reason as the station – the impossibly steep approach. But steep hills don't deter armies, so Mickley had its brief bridge, and a fine one too. Portable, versatile, quickly built Bailey bridges were a brilliant idea and made a great contribution to winning the war. Practice was needed at building them and Mickley contributed its share of places, but alas the bridge had to go – the Army needed it elsewhere, and not just for getting pitmen across the river to work. They had to go on pitting their lungs against the wind in the sometimes vain hope of rousing the boatman who was also mine host at the tavern, a long shout from the river; or they could walk the two mile detour by Ovingham bridge if the river was in one of its foul moods – only fools meddled with the Tyne in a temper.

Some of the continuous stream of gravel lorries plying from Christer's works by the river could have made good use of the bridge to save the testing haul up the hill, and the signalman's efforts opening and closing the heavy wooden crossing gates. Mickley signalmen were kept pretty busy, what with trains and gravel lorries and bridge builders and although mechanical ingenuity came naturally to the Victorian railway builders, they didn't skimp on hard work. The gates were worked by a system of wires and pulleys and a wheel like a ship's steering-wheel in the signal box, which was up a mountain of outside steps. The wicket-gates for line-crossing walkers were locked from the signal-box when a train was due, so pedestrians needed patience – Mickley traffic failed to justify a footbridge. One of these signalmen, Blackburn by name, took upon himself another duty – Lifeguard. He was a fine swimmer and was called to the rescue whenever a child got into difficulties during the summer drowning season – alas all too often a sad too-late.

Not only village children died in the river – one of the bridge-builders perished too ...

By a strange coincidence, some years later I stayed on the Isle of Arran with a chap, Matthew Laird, who had been a Major in the Royal Engineers at Corbridge. He told me that he had been in charge of the bridge-building at Mickley and how distressing it was when one of his men died when he was injured and fell into the river. Not all our heroes died in foreign fields, nor by bombs and bullets; the sacrifice was no less.

He, this anonymous soldier, was the only casualty of war who actually died in Mickley. The river though, and the pit, went on taking their relentless toll.

The Partings

We got to know our 'own' soldiers pretty well, but none stayed very long; in the course of four years we had the company of, as well as those already mentioned: the Border Regiment, Welsh Reg., Manchesters, Royal Berks., and the South Staffordshires. Some got to know our local lasses well enough to marry and return to after the war, to add more unusual names, such as Hignett, to our list. There was an inexorable increase through the war years, of servicemen throughout the area, in all shapes and sizes and nationalities and it became difficult at times for locals to get into a pub, let alone get a drink, and dancing at the Queens Hall, or the Oxford Galleries or Old Assembly Rooms in Newcastle was a close-packed shuffle. They were everywhere, these soldiers, in every nook and cranny – and became almost fluid, like ants, in 1944.

They came in convoys through Mickley, going this way, going that – mile upon endless mile of lorries, armoured-cars, bren-carriers, odd looking things called 'jeeps' that the Americans had given us, tanks and tankers; big guns, little guns, ammunition and field-kitchens – tins of Carnation milk. Despatch riders on motorbikes and MPs (police, not political), released from rounding-up wayward soldiers, fussed about like old hens, with maps on boards, directing the traffic.

Important looking Staff cars passed, sporting pennants and red-banded hats.

Overhead the fighters practised but not now to defend our land; another game was afoot. One force-landed in a field where the searchlight had been by Ovington, and was ignominiously taken away by road. One less fortunate crashed at Whittonstall, in sight of the cabbage field of Wheelbirks, and the remains of the 20 year old Australian pilot were found in the buried wreckage of his Spitfire in 1980 during open-cast coal-mining operations. Spitfires from on high went deep into soft earth.

Other flyers frightened the fish in the river – what's all this about low flying?

The remaining searchlights were used only to finger-point the way home for lost bombers with broken radios and often men, returning from the ceaseless battle in the night skies of Germany. A Wellington crashed at Stagshaw, where the peasants' unfit horses had mustered, and all five of the Polish crew perished; a Stirling hit a house at Acklington, killing occupants as well as crew ... The remorseless struggle went on, but happily it was no longer necessary to reassure – 'It's all right, it's one of ours'. They were all 'ours' – thousands and thousands of them; the air was never still, and the music of Allied aircraft engines sounded very sweet.

On the ground the great mass of khaki-coloured humanity slid slowly south like a huge brown glacier; most of it seemed to pass through Mickley.

Passenger trains were cancelled or very severely curtailed; getting to the Queens at Hexham became a major problem for ATC cadets in Prudhoe! But as for me, I left this fuss behind and went off at last to the RAF.

Going south by train, every siding, every line, was chock-a-block with wagons full of guns and tanks.

For the time being I could no longer keep an eye on dear old Mickley, but after all these centuries perhaps it was well able to take care of itself. It soon settled down to the quiet, apart from the hob-nails and the poss-sticks, when the Inns of Court rode south as the tide of war swept once again over France. Tears were shed, and the local lads stood a chance with the girls again.

Another strange feature of this war that is only now remarked, is that parents fussed less over their departing sons and daughters than they do now when seeing them off to college.

The Cosy lost a few customers – quite a lot – and the pubs. But if you wanted up-to-the-minute news of how the war was going, it was in graphic although censored detail, at the cinema, and many people went just for that. In Newcastle there were two cinemas showing only newsreels (and cartoons) continuously.

Newspapers, small though they were in wartime, mostly two broadsheets, were full of maps of Normandy and places east and north, covered with arrows pointing in different directions. The end was in sight, or so we thought.

In Ned Brown's field, above the Nissen huts, the zig-zag trenches had been filled in, leaving their image that is visible yet if you know were to look. The Nissen huts stood empty and sad and the church got its Mission Room back, a bit worn and minus its Saturday night 'hops'. Johnny Nichol kept Norfolks' bus in his garage again, and weeds quickly cloaked the churned-up parts of High Close Wood and hid bits of tanks and scout-cars and live ammunition, for discovery years later. The coiled barbed-wire in the streams and gullies took twenty years to rust away, and the mortar and howitzer emplacements are there yet, overgrown but recognisable. But in 1944 the mantle of war receded from Mickley.

The stone War Memorial in St George's Church names seventeen of the Parish who failed to come home. This time there were two Bells and two Rosemurgeys and another Scott. There was also the first sad loss of a daughter of the parish – Sheila Markham Brown. She was an Army doctor and died, I believe in Italy, but can't be sure, when the lorry in which she was travelling overturned. In her memory her father had the church organ electrified – it had been hand-pumped – and when he died a font cover was dedicated to him. The Browns were of that part of Mickley which now prefers to think of itself as Stocksfield.

A Fresh Start

The battle over, a grateful nation organised Welcome Home funds to mark its appreciation of those who returned, and made a better attempt than last time to order its affairs towards an improved 'land fit for heroes'. Mickley had fewer service folk to welcome than in 1918 and there was no extravagant talk of homes either for heroes or nurses; the 'thank you' was to be personal, and the village still was not a wealthy place.

Not everyone came home when the final whistle went – the demobilisation was orderly and spread-out. Besides, our erstwhile allies were still in fighting mood and of a mind to continue where Germany left off. My father when he returned from his war made a bonfire of his Army kit; we had to preserve our uniforms in case they were needed again – our pay-books contained a railway warrant and an order, cashable at a Post Office, for 2/- to enable us to rejoin our units. It behove the country to keep its sabres sharp, and it was more than three years before all the amateur fighters returned. Some chose to live elsewhere, where they had met girls and married, or the grass looked greener.

When the time came for the 'Welcoming', a meal was laid on in the big room above the Club where the Leek Shows were held, the room was full and, as ever, the womenfolk did their stuff with a good spread in spite of rationing being tighter than in the war: the country was on its uppers. I recollect only two servicemen being present – Tommy Spicer, air-gunner, and myself; we happened to be on leave. Speeches were made and went on for ever – Councillors never did know when to stop, and I was acutely embarrassed because neither Tom nor I, nor anyone else, made reply. Servicemen are no good at speeches – we weren't anyway. I hoped afterwards that no one was offended. It all seemed a bit flat, but we got £5 each, which was welcome, and some people did enjoy making speeches.

Stocksfield warriors got £5.10s. and teak seats made from the decking of redundant warships, placed about the village (for them to sit on in their old age?) with little brass plaques saying 'Welcome Home'. The seats were well used but got vandalised in the new kind of civilisation that lay ahead – but they lasted longer than my £5!

In 1869 the editor of the *Hexham Courant*, then in its fifth year, deplored the fact that, although the Reform Bill had made it theoretically possible, no working-class men were able to make their way to Parliament. 'Their knowledge and experience of the problems of the working class was sorely needed', he said. In 1945 the educated, enlightened, and in many cases widely travelled masses put their representatives firmly in power for the first time and brought about what might be termed the second bloodless Revolution in English history.

This is no place for an analysis of the 'socialist experiment'; how it affected Mickley is my concern. Total State control of the nation's affairs was the dream and aim; to right the wrongs, spread the wealth. The big snag was that there was not much wealth left in a nation that was weary and bankrupt after fighting two devastating wars on behalf of a Europe incapable of ordering its own affairs in a civilised manner, and not even grateful. And done down by a USA still thinking Independence grudges and bent on ending British world power while creating its own.

Everything within reach was Nationalised, to the great delight and high hopes of working people; 'liberation of the downtrodden masses' was at hand. But there was not enough food, even bread was now rationed. There was not enough coal, and factories had to make do with worn-out, obsolete machinery. Life in post-war Britain was pretty grim – the winter of 1947 was a nightmare and there was not much more than hope to live on; but the pitmen of Mickley were on their way up – they were 'Nationalised'. Which meant that they no longer had to drag their weary boots over the hill to Hedley pit and back – they went by special bus and it didn't matter if the seats got dirty. After work they were bussed to West Wylam colliery where not only the coals were washed – there were showers for miners, with oodles of hot water, and they changed into clean clothes for the bus-ride home. No more bathing before the fire, except for wives and children.

Oh yes, of course, the pay was better and high time too; but although there was much needed investment in machinery, working conditions in pits like Hedley could not be made much better and there was talk of it being unprofitable and running out of coal. But the new regime was welcome, and miners raised their heads – they were the bosses now. Actually they weren't and soon realised it; there were in reality more bosses than before: the previous ones were shuffled around a bit and added to and they, not only the workers, were better paid after Nationalisation. Civil Servants started to poke their fingers into things – we'd never heard of them, in pre-war Mickley – except for the man at the Dole.

The extra money brought in some of the nicer things of life to the Rows, but they were still the Raas with netties and none of those wonderful electric washing machines with powered wringers – the electricity supply, which was not much improved on 1908 and was neglected in the war, didn't run to washing machines. Some housewives had hand-operated machines, some had zinc dolly tubs, but for many, washday was still muscle work with the poss-stick. But the noise on Mondays was becoming more subdued.

Electric irons were just about possible if too many people didn't use them at the same time while the radio and lights were on. They were plugged in to an adaptor in the light socket, as there were still no power points, and the connecting flex dangled. At first only the more expensive irons had thermostats so inexperienced ironers still got their cheeks scorched, and lots of tables and those newfangled ironing boards boasted iron-shaped burn marks. One iron I know of burned its way right through the table, two leaves at that, and had started work on the floor before it was stopped. They took a lot of the hassle out of ironing and were not as frightening as the gas-irons still in use in the houses that colliery electricity hadn't the strength to reach. The pit electrician knew when someone had been naughty because the fuse at the end of the Raa blew and he had to mend it. Mains radios replaced the old faithful battery sets that had seen us through the war and better still, radiograms made an appearance. They resided in cabinets as big as coffins, so that the furniture had to be rearranged; they had lids that lifted for operating the knobs, and automatic record players that could go through ten records in succession without anyone having to jump up and down. There was not even a handle to turn and the needles had long lives and were gentle on the records, but records were still brittle and turned at 78 RPM for 4 minutes a side. Fortunately the electricity supply improved somewhat and those who spent their new wealth on such devices could show them off and entertain half the village on Sunday mornings, full blast with the door wide open, while the dinner cooked in the round iron oven and the room was as hot as Hades. Gracie Fields might sing Ave Maria, or Bing Crosby his latest, or Foden Motor Works Band

EARLY WASHING MACHINE AND DOLLY STICK

put Mickley Band in the shade although not out of business; they got back to their practising and emerged on special days, as before; perhaps not quite up to radiogram standard but 'live' and entertaining – especially on New Year's Morn!

One of the more adventurous ways of spending saved-up cash was on a 'real' holiday. Now the only such event of that name in old Micelee was a 'Holy Day', to be spent at Church or playing games – when the Church was looking the other way. Or in more recent Mickley times, a day at Whitley Bay courtesy of LNER, or a charabanc trip in the country for a picnic, which was fun if it didn't rain, because the early charas were merely open shells with seats that lifted on and off flat lorries. It often rained on Charabanc trips. By the time miners had enough money for holidays, Norfolks' buses and Frazers' at Prudhoe (who only ran excursions and pit buses) were dry, comfortable and reliable if somewhat coaly should you happen on the pit bus, and quite suitable for long-distance travel. Making LNER into British Rail and painting the carriages 'plum and spilt milk' couldn't save trains from the internal-combustion engine – Mickley holidaymakers went by bus – all of them together. There is strength in numbers!

You may think it good to get away from the folk you work with and the neighbours you never see but cannot stand with their barbecues and shared 'music'. In 1950, if you had never been away from home, shared a nettie with your neighbours, knew when they went – and all about them and their affairs; still worked in discomfort and danger and relied on your 'marra' ; then you needed the support of your peers when venturing into the great unknown of hotels and boarding-houses in far-distant places of strange languages and customs and unusual food. Blackpool was Mickley miners' equivalent of Livingstone's Darkest Africa. On the first great holiday occasion they went in four buses, like the Northumberland Fusiliers off to Flanders fields, and were 'seen off' by those who lacked the spirit of adventure. They lived all together, like a swarm of wayward bees, drank a lot of beer – probably complained because it wasn't what they were used to – sang 'Blaydon Races' to the discomfort of other holidaymakers who spoke strange languages and couldn't understand good Geordie English, spent all their money – why else would they go, and were glad to get home but what a time they'd had. What an adventure!

"Nivvor agien," some said. Others couldn't wait for next year and more of the same.

The Village at Peace

Few villagers had motorcars – they were for shopkeepers, Managers and the like. Cars seemed to be owned by townsfolk and before the war a great Sunday pastime was watching the cars go by, twixt town and country and back again. They were handsome things in rich colours of a variety of makes that confounds the memory. They were laid up during the war, those that weren't requisitioned, and emerged from their dusty corners to resume normal life when even working folk aspired to be car owners. There were not enough to go round and petrol was still precious, but I blued £47 of my Service Gratuity (not quite a 'golden handshake', but a little 'thank you') on a 1929 Morris Minor with a canvas roof and a cloud of blue smoke from where the engine threw oil on to the hot exhaust manifold. It could achieve all of 40 mph with a following wind, bouncing as high as the hedges, trying to get away from the smoke. It was fun while it lasted which was not long. It breathed its last gasp alongside, and to the entertainment of the queue outside the Empire Theatre in Newcastle on a wet Saturday night. Who needs buskers?

Some farmers had cars, and a lot of people resented this, because farmers were 'featherbedded'. Memories are short – not so long ago farmers poured milk down drains and left their fields to weeds because their food was not wanted. But there is nothing like the threat of starvation to focus minds on the importance of food and farmers, and one of the great achievements of the war was the way in which farmers fed the nation. It could not be done again – food now seems to come from factories and I don't think a war could be fought on it anyway. I doubt if the Reivers of Tynedale would have got far, towing a freezer full of pizzas.

Thomas Humble, of Eltringham Farm ran a Sunbeam Talbot, and beautiful it was; it graced the village. He had a tractor too, as had most farmers by now; traditional farming, that had fed the nation to greatness was declining and horses disappeared from Mickley farms, having worked through the war. The smithy on the hilltop had closed and become a cottage in 1928 when the Wrightson estate was sold, so the wartime horses had to walk to Stocksfield for their shoes.

Dairy cows, but not maids, lived on at one or two farms, although the milk was no longer sold around the village but went away in churns left on wooden stands at the roadside, for daily collection by lorry and treatment to clean it up and make it safe to drink, in the Co-op Dairy at Stocksfield. Even Ned Brown of Hallyards succumbed to the move for clean milk. Ironically, only Hallyards now has a dairy herd, the others gave up in the face of regulations and controls – and 'unsocial hours'.

The Co-op Dairy was an interesting place where milk was gathered, filtered to remove the filth because many farmers no longer bothered, and pasteurised to kill the bugs, bottled, then redistributed for doorstep delivery. In Mickley this was done mostly, into the 1950s, by a pretty girl with a high-fashion, piled-high hairstyle, driving a horse-drawn flat cart; at one time it was the horse that had its hair done up. She put a glow on the pit face of Mickley. Interesting machinery in the Dairy, unusual in its day, was capable of washing, sterilising and filling thousands of bottles a day – or just breaking them, according to its mood; it was worth watching, just on the off-chance. It was the lorries though, that endeared the Dairy to many hearts.

Any Mickley serviceman arriving late at night in Newcastle, but not too late, could have a word with the Stationmaster (he was human, his gold-braid was not of a military nature), who would arrange for the last train, the fast express Stranraer Boat Train, to stop for a brief moment at Stocksfield to allow him to alight. The railways at their best. If he arrived too late even for this special service, he had the choice of being miserable in the station until the buses started, or walking the night streets to the YMCA.

Too late for the train on my first late-night arrival in Newcastle, and shunning the waiting, I set off to walk the twelve miles home – if Bewick could do it, so could I. He didn't have to walk Scotswood Road at dead of night, and he had a cudgel, that I would have been glad of; it was four miles of unmitigated fear! Policemen, I heard, walked in threes along Scotswood Road at night. I was never so glad as when I reached Blaydon and was hotfooting it for the open country and safety, when along came a lorry laden with crates of empty milk bottles, stopped, and offered me a lift. I sat in the cab right to my door in Mickley and was firmly told by the driver to wait in future outside the station portico at four o'clock and a milk lorry would stop for me and any serviceman wanting a lift westward. Sure enough, they never failed to stop, these kindly gentlemen of the road. Their cabs unfortunately, not being designed for passenger transport, had limited capacity so there were times when there was only 'room on top', but not like double-deckers – flat-out atop the knobbly milk bottles, which was not much fun but got you home.

My last night-ride home was aloft on the crates in a blizzard and I should have walked. With neither snowplough, salt, grit or even decent lights or windscreen wipers, and certainly no washers or heaters, motoring in the snow in those days was not for the chicken-hearted. On my stack of snowy bottles I felt like Scott without a tent – but mobile, which at the time did not seem such a good idea.

I got home to find Rosedale without a fire – coal-less in a village of coal. This was peacetime, and we were the supposed victors.

Shortly afterwards drivers of milk lorries were forbidden to give lifts, on pain of instant dismissal. A group of lads, given a late-night crate-top lift from Hexham, had amused themselves all the way to Stocksfield by throwing empty bottles into the roadway and through windows. Too late for them to do a stint in the Burma jungle unfortunately; by then there were no longer servicemen needing lifts and the Dairy was obsolete, worn out and was closed and swept away to make way for houses.

The Bewick family departed too. After 250 years at Cherryburn they just disappeared from the scene in about 1945 and took no further part in the story of the village, of coal-mining, or of art. But they left their mark, played their part, a bit like the Baliols of Bywell, in their own small way.

Cherryburn became occupied by an academic, and there are few of those to be counted in this story – certainly not like Professor Clemo. With a name like that he must have been another Cornish influx, but was certainly not a miner. He fitted comfortably into the rural scene, although he was a chemistry man at Newcastle University and had a small laboratory at Cherryburn where he did things with cigarette smoke and Newcastle city air. He separated from cigarette smoke whatever it is that is supposed to cause cancer and got requests for his papers on it from all around the world – addressed to: 'Prof. Clemo, Mickley, England'. Whether it was his renown or that of Mickley which guided them here I'm not sure – perhaps it was the dedication of the Post Office. I wonder if he'd have got them, addressed to 'Micelee'? He reckoned diesel fumes to be worse than cigarette smoke.

Being a countryman at heart he kept a cow for milk and its calf each year for selling-on, and made his own butter – sometimes pretty rancid. He kept hens for eggs and eating and the wooden-hived version of the hovel-dweller's honey bees. His hives leaked like sieves when they were taken to the moors and the now distant heather for the autumn honey harvest. He tried to persuade them to stay 'in-hive' for the journey by stuffing carbolic-soaked rags into the gaps. Had I been a bee in a Clemo hive my only concern would have been to get out and away – which they did! To the heather in wartime with a group of other beekeepers and their hives, on a lorry at dawn was bad enough, but nothing compared to when he took to coming with me and my hives in my small van. We turned a few heads, believe me, driving along in veils and bee-keeping gear, in a van full of loose bees!

He had his garden full of fruit and good things, and a pig for killing at Christmas, with all the old-fashioned concomitants of pig-killing to share around. Real home-cured bacon hung from the beams of the Victorian kitchen that Thomas Bewick didn't live to see: he had died worrying about the dilapidated state of his beloved cottage-home, which now housed the Professor's cow – until one day she was startled by a pheasant into knocking the eighty-odd year old hand-milker off his stool. Gave him a right old shaking and bruising, it did, and brought to an end the practice of keeping a cow for the family milk; his was the last house-cow in the village, and he probably the last great character of the village. He wore knickerbockers and odd hats and a net shopping bag over his head to keep the bees at bay – but now he got his milk in bottles.

Changes came along pretty steadily. Charlie Hall retired having sustained the school through the war years and terrorised the children as Hitler never could. Miss Murray also left the teaching scene and the gap they left was filled by two 'Emergency Trained' teachers. These were candidates selected from the Services as being suitable for short training (two years instead of the usual three) as teachers, regardless of their academic qualifications. They caused a lot of resentment amongst 'real' teachers, and had to be twice as good just to be as good. Many of them were as good – and better. The two who taught at Mickley, oddly, were both called Robson, and both were ex-RAF, one a pilot, the other a navigator. The former pilot, DFC., died recently in retirement, falling out of a tree, off a ladder – a cruel irony. The other Robson lives in the village by Holywell, where Bewick played when dodging school.

Dave Carr with his wooden leg retired from the Post Office, which reverted to use as a house only. The small amount of mail that Dave handled (miners got little except football-pools and they all got those, warranting a special delivery) had arrived by bus. It still came by train to Stocksfield, where it was separated, put into a bag, sealed and taken to the bus-stop to await the 7.25 am bus; it was then padlocked to the pole that passengers hung on to while waiting to alight. Dave Carr waited at the bus-stop by Mickley Club and unlocked the bag from the pole; on Mondays it contained cash for pensions! After Dave retired, without a golden, or any other, handshake, and no party, the part-time postman went to Stocksfield PO to sort the mail and brought it back by bus in his satchel. The new sub-Postmaster, another ex-serviceman who, with his wife, also ran Stocksfield PO and shop, brought the pensions by car to the slightly less scruffy Mickley PO in the little old stone building that had been Rington's tea depot until the war put paid to house to house tea delivery by pony and cart.

The need for stallions departed with the need for foals, when tractors and lorries finally completed the rout of the heavy working horse, so Mr Knox, whose outbuildings had housed Rington's and now the PO, was no longer a familiar sight with his huge horse, plodding their way around the local farms where he was paid only the price of a 'service' for a replacement horse. He became too old for all the walking anyway. After he died, and then his wife, the Fosters moved into Eltringham Cottage.

Without rattling gravel-works and toiling lorries, and without poss-sticks now, the drift long closed and coke works demolished, tranquillity returned to the village. Men came quietly home in buses, some of them wore Wellington boots where the going was wet (sales of dubbing slumped) so even walking miners walked quietly. Those who worried about stones crushing their toes could buy 'safety' boots with steel toe-caps, at the pit canteen, which usurped the Co-op in providing boots and food at a discount – but no Divi. Pit canteens were like wartime British Restaurants in ensuring that workers were well fed at modest prices. They also saved housewives the trouble of cooking dinners on open fires and in round ovens, but most miners, the older ones anyway, still preferred 'home cooking'.

The wartime innovation of school meals did much the same for children, ensuring one good meal a day, and incidentally helping the trend towards working mothers, or should I say: 'going out to work' mothers – Mickley mothers had always worked, and how they worked. 1940s school meals were prepared on Army lines at the central cookhouse in the village hall at Stocksfield and distributed in aluminium boxes to the schools by van, and served by the teachers, who could turn a hand to anything when the need arose. The meals were eaten at the desks which in those days sloped, which must have been a bit tricky for the soup. Eventually a canteen – cookhouse – gymnasium was built at every school (to save the spilt soup?). A gymnasium at Mickley? The Mission Room had doubled as one – fifty years earlier, but miners really got enough exercise. School meals in the days of Mrs Brown were pretty good – like home cooking, rather than Army fare. But they didn't get napkins or pudding forks!

Meanwhile, back at the Raas, the housewife was having a slightly easier time; no water to carry, clothes to poss or baths to prepare – not so much dirt. Some aspired to carpets, and vacuum cleaners. Children were away all day and needed only teas at home – in theory: as I remember them, children had voracious appetites that needed continuous stoking. But there was a little daytime respite while they and the men were away and the place was quiet.

The whole nation fell silent and sad when, in 1952, their beloved reluctant King and wartime comrade, George the Sixth died, having earned one of man's greatest epitaphs : 'He did his Duty'.

The new young Queen brought not only new hope to a tired nation, but Television to Mickley – or nearly. Like most innovation, it took a long time to reach the backward North, and longer still to reach the Raas, which were screened from the transmitter by the hill behind. The ambitious bought sets and went to a lot of trouble, such as fitting aerials on long poles, to try to get a picture, which at best was pretty bad and only black-and-white anyway.

The Coronation in colour was at the cinema, but later. For most people it was in word-pictures through the mains radio, clear as a bell and painted by masters of the art of spoken English. This was the very pinnacle of broadcast speech and helped to consolidate BBC English as the standard language of the nation. What would Caxton have said, he who had set about standardising English in print?

A second-hand Coronation was no good to me so, after working till midnight decorating the front of Rosedale with flags and patriotic decorations, I set forth at 4 am on 7th June 1953, for London – on my bike!

Not just any old bike – they had come a long way since Angus's Velocipede brought crowds to Pilgrim Street in 1866 and bicycle mania swept the country. Mine was good; it was a 'sit up and beg' Raleigh with Sturmey-Archer three-speed gears and the chain running in oil in a chain-case – and a seat like an armchair.

It was really my father's; he had bought it from Coulson's bicycle shop in Prudhoe in 1938, after perusing for ages the enticing glossy catalogues – as big a decision as buying a Jaguar today! He settled for the best, on the same principal as buying a radio, and not a lot different in price – at £4: more than a week's wages. For the first and only time in his life he went into debt and paid for it in weekly instalments over a year. By the 1950s he had given it to me every Christmas for four years, so I felt it must be mine – unless he needed it again!

I cheated, because I fitted a two-stroke petrol engine to the rim of the rear wheel and got to London, 270 miles, in 14 hours, with a following wind, on 2/6's worth of petrol (12 metric pennies). There was not even a parking problem for a bicycle in crammed-to-the-rigging London – I just chained it to the railings of the Chevrons Club in Baker St (alongside Sherlock Holmes) and stayed overnight for 1/9d. In the morning I watched the procession pass on its way to the Abbey, returned to the club to watch the ceremony on television (London of course had it first and best, but only black-and-white), then back to the crowded streets and the return procession. It certainly knocked Mickley Band into a cocked hat!

Suddenly and miraculously the streets were empty except for armies of workers clearing up the mountains of rubbish left by people who had camped-out in the streets for days to secure vantage points. The amount of rubbish, and the speed at which it disappeared, astounded me; I concluded that Londoners were used to that sort of thing. The streets were clean and tidy in time for the remarkable evening fireworks display and street revelry.

It took me twenty-six body-numbing hours to get home, against an Arctic wind (wasn't dressed for it), and went to sleep freewheeling down a long hill near Durham. Have you ever slept on a bicycle? Fortunately the grassy bank I hit was soft.

I was probably the only person in Mickley to go to the Coronation. 'Nivor agien'!

Even when the North-east's own transmitter was built in the late 1950s television still couldn't reach the Rows – removing all that coal hadn't lowered the hill enough, so only the better-off at Old Mickley and Mount Pleasant sported those strange horizontal aerials on their chimnies. Aerials signalled not only television and status, but the death-knell of the Cosy – and the Electric (it had changed its name to the 'Rex', but not as far as we were concerned) and even, eventually, the Rio. Aerials made ideal places for jack-daws to hold conferences.

Not until 1959, when a master-aerial was erected at Mount Pleasant, and a wired relay system run to West Mickley, Branch End, and through High Close Wood, did television reach the Square, by which time it was too late – the Raas were doomed.

Nemesis

Disposal of waste had exercised the minds of men since they first began to produce it in noticeable quantities. Matters came to a head in the crowded 19th century, and the problem was largely overcome by the provision of piped water, sewers, and WCs in urban areas. But the introduction of ash-closets was the limit of progress in Mickley and there remained no prospect of a change without drains and an adequate water supply, neither of which was available until the turn of the century. Even then, there was always the vexed question of finance and the will to get on with the job – and progress was further delayed by two major wars.

By 1946 there was no excuse for netties, especially those across the main road from High Row South. Apart from anything else, while dodging horses had been within reason, high-speed motorised traffic posed serious problems to those in hasty need. But not for another ten years were plans formulated for getting rid of the ash-closets of the Square – and then the scheme involved getting rid of the houses that went with them – slum clearance, it was called.

In the meantime, backed by a subsidised, fervent Socialist zeal, Prudhoe Urban District Council set about converting ash-closets to water closets in other houses throughout the area, setting-off the costs against the considerable long-term savings to be made in the huge costs of emptying and disposing of the contents of hundreds of these noisome 'little rooms'. They gave £30 to each house-owner towards the cost of the conversion, and a free galvanised dustbin for the ashes and the tins and bottles that were an increasing part of life. Papers could still be burned on open fires and some was still used for toilet purposes, but it blocked the drains, so people were faced with yet another living expense – toilet rolls: 'Izal Germicide' – like grease-proof, in rolls or squares, and 'medicated', whatever that did.

All the brick houses built in Mickley after the turn of the century got WCs, including Rosedale and the Managers' houses, but they were still across the yard and operated by chain. The trouble with the Square was that it was ill-designed for WCs and would cost a lot to adapt. Besides, the houses were 'unfit to live in'.

In post-war Britain, slum clearance was the order of the day. Heroes this time would have their homes fit to live in – Council houses. A great wave of

Council house-building swept the country, especially in places like Prudhoe, which boasted more than its share of slum; semi-rural slum, mind you – the views and the air weren't bad. In addition to the Square, the whole of New Eltringham, Low Prudhoe, and West Wylam, most of them stone-built ('very desirable' today), substandard miners' cottages had the death sentence passed on them. There would be an end to mining villages: 'we'll have you all together, one big happy family, in fine new houses (where we can keep an eye on you?), with bathrooms and WCs but nowhere to put a car or for children to play. Would Socialist workers afford cars?

Why not build Council houses in Mickley? argued Mickley. "No way," responded the dominant, reforming Socialist Vicar Chairman of Prudhoe Council (who had streets named after him), "the sewage works will take no more WCs. – we will wipe Mickley off the map." This promise reminded me of Hitler's boast of what he would do to England and Churchill's reply – "Some chicken – some neck". Sure enough, the other pit villages died, but Mickley hung on, and kept its neck (the new part) – but the Square went, and it had just got television!

The Exodus

The place all fell apart at once, in keeping with the local saying, 'When they go – thay aal gan t'githor'.

Lock, stock and barrel they went, the mining folk of the Square. As Prudhoe blossomed with Council houses, the removals vans prospered, lino and carpet sales rocketed and there were high hopes of a great new life – tempered not a little by the sadness of leaving 'home'. Not only home, but a way of life that was unique and vanishing for ever except in the recollections of sentimental old men.

The young adjusted, after a fashion and the way of the young. Women had an easier time in their easier homes, except that it was a longer walk to the Co-op in Prudhoe. Older transplants found taking root more difficult and were to be seen wandering the streets of Prudhoe looking for what was lost and never could be found. They knew not what it was, but missed it very badly; they couldn't even find their neighbours.

It took about two years to clear the miners and their possessions; the mangles and the round ovens went for scrap and the slates were carefully salvaged for re-use – the only things in the Square that had appreciated in value through the years. Then the bulldozers moved in, that had replaced 'Churchills' in peacetime factories. The air was filled with dust – lime, but with a fair levening of leftover coal, and when it cleared the place fell silent once again, but a deathly silence – the Square had gone. It went to fill a hole in the ground – whence it had come, I suppose.

Phoenix Arises

The body was amputated, the neck survived, and the heart – the school – it only just kept beating. Without children, what is a school? No more than about forty children could now be mustered and the threat of closure loomed. However, the situation was alleviated by bussing-in pupils from Prudhoe where there was an acute shortage of school space – due to the influx of children from Mickley!

Without customers (and they weren't going to bus from Prudhoe), the shops, which had almost outnumbered houses, withered. First Mrs Truman gave up; she was getting-on anyway and there were very few houses remaining at her end of the village. Someone tried her shop as a butchers when the Co-op butcher's closed, but it was a forlorn hope, as was an attempt at selling electrical goods, which were now fashionable and helped by the recently created North Eastern Electricity Board (Nationalised electricity). They took over the supply from where MCCo. had left it and put it on new and bigger poles with blue streetlights that lit the dark corners which had few lovers to occupy them, and made lipstick wearers look a week dead. But even more electricity couldn't sell goods to departed people, so Trumans' became just a bigger house.

For want of hobnailed boots the cobbler's closed; the barber struggled on for a while then the room, like its neighbour the erstwhile PO, reverted to its intended role as a sitting-room, followed shortly by the 'Dolly Sisters' shop

COBBLER'S SHOP TODAY

– it wasn't worth sitting around all day just to sell a ha'porth of sugary black-bullets.

After the war, when he had little use for his garage except for storing Norfolks' bus, Johnny Nichols sold it and the adjoining field, where had stood the Nissen huts and anti-aircraft Bren-gun, to a returned soldier from Prudhoe, one George Lowdon. At that time a lot of what was euphemistically described as 'Government Surplus' came on to the market; with not much in the way of a war going on they had little further use for it. So there were shops where you could buy anything from a billy-can to an aircraft compass or altimeter (which made good barometers if you knew how), tin hats to spare socks and boots and uniforms – possibly even 'Churchill' tanks – Battle-dress made good work clothes for those who could overcome the aversion. George Lowdon sank his 'gratuity' on an ex-army 3-ton Bedford lorry and parked it on the roadside. He then proceeded, like all our previous entrepreneurs, to work all the hours that came, lorrying chalk from the mountain that had arisen on the banks of the Tyne by De-Umphraville's castle. This chalk was a by-product of the activities of the I.C.I. in the big, ugly, dirty factory with cooling towers and boilers and smell, built by the Government early in the war. Its war-work was supposed to be producing ammonia, but it appeared to produce, apart from night and day work for a lot of local men and women, mostly little brass cigarette-lighters, and boiler ashes. These could be had for the cost of transport, if you had somewhere to put them, and would yield enough good coke to keep your greenhouse boiler going. And this useless chalk stuff. Pity it wouldn't burn on greenhouse boilers! It built up through the war years into a veritable mountain, a long ridge like Helvellen Striding Edge, and hid the ugly factory-works from sensitive Ovingham eyes. Mind you, it was an eyesore in is own right. Some bright spark, probably one of those newfangled Civil Servants that all the jokes were about, thought up the idea that this white powder, containing a little lime, could be beneficially disposed of by spreading it about the countryside, which had not been much limed during the war.

Every ex-serviceman who could drive, it seemed, bought a lorry and transported chalk to the fields: it set up many of the firms that now run container-lorries to far-distant Continental places. The air over England and a fair bit of Scotland, was white with flying chalk and the roads around Prudhoe once again full of army lorries, in different livery. However, like the 'Seven Maids with Seven Brooms' and the sand of the seashore, they just couldn't get it clear and most of the chalk mountain is still there, although re-designated, from 'That eyesore', or 'The White Elephant', to 'Site of Special Scientific Interest', where one or two butterflies flit about. It still shields Ovingham eyes from factoy buildings but is an eyesore by any standards – and the ICI long gone.

George Lowdon worked long and hard at moving chalk and was able to buy another lorry, and another, and another. When the roadsides could no longer accommodate them he bought Nichols' garage, employed a mechanic to keep them going, and parked them in High Close Wood where the tanks had been. Soon a substantial brick garage replaced the old wooden structure, with 'Mickley Garage' proudly above it in big letters. Four electrically-operated petrol pumps replaced 'Cleveland Discol' and its 'Esso' mate. There was a kiosk selling sweets to children on their way to school, now that 'Nichols General Dealer' had become 'Valerie's Hairdresser' after a time as 'Twists' Shop'. The garage kiosk didn't last; apart from the risk to children crossing the road being greater than had been going to the nettie, there were precious few children at the school. But the garage had an office in place of the wooden chip shop, and toilets (WCs of course), and a new activity; a retail coal and coke business in the field above, which Mrs Lowdon ran, as well as the business side of the garage. Most of the businesses of the village were man-and-wife partnerships.

Where Nissen huts had stood and Bren-carriers cavorted, the entrepreneurial George built himself a stylish house, as befits a successful man. He did not have to go far for his fish and chips – they were now at the bottom of his garden.

Rather than join the flow of miners from Mickley to Prudhoe, the Simpsons saw the opportunity to stick with the village when the Co-op Manager's house came vacant (the future for Co-op Managers became as uncertain as that of miners). They bought it and set up fish and chips

EX-ARMY COOKHOUSE AND CHIP-SHOP

opposite, in the obsolete Army cook-house cleaned up a bit. They prospered for a time and looked more permanent in their concrete redoubt than the wooden hut chip shop that had gone to make way for George Lowdon. The fish and chips were good and it was still possible to round off an evening at the Cosy in the traditional way with chips wrapped in newspaper, but not the *Herald* any more – England was going Middle Class. The paper was lined with grease-proof to protect you from the printer's ink.

The chips and some of the remaining shops survived a little longer, living in hope because – now here enters treachery ... Never trust politicians, even small amateur ones. Having assured the people of Mickley that there would be no new housing there, before the ink was dry on their mendacity, Prudhoe Urban District Council had approved the building of almost a hundred private houses, and laid a sewer all the way to the new sewage works at Prudhoe – to cope with the extra WCs!

Any hope that the 'incomers' brought, of a revival of the 'old style' Mickley and its shops soon faded. Their lifestyle and aspirations were as different from those of the miners as were their 'semi-detatched', 'split-level', or 'link' houses with built-in modernity from the Raas from whose rubble they rose. They certainly didn't live like miners and shop at the Co-op. They had mortgages and fancy washing machines, fridges, freezers carpets, vacuums and televisions. They increasingly had cars, and garages to put them in, and shopped elsewhere. The age of the motor-car was truly at hand. The bus service began its decline.

Riding Dene Estate – a confusing misnomer, thought up by substandard small politicians – was built with coke-fired stoves for heating, perhaps just to keep faith with the village past and the coke was on hand, keeping Ruby Lowdon's business busy. But rattling and fueling stoves at night and in the mornings kept the neighbours awake and now oil and gas from the North Sea had coal, coke and steam on the run. Just as coal and steam had driven the working horse out of business not so very long ago, so now gas took on the role of heating homes and cooking food and drove coal almost out of business. It made life even cleaner and easier for housewives, but even they were to be driven out of business. 'Housewife', old style, was as demanding and honourable a business as any – but worse paid than most, so the need to pay the mortgage, the car, the gas bill, demanded a better return and the 'housewife' had to find other – better paid – occupation.

My old mother complained that she couldn't get her oven hot enough for baking bread with the newfangled 'North Sea Gas' – when the tide was out!. Neither was it much use threatening to 'put your head in the oven' when things got too difficult – it wasn't poisonously lethal like coal-gas. It could still blow your head off though, given the chance, and could sneak up on you in the night.

Apart from compounding bitterness in the displaced miners of Mickley the building of Riding Dene saved the village school from closure, even though modern homes seem to be able to house only 'two-point-something' children, compared to the 'sub-standard' Raas which had up to sixteen. It also became 'this desirable residential area' in estate-agents' parlance; what they could have done with 'stone built', had the Raas been up-graded in the manner of old farm buildings, instead of being 'wiped off the face of the earth'.

The End of the Pits

The euphoria of working men 'owning' the nation's resources faded and died in Mickley and Prudhoe in a few years after the clearances. Not only were the miners re-housed for 'their own good', but the pits that were their raison d'être, the heart of their lives, were deemed worked out, and closed. Low Prudhoe closed in 1947; West Wylam and Hedley lasted until 1960–61. Local miners argued, as could be expected, that there was plenty of coal; officially, it was too expensive to work by modern methods. More cause for bitterness.

So the only coalmining in the area after at least 300, and possibly 2,000 years, was the little drift mine at West Mickley, privately owned by the Bewick family and employing a handful of men. Mickley Collery at its peak had about 300 men; Mickley Coal Company, in all, upwards of a thousand.

So Mickley was one of the first areas to feel the cruel effects of the progressive elimination from Great Britain of the coal-based heavy industry that had fueled and financed her Greatness.

No amount of bathrooms and WCs, electic cookers and washing-machines, television sets – or Social Security – could replace the lost heart of Mickley when the pit closed. These were unhappy, traumatic times, not only for the miners – everyone was affected.

Little prospers without people, work and money and in a short time only a skeleton of the old trading set-up remained. All of the separate Co-ops combined to become 'North-Eastern', then just 'Co-op', and the Blaydon closed; there was no need for two branches in Mickley. West Wylam – the 'Store'- lingered a while and died progressively. First the butchers, then the cobblers, then the drapers. The eldery, lady-like, lonely Miss Young, who ran 'the Drapers' for as long as I could remember, retired to her dismal little cottage that had been the toll-house at West Wylam when hawkers were charged for entering the streets. She would miss the company of the customers. Finally, and sadly, the grocers went; all those smells and flavours – gone for ever and only ghosts remaining – and hungry mice.

Television ruined the Cosy. Patrons could have travelled to cinemas by car, bus or train, as well as on foot, but why bother? It could all be seen at home. Not quite like 'going out', and there was no snuggling in the side-seats, or fish-and-chips on the way home – in fact it was a form of deprivation for young people. But dressing-up was unecessary for watching the small screen, although I believe that some traditionalists did! and you could make a cup of tea – or have an ice from the fridge. And you didn't get wet or cold. I took my wife to see the last film at the Cosy, and we sat in one of the double seats at the side and ate choc-bars. I'm not sure that we were not the only ones there; we saw Gina Lollibrigida and the film was not very good. But I was there at the bright beginning of the Cosy, and at the unhappy end.

The chip shop gave up, and so did Jeffrey's, General Dealer, leaving Wormald's next door as the only shop in the village other than the newsagents/PO. Eric Wormald had spent much of the war years in the hands of the Japanese while his wife kept the shop going and he, at least, lived to come home, unlike the previous occupant who had gone to the Great War. They kept the shop going until long after retiring age.

The sub-postmaster retreated to his sorting office at Stocksfield and the PO moved across Station Bank into Johnston's the Newsagents which became the all-purpose Village Shop – but not quite up to the old Co-op in scale!

Alan Foster was the last of the village 'entrepreneurs', and an 'incomer'. He was an electrical engineer and saw a need for and thought up a paint for a particular purpose in that field. He marketed it under the name of 'Finnegan's' – which name he never satisfactorily explained, to me anyway. He lived in Mr Knox's old house, Eltringham Cottage, and mixed his paint where the stallion had been stabled, but struggled to sell it. Then he found that it had rust-proofing properties and it took off, under the name of 'Hammerite'. So he then put his mind to serious rust-proofing – there was certainly scope, in a world full of rusting motorcars – the result was 'Wax-oyl' and a fortune for Alan. He expanded from the stable and his wife as staff, to the vacant garage of a failed lorry owner, at the site on Stonygate Bank where the Bewicks had had their coke ovens and, like them, gave employment to a few of his village neighbours. He supplied the Armed Services with Waxoyl for protecting their equipment in the Falklands War, so the garage in turn became too small and he bought the old earthenware pipe works at Eltringham which had been put out of business around 1970 by plastic sanitary pipes. Alan went from strength to strength, set up international subsidiaries, and eventually his firm became too big to handle and he sold out – for millions. His was a classic story of success which, like great drama, ended in tragedy. One of his two sons suffered burns in a petrol accident and the other died in a road crash, then he himself died young. The factory grows bigger and bigger, is a major employer in the area and is now owned by ICI. It retains in its midst a stone-built morsel of the old fire-clay works, as one of the very few surviving reminders of the Coal Age.

A Different World, New Face

Nothing now is to be seen at the 'Junction' except hand-opened crossing gates, since the signal box was demolished. With gravel extraction finished, eight of the twelve Railway Cottages demolished (slums, you see), and no-one drowning since the Rex cinema at Prudhoe was converted into a swimming pool, nor even needing help to call the ferry, Harry Nicholson (who told a good yarn of his Navy days and saving the Admiral's daughter but now had difficulty in finding an audience) was able to pull his last signal and retire to a council flat in Prudhoe. The Hare and Hounds pulled its last pint and was demolished in 1962, after no-one knows how many years, and no-one seemed to notice – but I still have a glasshouse made from some of the roof timbers. The post-box went at the same time, after a hundred years. After perhaps a thousand years, with no ferryman now in the pub to row the boat and few wanting to cross anyway, the ferry came to an end; young Nora, the last of ferry-rowers, took on the job of delivering the village mail. The last two Railway Cottages became one, 'Riverside House' – painted white and electrically heated. The peace of Bewick descended o'er Eltringham, disturbed only by the farm tractors and an occasional train that doesn't even spare a sideways glance at what was, not so long ago, the industrial nub of Mickley. It had taken some time, back in the late 'fifties, to get used to the strange two-tone hooters of deisel trains and it is now a rare pleasure to hear the proper whistle of an occasional special steam excursion – perhaps the 'Sir Nigel Gresley' as it graces the valley with its passing presence. Crowds turn out to see the few remaining examples of the art and craft of steam.

Up the hill the Miners Arms closed – no miners. The pub, though old and simple – it might have been preserved as an example of a pitman's pub – was not a candidate for demolition, being sandwiched between other houses and all of them 'fit for habitation', so it went 'private dwelling', and with the others – 'Eltringham Cottages' – has kept pace with thinking on housing standards – double-glazing, central heating, make-believe shutters and all that. This pub, and the Hare and Hounds, was where inquests into pit deaths had been held and strangely, the last publican was tragically killed in an accident, not in the pit, but going to work as a part-time post-woman when she rode into the back of a lorry on her moped.

The Social Club survived. Miners were no longer virtually the only members, and they could travel from Prudhoe and bring their wives – no longer confined to the kitchen, the Co-op and the Cosy for the 'entertainments' and the 'Bingo' that had been 'Housey-Housey' in the days when it was illegal. They were even taking to drinking! The annual 'Leek Show',the last bastion of Northen miner's character, maintained its vigour; although the leeks have become all scientific and chemical and covered in rust for lack of the protective veil of sulphurous fumes from coal combustion. Coal smoke no longer keeps at bay black spot or mildew on roses either, but neither does it belabour the lungs – not, I venture, that it was ever much worse, or even as bad, as the secret vapours of oil combustion. The Club is losing out to the new style of drinking, fancy pub-with-food-with-children, and is but a shadow of its former self.

The old school had a close call, declining to two teachers and about thirty children and oh dear me, the educational standards hit rock bottom; least said ... However, it survived not only pupil-starvation, but 'New Age' teachers and continual educational reforms. The ghosts of Charlie Hall and Teachers Past must have wrung their hands and gnashed their teeth in despair. With increases in the leaving-age and an increased population, the older children had to be diverted to Prudhoe and go by bus – by bus to school, I ask you! How can a country child observe the natural world from a bus – still less from a car? Village children are motored to school now, even a few hundred yards, and a fine road hazard they are too, at the gates. Mr Bryson would fairly crook his finger at some of these drivers.

'Associations' became quite popular, and 'Communities' so a 'Community Association' was tried when the 'newest' village had settled in. It explored the possibility of making the then unoccupied Blaydon Co-op into a Centre, but it all fell through, sacrificed on the altar of apathy and self-interest, and the shops became two houses, with numbers. They filled-in the housing gap in Riding Terrace, which was at last completed as 18, 20, 21, 19, 22 & 23. I do wish the two conversions had been given names – 'Drapers' and 'Grocers' perhaps? Would not that have been fitting and attractive?

The original fervour of Wesley and his like was long faded and the squalor and deprivation that sustained it no longer relevant; post war attendances declined in the churches, nor were there enough Hubbucks to fill 'their' chapel, so it, the original Mickley Methodists Chapel stopped singing and became a house – 'stone built', with clematis at the door. Fate was less kind to the 'United' Methodist, alongside Rosedale. Although some of the faithful made the journey from Prudhoe, the singing became noticeably thinner, until it could barely be heard even with the door open and the birds silent. Significantly, the visiting preacher billed on the board as Rev. T. E. R. Morrow (I swear it!) didn't turn up so – termorrow never came! The End was nigh! I believe my sister would be the last person to be married there, in

1963, by the Rev Mitchell, and her firstborn would be the last to be christened there. Then the place became an electrical parts warehouse for a time, then fell into decay and dilapidation. There had never been a belfry – Methodists didn't go in for bells, perhaps they all had watches – but there were bats in the roof, and swallows in the summer.

One of my saddest sights of Mickley was seeing the swallows arriving weary-winged after their long flight, to find their holy summer residence being demolished. They sat around on the electricity wires for a time looking disconsolate (believe me, they can), then took themselves off – to the Estate Agent's and a 'superior' residence, I like to think. There are few homes for swallows in Mickley now, superior or otherwise, and the house-martins are discouraged because they make a mess. Neither do the skylarks sing, but there are no picnicers to hear, so does it matter?

The proud foundation-stones, commemorating Methodists of note in order of merit – Sydney Bates Esq., etcetera – were taken off to a dump.

Houses in a short street took the place of the Chapel, nicely named Chapel Row; this was no 'Raa'. No sooner was it occupied than there were complaints about the mess at the garage opposite – one of the few remaining places of employment left in the village. The first notes of the now common chorus were heard "We came here because we thought it nice, and intend it to remain as it was." 'As it was' would have seen them away in a day!

Rosedale changed hands, and appearance, and has grown to three times the size, is no longer recognisable in fact, but the 'River Mick' still flows through the garden, if the present sons are not too grown-up and computerised to play in it. I expect they are.

The after-the-war Reading Room, after a time with a hole in the roof and brief residential occupancy by our Co-op cobbler, was restored as a reading-room until the miners departed, when it no longer had a role. They were an awful miss in the village, those miners. It was under threat for a time, of becoming the 'High-Lo Night Club' (up and down stairs!). A Night Club in Mickley? Common sense prevailed and it became a place for repairing washing machines and vacuum-cleaners – in itself a wry reflexion on the changing nature of the village – against a back-drop of poss-sticks and hooky mats. This business was successful and became part of the Hexham firm Robinson and Cowell and the Room fell empty again, until it switched allegiance and settled for being a modest and rather drab St George's Church Hall in an exchange for the original rather fine hall – the Mission Room, which was condemned as unsafe. After a time as a fountain-pen warehouse it now houses, inappropriately I think, but successfully, a place for mending cars. The world is full of cars needing to be mended. The thumping and bumping and the weight don't seem to bother the hall.

The redundant Co-op – the 'West Wylam' – well built and in a prime trading position, but with parking suited to the horse age, had to do a bit of

WEST WYLAM CO-OP AS IT IS TODAY

hopping around to survive. First it did quite well as a builder's yard, with the grocery dept. making an excellent joiner's workshop and the draper's shop supplying the vogue for 'Do it Yourself', with tools and hardware. Now that was a new one, in a village where if it had to be done, you did it – even if it risked your being flattened by a wayward tree!

Messy fibre-glass mouldings (car wings and things) made temporary use of the cobbler's, and a pony lived in the butcher's for a time. Most little girls seem to aspire to a pony these days (dolls must be 'old hat') and another one, belonging to George Lowdon's grandaughter, lived in the ex-chip-shop, and in some style, with 'Bona Vista Stables' over the door! Riding ponies, I believe, now outnumber the working horses of yesterday.

For a time after the building business gave up, the Drapery Dpt. dealt in glass – double glazing and plastic windows – but then a man named John came along and set himself up as definitely the last of the village 'characters'. We joke that he is attempting to usurp my role as 'Village Idiot'! He filled Miss Young's old domain, and all the nooks and crannies that the hungry mice had vacated, behind and above the grocery, with 'junk' and called it 'Jiggery Pokery'. He offers the junk for sale but would prefer to swap it, in the manner of the Wizard or Rover of his childhood, for something more interesting. If he does sell anything, the price is for negotiation and based on the principle that guided old-time doctors – the ability to pay. Real bargains are there for the poor – and the interested. John Jewitt would rather sit exchanging yarns with an old codger, talking of bygone days, than attend to business – while his wife provides the tea and scrumptious home-made cakes to go with the chat. That is in the tea-room, where the rolls of cotton once perfumed the air, and the Old Mickonian might still be aware of the ethereal vapours.

The homely policy of simple trading – this is no 'antique' shop – in old throw-outs has earned him a reputation (he claims notoriety!) that has brought press and radio notice and people from far and wide to see the ever-changing bits and pieces from the past. No museum this – the same thing is seldom seen twice, and it can be bought, but only if John thinks you worthy to be the new owner! Here, in the old Co-op, might be found and perhaps bought, a poss-stick, mangle, or a tin bath, if you fancy a soak by the fire – memories of Old Mickley preserved.

Some of the rabbit-warren of rooms up the rickety stairs, worn hollow by generations of up-and-downing grocer's boys, change their function from time to time and become book shops, furniture, flowers, hairdressing – almost like a miniature Metro Centre but more interesting.

Interesting in a different, more orderly way, next door in the Grocery of late a joiner's shop, one Chris Bacon works where the hams once hung, and maintains a strong link with Mickley's past. An Academic (yet another one, in Mickley?) and practical printer; he produces works of art and high-class printing, some of it on old-style presses, and does demonstrations for the interested. Visitors can look around and see what printing in Bewick's time was all about. Call it, if you like, a working museum of hand-printing, helping to keep alive the art of engraving, including that in wood, Bewick style.

Cherryburn Now

Down at Bewick's home, when Prof. Clemo, the only occupant ever other than a Bewick, shuffled off, there came a threat of going 'modern'. The Professor had kept everything much as it was when the Victorian house was built and the cottage vacated, but uncertainty followed on his heels. Fortunately a group of enthusiasts saved the place, restored the cottage to something of its former state, and made the house into a Bewick Museum. The Philistine Council forgot, or didn't bother, to sweep the streets when our Queen Mother visited Mickley in 1988 to open the museum and the village schoolchildren weren't invited; there was no room for them by the time 'those that mattered' had their place – Councillors and the like. Bewick would have had something to say.

However, the Birthplace, as it is known, gained an award for the Best Museum of the Year, whatever that means. It is a pretty lifeless thing now that it is in the 'safe' hands of the National Trust, but is still worth a visit, if you can find a moment when it is open. Visitors looking for Bewick find signs proclaiming 'Mickley Square'.

The nature of Bewick, his life and times, cannot be preserved or re-created in a museum; the atmosphere, the smells, the ambiance, are all wrong. We can only imagine it – like coalmining – or the Co-op ...

The Cosy Reincarnate

The Cosy has outlived its rivals at Prudhoe but not alas, in its original form. All three cinemas changed their roles; the Rio to a Bingo Hall before making way, with the precious Park (where I had played many a happy wartime game of tennis) for Prudhoe's very own 'Supermarket' – Co-op, of course. The Electric (or Rex) became one of PUDC's most worthy achievements, costly and controversial though it was at the time – a swimming pool, nothing grand. It put an end to the toll of drowning at the Junction 'Lido' and taught a lot of children to swim, apart from being one of the last sources of cheap pleasure in the area. It eventually paid the price of being old and was bulldozed to make way for others paying the price for being old in one of those fashionable, can't say popular, Care Homes. 'Care' used to be at home in the Raas. Anyway, it's where 'Norse' Stokoe now resides.

The Cosy did a chameleon act in order to survive, and turned itself into a Masonic Hall (some chameleon!). Even this was not enough, although it went on for some time, and it has now changed colour again – into the 'Glendale Functon Suite' – cream coloured and more modest than the name implies, but one of the last of the worthy entrepreneurial efforts in the village.

The fellow who followed ex-POW Eric Wormald into the shop at 18 Riding Terrace made it into a cake shop – a CAKE shop – in Mickley! He kept a snotty-nosed little boy for poking his finger at the cream-cakes. Snotty noses are no longer the vogue in Mickley so the cakes and their keepers didn't stay long, and it was not much cop as a shop when Colin Russell and his wife took it on.

This couple were cast in the mould of the Shopkeepers of Mickley of Yore and bent their considerable efforts to revitalizing the shop – as far as that may be possible in the face of Supermarkets and the motor car. Quality of service in the best traditions of shopkeeping are simply not enough any longer to assure success, so when another opportunity came their way, the Russells indulged their ambition and set up an establishment in the 'Masonic', or 'Cosy', where the buses used to stop, and they called it the 'Glendale' – a kind of Club. A place for convivial gathering-together, for eating and drinking and dancing and having fun, and run in the same spirit as such places used to be. It is available for the Old Peoples' Christmas Treat and for any gathering the Village fancies. They have even made a brave attempt to make the outside look attractive – something, I venture, that no one has previously achieved with the outside of a cinema.

Jack Ward's is another story, typical of how a man with an idea and the will could succeed in Mickley. He worked as a jobbing gardener around the houses of Stocksfield which didn't justify a full-time gardener, and sold a few bedding plants to supplement his income. A few became a lot – on to greenhouses and nurseries on a not ideal, steep, north-facing but cheap to buy field, on the eastern edge of the village, where the wagon-way from the pit at West Mickley to the Pipe-works emerged from its tunnel under the road. The garden was a proper horticultural nursery, where plants were grown – in soil, if you can believe it, and real tomatoes could be bought, fresh from the plant, and all the bows on the plant ties faced the same way, at the same height. He had a fruit and vegetable shop in Prudhoe, run by his son, and became a forthright and respected Councillor.

Jack Wards' is now 'Tyne Valley Garden Centre' where everything is bought-in. Teas and ornaments and instant gardens, and Reindeer at Christmas reflect the times, but it is much better and more pleasant than many of the warehouse-style places that now dominate the gardening scene. It is a much needed place of employment in the village, and, with Cherryburn and Jiggery Pokery, makes a good day out.

All Jack's glasshouses and paving and quick run-off of rain played havoc with the drainage of the football field on the slope below and cost a fortune to remedy.

The church on the hill never relied entirely on miners, so was better able to withstand the shock of the dissolution of the mines than were the Chapels. Nevertheless, it was at a low ebb for some time before the last of its vicars, the Reverend Jim, pulled it together. The Reverend J. Symons was a man of the people, could cut as good a 'short back and sides' as the next village barber, grew a tidy leek that won the Show, and was no mean hand with a shotgun – just the man for Mickley. Recently retired after thirty years as incumbent, he has not been replaced. The strand of piety that links the Church and people of this country does not hold the fabric together, and in the absence of tythes and wealthy patrons, small churches have difficulty in affording vicars, who no longer work for love alone. At the same time it must be said that St George's keeps a full house and recently raised £12,000 for structural repairs in no time at all. It is a shame that it no longer justifies a vicar – nor a Parish Hall. The old Welfare Hall, the Reading Room, has now become the 'Community Centre'. The New Folk of Mickley will have to shake themselves if the Reading Room is not to go the way of the Chapels – into a dwelling-house – or rubble.

Of the old rivals of the Church in the village, only the Club survives, supported at Mount Pleasant by the little old pub – the Blue Bell, now minus its sawdust and spitoons and all done up for serving Sunday Dinners and Bar Meals. Around the corner the Methodists soldier on in their modest brick Chapel, which will have little future when the faithful Old Worshippers go. Maybe those of a Churchy nature will have to 'commute', like workers, shoppers and the sick ...

There would be no point now in putting a notice on a child's writing slate in the window of No 4 Riding Terrace displaying your house number. The Doctor wouldn't know what it meant: no, if you wanted him (or her), the proper procedures would have to be observed and you would, with luck and a telephone call, call into play the whole panoply of National Health Service facilities, technology and all – which is awe-inspiring. In the end you will die nevertheless but probably less painfully than Robert, son of Thomas of Eltringham, on his pile of heather in the hovel on the hill in the Clearing in the Forest. He would today have a better chance of living to a ripe old age – there would almost certainly be a Preservation Order on his killer-tree! His life, long or short (and medical wizardry doesn't really assure long life),

LOOKING UP WHERE ONCE WAS LOW ROW SOUTH

would probably be pretty purpose-less and trivial – but comfortable. He might have to journey ten miles by car to do his 'convenience' shopping – and back, if his car hadn't been stolen when he wasn't looking, and would spend most of his time in the company of computers, television, Hi-fi, and MacDonalds. He would find no hovel in Old Mickley, nor even a farm – they have all become 'desirable residences' and most of the occupants will never have seen a chicken other than a 'broiler' on a plate.

Only two working farms still work and only one – Eltringham Farm – has resisted the clamour for making farms into follies, it still seems like a farm where real farmers could feel at home, and there may even be a corner where the skylark sings and there is a grassy bank to lie on 'midst the harebells. I cannot be sure – I haven't heard a lark for years.

Hope for the future resides in the steadfast old school – monument to Mickley Coal Company (should there be a plaque?), and perhaps a reminder to us to think carefully on what we are doing and where we are heading.

The school is alive with activity again, even has a 'Victorian Classroom', where the teacher would not dare to use a slap, let alone a strap, and the football team would be very small. The children come mostly in cars to school, some from Prudhoe, where they live in houses with TWO WCs!. They play with computers, not 'chucks' and I would love to show them how to spin a top.

When these children grow up they will be able to get their milk at the petrol-filling station, but they will find no food in the village – that is for sleeping in. When they grow old – if they grow old – they will go away and live in 'Care', with Silent Springs and Starless Nights.

High Close Wood goes on – it has bluebells yet, anemones and primroses, and the trees grow dense where the Jays and rufous Squirrels go.

Finis

Note.

Chris Bacon no longer has his Printing Workshop in the old Co-op, which is now a shop selling 'habber-dashery' and children's clothes. Habber-dashery and Jiggery-Pokery together, how nice!

Sadly, the last 'Dolly Sister' died, and Nurse Stokoe is in 'Care', in the Red Brick House, at Prudhoe.